Better Houses, Better Living is the successor to *Build It Right!*
which was used primarily by people who were building custom homes.

Better Houses, Better Living significantly broadens the content to make it current and to be useful to anyone considering the purchase of a home, the remodel of an existing one, or the design or construction of a new one.

What Reviewers Said

"The title of this new book (*Build It Right!*) should be 'Mistakes to Avoid When Building Your New Home.' Author Myron E. Ferguson offers a room-by-room house tour and shows good features to emulate and bad features to avoid.

"Whether you are custom-designing a new house or buying a tract or resale house, this book is must reading. Its practical advice shows features to avoid, those to include, and how to solve home design problems. On my scale of one to 10, it ranks a solid 10."

Robert Bruss, Nationally Syndicated Real Estate Columnist

"Myron Ferguson has studied details in his own home and in more than 700 other new houses...The product of this research is *Build It Right!*, a book that is as interesting for its anecdotes as much as for its advice...cautionary tales are woven through chapters on selecting a lot, house designs, whole-house systems, the kitchen, bedrooms and baths, and finding and working with a builder. The...book includes diagrams and photos that illustrate significant points."

Robert Wilson, Editor, *Better Homes and Gardens Building Ideas*

"The book reads like a home tour with someone who is very focused on how a home works. Ferguson picks up a lot on his radar that most of us would never think about — at least until we moved in.

"People building custom homes can use the book to avoid the problems described. Tract-home buyers might be able to avoid them, but Ferguson wants them at least to realize what they're getting into."

Linda Shaw, *Seattle Times* & Knight Ridder Newspapers

"If you're building a new home or remodeling the old homestead, *Build It Right!* will help you plan and complete the project with maximum results and minimum headaches. Myron Ferguson has given the consumer a great tool to use in navigating the pitfalls of the design and construction jungle."

Jordan Clark, President, United Homeowners Association

"'Build It Right!' offers a breezy style that gives homeowners an overall look at the phases in building your own house...The most interesting nuggets are the anecdotes and photos of common mistakes builders and designers make and consumers often fail to catch."

Mary Sit, *The Boston Sunday Globe*

"New-house how to...If you're gathering material about...a house, you might add 'Build It Right!' to your collection. It's by Myron E. Ferguson, a systems engineer, who was dissatisfied with his own new home.

"He takes the reader through one spot at a time—how to plan your attic if you want to use it for storage, how to avoid doors that swing awkwardly."

Judy Rose, Homes Editor, *Detroit Free Press*

"This Book Is a Must for You...He (Ferguson) provides hundreds of tips on design and building materials...He explains how to assess existing floor plans and how to modify them, how to work with an architect and how to find a competent builder."

Around the House, Les Hausner, *Chicago Sun-Times*

"Which way do the doors swing? Will headlights from passing cars shine into your living room? Is there a light above the kitchen sink? Are the tile floors slippery when wet? Is there a light switch where you'll need it?

"A few hours spent reading this book will sharpen your critical eye as you visit models, compare one home with another and talk with builders and sales agents. Ferguson avoids jargon and tech talk and writes for a consumer audience."

Judy Stark, Homes Editor, *The St. Petersburg Times*

"If you're prospecting for a new home and would appreciate having the expertise of an engineer who has extensively researched the good and bad in homebuilding, here's your opportunity.

"*Build It Right! What to Look for in Your New Home* is a detailed and enlightening book that can help you to a better home."

Robert E. Trea, *Hanover Sun*, Hanover PA

"Do any of the following scenarios sound familar?

"You enter your new home after dark and spend minutes searching for the light switch, which is inconveniently located several feet from the door.

"In the meantime, you stub your toe and trip over the cat.

"These sort of aggrevations plague homeowners every day.

"Want to avoid them? Read Myron Ferguson's newly-revised book, 'Build It Right! What to Look for in Your New Home.'"

Kelly Humphrey, *Northwest Florida Daily News*

Better Houses, Better Living

What to Look for When Buying, Building or Remodeling

(Also Recommended for Realtors®, Designers and Consultants)

Myron Ferguson
5/27/05

MYRON E. FERGUSON

Author of *Build It Right!*

HOME USER PRESS
SALEM, OREGON

HOME USER PRESS
1939 Woodhaven Street NW
Salem, OR 97403-1854

© 2004 by Myron E. Ferguson.

Published by Home User Press, 1939 Woodhaven St. NW, Salem, OR 97304

1st printing 2004

Publishers Cataloging-in-Publishing
(*Provided by Quality Books, Inc.*)

Ferguson, Myron
    Better Houses, Better Living: What to Look for When Buying, Building or
    Remodeling/Myron E. Ferguson.
        p. cm.
        Includes biographical references and index.
        "Also recommended for realtors, designers and consultants."
        ISBN 0-9654856-1-7

    1. Building-Defects. 2. House buying. I. Title

    TH441.F46 2004   643'.12
                                  QBI04-200246

Library of Congress Catalog Control No. 2004108126

Printing history of *Build It Right!: What to Look for in Your New Home*, Revised Edition
            1st printing 1997... 8th printing 2004

This book is a work of advice and opinion. Neither the author nor the publisher is responsible for actions based on the content of this book. It is not the purpose of this book to include all of the information about getting a better house.

Every effort has been made to be as complete and accurate as possible. However there may be typographical and content errors. The book should be used as a general guide and not as a totality of information on the subject. Further, materials, techniques and codes are continuously changing so what is here may not be current when it is read.

Home User Press does not endorse the use of any product or service. References to them are for informational purposes only. The purchase and use of such products or services are wholly at the discretion of the purchaser.

Cover design by RL Graphics
Cover illustration courtesy of Alan Mascord Design Associates

Author's Preface

It's not what you look at that matters, it's what you see.

Henry David Thoreau, American essayist and philosopher, (1817-1862)

Thoreau's philosophical comment is just as applicable to the houses we buy as to the rest of life. A major objective here is to help you see what people too often miss when they're buying or redoing a home, when they're changing their dream to reality.

Better Houses, Better Living is the culmination of over twelve years of research, eight years of it since the revised edition of *Built It Right!* was written. I have looked at about 2,800 new homes, in many parts of our country and Canada, and in Santiago, Chile, and have had the benefit of interesting and informative discussions with people who bought the book at home shows and who ordered it on the telephone.

Even before *Build It Right!* was published in 1994 I was well aware that much of the information in the book was just as applicable to tract and spec homes as to custom homes. I received a number of comments to the effect that there should be a book for these other buyers of new homes. At the same time, the feedback I was getting was that the parts of the book about basic designs were the most useful.

These inputs led to *Better Houses, Better Living* where the stress is on what makes a home a better place to live—regardless of who designs or builds it and regardless of whether it is in a tract, is a spec house, is one that is customized or is an older existing house.

When trying to explain the user-friendly and user-hostile things I've seen in new homes, I always feel more comfortable when I can show what I mean visually. This led me to significantly increase the number of illustrations in this new book. There are over 500 photos and drawings. Combined with explanatory text these make it easier for the reader to understand the points that are made.

And the question of gender comes into just who will get the most use from the book. I've heard it said many times, "they were built by men", something which is generally true, Or, if they weren't, they were designed by men who are more concerned with the structural details than the housewife who uses the kitchen, for example, several times a day.

But user friendliness extends to parts of the house where, generally, it's a man's domain. For example, whether to use a tank type water heater or go with one of the newer tankless units. Or the various kinds of wiring needed in today's digital age.

There is useful information in the book for everyone.

A large proportion of the houses I've looked at were in tracts made both by large national companies and by smaller local builders. They ranged from starter homes to large expensive ones. The problems I saw, however, were universal. The photographs will help buyers recognize the problems when looking at models and the drawings will make it easier for the custom-home buyer to see them when they are on paper.

As I continue to look at houses I am still occasionally surprised to see things that are new to me—both friendly and unfriendly. By the time you read this I will have started a new collection of notes and photos. These will become available on the Web and eventually as part of a future edition. When people have more data available to them, the better will be the houses that they buy. And this, in turn, will lead to better homes being designed and built.

I can use your help, too. If you run across something that you feel is particularly good or bad, tell me about it (telephone, FAX, and Email and snail-mail addresses below). You'll have my thanks and the thanks of others who follow you in the process of getting a better house.

To complete the data that should be in a preface: I retired from a career as a satellite communications system engineer before moving to Oregon and buying a new home in 1990. The Oregon home, a spec house, was the trigger that made me take a closer look at what builders were making and selling. After looking around I decided that ours wasn't as bad as many others. I also decided that I'd turn my engineer's way of thinking to good advantage by helping people get more user-friendly homes. Which led to *Build It Right!* and then to *Better Houses, Better Living*.

I took all of the photos (aren't digital cameras great?) and made the drawings myself.

My particular thanks go to Dick and Mary Lutz of DIMI Press who published the first edition of *Build It Right!* and who encouraged and helped me to set up Home User Press to publish the revision and now *Better Houses, Better Living*.

And special recognition is due to Annell, my thoughtful and patient wife, whose help has been an essential part of getting this book into your hands.

Myron E. Ferguson
Home User Press
1939 Woodhaven Street NW
Salem, OR 97304-1854
E-mail: Info@BetterHousesBetterLiving.com
www.BetterHousesBetterLiving.com
(TEL) 503/391-8106
(FAX) 503/375-2939

...

Contents

Section I
Getting Started

CH. 1. RUDIMENTS OF HOMEBUYING - 9

"It's the Biggest Investment..." 10; Why Learn About Home Buying? 11; Homebuyers 12; Trade Associations 14; Real Estate Sales 15; Lenders 17; Home Builders 19; Remodelers 21; Designers 21; Governmental Agencies 22; Enter the Internet 23.

CH. 2. BUYING OPTIONS - 24

Your Options 25; Remodels 25; Pre-Owned House 26; Spec House 27; The Tract or Production House 27; Custom Houses 29; Owner-Builder 31; Building Systems 31.

CH. 3. HOME DESIGNS - 35

Design Considerations 36; Designs 37; Floor Plans 40; Home Designers 44; Getting Your Design 46.

CH. 4. LOTS - 49

The Lot 49; Zero Lot Lines 56; Country Lots 56

Section II

The Systems

Section III

The Kitchen

Section IV

The Rest of the House

On one of our trips my wife and I had dinner at Ray's Boathouse, a picturesque Seattle restaurant set on Puget Sound with a view of the Olympic mountains. We watched the lights of the boats coming into the ship canal until our dinner was served. We commented to Jennifer, the server, about the setting and how attractively the food was presented. She thanked us and then added, "but wait until you taste it." She was right; it was even better than it looked.

We couldn't help but think about the parallel between her comments and a new home. It should be attractive and in a nice setting but once you get past the looks there needs to be something for you to appreciate and enjoy or the looks don't mean a thing. Bon appétit.

Introduction

"Houses are built to live in, not to look on; therefore, let use be preferred before uniformity, except where both may be had," wrote philosopher Sir Francis Bacon almost 400 years ago.

Then in the late 1800s noted architect Louis Sullivan said the same thing with his "IDEA" that "Form Follows Function."

The years go by—but whether it's 1600, 1900, or 2000+, some things simply don't change.

Are today's houses the best available for the money? As we will see, most definitely not! As long as more thought is given to aesthetics and little, if any, to function, people will buy what they perceive is attractive. So that's what gets built. But, why shouldn't you have a house to, as Bacon said, "live in " as well as "look on?" You should and you can.

Welcome to the world of houses and homes, a world as imprecise and varied as the people who live in them. Nowhere does our individuality show more than in our choice of homes. We have this dream of something that is different from anyone else's, something worthwhile that we personally are responsible for, something that we work for and can be proud to say is ours.

The idea that a home is the "American Dream" may be a marketing stratagem, yet it has an underlying truth that we all understand. This dream is an edifice that one stands and admires—the flow of the roof, the beckoning of the entry, the magnificence of the whole. Inside, the furnishings are also of dream stuff, making day-to-day living luxurious and relaxing.

If you get the opportunity to read Louis H. Sullivan's, "The Autobiography of An Idea," you will find it an interesting commentary on the architectural practices of the late 19th century, the practices that led to his "Form Follows Function." The book is long since out of print (it was first published in 1924). But you may find it, as I did, in your local library. It is an interesting way to spend a few hours.

Our Mission

It may surprise you to find a mission statement in a book that's sold in the general book trade. But our experiences of the last 12 years have made it obvious that most homes are neither designed nor built to best suit the needs of home-owners, the people who live in them everyday. We think this can and should be improved. Hence our mission—to help people who buy houses to get better, more livable homes.

That houses are this way is nobody's "fault." For hundreds of years more attention has been given to how homes look than to how well they work for the homeuser. It's been a matter of putting "form over function" as characterized by Louis Sullivan in the 19th century. It's still that way. Yes, we have beautiful machines and materials that didn't exist in his time but people still buy houses, in large part, because of the way they look rather than how it will be to live in them. And, as long as people buy homes for this reason, it's not going to get better.

We want to change that, not by degrading the aesthetics, the looks, but rather by upgrading the attitudes of buyers, designers and builders in matters of function.

Our objective is simple:

> **To help people get better homes for the hard-earned money they spend on them.**

Home building is a highly competitive business. The objective, as with every successful business, is to maximize the bottom line. Houses must be acceptable to the target market, the buyers, while keeping costs as low as possible.

To make a change in the way things are done means changing things that may impact on the overall profits of the builder. That's why *Better Houses, Better Living* is here. When people choose homes with function as well as looks in mind, it will get better. *Build It Right!* had an impact but there's still a very long ways to go.

We want this book to be read not only by the people getting houses but also by builders and the people who design them, designers and architects.

User-Friendly

A term, taken from early computer jargon, that you'll see time and time again is "user-friendly". A dictionary definition is "easy to use" which is exactly what this book is all about. Homes should be easy to use as well as easy to look at and be impressed by.

Doing It

The first struggle in making our new-home dreams a reality is, for most of us, simply money. Instead of the wooded estate, we know we'll have to settle for the cottage in a neighborhood of peers. Yet we can't forget that dream, so we compromise here and take less there, making sure we express ourselves in the process. And we find lots of people who want to help us along the way— people who make a living at helping the dreamers into the real world. They show us what others have done, they find out about our dreams, then work with us to get the best we can with the resources we have.

These helpers we know as real estate people, designers, architects, builders, inspectors and remodelers. They have experience in the many facets of homes, experience that we must draw on to avoid disaster. Without them our dreams would never leave the realm of the ethereal. And, of course, we know that people are not perfect so we try to find the helpers who will be the best for us and our goals. They will be our advisers as well as the suppliers of goods and services.

We try, yet it doesn't always work out as well as we had hoped. Sometimes we find that we simply cannot have what we want with the money we have. Or there are practicalities like building codes that keep us from getting there. And still other times, and this is the most painful, when we're through with the whole process, we find that our dream isn't as dreamy as we had expected.

The professionals may help us get what we want, but what happens when we don't know what we should want? We learn the hard way—whence come the expressions "if we had only thought of it before..." and "if we had it to do over again..."

Designers create houses they believe are what people want, builders build them and consumers, with their limited experience, buy them. Of necessity, we consumers depend on the designers, builders, and sellers to give us the best we can get for our money. But these professionals, in their efforts to please, come up with what they think people want—which is why people buy what is produced. Houses to "live in" aren't part of the equation. From Bacon to Sullivan to today, it's the same story.

While we won't make much of a change in the way the housing industry does its business, you can sure do something about your own home! In most cases there is little conflict between form and function, between how it looks and how it works. Rather, *it's simply a matter of remembering function.*

Home Building - A Perspective

During my lifetime home building has come a long ways. The more-or-less starter home of today would have been an extravagent mansion. The availability of materials and the ways to use them make possible the impossible. And that metamorphosis is still going on. From an historical perspective, what has happened in the maturing of our country is paralleled in the home-building industry. When you stand back and look at it, you can't help but be impressed by the tremendous changes.

As with any growing entity, there have been and are problems. The automoble industry has grown up at the same time - only faster. Their problems of designs that were "unsafe at any speed" were changed under the mandate of Congress. With houses, the enactment of building codes that make houses safer places to live is still evolving.

With autos the number of defects in cars coming from factories led to ratings companies that categorized cars and manufacturers. This in turn impacted on the market-place and forced manufacturers to pay more attention to the quality of their products so that today's cars are virtually defect free. The same thing has not happened in houses, in part because of the huge number of builders. But the idea is gaining momentum and such organizations as Consumer Reports and J. D. Powers and Associates have come into the picture.

From a different direction, the federal government, through the Department of Housing and Urban Develvment (HUD), is actively developing techniques that will bring the industry up to today's industrial standards. New processes are evolving that will eliminate many of the serious defects that plague new houses today. Modular homes, built largely in factory surroundings, are coming more and more into prominence. Processed wall panels that both reduce the use of lumber and are less prone to defects are being adopted by builders, large and small.

It is and will continue to be an interesting industry to watch as it moves farther into the 21st century.

And it's not difficult. None of the facets of home design and construction discussed in this book are complicated in themselves. As you read about them you'll say, "Now that makes sense" and you're on your way to a better home.

The many decisions will inevitably involve compromise. You'll need to prioritize your objectives, to decide which of the many things you'd like to have are the more important and which are expendable. Cost may be the biggest factor but it isn't the only one. While the stress in *Better Houses, Better Living* is on functionality, don't hesitate to express yourself by choosing something that looks better to you even if you compromise functionality in the process. But make these decisions knowingly; don't just let them happen. It is one of the purposes of *Better Houses, Better Living* to help you understand the pros and cons of each compromise

and so make your new home reflect *your* personal likes and dislikes. Whether you remodel, buy an existing house or a new one, the more you know about what you want, the better will be the house you'll get.

Viz-a-viz "Build It Right!"

That first book, first published more than a decade ago, has helped over 30,000 people get better homes. Here we take those ideas into more depth, to recognize the materials and techniques that have become available and to broaden the content to specifically include anyone buying or remodeling a home.

We've taken advantage of digital technology to take literally thousands of pictures to better portray the points we make. You'll find 462 of them in this book vs. 64 in *Build It Right*.

ABOUT THE AUTHOR

Before he retired and moved to Oregon in 1990, Ferguson spent his professional career as a telecommunications systems engineer. He helped bring satellite communications to the world, working on the first satellite stations in a number of countries on 5 continents. His education and decades of engineering work made paying attention to detail an inherent part of his way of looking at things.

In Oregon he quickly noted how things in his new house were not made for the home user, but rather for the convenience of the builder and subcontractors. User friendliness and function, which had been an integral part of his satellite communications systems designs, were not (and are not) a way of thinking for home designers and builders. This started his second career, an author and publisher of books for homebuyers. He has written two editions of "Build It Right!" and is gratified that the book has sold well so that he can say that "over 30,000 new homes are better because of it."

His forté is in the details. He leaves the "big picture" to architects and home designers who focus on how a house looks, its spaces, the flow and how it pleases the senses. He wants to help people get that better house that'll make living in it more enjoyable.

He wants to get his message of thinking of the home user through to home builders as well home buyers. And he urges the designer and architectural communities to incorporate this paying-attention-to-detail into their work for new houses and for remodeling.

The Internet as a Resource

Another thing we've done to bring the whole subject up to date is the extensive use of the Internet as a source of additional resource material that could never be included in the book itself. You will find over 140 superscript references to URL's. They are listed in the after matter of this book (p. 320) and, to make them easier to use, the references are also included in our website <<www.BetterHousesBetterLiving.com>> where you can click on them as easy links to the resources without out having to copy the often complex URLs from the book.

At the same website you'll find updates to the information printed in book—including the resource URLs. And a place for comments and suggestions that could help other homebuyers.

What's Here

The reader is reminded again and again that the subjects covered in the book are not routinely considered in home design and construction—it's very much up to you if they are to be a part of your home.

Every time I talk to someone about their home I am reminded again about how many decisions must be made. The book couldn't possibly cover all of them because everyone's situation is different—and we wouldn't really want it otherwise.

On the way to making your dream a reality you will have to make a number of compromises involving costs and personal likes and dislikes. But the availability of materials and the skills of the tradespeople can also make you veer away from what you'd really like. With *Better Houses, Better Living* you'll have a better understanding of what you're getting and what you're giving up.

The material in *Better Houses, Better Living* isn't sensational. It doesn't deal with what happens in a few dramatic disastrous cases but with what happens day in and day out in house after house—in other words with what could happen in your home if you let it. And what's nice is that you don't have to be a graduate engineer nor an architect nor an interior designer to take advantage of the information that's here. You will find that most of it is just a matter of having it pointed out and you can take it from there.

Section I of the book starts with an overview of what's involved in getting that dream home. The second section deals with the systems that are a part of any house and with the pieces and parts that are found in every room. Section III is about the kitchen, that most talked about and most used and abused room in the home. Section IV is about the rest of the house: bedrooms, bathrooms, garage, etc.

At the end, there is the back matter—the list of Internet Resources, a glossary and the index.

SECTION I

> *The minute you settle for less than you deserve, you get even less than you settled for.*
> Maureen Dowd, New York Times columnist (1952-   )

Getting Started

Maureen Dowd's philosophy is just as applicable to houses as to anything else—we should never settle for less than we deserve. The problem is that we often don't know what it is that we do deserve.

Here we take a broad look at the homebuying process in four parts to help you in identifying what you can afford and what you want in your home. Generally, remodeling involves similar considerations. But it is an introduction, no more.

⇨ Money. Chapter 1 includes an overall look at the loan and lender scene as well as a broad look at the real estate business and at the homebuilders and their associations.

⇨ What. Chapter 2 is a discussion of the different kinds of houses you'll find are for sale ranging from older homes which may need remodelling to custom and owner-builder homes.

⇨ Design. Beginning with floor plans and where to find them, Chapter 3 is a start to help homebuyers in formulating a list of wants and don't wants in their new houses.

⇨ Where. Lot considerations, the good and the not-so-good, are the subject of Chapter 4.

These are all introductions to the more detailed aspects of homes that are the subject matter of the rest of *Better Houses, Better Living*.

Chapter 1

Rudiments of Homebuying

A comfortable house is a great source of happiness. It ranks immediately after health and a good conscience.

Sydney Smith, British preacher & parlimentarian (1771-1845)

In this chapter:

Most of the time, getting another home means going through the process of buying one. This chapter, as the title indicates, reviews only the rudiments. If you are remodeling, you may find the discussion of the overall homebuying picture interesting and, probably, useful.

If you have already committed to a house, consider this introductory chapter as entertainment that may still be useful.

Homebuying has many facets as any of us who have been through it can assure the neophyte. There are questions of how much you can afford, and of just what you want...and the inevitable compromises between those two things. There are many people who make a living helping people get their new homes. Most of these are competent, a few are not.

It may seem simple at first—after all there are many houses for sale—so surely you can find what you want. Or, if you can afford it, you may well consider having a home built to meet your needs and dreams.

And, if you are inclined that way, you can go the owner-builder route where you take on the responsiblity of overseeing having your new home built.

Or you may well figure that it'll be better for you and your circumstances to remodel the house you have now to make it more in keeping with your life style and with modern day materials and appliances.

But, always, we should keep in mind that some-day the house will be sold and we want to do what's reasonable right up front to be sure we get a fair price when the time comes.

In this introductory chapter to *Better Houses, Better Living* we take a look at the broader aspects of buying and remodeling a home. It is not our purpose here to go into detail about the many aspects but rather to give you the background to help put the discussions that follow into perspective.

Note that the primary focus of the book is to look at homes from the homeuser's point of view, not the builder's, the seller's, the Realtor's®, the banker's, the designer's and not the architect's, but yours.

A most important aspect of this, and here we've borrowed terminology from the computer industry, is that we firmly insist that a home should be "user-friendly", i.e., that it be made with the homeowner in mind and, most importantly, with how you use the home day in and day out.

How the house looks is important both for your own satisfaction and for the time you want to sell and move on. The same considerations apply to how the house "feels", how comfortable the home user is with the floor plan and the myriad of details that make up a room and the house as a whole.

Home building is a business, pure and simple. The builder and all of the people he calls on for goods and services are there to make money. As are the ancillary companies who are involved when you buy, build, or remodel a home. Builders build what their experience and research tells them will make them the most profit in a very competitive business. And, of course, that's what Realtors® have to sell.

What you buy and what you live in are the products of these businesses. The problem we focus on here is that user-friendliness has not been a major consideration in how houses have been designed and built. Some are much better than others, as you will see when you start including it in your assessments of houses and floor plans.

Builders build what they perceive the customer wants and and the real problem is that most people haven't paid attention to the details that are involved with user friendliness...details that they discover after they move in and then have to live with what could have done better.

This will change. The intervention of the Internet into the traditional ways of doing things is having an impact. People can more easily see what's good and what's not so good in a house while sitting in their own home in front of their computer terminal. This includes looking at floor plans and at ideas about how to make a house more attractive both inside and out. We welcome these. It helps in the learning process that everyone should go through before spending a dime.

If you could get help from somebody who understands all of these things, that would be great. Unfortunately, that time hasn't come...but it will as user friendliness becomes something that more and more buyers include in their decisions.

Right now you're pretty much on your own. It shouldn't be that way but it is. So exercise *caveat emptor,* buyer beware, and go get the house you want.

Homebuyers and homebuying make up one of the most important parts of both our culture and our economy. We are tied to where we live and we spend large portions of our incomes to provide homes for ourselves and our families. This is not news but it is easy to overlook its importance to our happiness and our day-to-day living.

"It's the Biggest Investment..."

How many times have you read, "It's the biggest investment you'll probably ever make", as if that's what home buying is all about? Probably so many times that you're sick of it. And it completely misses the point! Homes are much more than an investment, they are where we raise our families, where we come for refuge from a stressful day, where we kick off our shoes and relax and enjoy our families, our TV's and the Internet, entertain friends---whatever we want to do.

But that's not what the real estate ads or sales agents stress because that's not what they're selling. They are selling products and there's big money involved. Price, interest rates and downstream resale value are important to all of us. And those are tangible things that get our attention, things that the real estate industry can focus on to get you to buy the products they're selling. But it's far from being the only important aspect of buying a house to live in.

Why Learn About Home Buying?

"Knowledge is Power"

This comment, attributed to Sir Francis Bacon, couldn't apply more than to the process of home buying. There are multiple steps involved, whether for an existing or a yet-to-be-built home. Knowing what you're doing is essential to save money and get that better place to live.

Here's a suggestion. Fanny Mae, a government sponsored Wall Street corporation that buys home loans from lenders, has an excellent 51-page booklet, the "Home Inspection Kit", to help buyers in the process of buying a home. It's a good, day-to-day document to have handy when you're out there working on your homebuying efforts. You can see it at their website where you can copy and print it out yourself[1A].

And note their observation which we support wholeheartedly:

"An informed homebuyer is a successful homeowner."

The American Bar Association has an on-line book, "ABA Family Legal Guide" which has several chapters that we will reference later. The introduction to Chapter Four on Buying and Selling a Home[1B] also makes our point very nicely (the emphasis is ours).

"A HOME IS THE LARGEST PURCHASE most Americans will ever make. If you are one of the millions of Americans about to buy or sell a home, **it's important to understand the ramifications of the decisions you will make.** For example, state and federal law, the economy, your personal preferences, your financial situation, the prevailing real estate market, current mortgage rates, and tax considerations, are among the many factors that affect you as either a buyer or seller. You will also need to work with a variety of people—attorneys, lenders, home inspectors, appraisers, and insurance agents, to name a few. In short, buying and selling a home is not the simple matter it might appear."

What's important for you to understand from the beginning is that you aren't going to change the way things are done but, at the same time, you should know what is involved and what's going on as you go through the process. By enabling yourself this way you will be able to get that better home and save money in the process.

Homebuyers often have another option— classes offered by the local community college or other organizations where the necessary rudiments are taught. For first-time buyers these classes are a good introduction to the complexities of the real estate scene.

The Freddy Mac, another government sponsored corporation, website has an excellent discussion of 7 steps that a buyer should take to be successful in his homebuying[1C], ranging from making a list of needs and wants to how to refinance your house.

About saving money

A rudimentary thought, that you've seen many times, is that it's better to make house payments than to pay rent month after month. This is obvious with regard to the accumulation of equity which comes from the payments you make and any appreciation in the value of the property with time.

But there are other ways to make money on your investment. First, every penny you save in the buying process is money in the bank. Second, and this is something that's not stressed as much, is that whatever money you may make with this investment may be tax free under current tax laws. It's better than earning it the hard way. So it really does pay to know what you're doing.

The team

Note that, in each case, you will need a team to help you. You need financing. Unless you feel confident that you can do it all on your own, you'll need a real estate buyers agent. You should have an inspector to look at the house, either before you buy it or as it is being built. And, in many cases, you'll want a real estate attorney to keep you from getting tangled in legal battles that could add significantly to the cost of the house.

Homebuyers

But people in the business often look at buyers in a different light. As a start, consider how three real estate agents categorized homebuyers (next page). When we are dealing with our feelings most of us use our hearts instead of our heads. What we need for home buying are both. Don't let your heart get ahead of your brain but use your good

sense to see what will make you feel good about your purchase for as long as you live in it.

These real estate agents see their customers as "fickle", "busy" and "impetuous" buyers who are not as concerned with the long term aspects of their decisions as the agents think they should be. It is a fact that we are a mobile society and do not stay put. We instinctively know that buying a home because of its future resale value is not a crucial thing because we're going to be moving on before this affects us greatly. Besides, who can foresee the future? So we tend to let our hearts take over and make decisions based on curb appeal, gut feelings and looks. Unfortunately what it may be like to live day after day in the house doesn't enter into the decision.

Money

We've just said that price isn't everything or maybe not even the most important thing. Yet it is the side of home buying that gets the most attention. When you go to a real estate agent, probably the very first question is, "Have you been to a lender or mortgage broker to see how much you can afford?" There, the loan officer will ask you lots of personal questions, check your credit rating and, using a set of guidelines, tell you how much money you can get for the loan and what down payment will be required.

The loan officer will also tell you what kind of loan you should get and what your monthly payments will be if you get the maximum you qualify for. It's up to you to decide if you want to be committed to that kind of expenditure month after month. Or if you want to have money left for new furniture from time to time, or to repaint the house if you don't like the color or to redo the yard. Or to take that vacation cruise you've always dreamed about. The options are endless, of course, and you'll be faced with making the decision of whether pouring everything into down payment

Homebuyers - Three Views

Whether or not you use a sales agent, look at what three of them told me as their view of homebuyers. There are lessons here, both in understanding yourself and in seeing it from the other fellow's perspective.

First

One agent characterized buyers as "fickle" meaning the agent will work with the buyers for a while only to have them go to and buy using another agent. The problem here is partly the first agent's for not finding just what the buyers were looking for and partly the buyer's because they didn't define to the agent just what they wanted. (Actually, this would be one criterion in sorting out good agents from so-so ones. If you get a good one who does her job correctly, this wouldn't happen.)

Second

A second agent classified 80% of buyers as "busy" and the rest as "independent."

Busy buyers are ones who don't think that doing their homework is important. They spend as little time as possible with a sales agent initially and are likely to buy the first house they are shown if it fits their perceived needs at that time. These buyers often justify their actions by saying that "we're only going to be living in the house a few years anyway, so it doesn't matter." (Believe me it does matter, both in having a comfortable house and in having a house with good resale potential.)

Independent buyers are ones that make up their minds with virtually no inputs from the sales agents. They think they know what they want and may spend an inordinate amount of time finding it---then decide it's not really the one after all. Using the services and experience of a good agent would save them a lot of time---if the independent buyer would only work that way.

Third

The third agent, one who specializes in being a buyers agent, describes buyers as "impetuous." His approach is to cater to this and learn only as much as he needs to get them to a house he figures they will buy. They do not spend time shopping or defining in much detail what they want. This agent, by the way, is one of the top producers in his company, a top franchisee in a big nationally-known corporation. (And what does that say for most buyers? That they're impetuous? Could be.)

You

Note that "fickle", "busy" and "impetuous" are different ways of looking at the same kind of person. But don't you be any of the kinds of buyer described here. Take the time to figure out just what you want.

and monthly payments is really that important. Remember that lenders are very astute and practiced at looking at your situation and deciding how much money they can prudently loan to you without taking excessive risks.

To them, risk is the possibility of losing money on the deal if you don't make your monthly payments. They balance this against the income that comes from getting you committed to the most interest money in your monthly payments they possibly can. It's a business deal to them, it's your future to you. Your happiness isn't a factor in their formulas.

Sales commissions

And don't forget that real estate agents are salespeople whose income is generally only from commissions and that the more you spend, the more they earn. Of course, *good* sales agents know that having the referrals that come from happy clients are needed for a successful career. For this to happen they also know how to help you get what you perceive as happiness. If you don't object to a house with a layout that will be a pain in the neck forever, that's your problem, not theirs. And when you figure it out later on, you'll blame yourself, not the agent, for being so unobservant. The more you know *before* you make your choice, the better off you'll be.

How many will you buy?

We've already commented on, "It is probably the biggest investment you'll ever make." That inanity can only be true once, if at all. If you bought just one house and lived in it until you leave this world, it probably would be OK, but that's not what happens. If you buy your first house when you're 25 and your last when you're 65 and move every seven years (close to the national average) you'll have purchased six homes along the way and clearly only one of them can be the most ex-

In discussions with a new-construction home inspector, he made the observation that the largest proportion of his customers are in the over-55 group. He feels this is becaues they are more likely to include practicality in their thinking than are younger buyers to whom getting their first home is such an emotional adventure that they tend to avoid any thoughts that might make it seem mundane. Unfortunately, many of them will pay for that later, of course.

I can only urge you to become an educated homebuyer before you spend a penny. Then, whether you buy an existing house or a new one, you can enjoy the euphoria that comes with getting your very own home.

pensive. You *won't* find the "biggest investment" banality anyplace else in this book from here on. Hopefully you *will* find down-to-earth info that will help you regardless of where you are in the cycle.

The rudiments are the same, whether it's your first home or one farther down the road. Know what you're doing, get good help and plan on spending a lot of personal time at it.

Trade Associations

Trade associations (groups of people plying various trades) have existed since the days of the medieval guilds and are most often beneficial. By focusing efforts in areas of their professions they can bring about changes that benefit everyone.

But do not be mislead to think that the association is there *primarily* for you, the customer. First, to do anything, they must keep themselves in existence and to do this they must serve their members. It is for their own benefit and protection that a bunch of competitors get together to form an association.

This shows up in several ways, one of the more significant being the political pressures they bring to bear at national, state, and local levels. It is to the benefit of all of these organizations to see to it that people keep buying new homes. So, when it is suggested that something be done to control urban sprawl, for example, you can bet the political action committees (PACs) will spring into action to let nothing, from high interest rates to taxes to growth boundaries, stand in the way of building more homes. For an industry it's a natural thing to do– it's why the association was formed in the first place.

On the positive side, these activities result in making home ownership available for many who couldn't otherwise afford it.

But there is a darker side, too. When it should be a matter of self-policing, too often trade organizations will stand up for someone that they should be riding out on a rail. And this, in turn, can lead to using the strength of an organization to promote and defend laws that are narrowly self serving.

Personal note: After the above was written, I came across a situation where a group of builders had their memberships in the local builders association (and hence in the National Association of Home Builders (NAHB)) revoked because of unethical practices. There **are** standards that can be enforced. Whether it happens often enough is another question. Lesson: be sure anyone you are dealing with is a member of the appropriate trade association–or has a good reason for not belonging.

There are four groups that have trade organizations which, even if you don't come into direct contact with them, will have an impact on you and the home you buy:

- ⇨ real estate sales,
- ⇨ lenders,
- ⇨ builders and
- ⇨ the designers.

Three of these organizations are discussed here.

Besides these behemoths there are national associations of home inspectors (ASHI[1D] and NAHI[1E]) and appraisers along with state associations which may or may not be affiliated with a national association. There are also national title companies and individual real estate attorneys whose services you may well have occasion to use.

Real Estate Sales

Brokers and agents

When you bought your first home, it probably involved a real estate agent who acted for you in the process—or so you thought. That may not have been the case but at least you trusted him/her and, if it wasn't all to your advantage, you never knew.

Recent changes in some states have blurred the difference between agents and brokers and it might be well for you to find out what the situation is in your state.

Real estate brokers and agents are licensed by the state in which they do business. They are obligated to obey national and state laws. Brokers assume the ultimate responsibility for real estate transactions—agents must get the broker's approval before a deal is finalized. It's a way to double check the legalities involved. Agents work with sellers and/or buyers in arranging sales or trades of real property, including houses.

A broker is bonded and must have several years experience as an agent before being eligible for a license. The owner of a real estate firm is usually a broker; large firms will have several. The relationship between the firm and the agents is not that of employer and employees; rather, while agents are affiliated with their firms, they are independent businesses in many ways. Competition is stiff. Agents in the same office compete with each other (and all other agents in the community) to get listings and to represent buyers and sellers..

The NAR

Most real estate brokers and real estate agents belong to a local Board of Realtors. In each state there is a state association of Realtors and nationally there is the National Association of Realtors (NAR)[1F]. This politically powerful organization with over 800,000 (!) members is the world's largest trade association.

The national association has a published code of ethics for its members. This code encompasses the relationships and interactions between Realtors® and between Realtors® and their clients. If you get a chance, take a look at it on their website. It puts pretty stiff constraints on what agents and brokers should do.

"Realtor®", "Realtors®" and "Realtor-associate®" are all registered trademarks of the National Association of Realtors. Only members of that organization are entitled to use these trademarks. Others should be referred to as real estate brokers or real estate agents. Note that, like many other trademarks, the terms are often used in a generic sense, that is, "realtor" instead of real estate agent, etc.

> **"®" Ever wonder? A curiosity-satisfying piece of information.**
>
> ® indicates that a name is registered by the U.S. Patent Office. The term Realtor® is registered by the National Association of Realtors. It identifies their members.

Not all brokers belong to the NAR. Some feel they can better serve their customers in non-conventional ways. If you know exactly what you're doing, using one of these renegades may well get you what you want at a significantly lower cost.

Real estate councils, etc.

You will see the initials "GRI" after some Realtors' names. Graduate, Realtor Institute is awarded to a Realtor after the completion of three one-week courses offered by the state association. This program is for brokers and associates who are involved with single-family homes.

A Certified Residential Specialist (CRS) indicates that an agent has taken extra studies in this particular area. (Aspects of home design are *not* a part of those studies.)

More recently REBAC[1H], a part of the NAR, is offering courses leading to the Accredited Buyer Representative (ABR) designation.

MLS

A multiple listing system (MLS), often sponsored by the local Realtors® association, is a list of all properties being sold by the members. These are put into a computer file that is accessible to the members who subscribe to the service. It gives the local Realtors the ability to sort through the listings and come up with those that closely meet the needs of a client. In the not too distant future, you'll probably find the MLS listings available on the Internet - many of them are today.

Who's your agent?

In the process of selling and buying a home, different agents usually represent the seller and the buyer. But, depending on the laws of the particular state, the agent that the buyer thinks is representing him may, in fact, be a subagent of the seller's agent. This can put the buyer at a significant disadvantage in the buying process. Some states have changed their laws so that a buyer's agent must truly represent the buyer and the laws are being changed in others.

But there is one aspect of it that you shouldn't forget. As long as the agent representing you, the buyer, is on commission, it is to his/her immediate advantage to make the selling price as high as possible—which, obviously, is not to your advantage. (The other side of this is that because an agent's long-term success depends on referrals from previous clients it is advantageous to do as well for a buyer as possible.)

One of the problems real estate agents have in representing buyers is that the buyer is under no obligation to buy through an agent even if the agent has spent many hours showing properties to them. To get around this, you may be asked to sign a contract with an agent in which you agree to pay him/her a fee whether you buy through him/her or not. Don't sign it until you are confident that the agent is competent, not only with regards to the legal and financial aspects of the transaction but also that he/she knows a good property from a bad one. Many do not. A good agent will be well worth the money. A poor one is a waste of time as well as money. Shop around and get references. And, even then, be sure you have a reasonable escape if things don't work out as you had expected, like having the contract run for a relatively short period of time.

Recognizing a market need, another type of real estate company has come into existence—the exclusive buyer's agency. These companies do not take listings; they only work with buyers. Their agents are paid a fixed fee—not a percentage of the selling price of the house. They are not salespeople but rather consultants and advisers to buyers. The exclusive agency concept is more strongly developed in some parts of the country than others. There are several national organizations of exclusive buyers agents listed in the Supplement F on Realtors®[1J].

But do be careful here, too:

⇨ Most exclusive buyer agents are no more qualified to warn you about defects in

the way a house is designed or built than are other real estate agents.

⇨ Be sure these agents' fees are independent of the selling price of the house so there is not the same incentive to keep the price high. Responsible buyer's agents expect this kind of an arrangement.

Real estate companies

Many local real estate companies are franchises of national organizations which, in turn, may be parts of a big Wall Street company. It is this environment that makes it ever so important for local governmental agencies to have control over the operations and actions of the local franchises. Fortunately, they generally do.

Lenders

There are two major trade associations and two federal-government sponsored companies that are parts of the financial conglomeration that is involved in lending money to build and buy homes.

The big lenders' associations are:

⇨ The Mortgage Bankers Association of America (MBA)[1K], and

⇨ The National Association of Mortgage Brokers (NAMB)[1L].

Unless the lender is a bank that keeps a mortgage in its own portfolio, it is sold on the secondary mortgage market. These may be other lenders, investors and agencies that then sell the loans to mortgage investors/agencies. Today the biggest of these are:

⇨ Fannie Mae[1M] rated #20 in Fortune's 500 companies in 2002 and

⇨ Freddie Mac[1N] #41.

Both are private, federally-chartered, stockholder-owned corporations. Fannie Mae was chartered by Congress in 1967 and Freddie Mac was chartered in 1970.

The MBA

The MBA's website says:

"MBA is the national association representing the real estate finance industry.

• The association works to ensure the continued strength of the nation's residential and commercial real estate markets, to expand homeownership prospects through increased affordability, and to extend access to affordable housing to all Americans.

• MBA promotes fair and ethical lending practices and fosters excellence and technical know how among real estate finance professionals through a wide range of educational programs and technical publications.

• Headquartered in Washington, DC, MBA represents more than 2,700 members involved in real estate finance and comprise more than 70 percent of the single-family mortgage market and more than 40 percent of the commercial/multifamily market, including: mortgage companies, mortgage brokers, commercial banks, thrifts, credit unions, savings and loan associations, savings banks, and life insurance companies."

For additional information, visit the MBA's website.

The MBA is the organization that is battling in Congress with the National Association of Realtors to allow banks to sell real estate.

The NAMB

The NAMB describes themselves as:

"Established in 1973, the National Association of Mortgage Brokers is the only national trade association representing the mortgage brokerage industry. With 46 affiliated state associations and over 16,000 members, NAMB promotes the industry through programs and services such as education, professional certification, and governmental affairs representation. NAMB members subscribe to a code of ethics that fosters integrity, professionalism, and confidentiality when working with consumers."

Note "fosters integrity." Neither the NAMB nor any other nongovernmental body can enforce integrity. One reason for this is the proliferation and, often, ineffectiveness of state statutes and rules that regulate the mortgage industry. The NAMB is currently sponsoring a model state statute to try to make some organization out of what is now a chaotic situation in many places. They do not, however, have a database of either the mortgage agencies on a state-by-state basis nor of websites where you can go to find information. Their suggestion is to get legal advice when you need it.

The secondary mortgage market

From Freddie Mac's website in 2003 re the secondary mortgage market (this info was not found in early 2004):

"If you think of America's mortgage lenders as retail stores where people go to get mortgages, the secondary mortgage market is their supplier. Freddie Mac, one of the biggest buyers of home mortgages in the United States, is considered a secondary market conduit between mortgage lenders and investors.

Lenders look to Freddie Mac and other secondary market conduits for the funds they need to meet consumer demand for home mortgages and multifamily housing. About half of all new single-family mortgages originated today are sold to secondary market conduits. By 'linking' mortgage lenders with security investors, Freddie Mac keeps the supply of money for housing widely available and at a lower cost."

Fanny Mae's role is similar.

As you might imagine, with the amount of money involved in a home mortgage and the number of them out there, this area attracts some powerful businesses. There are many ways to get a loan, some of which cost much more than others. The U.S. government has gotten into the act, too, by: (1) setting up several agencies which are primarily there to help the low-income buyer get his own home and (2) generating laws and rules to protect the homebuyer—at least to some extent. It is truly a complex set of confusing interactions.

One of the first things a prospective homebuyer should do is to find out just where he/she stands relative to the loan scene. Mortgage company loan officers are in a position to help. Good real estate agents can too.

And today we have the Internet as another. The companies that check credit ratings are called credit bureaus which Freddie Mac's website[1O] defines as:

> "A company that gathers information on consumers that use credit and sells that information in the form of a credit report to credit lenders."

Three of them are:

➪ Equifax[1P]
P. O. Box 740241
Atlanta, GA 30374
(800) 685-1111

➪ Experian[1Q]
National Consumer Assistance Center
P. O. Box 2002
Allen, TX 75013
(888) EXPERIAN [(888) 397-3742]

➪ Transunion LLC[1R]
P. O. 2000
Chester, PA 19022
(800) 888-4213

Home Builders[1S, 1T]

Houses are complex structures made of many different materials from many sources. The suppliers of these materials are large industries in themselves: lumber, windows, doors, plumbing, appliances, etc. It is the home-building industry that puts these together into marketable products that are attractive and functional. If there is one thing that characterizes this industry, it is the number and diversity of builders. Unlike other major industries in today's world, there is no big name, no "big three." Most builders do only a few houses a year and even the largest builder, although it is a Fortune 500 company, makes less than two percent of the country's total number of new houses.

Given the large number of builders you shouldn't be surprised to find all kinds of people in the business of home construction. As with any profession, there will be the able and the inept, those who take pride in their work and others who don't care, those who build with the customer in mind and those whose end-all is the

This national builder is well up on the Fortune 500 list of the country's largest companies. Management is responsible to stockholders, not homebuyers.

almighty dollar, those who are honest and forth-right and others who are litigious and a disgrace to their industry. They're all out there.

When you buy a car, there is a large but finite number of options. In homes. the choices are virtually unlimited. From the homebuyer's perspective, this is both good and bad. There is the opportunity to get exactly what you want and can afford. With this freedom goes the flip side, you better know what you want, what's right and what's wrong for you.

Builders are small- to large-sized businesses and they *must* understand the business side of what they're doing or they invite disaster. And, unfortunately, when they do happen, those disasters usually involve everyone around them: suppliers, subcontractors, *and* customers.

As the manager, the builder's staff should know good and not-so-good materials and workmanship. Scheduling and coordinating material deliveries and subcontractor work are critical and oversight during construction is crucial. Inept and don't-care builders turn things over to the subcontractors and accept whatever happens while good builders stay right on top of the work, with competent on-site supervisors who insure coordination and get boo-boos fixed before they get locked into the fabric of a house.

If the end product is to be acceptable to the customer, the builder must know what's to be built. When it's a custom house or a remodel, the customer tells the builder what's wanted. If it's a tract or spec house, the question is one of marketability and the builder makes what his research tells him is most likely to sell. The common thread here is that the builder is responding to his conception of the marketplace. And as long as buyers don't insist on functionality, along with aesthetics and structural soundness, then functionality will usually suffer.

For an older home, the same considerations are involved. The original builder left his mark and then the owners made their changes, both good and bad.

And where does all this leave you, the prospective homebuyer? Do you buy an existing house or a new one? Or do you decide to remodel your old home? In every case, you need to know as much as you can about what you want—not only in the size and location of the house but also in its design and workmanship. And, most importantly, from the point of view of the person who's going to be living in the house, being able to see how livability is an integral part of all of this.

Organizations

Most builders belong to a local or regional builder's association that is affiliated with state and national associations. These associations have the words "home builders" or "building industries" in their names. The National Association of Home Builders (NAHB), is the trade association for the industry at the national level.

The National Association of Home Builders (NAHB) has 205,000 members and over 800 state and local associations[1T]. The membership includes a number of the Fortune 500/1000 companies.

The associations, at all levels, represent members before various governmental agencies. They sponsor and work for legislation benefiting the building community. Membership comes from all areas of the building trades. It includes remodelers and small, medium, and large volume builders. Associate members include subcontractors, materials dealers, house designers, lenders, and Realtors®.

Membership in the local association is seen as giving credibility to the member. The building community recognizes NAHB membership as a sign of professionalism.

At the local level, the home builders' associations provide group insurance programs, sponsor seminars, and hold periodic meetings and social events. These activities are for the purpose of education, business contacts, and general assistance to the members.

On the national level, the NAHB tests and approves new building materials. It has a number of services available to its members that are intended to provide help in areas of home building. It lobbies at all levels of national government to "ensure housing remains a top priority during the formation of national policy." Individual members are asked to bring the NAHB message directly to their representatives in Congress. The NAHB has the third largest trade association Political Action Committee (BUILD-PAC) in the country, raising over $2,000,000 every four years.

It publishes monthly magazines along with other data available to the members upon request. The NAHB sponsors educational seminars and the country's largest trade show.

Builders aren't required to belong to the local association. A few don't. (But don't forget our earlier admonition that it's a yellow flag if they don't—be careful.)

Regulation

Builders are among the least regulated major industries in our country. A few states require builders to take and pass examinations before being licensed or registered. Most do not and in a many states all they need is a business license.

They range in size from single carpenter/builders to large national companies with operations in many states. A number of them are in the *Fortune* list of the country's large companies.

The lack of strict regulation has led to many abuses which, in turn, have led to an increasing number of serious defects in new houses. These have resulted in claims, law suits and an increasing bitterness on the part of home buyers.

The problems arise primarily from three factors:

⇨ A lack of enough competent help, mostly at the subcontractor level,

⇨ A lack of competent and/or adequate supervision at the builder's level,

⇨ An inability or unwillingness to change their method of doing business to adjust for the first two factors.

A HUD report comments that the homebuilding industry hasn't yet gotten into the industrial age. The knowhow to do this is available, the incentives are not.

This is all discussed in Web Supplement E[1S].

Remodelers

Most remodelers are members of the National Association of the Remodeling Industry (NARI)[1U] and of the associated state organizations. You'll find that some remodelers specialize in particular areas of a house, like kitchens, others will do interior areas that do not require changing the exterior and still others include the whole house in their areas of expertise. Again, references and taking a look at what they've done for someone else is your best way to find the right remodeler for you. If there is a yearly remodeler's tour in your community, that is a good way to see what can be done and to learn something about the individual remodelers.

Designers

There are two organized groups whose members design houses, the American Institute of Architects (AIA) and the American Institute of Building Designers (AIBD). And there are many designers who don't belong to either of these. In fact, a significant number of small builders do their own design work. Watch out for these, many of their designs show their lack of experience and in-depth knowledge.

What to expect from an architect and designer is discussed in more detail in Chapter 3.

Generally, if you hire an architect, you can expect to pay more to have the work done but it is less likely to be a commonplace design. Architects will put more detail into their plans, leaving fewer decisions up to the builder and his subcontractors. Architects will usually, for a fee, keep an eye on the house during construction. This may be helpful if there are unusual design features. Depending on what your new house is to be like, you may be better off with an architect or you may find a less expensive building designer is just fine. Chapter 3 shows an example of an upscale house where an architect wasn't used. The basic design was OK, the construction was not.

Two things to be careful of:

⇨ There are good and bad, both architects and designers, and

⇨ Neither is likely to be sensitive to user-friendliness in their designs. That's where and why you should plan on being involved in the process whether a simple remodel or a complex new home.

Governmental Agencies

Building codes

Each state has its own set of laws and rules with its own set of commissions and agencies. About half of the states do not regulate builders in this area. Many states do not have building codes but leave this up to the local governments.

Until a few years ago the state agencies turned to one of several organizations for the basic code requirements. The differences in these just added to the proliferation of building codes across the country.

Now this is being pulled together into a set of agreed-to codes that the state agencies can use as the basis for their own. This all comes under the overall umbrella of the International Code Council (ICC) which is in the process of generating a number of new standards. The ICC website page[IV] is a list of the codes which are available. (We are not suggesting you should buy them, but the list will give you an idea of what's covered.)

Real estate agencies

Real estate sales are more controlled, each state having a real estate commission. The Association of Real Estate License Law Officials, ARELLO[IW], is a good source of information about the individual state agencies.

Federal agencies

There are federal and state government organizations with special programs dedicated to making homeownership possible for first-time and other homebuyers who would could have problems meeting the requirements for getting a mortgage loan and becoming homebuyers.

It is well to become aware of exactly the situation in the location where you are thinking of building or buying a home.

Federal agencies include:

⇨ HUD. The Department of Housing and Urban development[IX],

⇨ FHA. The Federal Housing Authority (a part of HUD) insures mortgages low-down payment to individuals, and

⇨ VA. The Veterans Administration guarantees loans to qualified veterans, sometimes up 100% of value of the home[IV].

Enter the Internet

As an individual you and your homebuying adventures are a tiny, tiny ripple on the surface of all of this. The ways things are done, and have been done for decades, are pretty well "poured in concrete", except for one thing - the Internet and its ability for communications and information dispersion.

Things are changing. You can take a first look at new houses, from big builders and small, without leaving your home. Ditto existing houses. The Internet is a plethora of information about houses, getting mortgages, what's good and bad in houses and about some of the despicable things builders and lenders have done.

And there's more. Because of the ability to disperse information on the Internet, there are books today that couldn't exist 10 years ago. There are websites and books that let you consider seriously being an owner-builder and the money it can save you. And there are websites that tell you, in detail, about the advantages of modular homes and how the factories for making them are spreading across the country. People *are* becoming enabled to take more control of their home buying, both in terms of what they cost and in terms of what they're getting.

All That Glitters...

Annell and I were checking out one of the models in a new subdivision by a national builder and we noted how open and bright the kitchen and adjacent family room were. However, the dishwasher location was not user-friendly. It was in a corner of the cupboards where it will be an irritation forever because, when it is being unloaded, the open door blocks access to the cupboards behind it, both upper and lower. (Chapter 14 is a discussion about dishwashers.)

Another couple came in and when the woman saw how attractive the kitchen looked her reaction was, "I love it. This is the house I want." We didn't stick around to see whether they got the house or not – probably not because there are so many other things that even the most emotional buyer will have to check out, like price and how many bedrooms. But the lack of sensitivity to the kitchen layout, where the woman would be using that dishwasher day after day, made me even more aware of the need to caution homebuyers to be more down to earth and not be carried away by their feelings.

And that particular builder's sales contracts have a very onerous binding arbitration clause in them which should also be avoided. This is another place where being practical can pay off in a big way later.

Chapter 2

Buying Options

> *That's the way things come clear. All of a sudden. And then you realize how obvious they've been all along.*
>
> Madeleine L'Engle, American author (1918 -)

In this chapter:

One of the first steps in buying a house or in remodeling an old one is to define just what you want. And one of those wants is a house that's easy to live in, i.e., one that is user-friendly.

This chapter reviews the various ways of getting that better home. These are a start for the rest of the book which discusses in more detail the things that make a home easier to live in.

You've put in a long day at work and you come home to relax and put the day behind you. What you don't need is a house that makes extra work for you or your spouse to fix dinner or that reminds you how far it is from the garage to the kitchen with what you've picked up at the store. What you **do** need is a home that doesn't have the irritations and inconsiderations that characterize so many of today's houses—you need a user-friendly home.

As you start your journey toward this better home, it may all seem simple enough. All you have to do is to find the home of your dreams, buy or build it, and move in. Ah, if only it were that easy. Very quickly you'll come to realize that it's a real jungle out there, with a tremendous variety of homes for sale, some of them with things you really like and others you wouldn't live with. Ever

Your Options

If you are thinking of remodeling you can:

⇨ Invest your time and money in remodeling your current house or

⇨ Buy an older home with the intent of remodeling it to fit your needs.

If you buy an existing house you may:

⇨ Buy a pre-owned home with the potential of good and bad that goes with it or

⇨ Buy a new house that has already been built (a spec house).

If you decide to buy a new yet-to-be-built home, one of your early decisions will be whether to:

⇨ Buy a house that is a copy or a modified copy of a model in a tract,

⇨ Have your dream home custom built,

⇨ Get a building-systems home, one that has significant parts made in a factory environment, thus avoiding most of the defects that occur on site, or

⇨ Build it yourself, the owner-builder method. This is often a combination of the custom and building-systems approaches.

Getting to know what makes a home user-friendly or -unfriendly should be an integral part of any decision making. Then, when you start looking at existing houses or at plans, you are much better equipped to recognize those features that you wouldn't want after you move in.

Remodels

If you like your current house but there are enough things that are out-dated or are a real pain in the neck that you're either going to change it or move, you may want to consider remodeling.

Remodeling may also be attractive if you're somewhat of an entrepreneur and run across a pre-owned house that needs a serious amount of work but which will be a real gem after it's done, both financially and as a place to live.

Unless the remodel is small and/or you're pretty handy and comfortable with rebuilding the house yourself, you'll want to use a remodeling contractor and, depending on the size and nature of the job, a designer or architect.

The design

Before a contractor can give you a cost for doing a job, he has to know exactly what's to be done. For small jobs, he'll talk to you about what it is you want and sketch up plans in enough detail to figure the costs of material and labor. You'll want to see these plans yourself to be sure it's what you thought you wanted.

For a major effort which involves changes in the structural elements of the house you should give serious thoughts to involving a home designer or an architect. They will draw up a set of plans detailing what is to be done.

When this happens before getting the remodeling contractor you can use the plans as the basis for going out for bids. Selection of the contractor is then similar to the steps you take with the custom house discussed later.

User-friendliness in remodels

As with new construction, you're the one who will be responsible for seeing that the job considerations include the user-friendly aspects discussed throughout this book. You'll find that, in general, this is not a consideration in anyone's plans.

Remodeling has a further constraint that will often require compromise. For example, a narrow U-shaped kitchen (*see* Chapter 18) with the sink at the closed end of the U, is inherently user-un-friendly. To eliminate it in an existing kitchen would usually necessitate a major change in the house itself, not just the kitchen. This can be quite expensive and you may decide to leave the basic kitchen layout unchanged. After all, it's the kitchen you've been living with for years already.

Pre-Owned House

Look in the "houses for sale" section of your newspaper and you'll find that used or pre-owned houses far outnumber all the others. There is a wide variety of houses of this type and, after you figure out this is the way for you to go, you will still need to narrow the field considerably. A real estate agent can help or, if you're starting out on your own, you'll have to focus your search using location, size and cost.

Another consideration is how old the house is. Older houses may be fixer-uppers that you'll need to remodel before or shortly after move in. Newer ones are usually closer to move-in condition but are more expensive.

Access to the Multiple Listing System (*see* Chapter 1) can be a real time-saver when you're sifting through all of the available houses.

With a pre-owned house you have the option of buying via the real estate community or getting one that's For Sale by Owner (FSBO).

Whether you use an agent or not, be sure you get an honest, competent home inspector. The few hundred dollars they cost can save you much more than that in the long pull.

Using a buyer's agent

Using an agent can save you money because they have access to listings of all homes for sale, they know the sources of financing and they can give you the advice of someone who's been spending years of his/her life in dealing with homes of

all sorts. What can be important in some situations is that a good agent will be up to speed on the requirements of what the seller is supposed to do, including proper disclosure. The agent will be able to keep you out of some of the pitfalls that exist. (Whether any given agent will actually do this is another question.)

FSBO

For Sale by Owner avoids the 6 to 7% commissions that are usually involved in buying a house. Obviously you need to know what you're doing, the pitfalls and the procedures, to go this route. But there are many thousands of dollars out there if you do.

There are organizations which are set up to help the FSBO seller get his house on the market, including Internet listings. They usually publish paper booklets, which you may find at your grocery store and postoffice, that let you see if there's anything there you might like. Some hold classes to help at a cost—but significantly less than the fees you'd have to pay a realtor..

Because the sales commissions are built into the price of a house, not having to pay for them reduces the cost of the house which, in turn, adds to the gain on the property when you sell it.

Sometimes a small spec-house builder will not use a selling agent but rather will sell using FSBO arrangements. This also avoids the 3% selling agent's fee.

Spec House

A spec house is one which a builder has built "on speculation" without having a firm buyer when it's started.

Here's another place where you may deal directly with the seller (the builder) and avoid a sales agent's commission. If you're sure of what you're doing, go for it. But you may not save as much as you thought you might because the builder will often have an agreement with a selling agent where that agent gets the commission regardless of who buys the house or how. You should save the buyers agent's commission, however - usually 3%. (But see below re Production houses.)

Whether you use a buyers agent or not, it will be very much up to you to be sure the house is going to work for you.

A home inspector is just as good an idea here as with the pre-owned home. He will often find something you would have missed, something that's far better having fixed before you commit to the house.

I f you get the idea that we firmly believe that it's far better to avoid problems than get into hassles to get them fixed later, you're right, we do! Sellers of all kinds are a lot more amenable before thay have your money in hand.

When you buy an existing spec house (Oregon, above, and Pennsylvania, below) you should know, good and bad, what you're getting.

The Tract or Production House

The dictionary says a tract is "an extended area of land," while production is "any tangible result of effort." With houses the two terms are used to mean the same thing. Years ago a tract got a reputation of something less than desirable and "production" came into being as the term to describe the methodology used to build more desirable houses.

They are *not* built on a production line like cars are at Ford or General Motors. Far from it. Generally there are a few models from which you pick one. You do get to personalize it by your choices of colors and, often, by having options on how the front of the house looks (the elevations.) But in terms of getting changes made to make the house a better place to live, i.e., to make it more user-friendly, that's usually not an option in tracts.

Tract houses are purposely easy to buy. First, you have an existing model that you can see in the flesh. And you don't have many decisions to make because most have already been made by the builder. Your main involvement is in deciding which house you want in which subdivision. Some builders do a much better job than others of thinking about the home user. When you know what to look for you'll quickly figure out which builders and which plans to avoid.

In reality, it's not often that your only decision is which floor plan. First, there's the lot—you usually have a choice of several on which the house can be built. Then, there are the options, frequently many of them, that the builder is offering. And, finally, there may be things you can have done that are not in the standard option package, things that

With a tract house, choosing user-friendliness becomes a matter of whether you buy the house or not. Don't expect the builder to change anything. (Colorado, above, and California, below.)

will make the house more cost-effective and a better place to live.

A word of caution here. I've seen many tracts where modern marketing techniques have taken over and, to get the base price down, builders have left out as much as they can and still have a house. They make it up with the options which everyone wants. (Would you, for example, want a house without an electric garage door opener? But many tracts don't have any!) Be extremely cautious when comparing tract models, it's often the cost of the options that make the real difference.

Tract houses are meant to be the least expensive way to build a house. The builder, who may also be the subdivider, plans how many houses of each of several plans are going to be built and then buys materials in larger quantities. He is also in a position to offer subcontractors continuing work which means he can negotiate lower labor costs. But the more he does this, the more rigid he has to be about not making changes.

There is yet another gain to be had by knowing what you are doing. When something is wrong or goes wrong in a new house within a year after you move in, your recourse is to turn to the builder or his warranty company to get it fixed. In the matter of home warranties the recommendation is made to avoid builders who use the legalities of the sales contracts to avoid taking responsibilities for their mistakes. Finding a builder who stands behind the houses he builds is one of the smartest and most empowering things you can do.

Here's another yellow-flag waver. When looking at some production houses, I looked over the sales contract to see what it had to say about warranties. I wanted time to study it and asked if I could have a copy. The request was flatly refused as being against their policy. Further inquiry told me that they only gave a buyer a copy after he had signed it. I couldn't even have gotten a copy to take to an attorney before signing. And this was a large national builder!

Sure, builders may not want their competition to see what their contracts say. But what about the buyer who's trying to protect himself? The whole area reeks of "who gives a damn about the consumer."

If it can be worked out with the builder, have an inspector who can keep an eye on things for you while the house is under construction. And don't you hesitate to watch what's going on yourself. And, if you run across a builder who forbids you or your inspector to set foot on the property while it's under construction (and there are these kinds who use liability issues as an excuse), you'd undoubtedly be better off to keep on going. That type of builder is so concerned with himself and his profit that it's quite unlikely he'll be anything but uncooperative if troubles do appear. How you, the consumer, fare is your problem, not his. And don't forget to ask about this when you're looking at models, a long time before you make any kind of commitment.

Something that's happening as this is being written is the awakening by some of the big production builders to the cost of having unhappy customers, either in the lawsuits that have resulted from their defective houses or in damage to their reputations. The obvious way to improve this situation is to build better houses, ones that are less likely to have some of the failings that past construction has had.

To this end many production builders are using more and more materials that are pre-manufactured in factory environments and shipped to building sites. One of the techniques is to use structural insulated panels (SIPS)[2B] in the walls of houses. These cost a little more but reduce the amount of on-site labor. They can result in significantly better houses in terms of defects.

Another variation on the site-built house is the use of insulated concrete forms (ICFs)[2F] where walls are poured concrete which use styrafoam forms that are left in place to act as insulation around the walls. These are sometimes used in conjunction with SIPs as the roof and interior walls.

It's something to look for and ask about when you are visiting production/tract model homes.

Then there are the real estate agents. Here are some words of caution.

Sales agents

When you are talking with sales agents at model houses, be sure you understand that you are dealing with people who are consummate professionals. They know their business—selling. They've taken detailed courses in how to hook peoples' interests and how to get them committed to buy a house. You are far better off to adopt an attitude that keeps your feelings out of the action. As Jack Webb used to say, "Just the facts, Ma'am."

Getting your own agent

This may sound unreal, but you won't pay more when you have an agent to help you find the house you want than if you don't because your agent will be paid by the builder! If you get a good buyer's agent, they're the ones who can help you be objective and not to be swayed by the persuasive chat that you hear from the builder's agent.

A word of caution. Before you start looking at models in a tract, be sure to tell the sales agent that you have a buyer's agent, otherwise the builder will just pocket the commission that would have gone to your agent. Better yet, have your agent with you when you first go to a tract.

But don't expect agents to point out user-unfriendly designs like registers in a kitchen floor (*see* Chapter 7). That's not been part of the agent's job and few of them are aware of how much actual help they could be.

A custom house lets you fit the house to its surroundings. (Arizona)

In every case, it will pay you to be knowledgeable about good and bad design and construction.

Custom Houses

We noted that tract houses are usually called production houses. Or they may be known as a "development." They're all pretty much the same thing. But not "custom" houses. Let's take a look at what a custom house might be.

The dictionary says re custom: "made to order." But note—in a *tract* the builder doesn't start building the house until he gets an order from you. So you could argue that production houses are custom and, believe it or not, some production builders do call their products "custom homes." (The largest builder in my state does this.) And "custom" is used all the way from production houses to houses where you have complete control over everything that goes into the house from

Custom houses may be modest or grandiose. They are all an opportunity for buyers to get what they want. But, again, buyers need to know what's good and not so good. (Oregon, above, and Florida, below)

initial design to the choice of lots, appliances, appearances, heights of ceilings, etc.

With a fully custom house you generally buy the lot on your own, get your own floor plan and house design, put together a bid package and go out for bids. You select the builder based on reputation and bid price. All the choices are yours, although you will probably work with the builder

This up-scale fully-custom house was a disaster. The exterior is being redone here. Regardless of how you buy your home, you can't be too careful—inside and out. (Oregon)

to fill in details such as appliances, finishes, etc. But these, too, can still be disasters as in this photo.

You'll find there is no hard and fixed rule about what you can customize when you're getting a truly custom house. First, there are zoning ordinances and building codes that have to be taken into account. There may well be deed restrictions that dictate what you may build. You'll find that many builders have lots reserved in a subdivision which can make your choice of lots an easier task. And they may have plans for you to start with, making that job easier, too. Truly, the words "custom home" can mean everything from a purely production house to one where you make the decisions about every tiny detail.

So where do you start? There are so many things that seem to need doing first: finding a lot, a house designer, financing, getting a builder—the list seems endless and all are big decisions. At this point, you might be tempted to back off and buy that "ho-hum" tract house in the local subdivision.

That's tempting, but getting a custom house is well within just about anyone's reach. But there is a lot of work involved. You'll have to figure out just what you want, not as a nebulous dream, but as something that can be put on paper and then built.

Among the reasons people get custom houses:

⇨ They want a truly one-of-a-kind house.

⇨ They don't want to be just another look-alike in a development.

⇨ They've found a special lot, often with a great view.

⇨ They're in an area where there are few tracts and these are all low-priced starter homes. So the choice is either a spec house or a custom house and, since most builders make both, buyers are more likely to get what they want if they have it custom built.

⇨ They want to do part of the work themselves and can work out a deal with a builder which will let them do this. Or they can act as their own general contractor and do as much themselves as they want.

⇨ They're willing to spend the time to shop for appliances, fixtures, cabinets, countertops, etc., and save significant money in the process.

Besides the usual process of hiring an architect or building designer and a builder, there are several alternative ways to get the made-to-order house that may appeal to you.

As an owner-builder you act as the general contractor and do as much of the construction work as you like. The carrot is a lower-priced home. Or you may want something specialized as this owner-builder did. He make his own environmentally-friendly house. But you MUST know what you're doing–including the intricacies of design and construction. (Colorado)

Owner-Builder[2C, 2D]

One of life's greatest satisfactions can come from starting from scratch and ending up with a home that's the result of your ideas, decisions and actions. You can even be your own general contractor! This may seem ridiculous to you right now, but it's not that difficult with the help of companies formed specifically to help you make decisions that general contractors make and to help you save part of the money that a contractor needs for overhead and profit.

Two of the options you have as an owner-builder are where you get the design and the materials for your house. These include "building systems" where significant parts of the house are manufactured in a factory and shipped to your site.

Building Systems[2E]

The building industry describes these generic kinds of building systems on their website:

- ➪ Kit homes.
- ➪ Panelized.
- ➪ Modular.

With a significant amount of work being done in factories under weather-controlled conditions and with better quality control, building systems offer three significant potential advantages over the usual site-built home:

- ➪ Shorter erection times. The pouring of the foundation and the construction of the house in the factory go on at the same time, not sequentially. And weather does not effect the construction, in time or quality.
- ➪ Lower cost.
- ➪ Fewer defects.

Kit homes

For these homes the materials are made in a factory, bundled into kits and shipped. Often these are log homes where the exterior is entirely logs.

This log-home is one class of kit home. Others may look very much like the usual site-built home. (Washington)

Some kits may include interior walls but usually that is left for the builder to finish on site.

Depending on where you live, companies will sell you, delivered on-site, all the materials you need for your house along with detailed instructions about how to erect it. They'll either sell you a pre-designed house (with its shortcomings) or will engineer a kit to your specifications (based on their standard models). You are responsible for making the arrangements to have the house erected.

Among your options:

- ➪ Do it yourself. (Owner-builder)
- ➪ Contract with a builder. (Custom home)

Panelized homes

Here the walls are factory made as panels and shipped. These generally include only the external walls but internal walls may also be panelized. The panels are erected on site and the finishing work is done as with a site-built house.

As noted earlier, several large production builders are moving to reduce the cost, defects and time required to frame new homes by using factory-made panels. It is a first move toward bringing home building into the industrial age.

At the same time, as an individual, you can buy a completely designed panelized home ready for erection on your site. You will have to find a builder who knows how to do this.

A few words of caution re structural insulated panels (SIPs) which are being used in more and more new homes. These result in very tight houses—there is no place for air to get in or out. There must be some means of air-to-air exchangers to get humidity, radon and other toxins out of the houses. These are usually special units attached to the furnace/air conditioner that keep the inside air from becoming stagnant.

Modular homes

If you live where they are available, modular homes are another way to get the custom dream you want. Modular homes are "stick built" houses that are made in a factory, broken into modules and hauled to your lot. At the site they are set onto prepared foundations. External connections to utilities are made. Items such as outside walks and steps are added.

The houses must meet the building codes of the states where they are to be erected and generally there will be an inspector within the factory who certifies that the home meets the requirements of the particular state where it is to be shipped.

A completed 4-bedroom modular home. (Pennsylvania)

A smaller modular home being set on its foundation. (Oregon)

Note these are not "manufactured" homes which are made to a different set of standards and codes than are modular homes. But not all modular home companies are created equal. Many are manufactured home companies for whom the change over to making modular homes was an easy transition. This is particularly true when they sell to states which have relatively loose building codes so that it is almost a case of calling their manufactured home a modular home and selling it.

And do be careful when you see the words "modular home". There are some unscrupulous factories which use the term for such things as sheds, for example.

There is a further caution. When you look on their websites, far too many modular-home companies include the garage in the "square feet" values given for their homes. This makes a comparison with site-built homes—which never do this—virtually impossible. When shopping do be careful.

The larger, more-experienced companies will offer a variety of homes ranging from "stock" designs to fully custom. You generally buy them through a homebuilder who has a working arrangement with the modular company and is responsible for getting foundations ready to receive the modular home when it arrives on site. In other cases, you buy the home from the modular manufacturer who takes the responsibility for the foundation and the on-site finishing—for a fee, of course.

When finished, well-built modular homes are virtually indistinguishable from site-built homes (*see* photos). They can be fully customized including design and materials. They have several advantages over the traditional way of building:

- ⇨ They are less expensive,
- ⇨ They are built in factories sheltered from the vagaries of weather,

➪ Workmanship is likely to be more consistent,

➪ Houses built this way take weeks on site to finish rather than the months for a typical site-built home, and

➪ Because the on-site preparation goes on at the same time as the building in the factory, the overall time from placing an order to having your home ready is significantly shorter than with site-built houses.

But there are downsides to modular homes:

➪ You may not find a builder of modular homes in your area. This, however, is changing as more people are buying them.

➪ You have to find the lot yourself. It's more like getting a custom house than a tract one.

Tim Carter, who writes the nationally syndicated column "Ask the Builder", is high on the modular home as the way to get a better custom home for less money but does set a lower limit of 1500 square feet as the minimum size below which the modular home is not less expensive than a standard site-built house.

You might take a look at his website to see his comments[2G]. In that same column he also points out the general dangers of dealing with the many inept home builders.

One of the more interesting trips in looking at houses was visiting two modular-home factories in central Pennsylvania. Things are set up on a production line with experienced, competent workers along the way, each doing his speciality on a continuous basis. It was all, of course, inside a big, covered building. Quality inspections were performed as each portion of the job was finished and problems fixed right there and then.

When you see such an operation and realize the advantages to the factory of buying in quantities instead of one house at a time and of providing continuous work for better employees, you can see for yourself how they can truly make better houses for less money.

If you get a chance, it is worthwhile to visit a modular-home factory. You can then make the comparison yourself between the controlled conditions in a factory and the open-to-the-great-outdoors conditions of a site-built house.

Chapter 3

Home Designs

Home is the most popular, and will be the most enduring of all earthly establishments.
Channing Pollock, actor, magician (1926-   )

In this chapter:
What home designs are, good and bad features, who uses them, who makes them. how they are sold, and where to put them are the subjects here.

Channing Pollock expressed it nicely in the above quote. While we may not be able to afford what we'd like, when we buy a home, we're looking for something that best fits our needs and our desires. It's a combination of aesthetics and practicality; of what it costs, what it looks like, how proud we are of what we've done, and how comfortable it is to live in.

The design of the house encompasses all of these and whether you're buying one that already exists, one yet to be built, or remodeling, checking the design is probably the most crucial of your decisions.

The floor plan reflects the practicality. It shows how the rooms are laid out, where the doors and the windows are, and where the appliances go. The overall design goes beyond this by taking into account how the house will look both inside and out. And it's right here that we start to see differences both in the quality of designs and in their details.

An important thing to keep in mind when considering the design of a house is how it may effect the resale value of the property. And this is true for a pre-owned house, a production house and, of course, for a custom house. A design that is eye-catching may be excellent for resale or, if it's unusual, it may be difficult to find someone interested in making it their own.

How to Use the Information in This Chapter When Considering a House

<u>Older Home.</u> When looking at an older home, you may want to consider how big a job it would be to remodel it—to bring it up to date.

<u>Newer Existing House.</u> With a newer existing house, you're interest is how well the design fits your needs and wants. You'll probably end up compromising when all the factors are considered but you'll know what you're getting into and won't be in for unpleasant surprises later.

<u>Production Home.</u> For a production house, you usually have some choices in such things as colors, counter tops, floor coverings and appliances. These are sometimes considered design items and their availability can make these choices a major factor in choosing which house to buy.

<u>Custom Home.</u> For custom houses, it's a whole different thing. You are not constrained to start with any particular design. You are free to look and choose. (We lump owner-builder with custom houses in these discussions. The buyer is in control.)

<u>Semi-Custom Home.</u> Check out your options and constraints. You don't have the freedom of a custom house but it should be possible to get the features you want. Kit homes also have this characteristic.

<u>Remodel.</u> This is an opportunity to get rid of any bad design features that the builder put in in the first place. But be sure you don't add some of your own.

AND ALWAYS CHECK USER-UNFRIENDLINESS.
WHEN YOU FIND IT, IT'S ONE LESS SURPRISE LATER.

Design Considerations

There are many design requirements and considerations that are involved in the planning and building of a house. Here, briefly, are some of them:

⇨ Location. This determines the general price range of the house. Subdivisions are generally done for a particular style of house in the same price range thus assuring that the houses will attract the same genré of buyer making them compatible in terms of surrounding houses and neighbors.

This is why you'll find, even in such developments as private golf courses, that the different subdivsions are made up of homes of compatible but different characteristics. This leads to the next two parameters.

⇨ Price range of the house.

⇨ Style of the house. This includes architectural style, size, number of bedrooms and number of floors

⇨ Terrain. A house on the side of a hill has different design requirements than one on flat land. Further, the soil and the ability to anchor the house to the hillside are factors. This can be a remodeling consideration as well.

⇨ Lot. The lot size and its location relative to streets and utilities. Particularly if there is a view, the lot can a have a big impact on the design of the house.

⇨ Local climate.

⇨ Local code and building regulations. These change with time and include such items as energy savings and the ability to withstand winds and earthquakes. They can effect what's done during a remodeling.

⇨ Homeowners' association bylaws.

⇨ Local customs. These are significantly different from place to place and they, too, change with time. (As a minor example, did you know that, while most places include medicine cabinets in bathrooms, there are some that do not?)

⇨ The builder's perceptions about what he can build the least expensively and sell for the greatest profit. This, of course, varies from one builder to another.

⇨ The buyer's personal likes and dislikes. And here, too, there are wide variations from buyer to buyer as well as over time.

⇨ The availability of appliances. These continually improve from year to year and can impact on design details.

⇨ Building material availabilities. Today there is a significant stress on energy saving and, with it, the tightness of houses which, in turn, impact on such items as windows and doors and on concerns for toxins and molds.

⇨ Whether it is a spec, production, custom, modular, or owner-builder house. The constraints for each of these are different. And the end houses will be different because they stress a different aspect of home building and buying.

It is from the combinations of these considerations that you'll see houses that look different inside and out in different parts of the country.

We've taken pictures of houses from around the country to give you a feeling for the wide variety you'll find (pages 38 and 39). While there are many differences, it is remarkable just much houses really are like those elsewhere. And, the design and building shortcomings that are the thrust of this book are found in all of them!

Designs

While this section discusses plans as if you're going to be getting them yourself, the details here are applicable to existing and pre-designed homes where they will help you see the things you'll want to watch for and what might be done to correct the shortcomings. They may also give you some thoughts for remodeling.

Floor plans that you see in magazines and on the Internet are scale diagrams of the layout of the rooms, halls, etc., in a house. There will be separate drawings for each floor.

House plans and house design packages generally include floor plans but not the other drawings needed by a builder to build the house. A basic problem with plans designed for sale via magazines, in catalogs or via the Internet is that the basic plans are of necessity designed to be used anywhere. This means that such things as the specific building codes where you live haven't been taken into account. Seeing that that is done is up to you.

If you are considering a to-be-built home, there are several distinct ways you can go about getting the design for your new home. The simplest is to find a house you like and have the builder make another one just like it. This is what happens in a tract or when you find a spec house that you'd like to see built on your own lot.

But you'll probably want the builder to make a change here and there and some tract builders may encourage this by offering an extensive package of pre-planned options. If you take this route to

AMONG THE CONSIDERATIONS IN THE DESIGN OF A HOUSE ARE THE COMMUNITY AND THE SPECIFIC LOT

1. Western ranch
2. Desert
3. Row Houses
4. Riverfront
5. Tract (OR)
6. Beach (CA)
7. Used (25-year old)
8. Custom (AZ)
9. Modular (PA)
10. Flood Plain (OR)
11. Custom (GA)
12. Tract (CA)
13. "Green" (CO)
14. Custom (CO)
15. Custom (CO)
16. Custom (FL)

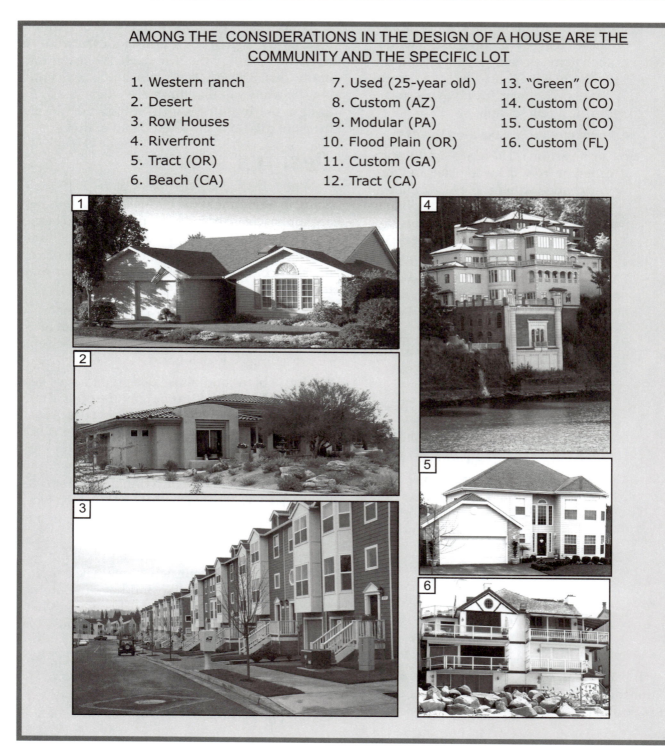

your new home, don't be discouraged by not finding exactly what you want. Some smaller tract builders are more than willing to consider changes to their standard offerings.

We did just that in our southern California house. We liked the floor plan and the way the model was finished but decided we'd like some changes besides those the sales agent offered. The builder was more than cooperative. Sure it cost us more money, but he was happy and so were we.

And the slower business is, the more agreeable the builder will be.

Floor Plans

General Considerations

The floor plan should make the house feel comfortable and easy to live in. Look at which areas will get the most use and where people will walk when getting from one area to another. You can do this in an existing house as well as one on paper.

Here are some other things to remember. As you become aware of them, you'll no doubt find still others you'd rather avoid:

➪ Is there a traffic path through the kitchen where culinary efforts will be under way? Is there a lot of traffic across the family room in front of the TV? It takes only a few minutes to decide if a floor plan makes sense in terms of how the house will be used.

➪ Consider the room arrangement and noise. Family rooms next to bedrooms can be a noise problem unless the wall between them is sound insulated. (*See* Chapter 12.).

➪ Is there an entry closet? Surprisingly, some designs don't include them. The same goes for linen closets. These are

often in hallways or, sometimes, in bathrooms. And, in some cases, there aren't any at all!

➪ Is the garage close to the kitchen? When it is, it makes for shorter trips from the car, particularly with groceries. In some house designs if the garage is on the right side of the house, it can do a good job of shielding part of the house from the midday or afternoon sun or winter storms .

➪ Is the kitchen close to the outside door where trash cans will be kept? It can be a major annoyance to have to travel through the whole house to take trash out.

➪ If you're planning a two-story house, be sure to include a half-bath downstairs. But be careful here too, these often have the "sidle" door problem discussed in Chapter 9.

➪ Bedrooms over the garage are virtually impossible to insulate against the noise of the opening and closing of the garage doors. Think twice when you see this arrangement.

➪ Is there a door out the back of the house? Surprisingly, some plans forget this. In other cases, the way out to the back is through the garage but the garage lacks a side door! (*see* Chapter 9.)

➪ One consideration in choosing your floor plan and house design is whether it lends itself to future expansion. This may be important to you or, at a future date, to someone else when they're looking for a place to buy.

➪ Some people object to being able to stand at the front door and look through the house to the kitchen. If this bothers you, watch for it. (Split level entries are often this way.) Or, since it could reflect on the resale value of the house, just don't have a house where this can happen.

⇨ Other potential problems with split levels include:

- Inadequate space at the front door (you should have room for both you and guests to comfortably stand).

- Stairs so narrow or twisted that it is virtually impossible to move furniture up and down.

- Watch where the guest closet is located. There is usually a half flight of stairs between the door and the closet. Don't have it any farther away than is absolutely necessary.

⇨ In the same category as being able to see the kitchen from the entry are objections to arrangements where you can see into a bathroom from the living area of the house. Even if you don't care, some day a potential buyer could.

⇨ Is there enough storage space? Because it isn't a showy thing, designers and builders often skimp in this area. Be sure there are places for brooms, vacuum cleaners, and things you may never need but want to save anyway—like the original boxes for electronic equipment.

⇨ Don't forget a place—a basement is great if you have one—to put seasonal items like skis, snow blowers and lawn mowers. If it isn't there, you'll probably need an external tool shed. Attic storage can be useful but needs to be planned (*see* Chapter 12).

⇨ The kitchen should be next to the formal dining room, if there is one. Separation of dining room and kitchen means many extra steps when serving food and cleaning up.

One story or two?

In deciding between a one- and two-story house, consider:

⇨ Stairs.

⇨ Space taken by stairs and outside walls.

⇨ Heating and cooling.

⇨ Lot requirements.

⇨ Shading from roof overhangs.

Stairs

Older people, even those without physical disabilities, prefer not to have stairs. Two-story plans with the master bedroom on the first floor are helpful but most often single-floor arrangements are the choice of senior citizens.

Space taken by stairs

A typical stairwell, including framing, is 4 x 13 feet which is over 50 square feet on each floor of space that isn't needed in a one-story house. Landings also take away from the useful floor area.

Outside walls

The area on each floor taken up by outside walls is included in the stated square footage of the house. (Square footage is measured on the outside, not the inside, of a house.) With two floors this lost area occurs twice, once on each floor. In a typical 2400 square-foot house, the floor space taken by the walls will be about 40 square feet more for a two-story house than for a single story with the same number of square feet.

Overall

For the same amount of square footage the single floor house will often be higher priced than a two-story unit. But don't assume that a two-story house is a better buy until you take out the floor space used by stairs, landings, and outside walls.

Heating and cooling

As you know, upstairs rooms are noticeably warmer than downstairs areas. Most builders don't do anything about this even through there are ways to correct it (*see* Chapter 7). It will cost money and is another item to think about when comparing one- and two-story houses.

Lot requirements

For the same amount of useful floor area, the two-story house takes up less of the lot. And in many areas the pressures for putting more houses in a given area are making lot sizes smaller and smaller. If this is the case where you are or if it is important to you otherwise, it may be the deciding factor in selecting your floor plan.

Shading

Roof overhangs can be used to shade windows on one-story buildings but not the lower walls and windows of two-story houses. This can be important in the desert and other hot climates—which is why most houses in Arizona are one story. And, every place, this lack of shade makes the summer cooling bill higher.

Simplicity

In general, the simpler the outside of the house, the less expensive it will be. A rectangular box will be more economical to build than a house with notches and zigzags in the walls. Similarly, the more complex the roof line, the more costly it is. Breaks in the roof line, multiple gables, and turrets add to the cost—as will hipped roofs. Steeply pitched roofs will be more expensive than those of moderate pitch because of the greater difficulty (and danger) for the roofer. You have to decide how much money to allocate for the sake of appearance (and resale).

Architectural fashions come and go. In the past we've had baroque, rococo, and Victorian. Today, it's colonials, gables, glass, and eye-catching interiors—about as far from the plain rectangular box with its plain sash windows as you can get. In many designs each room seems to need its own gable, including the entry. Look at how many new houses and designs have glass above the entry and glass across the front of the house. And note the lack of continuity—they look as if the designer took pieces from wherever he/she could find them and stuck them together. Who knows which direction the pendulum will swing next, but history's lesson is that what's faddish today will be passé tomorrow. And that can be an expensive lesson at resale time.

The message: don't too get carried away with today's "in" thing. Have enough roof-line breaks to be interesting but don't overdo. Have enough glass to make the interior light and appealing but don't make it a fish bowl. Keep the interiors open for family togetherness but make sure there are private spaces too. And above all, keep it user-friendly.

How many square feet?

Use the number of square feet shown on a floor plan only as a general guide. In many houses and plans there is useless space that still costs to build and heat—space that could often better be used elsewhere. We address some of these areas here. How they affect your ideas about a particular house design is an individual matter.

Conventional wisdom has it that a two-story house is less expensive per square foot than one story because of the smaller foundation and roof for the same number of square feet. This is true if you stop right there but it doesn't account for the non-living space taken up by stairs and walls as noted previously.

But these aren't the only places where unused space is included in the overall square footage. Some master bedrooms have a large space in the center of the room whose sole purpose is to make the room look bigger. Even kitchens sometimes end up with space that isn't used. (This is unfortunate, because it will mean more work in such a kitchen than would be needed with a better design.)

Other places to look for useless space are in the centers of walk-in closets and pantries. To be sure, you need to have a place to stand, but good design will minimize the amount of space required. Eliminating the walk-in pantry is one way to avoid the waste. Cabinet-type pantries with pull-out shelves make much better use of the space than does a walk-in unit, although they're not as pretentious and they may not be as convenient.

Similarly, eliminating the walk-in closet would also save space. While walk-in closets are popular today, wall closets have more useful space per square foot of floor than do walk-ins. (Eliminating walk-in pantries and closets also solves the problems of where to swing the doors. The whole thing is very much a matter of personal give and take.)

You'll often find unused space in hallways. Where a second-story bridge is needed across an open space between two upstairs bedroom areas you have an example of aesthetics first, followed by utility. (A basically different plan would obviate the need for the bridge. But it may still appeal to you—as it has to many others.)

User friendliness

One of the facets you'll want to be careful of in any plan, whether it's an existing house, one yet to be built, or a remodel is that some care is taken to be sure there aren't things in the plan that will be a pain in the neck to live with. (Like a refrig-erator in a corner where you can't get a door fully open.)

The concept of user-friendliness in home designs is explored in detail in succeeding chapters. When you have a custom house built or you're remodeling, you've got control—make it a better home. And be cautious here, too, because this is often a subject that neither builders, plan designers, building designers nor architects pay much attention to. It's usually very much up to you.

NOT user-friendly. The left (freezer) door will hit the wall. You'll never get it all the way open nor be able to get the freezer bins out (see Chapter 15.) And don't be in a hurry to use stainless steel (Chapter 18).

This might be a good time to take another look at our website and see the floor plan for the *Horrid Little House* with its multitude of typical, horrid places where you can make your home better by controlling the design and floor plan[3A].

Our *Horrid Little House* would, indeed, be terrible to live in but, as noted earlier, I've seen everyone of those horrors time and time again in the new homes I've looked at.

It is my hope that the examples in that floor plan will make you more aware of just how prevalent these things are. Then, when you're looking on your own, you'll be able to nod and say to yourself, "Aha, I don't want that."

This was brought home to me during a "Street of Dreams" tour I took recently. As I was looking around the master bedroom suite, I saw one of my favorites, a "sidle" toilet. (This is where the bowl is in a room so small that you have to go in and sidle back between the bowl and the wall before you can close the door.) I was getting ready to take a picture when a woman asked me what was so interesting. When I explained, her face just lit up. Seems she was the interior designer for that builder who hadn't paid much attention to her comments about the room. For me it was nice to know that someone else could see the obvious.

A "sidle" toilet. The interior decorator didn't like it either. (Chapter 20 discusses this user-unfriendly arrangement in detail.)

Home Designers

If you are buying an existing house, the rest of this chapter will not apply directly to your home purchase activity. If the house is in a tract, you may be able to see the problems in the model and make some arrangement to have them corrected in your own house. If you are considering a major remodel, this information may be helpful.

Watch the details

Some plans are much more detailed than others and you need to be careful with both kinds.

⇨ The undetailed ones ignore the placement of heating registers, electrical outlets and switches, TV outlets, the way doors swing, and even whether they are swinging, folding or sliding doors. The builder then leaves these up the subcontractors which, for you, is like playing Russian roulette. When you can, get the message through to the builder about just how those things should be handled.

⇨ The opposite are the plans that detail where everything should go—but they may not have them where they should be. Again the builder leaves it up to the subs who will generally follow the plans. This time you'll have to go over the plans with a fine-toothed comb to be sure things are right. Either that or get an architect or building designer who knows about user-friendliness. And that may not be easy.

As a general rule, it's a good idea that the plans be as detailed as you can get them. Otherwise builders and their subs will do things just like they've always done them—whether it's what you like or not.

Architect or building designer?

Most building designers are members of the American Institute of Building Design (AIBD)[3B] or the American Institute of Architects (AIA)[3C].

The AIBD

From their website:

The American Institute of Building Design is a nonprofit professional organization dedicated to the development, recognition, and enhancement of the profession of building design.

The AIBD started in California in 1950. It now has members in most states. It is not a cohesive organization nor do all plan designers and vendors belong to the AIBD. Because of it's West Coast roots, there are a significantly larger proportion of today's members in California, Oregon and Washington.

AIBD members sell building plans via catalogs and, of course, via the Internet. They will modify existing plans or generate new ones. Their range of experience and expertise varies widely. If you are considering a house that doesn't have some unusual design feature, you may find that getting a plan from an AIBD member is the right choice.

Building designers, are in general, not required to be licensed in the states where they operate but their responsibilities for the designs they create will depend on the state where they are. You should check their insurance coverage (Errors-and-Omission and Liability) before you hire one.

The AIA

If you go to the AIA website page[3E] and click on the button "Why an AIA Architect?", you'll find this description of an architect:

Like doctors and lawyers, architects are licensed professionals. The title "Architect" may be used only by an individual who possesses a state license to practice architecture. They are the only professionals in the construction industry who are ethically bound to represent you, the building owner.

Professional qualifications generally include:

*

College degree from an accredited school of architecture, requiring five or more years of professional studies.

*

Three years of internship under the supervision of licensed architects.

*Passage of a rigorous five-day examination

Only those professionals who have fulfilled these requirements, or other requirements as stipulated by each individual state, may legally call themselves architects and practice architecture in the jurisdiction granting the license. Individuals may be registered, or licensed, in more than one state by means of reciprocal licensing agreements among the states.

Unlike the AIBD which focuses on residences, AIA members are involved in all aspects of building design. Some do residential design as the main part of their practice, others only occasionally. You can look at their "Residential" Web page(s)[3D] and click on the various buttons to see what the AIA says an architect can and does do.

Of particular interest to homebuyers is this from the AIA page "What an Architect Can Do For You"[3E]:

Building is a long process that is often messy and disruptive, particularly if you're living in the space while it's under construction. Your architect represents you, not the contractors. Your architect looks out for your interests and smooths the process, helps find qualified construction contractors, and visits the work site to help protect you against work that's not according to plan.

The problems that Lilly and Robert had (picture on page 30) could have been avoided if they had used an architect to look out for their interests and visit the construction site to watch the work while it was underway. Actually, there is another way to be sure your house is being built according to the specifications of the contract. If you can find a home inspector who is qualified to inspect new construction, he should be able to watch out for you, too.

Which?

Whether to use a building designer or an architect is a matter of money and comfort. If your house is modest and you find a plan that fits your needs with little or no change, then a designer is probably OK. If your house is upscale or has some unusual features, then an architect might be the better way to go.

Another part of the decision process is just how competent your builder is in building the kind of house you want. If he does a good job working from blue prints without conferring with the person who designed the building, then you may be OK without an architect but do get a new-construction qualified home inspector—if you can find one and if the builder will work with him.

To find such an inspector you can contact an inspection school that gives classes in new-home inspection. The Inspection Training Associates website is a start[3I].

Getting Your Design

There are several different design business areas and some designers work in more than one of them. The discussion here is meant to help you understand what you're looking at when you see a fully custom plan, a plan in a newspaper or magazine, one in a catalog you pick up in the supermarket or bookstore, or on the Internet. Note that home designs can be drawn by anyone, qualified or not. He/she may be a registered architect, an experienced designer or a beginner who works at it evenings and weekends. Or it may be someone who doesn't know what he/she is doing and does it anyway.

If you're buying an existing house you probably won't need the services of a designer unless you're considering a major remodel.

If you decide to have your new home custom built, you will need a set of plans for the builder to work from. Your options are to:

⇨ Use a set of existing plans from a magazine, catalog or the Internet. Whatever changes you want made are done by you and/or the builder. You don't use a designer.

⇨ Use a set of existing plans and have them modified by a designer. Be sure to be careful of copyrights, it's easy to infringe. Internet sources of home plans usually include a way to get plans modified to meet any different requirements you may have.[3F, 3H]

⇨ Get your builder first and then choose from his available plans. He has them modified them as you wish. This is what happens with a semi-custom house.

⇨ Have plans made from scratch by an architect or designer.

And a word of caution re the plans you will see in magazines, on the Internet, etc. They may not meet the requirements of your local building codes.

This was made clear to me when looking at floor plans on the Internet which are all for 4" exterior walls. In Oregon, where I live, this will not meet the R-values required by our state energy codes. If you were to buy a set of these plans you'll pay significantly more to have them modified to get the required 6" walls. Of course, your builder may well be able to do this without having the plans redone. But it's another thing that will require your attention that a set of locally made plans would not.

The custom designer

The custom designer provides a service. He/she works with a client to find out what the customer wants and what they can afford. The object is to satisfy the customer. While they may proffer advice and suggestions, the end product is the result of customer inputs. In general, the designs are user-friendly only if this is important to the buyer.

The same word of caution: the need for you to know what you want is as important here as with any other way of getting that house.

Architects, for example, will probably be more geared toward the aesthetics of the design than designers. Their education and training makes them see building design in terms of spaces, flow, charm, and feeling than do the designers who tend to focus on the mechanics of how it is to be constructed.

The external look will be important to you and you'll need to have a good idea of what you want, or will have to choose among the several options which they'll offer you.

Existing designs

If you haven't done it already, take a look at any national home magazine and you'll find full page ads for catalogs of home plans. Or you'll find pretty pictures of houses with floor plans—along with offers to sell you the whole set of plans.

The Internet is another place where you can find many thousands of floor plans for sale, either by the companies that make them[3F] or by companies that act as the retail outlet for many different designers[3G].

These marketers gear their products to what they can sell—to what they think individual people are going to buy. For this market, repeat business is not a major consideration (after all, once you've built your home you're no longer interested in plans) so what goes into the plans is what the publishers think will sell right now with little concern about your future. There is no incentive to make plans other than what will appeal to most people—or to a specific group of people like those who read magazines on country living. And there is little reason for plan producers to be concerned about user-friendly designs because, unfortunately, most people don't think about the things we're discussing here.

In either case, don't expect user friendliness, as we are discussing here, to be a factor in the house designs.

The others

There are people who do plans as after-hours projects. These include builders and "draftsmen" who aren't qualified or can't make a living as designers.

A word about builders who do their own plans—and this includes small tract builders. Without a doubt the worst designs I have seen—and I've looked at well over 3000 of them in the last

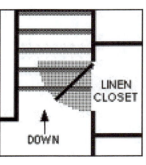

This linen-closet door swings out over the stairs! Incredible! (Designed by the spec-house builder himself.)

ten years—are ones that have been done by builders who seem even more removed from the end user than professional designers. The diagram and photo, for example, (previous page) show a a house whose plans were made by the builder.

A full set of plans will run you many hundreds of dollars. There will be multiple copies for the builder and his subs. They should include a list of materials so that the builder doesn't have to make it up himself.

If you find one that looks close to what you want (and there are enough of them that this should pose no problem), you can talk to whomever is going to make the changes about whether to get the full set of plans and/or, maybe, a set of reproducibles which can be marked up.

Chapter 4

Lots

The house of every one is to him as his castle and fortress, as well for his defence against injury and violence, as for his repose.

Sir Edward Coke, British jurisist and politician (1552-1634)

In this chapter:

This chapter looks at one of the first considerations when deciding on a house, its location.

The lot is more than a place to put the house. Here we look at the restrictions which may exist, the question of water and how it can impact the lot as a place to live, and several other aspects of a lot that are easy to overlook initially.

The Lot

Wild fire, wind, flooding, tornadoes, earthquake, hurricanes, winter ice, or summer sun—which is of more concern where you're thinking of that new home? Or is it the CC&Rs, the building codes, or the price? Every one of these should be taken into account when you looking at the lot where your home will be.

But, above all, location—length of commute to work, suitability of schools, neighborhood, distance to shopping, and taxes. Some lots are special because of the view they offer. Other locations may be important for personal reasons.

In this chapter several additional aspects of lots are considered, aspects that are easy to overlook in the enthusiasm of getting a home. These considerations apply if your new home, custom or tract, is to be built on it. With an existing house, you may well change your mind when the lot considerations are taken into account.

General

CC&Rs

If they exist, deed restrictions or the CC&Rs (Covenants, Conditions, and Restrictions) can be crucial. (These are discussed in detail in Web Supplement D[4A].) They restrict what you can do on a piece of property, even what kind of house can be built on it. You'll

Different strokes for different folks. Lots in special locations have their own sets of deed restrictions.

have to sign a document acknowledging that you agree to abide by the CC&Rs before you get title to your property. DON'T WAIT UNTIL THEN TO READ THEM.

When you're looking at a house or just a lot, the sales agent may not tell you that there are any CC&Rs[4B]. You should ask and get a copy if the property interests you.

At other times agents may make a big thing of telling you how great the CC&Rs are, how they really add value to the property. What they may not tell you is that CC&Rs are not worth the paper they're written on if they're not enforced. (Many CC&Rs are for the convenience and protection of the subdivider and, as such, are worthless as protection for the homeowner.)

Before you buy your property, read the referenced Supplement D and then read the CC&Rs. There might be some constraints, or lack of them, that would make the property unacceptable to you. As a final step, check with other homeowners

in the same subdivision and see just how effectively the CC&Rs are enforced.

Zoning

Check the zoning to see that it's compatible with your plans. Generally, if it's being sold as a residential lot, it is zoned that way. But if you want to use it for a business also, you'll need to be careful.

Finishing

If you're buying just the lot, is it "finished", i.e., are the street and utilities up to the lot line? Has the city approved it for building? If not, you could be out a significant expense in getting it ready.

Taxes and fees

⇨ How much are real estate taxes?

⇨ How much are homeowner association(s) fees?

⇨ What assessments exist on the property?

The house and the lot

Look at how the house fits on the lot. Usually there are local constraints, either CC&Rs or ordinances, on the amount of front, back and side setbacks required. (A setback, usually measured in feet, is how far the edge of the house must be from the edge of the property.) Consider the driveway and the front walk. If you want a garden or an RV pad between your house and the adjoining one, is there room?

If there are, or will be, houses on adjacent lots, check how much privacy you'll have. Wooden fences, common in the western states, might be all you'll need. When the adjacent house has two stories or when it's above yours on a hillside, neighbors may have a great view of your back or side yard—and into upstairs bedrooms.

Garage

Is the lot wide enough for a floor plan that has the entrance to the garage facing to the side of the house? If that's what you have your heart set on, be sure there's room for the driveway. Or that the house is on a corner.

Wind

In western coastal areas there may be persistent on-shore winds, especially in the afternoons. These are often strong enough to be downright annoying, particularly when you have to fight them for several months every summer. You can find the same problem if the lot is in or at the mouth of a gorge or canyon.

That nice little creek

At the other end of the spectrum are houses or lots alongside an easy meandering creek where the most threatening things are the frogs that croak all summer. Then comes the once-in-a-lifetime flood. If you're lucky, you'll have flood insurance. If you're not, cleanup can be costly. The best thing, of course, is to not have a house there in the first place.

Owning a house in a flood plain is always risky.

Hillside lots

Hillside lots are attractive because they often include a view. You can expect to pay a premium for these lots in two ways: 1) the price of the lot itself will be higher than others of comparable size and 2) foundations and excavations are more expensive. If the lot is remote, there are other considerations (roads, water, utilities, sewers). A builder can give you some idea about the extra cost of having a house there.

Hillside lots are a real danger in areas where wild fires may occur because fire races up hills and can be uncontrollable. A more subtle problem

Views are great, but hillside lots can have problems, too.

is that fires may not destroy your home but, because they destroy the vegetation, they increase the likelihood of mud slides the following rainy season.

Some areas are known for the number of houses that have slid down the hills over the years. If you want to build or maybe even buy there, consider having an engineering study done to see if there is a problem and what the cost would be to remedy it.

When a house is on a hillside lot and the garage is cut back into the hillside, you may be giving up a side garage door. You should factor this into your planning.

Lots with great views can have problems with winds. They often sit on a bluff overlooking a scenic river valley. The problem is that such views are often just where winds blow almost constantly. Strong winds blowing against windows cause noise and, when the winds are continuous, the noise can become depressing. (These considerations can also be a constraint on what kind of siding you are going to have on the house because vinyl siding, for example, often rattles in the wind.)

Before you pick a location for its view, find out what protection, like CC&Rs or local zoning ordinances, that you have to prevent someone from building, or even planting trees in front of you and blocking that valuable asset.

Ground water

In many places, rain water soaks through the top soil, hits an impenetrable layer of clay and then runs down whatever way the clay may be sloped. This is "ground water." It is in the ground and can be a severe problem even if it is not visible.

How can you tell if ground water is present? If the lot hasn't been graded clear of vegetation, be suspicious when you see a heavy thicket of greenery. Ask to see any engineering reports made on the lot or the subdivision. Talk to neighboring property owners to see if they've had water problems during the rainy season.

The presence of ground water will often mean extra expenses for foundation and drainage. And, if not taken care of properly, it can be a source of problems later in either a crawl space or a basement.

You'll need adequate drainage to catch the water before it gets to the foundation. If the lot is below street level one of two things is needed:

- ➪ A sump pump to get the water back up to the storm drain in the street. Sump pumps can be noisy and may cause maintenance headaches when they're in a crawl space or basement.

- ➪ An easement so that a drain line can be run across an adjacent downhill lot to a street below. Check to see if the easement exists.

Also, check what happens to water from an adjacent lot located above yours. If it runs on to your lot, ask what's being done about it. If you're not satisfied, find another lot—or you may be faced with a lake in your yard or the need for a special drain when the rains come.

Other

Check the orientation of the house relative to the sun and the street. One school of thought is that the kitchen should face east. North-facing kitchens lack sunshine all of the time, while south- and west-facing kitchens get the summer sun when you may not want it. For a house yet-to-be built, sometimes reversing the plan will make the arrangement acceptable; other times you may decide that the lot and the house just aren't compatible.

A home on a river (or lake) can be impressive.

Another concern you should have with the lot is the steepness of the driveway into the garage. Steep driveways have two problems: 1) if there's an abrupt change in slope, part of your car may drag and 2) in icy or snowy weather you may not be able to use your garage, particularly if it's facing north with no sun to help the melt.

If your prospective house/lot is close to farming areas, take a drive around to see just what kinds of farms may be there. Dairy farms generate odors that even gentle breezes can waft for a mile or so. Similarly mushroom factories, which use manure to grow their products, can be a source of unexpected and unwanted odors.

When a plot of land is being subdivided sometimes there will be a set of power poles running along one or more sides of it. Lots along those sides will then have the power and telephone lines in front of their houses. People may have lived this way for many years but they shouldn't have to do it now—not in newer homes anyway. If you make an offer on such a lot, take into account that its value is lowered because of the poles.

Utility boxes

Utility boxes are often forgotten when people look at a piece of property. When utility wiring is run underground, the power company must put their transformers someplace. In some areas these may also be underground but, if they're not, they're an eyesore, especially if the box housing the transformer is in front of your house. Above-ground boxes for TV distribution amplifiers and telephone junction boxes, while not as big as power transformers, will also look better down the street.

Steep driveways will be a problem when there is snow or ice. (This one is made worse because it faces north, making things slow to melt.)

Utility boxes always look better in front of someone else's house.

You don't have much to say about where utility boxes will be located, but at least you can see where they are when it comes time to select a house or lot. Likewise, groupings of mail boxes furnished by the Postal Service aren't things of beauty and would be better placed away from your lot. When it comes time to sell, prospective buyers will see things like this. (For the USPS it's a case of function not form.)

Far-sighted land developers can do something to reduce the visual impact of these functional things. In some tracts subdividers build housings that include more aesthetic-looking mail boxes. These cosmetic housings improve the appearance of the boxes and have an impact on the perceived value of your property.

Noise

Traffic and traffic noise will affect the selling value of the property.

We moved into our house in northern California when the nearby freeways had little traffic. When we put the house on the market 15 years later, we had more than one prospective buyer pull up in front of the house, stop, listen, and get back into the car and drive off.

Take the time to find out what future traffic patterns are planned around any lot you consider. Stay as far away from freeways as you can and at least a block away from what could become a major arterial.

A couple we know chose a lot in a large subdivision when the builder was just starting construction. It was close to the golf course clubhouse, making it convenient for golf, dinner at the club, and the other social amenities they desired. The lot backed up to a street that had no traffic; in fact, it dead-ended just a block away—a quiet, ideal place to spend their retirement years.

Over the next several years they found out what the sales agent hadn't told them. Their quiet dead-end street was no longer quiet or dead-end. As the subdi-

vision grew, so did the street, both in length and in volume of traffic. It is, in fact, a very busy arterial. They have decided to put up with the noise rather than go through the stress of moving again. But the reminder is always there—you can't be too careful when choosing the location for your home.

Outside noise can come from sources other than traffic. Check how close the house or lot is to an airport, commercial or military. Even though planes may not be flying overhead when you visit the lot, changes in weather can cause changes in air traffic patterns. It's not what you need in your nice quiet neighborhood.

Railroads, even those several blocks away, can generate noise you'd rather not have. Don't be like the guy who bought a house close to a railroad track and, after waking up night after night for several years, wrote a letter to the local newspaper complaining that the railroad company should use the tracks only during the day. Check things like this out before you buy.

Corner lots

There are pros and cons about corner lots. You have an abutting neighbor on only one side but you still have two sides of the lot on a street, making for more maintenance of lawns and shrubs and, at the same time, your backyard becomes visible from the street.

These lots are favorites for people on foot or on bicycle who like to cut corners . It may take a fence to stop them (if allowed by local ordinance and the CC&Rs) but that may not be aesthetically pleasing to you.

On the positive side, a corner lot gives you two ways to access a street. For example, your garage can be facing the street in front of the house while the driveway to an RV pad can be on the side street.

If you buy a corner lot and the front of the house faces the same street as the garage, be sure the garage side of the house is away from the corner.

This garage is, correctly, away from the corner.

The garage should __not__ be on the corner side of the house.

A house at the end of an intersecting street may have headlight problems. This one has the garage where lights will hit. Good.

You may have to reverse the floor plan to do this. There are several reasons:

⇨ It's safer to back the car out of the driveway.

⇨ The garage side is where you're more likely to have an RV pad and garbage cans—items you'd rather not have on the street side of the house.

⇨ The side of the house away from the garage is often more attractive from the streets.

Lots and headlights

While driving at night in a residential neighborhood watch where your headlights hit, particularly on high beam. When they hit the front of a house which has sidelights around the door, there will be a flash of light in the entry. When they hit a bedroom window, special attention to window coverings will be needed if sleepers are not to be bothered.

Curving streets and intersections also have the potential for this problem. When checking out a lot, see if cars coming from either direction will be directly facing the side or front of the house. If so, you need to take a close look at where windows are placed in bedrooms and entries.

While upstairs bedrooms won't generally get the full brunt of headlights, they will get some of it. And, if the street is on a grade, even they may not be spared.

There are three types of corner lots to watch for:

⇨ When the lot faces the end of an intersecting street, look at the design of the house to see if headlights of cars coming up the street will hit the front of your house. And you may have second thoughts, too, about the possibility of a driver who is inattentive and forgets to turn. In general, these are not the most desirable lots on the block.

⇨ In a common four-way intersection, all the corner lots will have headlights swing across them as cars turn. Even houses on lots next to those on corners may be affected.

⇨ About as bad is an L where both streets end. Houses on corner lots face down one of the streets, with the same considerations as the previous situation.

Both of the families on this corner get headlights shining into their homes.

A cul-de-sac is attractive for young families because the closed end can be a relatively safe place for the kids to play. But, for lots at the end, headlights will swing across the fronts of the houses as cars loop around the end of the cul-de-sac. You probably won't want bedrooms there.

Zero Lot Lines

Some subdivisions use zero lot lines, meaning one wall of each house is located on a property line. In some cases, two houses share a common wall, so that from the street, the two houses look like a duplex. In other cases, each house is separate, with all houses in the block placed on the same side of their lots.

If you consider a house on a zero-lot-line lot, be careful to understand all that that entails. There will be some definite restrictions on what you can do (including a requirement that you use the subdivider as the builder of your new home).

A monetary caution about zero-lot-line tracts. They are, of necessity, associated with a homeowners' association which is responsible for street-side landscape maintenance and fire insurance. The association dues can be sizable.

Country Lots
Oakland, Ca. 1991

Owners of houses in the country, or even in cities next to an undeveloped area, need to be concerned about the danger of wildfires. In Oakland, California, in 1991 fires destroyed many hillside homes and, as a result, a number of jurisdictions in the state enacted special local building codes. These require that homes built where there is a danger of wildfires take extra precautions to prevent the house from burning. If you are going to build where this may be a concern, be sure to check what it may mean in extra building costs. It can, for example, be prohibitively expensive to run a water line for a fire hydrant to your lot. You'll need a nonflammable roof—and that, too, will add to the cost.

If you are looking at a house built on a hillside in California before 1991 or a house or lot anyplace else in the country where there is a danger of wildfires, look carefully at both the surroundings and at the design of the house to see if there could be the potential of disaster there for you..

The lesson here is to consider the possibility of a wild fire before you make a commitment to a lot in an area like this.

Just lots

When the lot you're considering is outside a metropolitan area, you need to remember water, sewer, gas, electricity, telephone, and roads. If you have to drill a well, you need a back-up plan in case the water you get is not potable. If you require a septic tank and leach field, you need to know the soil is suitable. The seller may be able to guarantee these things; otherwise make any offer on the lot subject to your approval of test results.

But before you do that, find out what the utility companies will charge to get power, gas, and telephone to the lot. Also, find out what the costs will be to have a road extended to it.

And look carefully at the wildfire danger if the lot is in a forested area. There is not only the danger of fires, the insurance on your home may well be significantly higher—if you can get any at all. This is particularly true in areas like San Diego and San Bernardino counties in California which suffered tremendous dollar losses in the fires in the summer and fall of 2003.

Another consideration, if you are looking at a country home, is that wild animals can make life pretty miserable if you have a yen for gardening, either floral or vegetable. Deer, particularly, can become very much attached to your efforts and fences to keep them out must be high and kept in good shape. Of course, raccoons and opossums are also critters that will make a meal on the results of your gardening efforts if you have a home where they live.

Easements

Find out if there are any easements on the lot and, if so, what they mean to you. Sometimes it means you have to give up any use of part of your property; other times it means you can't use it for some purposes. Find out before you buy.

Don't be like one couple I talked to who looked at a lot with a real estate agent. The lot and the neighborhood suited them fine. Sure there was this ditch across the back of the lot, but they'd get that filled in when they did their landscaping. It was later that they discovered the ditch, which is six feet wide and three feet deep, is covered by an easement. They can't fill it in because it's for rain water that flows all winter. They're now looking at an expensive drain if they want to use the rest of their lot.

Special assessments

If you're buying in a state where they may exist, be sure to check for "special assessment" or "local improvement" districts. In a number of states, local jurisdictions can set up special assessment districts so that new home buyers pay for the streets, sewers, and other utilities to service new subdivisions. This seems fair enough. But, if buyers first learn about when they get their tax bill and find a large payment due on the assessment. That *isn't* fair!

For example, there were the folks in Vancouver, Washington who found out in 1997, a year after they moved into their new homes, that there was a $4000 local improvement district assessment on their lot to pay for new roads.

It is a shock to new owners to find they owe a large, totally unexpected, special assessment. Not all sales agents or builders are quick to volunteer the information—it could make you decide to look elsewhere. Ask!

SECTION II

The Systems

In this Section the discussions are about the systems that involve the entire house rather than a single room or area. As with every part of the house, decisions must be made about the components in these systems. If you can make the decisions, you control what you get; otherwise it's up to the builder and the subs. And you will get what they want—or don't care about.

The electrical, plumbing, and heating and air conditioning systems are described along with some aspects to help you in deciding what's best for you. Doors, windows, fireplaces and stoves, and security systems each have their own chapters.

The last chapter of Section II includes the important subjects of storage, noise insulation, floors, and ceilings.

A note about terminology: the almost universally-used interior wall covering is variously known as "sheet rock", "dry wall", "gypsum board", or "gyp board." The one and two family dwelling code calls it "gypsum wallboard." We stay away from brand names and simply use "wallboard" throughout *Better Houses, Better Living*.

Chapter 5

The Electrical Systems

> *Everything should be made as simple as possible, but not one bit simpler.*
> Albert Einstein, physicist (1879 - 1955) (attributed)

In this chapter:

Homes have more than one electrical subsystem including, power, video, sound, telephone, and computer connections.

Here each of these is reviewed and suggestions made to make the home both more attractive and a more comfortable place to live.

There are several distinctly different electrical subsystems and with each it is helpful to be aware of the good and not so good ways your home might be equipped. The choices involve matters of both form and function:

⇨ Form because lights, switches and outlets are an integral part of how the home looks and

⇨ Function because when lights, switches, outlets, and connectors are properly placed and used, they make a house a more enjoyable and user-friendly place to live.

And there's the matter of building codes. Misused components can pose a threat of electrical shock and/or fire to the occupants, so building codes go into detail about what may be used and where it may be placed. Whether in an existing home or a new one, it is useful for the homebuyer to have some understanding of what should and should not be done.

In this chapter the focus is on the functional aspects which are general to the whole house. Later chapters consider some of the interrelationships between other subsystems and the electrical components. (For example, how the home is framed can have definite functional impacts on the electrical system.)

Power

The major subjects dealt with here include:

⇨ Electrical outlets,

⇨ Light switches,

⇨ Ceiling fans,

⇨ Electronic equipment interconnections and controls and, finally,

⇨ A discussion of the interplay between the electrical components and a number of the other parts of the house including:

• Kitchen,

• Dining room,

• Bathrooms,

• Closets,

• Thermostats,

• Alarm systems,

• Laundry,

• Garage, and

• The exterior.

In all of these, as the buyer, you will need to take a look at what's in an existing house or what's planned for a new one. Many of them can be changed either before or after you move in. You balance the costs of making those changes against just living with what's there.

What color do you want for the cover plates on switches, outlets, TV connectors, and telephone jacks? These are among the few things that can be changed later without tearing the house apart but it will be one less thing to worry about if it's to your liking from the get-go.

With both outlets and switches you'll have the opportunity to choose which of several available colors you'll want to use. Generally the same color is used throughout the house but you may want to go to a different color in a special room. It's all up to you and, since color is a wholly aesthetic matter, let your heartfelt desires take over.

Outlets, a.k.a. Receptacles

Indoors

General

The heights of outlets above the floor should be the same throughout the house, twelve inches is the norm. This is generally (but not always) a matter of aesthetics rather than function and it will look better if all of the outlets are the same height.

The increasing use of SIPS (structurally insulated panels) for walls locks this into place more firmly because the locations of the electrical runs are more or less fixed by the SIPS manufacturer.

Take a good look at the locations of outlets on walls where you'll be placing furniture. When they are behind headboards, sofas, or dressers they are a major problem for plugging in lamp cords or anything else. Codes specify the maximum spacing between outlets so that lamp cords aren't strewn all over the place. Section E3801.2.1 of the 2000 International Residential Code (IRC) says,

"Receptacles shall be installed so that no point along the floor line in any wall space is more than 6 feet, measured horizontally, from an outlet in that space. Receptacles shall, insofar as practicable, be spaced equal distances apart."

If this concerns you, check your local code requirements—they may not be the same. Codes change with time and you may find older homes where this rule wasn't followed. Just remember that the farther apart the outlets are, the greater the likelihood of having an extension-cord mess with the resultant inherent danger of a fire.

Did you ever try to plug in a lamp on a triple dresser when the outlet is centered in the wall behind the dresser? If you have, you'll understand the reasoning behind this next suggestion.

There is nothing, other than cost, that prevents outlets from being closer together. If there is a problem with furniture placement, then, if you can, add one that will be easily accessible with the furniture in place. Otherwise it's one more annoyance you'll have to live with.

You may want to consider outlets in the floor in areas where getting power to a lamp would mean a cord across a walking path.

Instant hot water

If you want instant hot water in the kitchen (*see* Chapter 6) you'll need an outlet under the kitchen sink. This is another one that's much easier to put in when the house is being wired than having it done later.

Toilet seats

You may want to consider a relatively new item in the bathroom arena, electrically heated toilet seats[5C]. These replace the standard seat. They do require that an outlet in the wall close to the toilet. And it must be GFCI protected (described below).

Outdoors

Today's codes require:

"At least one receptacle outlet accessible at grade level and not more than 6 feet, 6 inches above grade, shall be installed outdoors at the front and back of each dwelling unit having direct access to grade."

Note that they should all be designed to be outside with a waterproof cover. The requirement for the front outlet is relatively new to the codes. You probably won't find it on older houses.

Both outlets are useful for electric gardening tools such as lawn mowers, edgers and trimmers—as well as the spit for your barbecue grill.

Front

While it may be primarily for gardening tools, the outlet on the front of the house is also very useful as a place to plug in your outside Christmas lights. As such you may want to consider having a switch, say in the garage, which can be used to turn the outlet and the lights on and off.

Alternatively, you might think about having a separate outlet (switched) up under the eaves specifically for the Christmas lights.

You can go a step farther with these Christmas light outlets and have a programmer built into the switch box in the garage (or wherever it is). These are, of course, cost items. And there is yet another option—remote control the lights (*see* below).

Rear

The outlet in the rear should be on a patio or deck. If there is natural gas in the house and it is brought to the patio/deck area, the outlet should

The electrical outlet and the gas stub should never be farther apart than these. When they are closer together there is more freedom in where the barbecue can be.

be close enough to the gas stub that the cord and gas hose from the barbecue can reach them easily. (Which, on a new home, you should have even if your barbecue doesn't use natural gas. When you sell the house, it'll be a plus.)

Basements and garage

Section 3801.9 of the IRC says,

"At least one receptacle outlet, in addition to any provided for laundry equipment, shall be installed in each basement and in each attached garage, and in each detached garage that is provided with electrical power. Where a portion of the basement is finished into a habitable room(s), the receptacle outlet required by this section shall be installed in the unfinished portion."

GFCI protection

In your house you have at least one outlet with two buttons labeled "Test" and "Reset." These are Ground Fault Circuit Interrupter (GFCI) protection devices designed to protect you from electrocution. (The buttons may not be colored as were the ones shown in the photo.)

A GFCI outlet.

Codes require that certain locations in the house be wired with these outlets to prevent you from being shocked if you accidentally touch a ground (such as a water pipe) and a hot wire at the same time. Old-time TV thrillers to the contrary, you won't be electrocuted if someone throws a hair dryer into the bathtub with you—as long as the dryer is plugged into a bathroom outlet. Bathroom outlets are supposed to have GFCI protection that instantly turns the power off without harming you. You should find these outlets on kitchen counters, in bathrooms, garages, basements, crawl spaces and outside the house. Even if the actual protection device itself is not present on each outlet, building codes require that outlets in those locations be tied to a GFCI-circuit someplace.

Outlets in which the GFCI unit is an integral part of the outlet are readily identified by the two buttons on them, one marked "TEST" and the other "RESET." If you do something that trips the circuit, you have to push the reset button to get things going again. Manufacturers recommend that you test the circuit monthly by pushing the test button to see if the power goes off, then push the reset button to get back to normal. This is something that most folks don't know or worry about.

You may find GFCI outlets that have a little light that comes on when the unit has been tripped. Because the test/reset buttons are not always that easy to see, the light can be helpful when you're trying to figure out why there is no power someplace in the house.

A word of warning. The requirements for GFCI are intended for your protection. They are not all inclusive. By code, the outlets that serve countertop surfaces must have GFCI protection. If your toaster has a short in it and you touch it and the water faucet at the same time, you won't be electrocuted. But, if you have a stove top mounted on an island or peninsula, the outlet(s) on the side of the island or peninsula may not be GFCI protected. Like the water faucet, the stove top is grounded and, if your faulty toaster is plugged into an unprotected outlet on the island or peninsula and you touch it and the stove top, it's jolt time!

Don't depend on GFCI protection to keep you out of trouble. Use common sense with appliances and tools. If one has a short or a frayed cord, don't use it. You may not have protection where it's plugged in.

A GFCI outlet costs several times that of a standard one. So builders and their subcontractors limit the number they use. They will sometimes run wires all over the place from a GFCI outlet to avoid putting in another one.

In one house I had, the only protected outlet is located in the garage and serves the entire house. Thus the outlets in both bathrooms, several in the kitchen, and the outlets outside the house were all tied to this one GFCI circuit. One day I unknowingly tripped the protection circuit from an outside outlet. Because no one had explained all this to me, I spent quite a while before discovering why there was no power in the bathroom for my electric razor.

You should expect to have a GFCI outlet in each room where protection is required. When an outlet is tripped, it can be frustrating and time consuming to try to find the GFCI protector when it's in a different part of the house—or the garage.

You'll have GFCI protection in the garage. In older homes, if there is more than one outlet only one of them may be protected. The one protected outlet is there for you to use for power tools. The others may be construed as being dedicated for freezers or other large appliances that, according to code, do not require protection. Similarly, outside the house you may have a special "T" outlet made to handle only a single plug rather than two. This is probably for a spa. Some building inspectors will let this go by without GFCI protection. If you have one of these, treat it with special respect. NEVER use an unprotected outlet for the rotisserie motor on your barbecue, electric lawn mower, edger, outdoor lights, or your spa.

Labels are available for outlets that say they are GFCI protected. These are worthwhile. It lets you know to look at the GFCI unit as well as the circuit breaker when power is lost.

As a rule, have the builder install more, rather than fewer, GFCI protectors. When there is one in each room that has protected outlets, it is easier to find the one that needs resetting.

Another suggestion is to be sure you know the location of the GFCI protectors for all of the protected outlets. Then when you need to reset it you won't need to search all over the place for the right one, as I did.

Remote Controls

Today remote controls are available for just about anything electrical inside or outside of a house. Here are some common ones. You may find others if you search:

➪ For TVs, VCRs, CD players, DVD players, radios and digital systems. These usually come with the sets and you know about them already. The distance over which these remotes operate is limited.

➪ For lights, good up to 100 feet. There are two types:

• One where the controlled part screws into a socket and a bulb then screws into it.

• One where the controlled part goes between an outlet and the plug on a cord. This latter is usually used with a table or floor lamp. An interesting possibility here is for outside Christmas lights where you may find it convenient to turn them on and off from inside the house.

➪ For ceiling fans. There are two different kinds of remotes for controlling the fan:

A remote controller for a ceiling fan.

• One that turns the fan on and adjusts only its speed - it's less expensive

• Another that lets you reverse the flow of air from the fan (up or down) as well as speed. Being able to reverse the air flow is a big help with a vaulted ceiling where it would take a ladder to reach the fan to do the reversing by flipping a switch. These remotes are more pricey.

Both have controls for the lights, on-off and dimming. Like wall-mounted fan controls, they are particularly useful where fans are not easy to reach. They are also convenient for being able to control the fan and/or lights in a bedroom when lying in bed. For new installations they avoid the need for putting switches and/or controls on walls as well as with the need for special wiring to the fans. Certainly consider using them in remodeling situations.

➪ For opening and closing curtains and drapes remotely. This is particularly useful when there are picture windows over a large bathtub (*see* Chapter 20). This could also be done with a wall-mounted controller/switch. Either way, there must be a motor on the curtains and power must be wired to it.

➪ For controlling a gas fire in a fireplace and its fan.

A downside to any of these controllers is the ease with which they may be misplaced. *(But we all know about that, don't we?)* Another is the confusion that arises when a number of them are lying around.

They may be more expensive to add after the initial wiring is done but for new installations, particularly in the case of ceiling fans, what is saved on wiring and switches may well offset the price of the remote controller.

Switches

If you are considering existing houses, give some thought to how important some of these aspects of switches will be to you in your choice of a home:

➪ For production houses, depending on how rigid the builder is in not making changes, you may be able to get some improvements made when yours is built. Or you may still be able to make some changes yourself after you move in. (Adding dimmers, for example.)

➪ For a custom house, if you are working with a building designer or architect when plans are being made, this is a subject you should spend some time with to be sure everything is carefully thought through and the details included in your contract.

➪ For a remodel, it will generally be up to you to tell the builder/remodeler the types of switches you want and where to put them.

Wall switches

Which type of wall switches will you want, the older flip switches or newer rocker ("decora") switches? They both work fine but rocker switches are perceived by many as easier to use and more in keeping with today's homes—a resale consideration. The rocker switches are a little more expensive but are an insignificant cost item in the overall. You'll also want to consider dimmers for

This was seen on a remodeled home tour. They're still around but probably should be replaced with modern switches which are easier to use and are more reliable.

lights, particularly in living, dining, and family rooms. But do make them user-friendly.

Since people tend to leave doors open, be careful of having switches behind doors. And, if there is a pocket door, beware—switches cannot be put in the pockets and, as with double doors, the electrician may have no choice but to put the switches in inconvenient locations. Thinking ahead could avoid this problem. Once built, it may not be an easy fix.

General Location

If there is a choice, have the switches and wall-mounted controls for the various lights, fans, and gas fireplaces put where you want them—electricians get paid by the number of switches, not by where they're located. As a guide, switches should be mounted in the room or hall with the light, outlet, or appliance they control and the center of the switch should be within six to eight inches of the entry to the room or hall. (And they should be the same throughout the house.)

In my house, for instance, the horizontal distance from the room entrance to the light switch varies throughout the house, more or less randomly, between 4 and 17 inches. After 14 years it's still fumble time when trying to find a light switch in the dark.

The heights of switches above the floor should be the same throughout the house. 45 to 48 inches is normal. If they're not that way in an existing house and it's impossible to do anything about it other than a significant remodel, it's a negative on your plus/minus list. For a tract house, the builder may welcome some constructive thoughts.

One custom/spec builder I knew waited until the house had been framed then walked through the house with the electrical subcontractor which is when she told him where switches and outlets were to be placed. If there is framing where there should be a light switch, that's too bad. The switch goes someplace else.

If the builder knows what's right, and if he cares, there would be no problem because it would be avoided with proper framing. This, however, is wishful thinking in far too many cases and you'll see switches all over the place in houses, models, and in those few floor plans that do spell out the switch location.

Three-way and four-way switches

When you need to turn a light or lights on/off from two different locations, a three-way switch configuration is used. This arrangement runs wires between the switches as well as to the light(s). The term "3-way" refers to the possible ways the switches can be controlled:

⇨ Off,

⇨ On at switch A, or

⇨ On at switch B.

Occasionally it is useful to be able to control a light or lights from three different locations—the top and bottom of stairs and an upstairs hallway, for example. For this, three switches in a 4-way arrangement are available.

They are commonly used in:

⇨ Halls,

⇨ Kitchens,

⇨ Garages,

⇨ Master bedrooms, and

⇨ Stairs.

At this outside garage door there should be two switches, one for the outside light and a 3-way switch for the lights inside the garage.

Rules for light switches

Because you use them everyday, locations of switches are significantly more important than for outlets. Electricians sometimes have their own ideas and sometimes they don't have any choice. When framers put studs so close together that there is no room for an electrical box to hold the switch, the electrician has to do the best he can. Good framers look at the house plans to see where switches would go and, if possible, make sure they don't put lumber there. Even better, the plans show where they're going to be and how to build the walls so there is a good place for switches.

Like doors (*see* Chapter 9), the unthinking positioning of switches is one the several irritating and least excusable things that a designer/builder/tradesman can do.

Here is our simple admonition about light switches:

**Put switches where most people would
expect to find them.**

When you enter a room your normal reflex is to look for the switch just beside the latch side of the door. Many, unfortunately, are not this way.

To have switches where most people would expect to find them:

1. Don't put a switch behind a door.

2. Don't put a switch around a corner.

3. Do put a switch next to a door (8" max.). The exception would be a double door (*see* below).

Some switch locations may violate more than one of these rules. They are just common sense and, generally, the rules are not followed for one of two reasons:

⇨ The person who makes the decisions about switch placement is more concerned about the speed and ease of installation than about user convenience.

⇨ The persons responsible for the design of the house pay more attention to how a house looks (form) rather than to how things work (function). The result is that they'll come up with an entry that they think is attractive, one where the switch locations are not a part of their thinking.

It is well to say again that contractors (and their on-site supervisors) usually are not experts in all areas of construction and must rely on their subcontractors to make decisions such as where switches should go. Standard home plans usually indicate locations for switches and fixtures, but often either the contractor or the electrician changes these as the house is built. The homeuser is frequently not a consideration in these choices.

Rule 1.
Don't Put a Switch Behind a Door

When you see a switch hidden by a door it's because nobody was thinking ahead. With this arrangement, when you walk into a room you have to walk around the door to turn on the light. This happens with both entrance and interior doors.

Probably what happened in the photos is that the finish carpenter and the electrician didn't talk

*A switch should NEVER be behind a door.
A Rule 1 no-no.*

to each other, so the door got hung on the wrong side and the builder was out to lunch. Nobody cared.

In one upscale show home, the double doors into the master bedroom suite had been removed for the show. As often happens in models, it wasn't evident that the light switch for the master bedroom and the key pad for the alarm system would be blocked by one door—or be several steps away from the other one. They should have been at the end of the door, not behind it. But that would have meant thinking ahead because the wall at the end of the open door is usually where framing studs would go and this might impact on just how long the wall should be. Keep your eyes open.

Another switch-behind-the-door incarnation. Here, when you come into the house, you have to go around the the door before you can get to the switch.

Rule 2.
Don't Put a Switch Around the Corner

The entry door photo (below) is an example of this rule breaker. It can happen at any door. There is

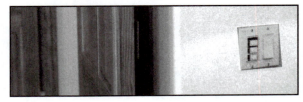

An entry door where the switch is around the corner. When you come in, it's fumble time. A Rule 2 no-no.

simply no room beside the door for the switch. A little forethought would have avoided the problem.

Rule 3.
Put the Switch Right Next to the Door

Another common arrangement you'll see with entry doors is a door sidelight right where you would like to have the entry switch. There are two solutions:

➪ As shown in the photo, make the entry door wall wide enough so that there is room for both the switch (preferably next to the door) and the sidelight .

➪ Put the sidelight on the hinge side of the door which solves both the switch and the security problems.

The location of light switches is a vexing problem with double doors because, as often as not, you'll have to take several steps after entering a

When the sidelight is moved away from the door it leaves room for the switch so that it can be right next to the latch side of the door.

room to reach the switch. You may get used to it, but you'll never be happy about having the switch in an inconvenient location. Ideally, there should be a wall that can be reached by opening the door 90 degrees with the switch right at the end of the door.

SWITCHES AND DOORS

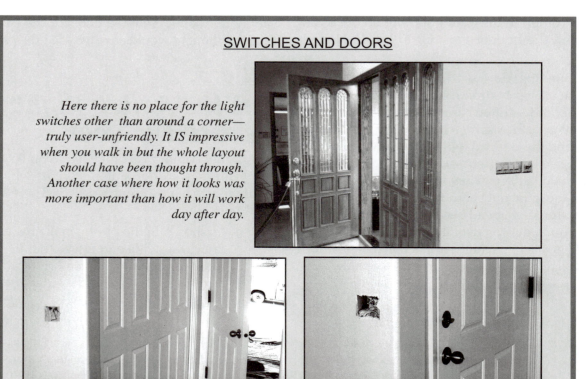

Here there is no place for the light switches other than around a corner— truly user-unfriendly. It IS impressive when you walk in but the whole layout should have been thought through. Another case where how it looks was more important than how it will work day after day.

With the guest closet right behind the entry door, the builder put this light switch around a corner several steps away from the entrance.

With the way the framing was put around this door, the switch has to go around the corner.

When this was finished, the entry light switch was several steps away from the door because there was no place to put it closer.

Here you must take 4 steps to reach the switch when you come into the house. At least it won't be behind an open door.

Entry doors are a place where lack of foresight gets the switches in user-unfriendly places. In some cases there is so much lumber around the door that there is no place left for a switch except on a far wall or around the corner—or maybe it's just easier for the electrician to put it there.

If there are double doors, both of which swing 180 degrees into a bedroom or den, consider having two switches in a 3-way configuration—one in the hall and the other switch inside the room at a convenient place.

The switch in the hall should be next to the side of the door that is normally used. And this takes some attention when the house is built to be sure the electrician puts the switch where it should be and that the finish carpenter then mounts the doors so the one next to the switch is the one that's usually opened. The best place for the switch inside the room will depend on the layout—next to the bed or a desk in the den may be convenient locations.

Switches and Fans

Exhaust fans

Have you ever gone into a bathroom and reached for the light switch but turned on the exhaust fan instead? When they are mounted side by side it's easy to do. In many houses in the Pacific Northwest fan switches are located nine inches to a foot above the light switch. If this doesn't seem too radical to you, give it a thought. While different to look at, they *are* more user-friendly. (For a discussion about bathroom exhaust fans *see* Chapter 20.)

At first I was completely turned off by the appearance of these switches but, having lived with them for many years, I've come to appreciate that you don't have to stop and think about which is going on —the light or the fan. I wish they were that way in bathrooms and the laundry.

One of these switches in a bathroom is for the lights, the other for the exhaust fan. Want to guess which to turn on when you want light?

Here the upper switch is for the exhaust fan. The lower two are for lights. The annoyance is gone.

(I did, in fact, change the arrangement in one bathroom, as shown in the photo.)

Ceiling fans

Ceiling fans come in a wide range of designs and prices. If you are going to have one in your house, you'll need to do some shopping. Here are some things to think about before it's installed.

What a fan is supposed to do:

⇨ In a vaulted ceiling—helps in heating, not cooling. Because the nature of hot air is to rise, it will accumulate, uselessly, as high up as it can get. When you're trying to get heat into a room for comfort, a ceiling fan in a vaulted ceiling can be used to blow it down—basically to stir it up, you won't feel the air but it will make the room warmer. This is particularly useful with a fireplace which throws it's heat right out in front of it where it will rise up to the ceiling.

⇨ With a standard ceiling, the fan is used to blow air on the people in the room. If it is close to the ceiling, it can be reversed to throw it's air upwards where it is deflected down over a wider area.

Most fans are made so that lights can be added readily if they aren't included initially.

Fans in vaulted ceilings are used primaily to distribute hot air around a room, not to keep you cool.

There are three ways to control ceiling fans and lights:

⇨ pull chains,

⇨ wall switches and

⇨ the remote controls discussed earlier.

Pull chains

A pull chain on the fan controls the speed of the fan. When lights are present, a second chain turns them on and off.

This is not usually convenient and, when the fan is high off the floor, it means getting something to stand on just to turn the fan and/or lights on. So what you'll often see is the pull chains combined with wall switches.

Wall switches

The same mounting approach can be taken as with exhaust fans: mount the light controls at normal switch height and the controls for the fan nine inches to a foot higher.

It's not absolutely necessary to have any wall switches associated with the fan unless it's so high in a room that the control chains can't be reached. However, for convenience, a common practice is to have an on-off wall switch for the fan and, if there are lights, to have a separate switch for them. This requires three-conductor power wiring between the fan and the switches rather than the two conductors needed for the fan alone.

A common unthinking practice is to run only two wires to a single switch that controls the fan and lights at the same time. If the home user wants the fan on without the lights, or the other way around, one or both of the chains on the fan assembly have to be used. When the fan is high in a room with a vaulted ceiling, it means getting up on a chair or ladder—hardly something you want to have to do—or to put a hook on a long stick that can be used to jockey the pull chains around.

An arrangement using separate switches to turn the lights (lower switch) and the fan on and off (upper switch). Chains on the fan control its speed and reverse its direction.

Yet, that's exactly what happened to one of my sons in his new house. In the family room, the builder had planned for a simple hanging light fixture. But our son had a ceiling fan and the builder agreed to install it. The proper wiring could have been provided but no one bothered—if they knew about it. There is now a ceiling fan with a light on it and there are only two wires from the switch to the fan.

Needless to say, when the fan is on, the light is also on and, when someone needs a light, the fan comes on at the same time—somewhat annoying when watching TV. It's either that or the long stick comes out. He's considering a remote control and, when that's installed, the fan will be usable again.

Instead of having two switches on the wall, there are units with both a fan speed control and a light dimmer that mount in place of one wall switch! The overall cost is lower than it takes to mount switches in separate boxes for the fan and the lights. In other words, it would be less expensive to have a wall-mounted speed control for the fan and dimmer for the lights than to have the two switches mounted a foot apart on the wall. But they still take three wires. (An important note: don't try to use a light dimmer to control a fan's speed. They are different beasts. You could damage your fan motor.)

At least one manufacturer of ceiling fans has a special unit that permits you to control the fan and lights as well as reverse the fan's direction from a single wall-mounted controller. (But you can't install one of these fans after the house is built unless the proper wiring is there from the start.)

If, in the future, it may be possible to replace a light fixture in a room with a ceiling fan, three wires are needed between the fixture and the light switch—not two. Also, the mounting box for the fixture should be strong enough for a fan. These should be put in place when the house is built although it is often possible to add them later—at a significant cost. Rather than do this, it makes more sense to consider using the remote controller discussed earlier.

Switches and Stairs

When the builder wasn't keeping on top of things and/or was one of those who just doesn't care, you might find a switch right behind the stair railing. This is just poor workmanship.

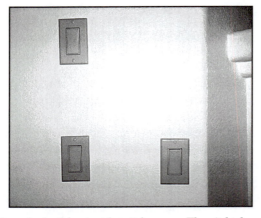

When the builder just lets it happen. The right-hand switch is for the gas fireplace. The other two are for the ceiling fan and light. The builder should have been on top of this but simply didn't care. The gas fireplace installer put in his switch and the electrician put in the other two. The result is neither attractive nor user-friendly.

A light switch behind the hand rail. This was a builder for whom user-friendliness was not his way of doing business.

Lights for stairs use 3-way switches with one switch at the top and one at the bottom of the stairs. If the stair light is also used for illumination of an area at the top of the stairs (a landing, hall, or bridge), it is convenient to have an additional switch there so you don't have to walk around in the dark after coming up the stairs. For this you may see or want arrangements using 4-way switches where any one of the three can control the lights.

Dimmers

Switches with dimmers are available for places where you'd like to be able to change the intensity of the lighting—the dining room chandelier for example.

A dimmer switch: adjustment above, on-off below.

They cannot, of course, be used with 3-way or 4-way switch arrangements.

Switches and Fireplaces

For gas fireplaces, the on-off switch should be close to the fireplace. It is not a good idea to put the fireplace switch together with those that control lights because it's too easy to turn the fireplace on accidentally and leave it burning. If there is a switch or speed control for the fireplace fan, it should be in the same mounting box as the on-off

switch or mounted above it—not on the other side of the fireplace. The photo arrangement, below, is not this way. It is not user-friendly. You may also be able to find a remote control for your fireplace if that suits your fancy.

Switches in Closets and Pantries

Don't forget lights and switches in closets and pantries. These are easily overlooked—until you move in. If you catch it in time, you can have these added to an existing design. Or it may be a small matter to have them added to an existing house, depending on where the house wiring is run. But be sure they're put in a user-friendly place.

⇨ In one house I visited, the switch is on the wall on the outside of the walk-in pantry but it's on the hinged side of the door that swings into the kitchen. To use the pantry, you have to walk around the door after turning on the light. If you can, don't let things like this happen to your house—or get it changed.

⇨ In another house the light switch is inside the pantry where it belongs—except you can't see it because it's under a shelf where it's hard to reach! Be alert to keep such annoying and unfriendly workmanship out of your house. If feasible, get such a switch moved to where it's more easily accessible.

The on-off switch is the one on the left of the fireplace. The one for the fan is on the right. They would be easier to use if they were next to each other...or, better yet, combined in a single unit.

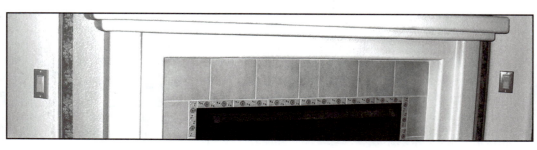

This switch inside a pantry is where it won't be blocked by stored items. Good.

Then they're put behind a decorative post to make it hard to even find them. What can I say????

⇨ Above all, don't forget that there should be a light in a walk-in pantry. In one tract I visited I couldn't find the switch for the pantry only to discover that there wasn't one! At night you'd need a flashlight. And all the models in the tract were the same way. *Caveat Emptor.*

Banks of Switches

You'll sometimes see switches arranged in a bewildering array of four, five or even six switches and dimmers in a single plate on a wall. It's something you might not think about until you have one. Most people will be unhappy with this forever because they'll never remember which one is for what. Far better to have the switches closer

A bank of wall switches is usually confusing at best—how are you supposed to remember which does what?

to the lights, fans, etc. which they control so that it's intuitively obvious which switch does what.

Entrance Capacity

The electrical system entrance capacity should be large enough for future expansion of electrical needs. In most houses a 200-ampere entrance is appropriate. You should get professional advice if there is any question. It is something that you'll want to check when you're buying an older home, particularly if you plan on changing over to an electric range or you have significant power tools.

Light Locations

The pros and cons of locations of lights in the various rooms of a house are discussed in the chapters for the individual rooms.

Electronics in the Home

First it was a telephone and radio. Then came TV, followed by tape decks, stereo surround sound, intercoms, computers, alarm systems...etc, etc. And it's all getting better and better.

We cannot hope, here, to cover everything that's available today to say nothing of tomorrow. Instead, we will note a number of things which you might want to consider in your next home, whether an existing one, one to be built, or when you are having a remodel done. Although it's always easier to put these things into homes as they're built, the kind of wiring that's generally needed is relatively easy to add at any time. And wireless interconnections are becoming more and more common. One company that makes virtually all of these things is Leviton[5A].

With houses where the wiring is already in place (existing houses) or when a design is firmed up (production houses) where you have to take what's already there, you may want to consider what would be involved in getting the system you want after you've moved into the house.

The areas we'll look at include:

⇨ Telephone systems,

⇨ Video,

⇨ Sound,

⇨ Computers,

⇨ Intercoms,

⇨ Alarm systems, and

⇨ Sound/video monitors.

Telephone systems

Telephone wiring

Telephone lines are most often run in cables from the central office to neighborhoods and houses. The cables may be overhead on utility poles or they may be run in conduits underground. In some remote rural areas they may be wires run individually on poles.

Until fairly recently, it was normal for the telephone company to run one or two lines from the cable on poles or in the street to each house. Now, because so many people have computer modems, fax machines and forever-talking teenagers, many telephone companies have upped this to five lines to new homes. These lines are there and can be activated at any time when the homeowner chooses to increase the number of phone lines to his house. Regardless of what is in the house already, more are available if desired but if they are

put in when the lines are run initially, it'll save money and time. However, this increased number of lines in the house leads to a different concern—how the house itself should be wired

The interconnection between the house wiring and the telephone company is usually done in a small plastic interface box found on the side of the house, often on an outside garage wall. The local telephone company runs a cable from the street to the interface box and the electrical subcontractor wires the house.

Older two-line method

The older method is for the electrician to tie all the telephone jacks together (in parallel) when wiring the house. Connections between jacks are in the walls of the house. They are permanent and difficult and expensive to change. It is okay for a house with only one or two lines where future expansion or changes are not expected. When you are considering an existing home and if you ever expect to need more lines, it would be well to check what exists in the house and how it is wired.

The flexible method

A much more adaptable method is to not tie the telephone lines together in the house but to run the two pairs of wires from each telephone jack to the telephone interface box so that any telephone jack can be connected to any incoming telephone line. The connections can then be changed quickly and inexpensively at any time. Then, if you want a separate line (beyond the initial two) for your teenager or for a business line, it can be added without rewiring the house.

The cost for installing this flexible scheme when the house is being built is more wire, which is not expensive—that and using an electrician who knows what he's doing. It becomes a more expensive proposition if it has to be done later.

Jack location

When the house is wired and if you have the option, you should indicate which rooms are to have telephone jacks and, if you and the builder are on top of it, the electrician will be told where the jacks are to go. If he's not told, he'll make his best guess, and this may not coincide with your needs.

In the kitchen, a wall-mounted telephone is often preferable to one that sits on a counter. At least on the wall it won't get in the way. And it's probably better if *you* decide where the terminal for this telephone is to be located.

Note that the modern concept of using the multi-connector plates shown below has a down side if you're not careful. Seldom will you want the TV cable jack and the telephone jack together. Generally, the TV is on one side of a room (bedroom or family room, for example) and then you'll want the telephone jack on the other side of the room, close to where you'll normally be lying or sitting.

Pick the place for the telephone jacks on their own, not for the convenience of the electrician.

Another option

If you have a small business in your home (and many of us do), you'll need numbers for your business telephone and for your fax machine as well as the one for personal use. With today's telephone systems these don't have to have multiple telephone lines, rather you can consider having multiple rings on one line. One example would be to have a single ring for personal calls, two rings for business calls and three rings for your FAX machine. Each of these would have a separate telephone number. This is more economical than having three lines, particularly if you have to rewire the house to accommodate them or have to have more lines run into the house by the telephone company. Of course, if any one of the numbers is occupied for extensive periods of time it ties up the only line in which case you'll need a second line for the long-talker.

FAX machines and answering machines are available that can be set to answer one, two, or

This plate mounts in a standard electrical box on a wall. It will hold up to six connectors for telephone, video, sound, and/or high-speed computer connections. Plates are available for one, two, three or six connectors. The connectors themselves snap into the back of the plate and can be added or changed at any time.

The Cat. 5 connector (upper right) is suitable for telephone or ethernet computer connection.

The coaxial connector (lower left) is usually used for video connections among TV cables, antennas, TV sets and DVD and VCR players.

Having the telephone and video connections on the same wall may not be very user friendly. Thoughts on where to mount the boxes and the plates are discussed in the text.

three rings. You'll need these if you choose to go this way.

Video cabling

The entertainment systems in today's homes may include surround sound and multiple choices of TV signal sources (cable, roof-mounted TV antennas, satellite antennas, VCRs and DVDs). These are often integrated into a single system which is both flexible and comprehensive. If you want such a system, let the builder or electrician know so that the additional wiring and cables can be put in place as the house is built. Or check and see if it can't be done with wireless arrangements.

Sometimes it takes a specialist to look the situation over and estimate the special wiring costs; other times the electrician can do it. It will depend on what you want. Unless you specify otherwise, usually there will be a single TV outlet in each bedroom and in the family or great room.

The TV outlets in a house are NOT wired together. Rather, each wall connector has its own cable that is run to a central location where the cables are connected to the antenna or to the local cable company. This connection uses little boxes, called splitters, with three or more cable connectors on them. These units properly split the signals to the various TV sets, VCRs, and FM sets. (If you have too many splitters you may also require a little amplifier which will necessitate provision for power to it. Again, your electrician should be able to give some guidance here. And, again, it should be thought out before the house is wired, if possible.)

The interconnection between the cable company and the house cables usually occurs in an area such as the attic where there's protection from the weather. In some locations (like Phoenix, Arizona) the interconnections may be outside the house. If there are many cables, an interconnection box someplace in the house or garage makes

it convenient to change the connections to the various outlets as needed. This is a nicety even when there are a relatively few numbers of cables. It makes it easy to change connections whenever you want.

For your TV, wall outlets are available that have the cable jack and the power socket on a single outlet cover plate. If mounted in the right place, these can help in hiding unsightly connections to the set.

The location for the TV outlet in the family room should be related to the location of the fireplace as discussed later in Chapter 21.

In a bedroom, for most people, the appropriate location for the TV outlet is one where they can watch their set while resting in bed. This suggests a location across the room from the bed.

And don't forget the computer (see below).

Sound systems

Sound systems are many and varied from simple ones in a room to those that permit surround sound in every room in the house—and the sound may be generated in multiple locations, radio, TV sets, tapes and CDs. Again, the kind of wiring you'll need will be a function of what you want. But, it should be a system that is thought through before you start. Certainly any wiring or rewiring that's needed will be easier if it's done in conjunction with the wiring of the other systems, telephone, video, etc.

Computer connections

To keep up with today's changing data-processing environment you'll need a high-speed internet connections together with either:

> ⇨ High-speed cables for tying more than one computer to that connection and for tying computers together or

⇨ Wireless connection for tying computers to the high-speed internet connection.

High-speed internet connections come:

⇨ Via a cable modem which must have access to your video distribution cable.

⇨ Via DSL (digital subscriber line) which is tied to your telephone line.

⇨ From an outside parabolic antenna which you purchase.

So it becomes a good idea to have a TV outlet and a telephone jack near the place you expect to put the modems and hubs that provide the interfaces between these outside lines and your computer(s).

The technology that is commonly used to tie the modems, hubs and computers together is called "ethernet". It uses a special, multiconductor, high-speed cable called "Cat. 5", a standard category in the computer industry. If computers are in your plans, you'll need to make provision for Cat. 5 cables in your wiring. Either that or depend on a wireless interconnection, a newer technology.

The outlet plate pictured earlier is meant to provide for this without needing multiple plates. The coaxial connector for the TV connection, a telephone jack and a jack or jacks for Cat. 5 cable connections can all be conveniently placed on one plate.

Again, you'll need a specialist to help you with these plans because they may differ depending on the make and model of your computers and their software.

Intercoms

Particularly with a larger home, it is often convenient to include an intercom system for communications between different parts of the house. While this is not generally tied with other systems wiring, it is less troublesome if it's installed ini-

tially. This is particularly true if you want a terminal at the front door because there the wiring will share the wall with insulation, something that isn't a problem on inside walls. The presence of the insulation makes it much more difficult to add in the wires than into an empty wall.

A wireless intercom system is relatively easy to install at any time.

Suggestions

Whether you're figuring out what to do in a new house or how to have an existing one remodeled to bring it up to date, it's probably a very good idea to invest in the wiring to put a TV outlet, a telephone jack, and a CAT 5 jack in each room. This will make the house both more useful and more resalable. While some prospective downstream buyers may not have an interest in such elaboration, it will become more and more of a real selling point as time goes on.

Other Electrical Considerations

In this chapter we have looked at the electrical system of a house from a broad point of view. There are a number of details dealing with specific parts of the house that are discussed in later chapters. These include:

⇨ Wiring for an alarm system, monitoring system, security lights, and the garage door —*see* Chapter 11.

⇨ Wiring around and under the kitchen sink—*see* Chapter 18.

⇨ Lighting for kitchen-counter work areas—*see* Chapter 18.

⇨ Lighting switch and outlet locations in bathrooms—*see* Chapter 20.

⇨ Chandelier placement for accessibility—*see* Chapter 21.

⇨ Lights in halls for closets and thermo-stats—*see* Chapter 21.

⇨ Light over the washing machine—*see* Chapter 22.

⇨ Garage lights—*see* Chapter 23.

⇨ Outside outlets should not be just anywhere—*see* Chapter 23.

Chapter 6

The Plumbing System

> *The fellow that owns his own home is always just coming out of a hardware store.*
> -- Kin Hubbard (1868-1930)

In this chapter:

There are two or three subsystems involved here, water, drains, and oftentimes, gas.

There have been ongoing changes both in the materials that are used and how they are installed. And, as with other parts of the house, some of these are more user-friendly than others.

For many decades water pipe was made of iron—with its rust problems and limited life. Leaks in walls of older houses were commonplace. Then came copper pipe which, while more expensive, offered such great advantages that iron pipe became pretty much a thing of the past. Today we have several types of plastic pipe that are less expensive and potentially longer lasting than copper.

In this chapter we look at these different types of water pipes, their pros and cons, and at two different kinds of drain pipes. Taps and faucets are generally a matter of personal preference and cost—except for exterior hose bibbs where a common arrangement is anything but user-friendly.

Plumbing plans are fairly simple and straightforward unless you want something unusual—like circulating hot water. There's no excuse for a layout that brings you a sudden change in shower water temperature when someone washes their hands or flushes a toilet. If you can check this in a house you're thinking of buying, it's a good idea. You should also check that outside hose bibbs are convenient and not located where growing plants will make them hard to get to.

Types of Water Pipe

While copper has been the most commonly used pipe inside new houses, one type of plastic, (CPVC) is approved in the Uniform Plumbing Code (the basis for many state codes). Iron and steel pipe is also approved when used properly.

Besides the metallic pipes, two others are OK for cold-water outdoor use:

⇨ Polyvinyl chloride(PVC)

⇨ Cross-linked polyethylene (PE or PEX).

Note, however, that a few states are slow to agree to let plastic piping be used in homes. But this is changing. You'll need to check in your own state.

One argument against plastic pipes is that they haven't been in use long enough to ensure that they won't cause trouble in the future—the old chicken-and-egg problem. And, in fact, there was a serious problem with polybutylene (PB) pipe and connectors that resulted in numerous lawsuits because of damage that was done to homes by leaky PB joints and pipes. Even though PB works well under some conditions, the problems that occurred were severe enough that many state codes do not allow it. Cross-linked polyethylene has been available for many years but bad experiences have held back its acceptance in some places.

One of the problems with any plastic pipe is that, if it is to fail, it doesn't do so for some time, from a few years to many depending on how it was installed and on its exposure to oxygenating chemicals. Whether you are buying an existing house or getting a new one, it would probably be a good idea to check what kind of piping is used or planned in the house. If it is plastic, then try to find out the expected life of that plastic in that location. Sometimes it'll be OK, other times you may change your mind about the house or the piping.

Copper

Copper is the material of choice by most plumbing subcontractors even though installing copper pipe takes more skill than plastic. Copper isn't without its problems, however. In southern California there have been reports of pin hole leaks in copper pipe presumably due to chemicals in the water. California allows plastic piping inside residences.

Chlorinated Polyvinyl Chloride (CPVC)

The white plastic pipe used in lawn irrigation systems is polyvinyl chloride (PVC). CPVC is similar, but unlike PVC, it doesn't soften when used for hot water. CPVC is 15 to 25 percent less expensive than copper. The installation times for CPVC and PVC are similar when done by experienced installers.

PVC can cause problems, too. This street was ripped up after 13 years to replace the connections between the water main and the houses. The problem was that the pipe was lying in the sun too long before it was installed and had become brittle—so the story goes. It broke years later. Plumbing, like many other things in houses, can wear out but probably won't if installed properly.

Polybutylene (PB) and Cross-Linked Polyethylene (PE)

Polybutylene and cross-linked polyethylene pipes are similar in that they are flexible plastics, they come in rolls, and require special fittings that are neither soldered nor cemented but are mechanical in nature. These fittings must usually be approved by local building officials.

Where allowed by codes, the flexibility of polybutylene and cross-linked polyethylene tubes and pipes makes it possible to use them in a different way which has definite advantages, both during installation and later when in use in the home. The main water line coming into the house feeds a manifold with multiple outputs. Each output connects to a single piece of pipe that goes to its own outlet: a faucet, dishwasher, toilet, tub, shower, or washing machine. Joints, elbows, and couplings are not needed.

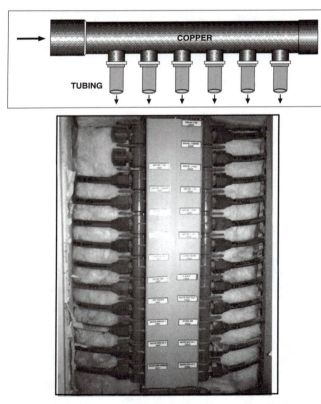

Two different types of manifolds. These offer distinct advantages over traditional methods of water distribution.

This results in faster installation than is needed for copper and a lower cost both in material and labor. Special tools and skills are needed for installation. (As with many other parts of the home, manufacturers' warranties are usually valid only if the installation is done by a trained tradesman. It takes skill, it is not a do-it-yourself operation.)

Because there is only one faucet per line coming from the manifold, turning on a second faucet has little impact on the flow to one already running. Thus, if you are taking a shower and someone turns on a faucet someplace else, there will be very little impact on either the amount or the temperature of your shower water.

Where they are approved, both PB and PEX are OK for hot as well as cold water.

Water Heaters

Be sure the size of the water heater is suitable for your family. The tendency for builders is to use the smallest (and least expensive) heater allowed by code.

If you live in earthquake country, you'll probably find that your water heater must be tied to a wall so that it's movement during a tremor doesn't break pipes, particularly the gas line which could result in a fire. Another, relatively recent requirement for areas that are particularly vulnerable is that gas pipe be a kind that doesn't snap during earthquakes.

There are two distinctly different types of water heaters available today:

⇨ The tank heater with which we are all familiar and

⇨ The tankless heater, introduced from Japan fairly recently.

Tank type

With this heater a tank of water is heated to well above the temperature at which it would be used for washing and bathing, usually about 140° F. This is a good temperature for cleaning pots and pans, but we mix it with cold water in our tubs, basins, and showers. The tank has a built-in thermostat that turns on the energy source (gas or electricity) when the water in the tank drops below a preset value—which it may with time and which it definitely will when the hot water is used and replaced with cold.

Today's tanks are well insulated and operate very efficiently—upwards of 80 to 90% of the available heating energy goes to heat the water.

Tankless water heaters

What they are

Tankless heaters, like their counterparts with tanks, can use either gas or electricity for the heating.

Tankless water heaters heat the water as it's used. There is no storage. When a hot water tap is turned on, the water is heated as it passes through one or more elements. You can preset the temperature to what's comfortable for you when it comes out of the tap somewhere around 95° -105°F. When taking a shower, for example, there is no need to use a combination of hot and cold waters...it's the correct temperature when it comes out of the shower head.

If gas is used, the gas is ignited when it's needed using an electric spark. With electric heating, the heat is turned on only when needed. Thus, if, for example, you are gone from the house for an extended period of time there is no energy wasted keeping gallons of water hot as happens with a tank.

Pros and cons of tankless heaters

Tankless heaters have several advantages:

⇨ They use energy only when hot water is being used.

⇨ With either type of heater, when a hot water tap is turned off, the pipe to the tap is left full of hot water and the energy to heat it is lost. But, because of its lower temperature, this energy is less for a tankless heater than for a tank-type system.

⇨ They are physically smaller. A typical system is about 14″ wide, 24″ high and 7″ deep.

A tankless water heater on the side of a garage. These outside units do not require exhaust vents and are less expensive to install than an inside unit. Note the small size, this one services a 3000 sq. ft. house.

And there are several drawbacks to tankless systems:

⇨ Their costs are significantly higher than a tank-type both in terms of the basic unit itself and in terms of installation. Typically, it will take three tradesmen to install a gas-heated tankless type: an electrician, a plumber to run the gas line and a craftsman who has been trained in their installation and operation. The overall cost can be expected to run two to four times as much as a tank-type heater.

⇨ If you want hotter water, for scouring out a frying pan, for example, it isn't there. (*See* auxiliary hot water, below.)

⇨ It takes trained craftsmen to properly install these systems. If one is not used, the warranty is seriously jeopardized. (It's another don't-do-it-yourself thing.)

⇨ Whether electric or gas, they depend on having electricity available to operate. There is built-in electronic "smarts" which senses how much water is passing through and which uses this info to control the amount of energy used by the heating elements. Gas units depend on a spark discharge to ignite the gas and, if the power is off, they simply don't work. How important this may be will depend on:

• How reliable your power is and

• How important it is to you to have hot water available even when the power is off.

Because of the initial cost differences, you'll seldom find tankless heaters in spec or tract houses. Their advantage comes into play when a lot of hot water is needed so that the lower operating costs will repay the higher initial cost in a relatively few years. For remodeling and a new house where you have the say, they are worth considering.

In the unit in the photo on the previous page the older house had used electricity for both heating and hot water. By changing the furnace to gas and putting in the tankless water heater the owner was able to get the gas company to run the line from the street to his house eliminating one of the costs of changing over to gas—which he did with the expectation that the pay back in energy cost saving would be relatively quick.

These units are an obvious consideration during any remodeling which involves the plumbing system.

Sometimes a further advantage for these units is that they can be mounted in weatherproof boxes and do not have to be installed inside. On the other hand, their relative small size makes them good candidates for mounting anyplace inside the house. Gas units will, of course, need to be vented outside which means you'll usually find them in the garage or outside in the weather. For more information, look at these four manufacturers' websites. [6A, 6B, 6C, 6D]

Instant Hot Water

When hot water is needed at the far end of the house, away from the hot-water tank, it is a matter of running the cold water out of the pipe until the hot gets there. This not only wastes water, it also wastes the energy that originally went into heating the water. There are two ways around this annoyance and waste: recirculating hot water and an auxiliary hot water supply.

Recirculating hot water

It is not clear how well a recirculating hot water scheme would work with a tankless water heater. If you might be interested in the combination, you should have a discussion about this with a plumber who has had experience with both of them.

Here we confine the discussion for use with a tank-type system.

You are already acquainted with recirculating hot water—or did you ever wonder how you got the hot water so fast in a hotel room? The process involves doubling the amount of hot water pipe in the house. One pipe carries hot water from the heater to the faucets and the other carries the unused water back to the heater. A small pump keeps hot water circulating through the system. The pipe must be insulated in both directions if it is copper. The plastic in CPVC, PB and PEX offers a certain amount of insulation in itself and additional may not be needed. WIRSBO, a manufacturer, says it's not necessary with their PEX. If you might consider recirculating hot water, check with the manufacturer of your piping and with your local building officials.

There's an initial cost for putting the system into place and an ongoing cost for the electricity to run it. Both costs are small, particularly when there is a timer on the system so that it doesn't run while you sleep. At least a part of the ongoing cost is offset by not having to waste water by running it down the drain until it gets hot.

CPVC, PB and PEX piping are attractive in recirculating hot water systems because they are easy to install, they don't have the potential noise problems of copper, and the plastic pipe itself acts as an insulator.

If you are looking at a house with this installed, it is an attractive asset.

For new construction, if your builder will consider having it installed, find out how much it would cost and then decide if it's worthwhile for you. For an existing house, you may be able to have it done, but it may be pretty costly, particularly if the plumbing is run where its accessibility is limited.

Auxiliary hot water

There are two different types of instant hot water heaters. They are meant to mount under counters and both use electricity to heat the water. The difference between them is in the amount of hot water they can deliver at one time.

Both are auxiliary in the sense that they back up the standard hot water system, they do not replace it.

Electricity is used to heat the water and is what you pay for the convenience. Gas is not used because of the venting requirements that would have to go with it. If there is an outlet under the sink where the unit can be plugged in, the installation consists of the plumbing that is required. If there is no outlet, connecting electricity to the unit adds to the cost.

Smaller units

These are meant for mounting under the kitchen counter with the water being delivered through a spigot mounted in the back apron of the sink. (Some sinks have an opening for such a spigot, for others you'll have to have it cut into the sink. It can usually be done in an existing sink.)

The amount of available hot water varies among units, 1/3 to 1/2 gallon being typical. Temperatures are adjustable, up to 200°F. They are meant to give you small amounts of water for a hot cup of tea or instant coffee, for example. Their attractiveness is their speed and convenience, you

A kitchen sink with instant hot water (the spigot on the right).

don't have to put water on a stovetop or in a microwave oven to heat it.

Larger units

This auxiliary hot water heater has a small tank of a few gallons of water (2-1/2 is typical) which is kept continuously hot at the tap where it is to be used. There is a picture of such a unit in Chapter 18 showing it mounted under a sink.

It is used both in kitchen and in bathroom basins. In kitchens it usually has its own spigot as described above for the smaller unit. For basins, since the amount of hot water that is used is usually small, the outputs of the units can go directly to the hot water piping to the basins. If you run out of water from the auxiliary tank, then it's a matter of waiting for hot water from the main tank.

Electric tankless heaters could be used to provide auxiliary hot water but their installed costs would usually make them unattractive for this application.

Water Pipes in Outside Walls

A good house design will minimize runs of water pipe in the outside walls because of the danger of freezing. Even so, you'll often find short runs of pipe for kitchen sinks and bathroom basins located there.

Outside walls in today's new houses are usually well-insulated. When water pipes are run in these walls, it is important that the pipes be kept toward the inside of the walls rather than the outside. And the wall insulation must be installed so that most of it is between the pipes and the outside wall and little or none is between the pipes and the inside wall. Plumbers and insulation installers understand this and normally install it this way. However, it doesn't hurt to check. (The use of toe-kick registers also helps—*see* Chapter 7.)

Nail Plates

Pipes running through studs or plates are always in danger of being punctured by wallboard fasteners—nails or screws that are 1-1/4 to 1-5/8 inches long and are driven into the vertical studs behind the wallboard. When the wallboard goes up, the installer can't see where the pipes are. Plumbers are supposed to put pieces of galvanized sheet metal, called "nail plates" or "safety plates," on the outside of the stud or plate to prevent the wallboard installer from putting a nail or screw there and inadvertently punching a hole in the pipe. The construction supervisor *should* check that nail plates are in place properly before the wallboard is installed, but they are sometimes missed. A good wallboard installer will also check these before he starts his work.

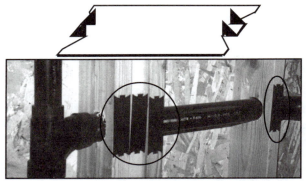

Nail or safety plates protect pipes during wallboard installation—if they are not forgotten.

Besides the obvious problem when an immediate leak occurs, improperly placed or missing nail plates can result in subtle problems that may not be seen for several years. Small leaks in drain lines are not always self evident and the dampness may be contained inside walls where it can rot the wood without being seen and provide an ideal environment for molds. There is also the possibility that a wallboard screw will penetrate a water or drain pipe but the screw itself plugs the hole—until it rusts out a few years later. If you

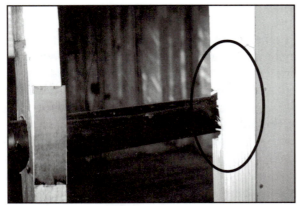

Nail plates do get missed!

can, double check that nail plates are in place to protect *all* pipes before the wallboard is installed. The builder's warranty for things like this lasts only one or two years. (Which is a good reason for having new-home inspections during construction.)

With an older home there is virtually nothing that can be done to avoid the consequences of this improper construction. If it's been leaking for a while, there's a chance the home inspector might catch it if he uses a moisture meter or if there are stains through the wallboard. Keep your fingers crossed.

Noisy Pipes

You can reduce water and drain pipe noise by paying attention to how the pipes are installed. As an experiment when you visit model homes, have your spouse turn on a faucet in one end of the house and see if you can hear the running water in the other. Some houses are significantly better than others in this respect.

Water running through a pipe is noisier when the pipe touches wood because the wood can act as a sounding board. Pipes should be kept away from joists and studs. Plastic piping used in water distribution systems has additional advantages here. First, most noise originates where the direction of flow changes abruptly and this doesn't happen with plastic in many installations. And copper itself will carry noise along the pipe more readily than will plastic.

Drain water falling from the second floor of a house makes noticeably more noise in plastic than in iron pipes. However, iron pipe rusts, so check its expected life in your area before using it. For either iron or plastic, wrapping with fiberglass insulation will help deaden the noise. In models you can check this by flushing an upstairs toilet and see how much noise you hear below it on the first floor.

Hose Bibbs

You'll want hose bibbs on the outside of your house. Most builders put in two: one in front and one in back. For most of us this isn't enough. If you have an RV pad, you should have a hose bibb there. In any case, an additional hose bibb on at least one side of the house is usually useful.

If you need hot water to wash your car, have a bibb installed in the garage, connected to both hot and cold water. (This works well with the utility tub in the garage as discussed in Chapter 23.) Be sure you take a hard look at the type of faucet that is used. The common faucet used for mixing hot and cold water restricts the amount of water that can be passed. This is not useful when a high volume of water at full pressure is needed.

For a not-yet-built house, make it known, either in writing or on a drawing, where you want the hose bibbs. Allow the plumber some freedom to minimize the cost of putting them in place, but be sure your wants are known. If it will be important to you, before you buy an existing house, check that the bibb locations are reasonably convenient.

In areas where there is danger of water freezing in hose bibbs, plumbing codes require a means of draining the water from the bibbs in the winter. Two methods are used:

⇨ A regular hose bibb with a stop-and-waste valve or

⇨ A frost-proof hose bibb.

Costwise, there is little to choose between the two approaches.

Stop-and-waste valves

Stop-and-waste valves are supposed to be installed in an accessible heated location where there is no danger of freezing. The "stop" part is simply a turn-off valve. The "waste" part is a plug on the valve which can be removed, if necessary, to allow water to drain.

The hose bibb is connected to the stop-and-waste valve with pipe that may be exposed to freezing conditions. In the autumn the home user must:

1. Turn off the water at the stop-and-waste valve.

2. Open the hose bibb and take care of any hoses which may be connected.

3. If the bibb and pipe don't drain by themselves, the waste plug must be removed to let the water out.

In the spring the above process is reversed.

Unfortunately, not all plumbers follow the code carefully and not all inspectors see that they do. In far too many cases the stop-and-waste valve is placed where it is not readily accessible, making it virtually useless. Basements and garages are the usual location. Hard-to-get-to crawl spaces are bad (and useless) spots for these valves.

If your builder or plumber insists that frost-proof hose bibbs are not a good idea, then you should insist that he put the stop-and-waste

This hose bibb may have a stop-and-waste valve— under the house in the crawl space. Because such a stop-and-waste valve would be impractical to reach, the plastic covering in the lower photo is needed to insure that the water in the bibb doesn't freeze—good only where you don't have really severe winter weather.

A stop-and-waste valve in a garage. By placing the turn-off valve well above the height of the outside hose bibb, the pipe and bibb will always drain and there is no need for a waste plug. But do note that you have to open the outside bibb and take off any hose as well as turn off the inside valve.

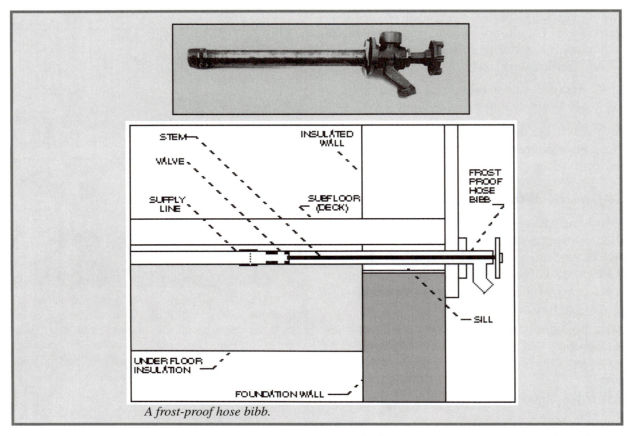

STEM

INSULATED WALL

VALVE

SUPPLY LINE

SUBFLOOR (DECK)

FROST PROOF HOSE BIBB

SILL

UNDER FLOOR INSULATION

FOUNDATION WALL

A frost-proof hose bibb.

valves where you can get to them easily and where pipes drain by simply opening the bibb.

Frost-proof hose bibbs

The frost-proof bibb (*see* above) includes a piece of copper pipe as a part of the bibb itself. This pipe extends the valve part of the bibb back into a part of the house that is heated and where there is no danger of freezing. When it is turned off, water drains from the exposed part of the hose bibb and no damage occurs.

There is a precaution, however. Sometimes hoses with closed nozzles are left connected so that the water cannot drain. This has happened often enough that plumbers in some localities have an aversion to using these bibbs at all. Properly used, they effectively eliminate problems with freezing.

Those builders who think that a frost-proof bibb is a user-friendly adjunct to their homes usually have a clause in their home warranties that the builder is not responsible for any damages if you don't take the hose off of the bibb in the winter.

Some Bathroom Niceties

Chapter 20 discusses some bathroom plumbing items which you may find interesting.

Gas, a Different Set of Pipes

When gas is used in the house, it is connected by the gas company to a meter on the outside of the house. From there pipes carry it to the several places in the house where it is used. These may include:

⇨ Water heater.

⇨ Furnace.

⇨ Gas fireplace.

⇨ Cook top.

⇨ Ovens.

⇨ Laundry.

⇨ Deck or patio for barbecue connection.

Because a gas leak has the potential for endangering both the property and its occupants, how the gas is handled is controlled by building codes. These vary from state to state at least in part due to the possibility of earthquakes, hurricanes, and tornados which could cause pipes to break. Some states require that gas lines in and under a house use flexible pipe which can give rather than snap when it is torqued. And natural disasters have caused some states to tighten down on these requirements in relatively recent years.

If you are buying a pre-owned home, it might be a good idea to find out if the gas lines in the house meet current codes and what the potential danger is to you if they do not.

Another thing to check is whether gas has been piped to the laundry room for a gas dryer. Generally, if there is gas in the house, it will be more economic to use a gas dryer than an electric one. When you are thinking about this, don't forget that here is another place where the attractiveness of the house for resale will be lowered if gas is not present in the laundry room.

When you are looking at new homes, not only check whether there is gas in the laundry room but look at the gas pipe. When you see pipes like

Gas lines to the laundry should be out where the connection to the dryer is simple and straight forward. It should NOT involve cutting into the trim or the wall behind the dryer. Again, incompetent work and inept supervision.

those shown in the photos it should wave a caution flag about the supervision given to subcontractors by the builder. After move in, the gas line to the dryer will have to be connected here and it really shouldn't be necessary to cut into the wallboard to make room for a coupler—as would be needed here.

Chapter 7

The HVAC System (Heating, Ventilation and Air Conditioning)

We can learn to tailor our concepts to fit reality, instead of trying to stuff reality into our concepts.

Victor Daniels, psychologist and philosopher (1941-   )

In this chapter:

The HVAC system is a major player in the overall objective of getting a house that has both comfort and energy conservation.

Some aspects of this that are seldom considered are the placement of registers which can have a significant effect on user friendliness.

The major emphasis is on the commonly used forced-air systems of all types. Other heating systems are noted as appropriate for special circumstances.

The HVAC system is much more than just a way to control the temperature. It, and how the house is built, determine energy efficiency, comfort, and your energy costs.

The mechanical subcontractor is responsible for the HVAC system, usually including design as well as installation. And, again, there is the on-going question of oversight. No one checks the design (see my personal story later in the chapter) and often the work is done by tradesmen with little or no supervision.

When you're looking at homes, find out what type of heating system is used. Most will be forced air, with electricity, gas, or oil as the energy source

HVAC Design and "Green" Buildings

An overall concern with the HVAC design and with the design and construction of a home is how well it saves energy. There have been a number of approaches to this problem. We touch on some of them here. You can find more detail in Supplement A[7A].

Some of the requirements are included in building codes. Other desirable characteristics are made attractive by the lower energy bills you, as a home owner, would have to pay. And it is right here where a big gray area appears, made even murkier by the fact that what's good in, say, Florida, is not at all appropriate in Minnesota. Unfortunately, many of the proponents of certain green-home features do not differentiate among different geographical climates.

For example, one proponent strongly recommends the use of light color roofing material. This may be fine in the southern states where the need to reflect the sun's rays is a primary concern—but not in the north.

The problems are two-fold. They do not consider that:

⇨ In northern states the desire is to get as much heat from the sun as possible, not to reflect it, and

⇨ There are other considerations besides the particular one they're pushing that need to be a part of any decision. (A roof that won't blowaway in a hurricane in Gulf and Atlantic seaboard states, for example, is more important than its color.)

While there is no question that more insulation around the living areas will reduce heating and cooling costs, stressing that while ignoring other places where heat is gained or lost can be misleading—or worse.

Then, sometimes, it looks as if the "Green" building people have a monetary axe to grind where they're pushing a product or process which, while it may be helpful, will never pay for itself in energy savings.

And, other times, they can come up with what is an obvious energy saving approach while conveniently overlooking the negative impact on the design of a home and not comparing this to the projected cost savings over conventional methodology.

For example, running heating ducts and return ducts in air-conditioned space will, without argrument, lose less heat then conventional techniques. At the same time, the cost of making a place for these ducts is not trivial in the construction of the home. Nor is the cost of any repairs that may be needed after the house becomes your responsibility.

And, of course, the question of air quality needs to be uppermost in the minds of everyone when it comes to the tighter houses needed for energy saving. It's a complex question that's addressed in more detail in Supplement A[7A].

but you may find something different such as hot-water baseboard, radiant floor heating, electric baseboard, or wall heaters. These non-forced air systems can be advantageous, particularly when most of the time you want to only heat a small part of the house. Their major disadvantage is that they cannot be integrated with an air conditioning system. Some comments about these follow a discussion of the forced air systems found in most homes.

Forced Air Systems

In forced air systems, air is heated or cooled and forced under pressure through a network of ducts to outlets or registers in various parts of the house. Usually there will be one such system per house, but in larger homes there may be more.

The basic energy source for forced air systems may be electricity, gas, or oil. Electric systems commonly use a heat pump because it is more cost-effective than heating the air with electric heating elements.

Heating involves collecting air in the house using the duct work, heating it and redistributing it. The air is heated by a burner in a gas or oil system or by the heat pump or heating elements in an electric system.

Cooling is similar. The cooling uses refrigeration techniques that take the heat out of the air in the house and send it outside. The machine that does this may be an air conditioning unit or a heat pump.

Note that, when there is a heat pump, it does both heating and cooling. This is accomplished by reversing the refrigeration process. For cooling, it moves the heat from inside the house to the outside and for heating it takes heat from outside and moves it inside.

Which heating and cooling approach is best for you will depend on the climate in your area, whether cooling is important to you, and on the relative costs of the available sources of energy. Your local heating and air conditioning equipment supplier can best advise you. (Don't depend on getting straight answers from energy suppliers—they sometimes have their own agendas.)

Of particular interest to us here are several aspects of the design of forced-air systems which impact directly on their effectiveness in making our homes comfortable places to live—and on the user-friendliness of the system.

System Design

Registers

There are two kinds of ducts and registers:

⇨ Those that take the heater/cooled air from the furnace and distribute it throughout the house. There will usually be at least one register for each room.

⇨ Those that collect the air from inside the house and return it to the furnace. There will typically be one of these for each section or wing of the house.

The registers for individual rooms and the return air should be well separated so that the heated/cooled air has a chance to circulate before it is pulled back to the system.

In one-story houses with crawl spaces, the heating ducts are usually run under the house and the registers are in the floor. The return air registers are then in the ceiling with the ducts in the attic.

With concrete slab floors, the ducts, and often the furnace, are in the attic and the heating registers are in the ceiling or in walls close to the ceiling. The cold air returns are then found near the floor level.

With two stories or when there is a basement, the registers may be in the floor or in the ceiling, a decision that the designer or builder makes.

Where the ducts are run in unheated parts of the house, such as the basement, crawl space or the attic, they should be wrapped with insulation to minimize heat loss. In heated parts of the house, such as between the downstairs ceiling and the upstairs floor or in inside walls, they need not be insulated and usually are not.

The forced-air heating system in our one-story house was designed by the mechanical sub-contractor—the builder simply hired him and depended on him to do the job right. When the first heating season came we found the bedroom end of the house was too warm and the living areas weren't warm enough. We closed the floor registers in the bedrooms to balance the system. In trying to understand why this was necessary, I found that the two areas have about the same number of square feet and that the basic design put about the same amount of hot air into each of them. However, because the living area of the house has a larger proportion of glass and outside wall than the bedroom wing, it has significantly more heat loss. The basic heating design did not take this into account.

⇨ For a new home, if you get the chance to have a knowledgeable person review the HVAC plans before they are implemented, you may be able to avoid problems arising from a faulty design. It may not always be possible to find someone to do this for you, but it is good insurance if you can.

⇨ For an existing home, you probably won't be able to do much about it, but knowing as much as possible may help you in your choice of which house to buy. And by all means check the temperatures in the various rooms. They should be warmer in the living areas, lower in the sleeping rooms.

⇨ When you remodel, you may be able to make up some of the shortcomings in the original layout.

Types of registers

Two different types of registers are commonly used for hot air; what you have will depend on where you live.

⇨ Registers that mount flush with the floor, ceiling, or wall are used almost exclusively in the west.

⇨ In other places registers may be a type that mounts against a wall just above the floor. They look similar to a baseboard heater. Their advantage is they are not a problem for foot traffic. Their disadvantage is that they are not as easy to clean as a flat register.

Register location

It has been standard practice forever to put heating registers under windows around the outside walls of rooms. This was done to offset the cold air that came off windows in the winter. With modern high-quality, double-glazed (double-pane) windows this problem is greatly reduced and the old rule is no longer as iron clad as it was.

For a new house, take a look at the model or at the mechanical subcontractor's plans before work is started on your own home. If you want to put a piece of furniture in front of a window see if the register can't be moved along the wall to where it won't interfere with furniture placement. (Make the arrangements to have this done before work starts on the house—it may impact on the cost of the HVAC system and on the price of the house.)

But don't do what I saw in a tract in York, Pennsylvania where the builder **was** thinking ahead. In the master bedroom he had moved the register to a different wall away from the window. Which was great except it was the only wall where the bed could go and there was the register—right under the bed in the furnished model! Which is, of course, OK if you want the underside of your bed heated.

COMMONLY USED HEAT REGISTERS

The styles and usages of heat registers vary across the country but there are some common practices that are not particularly user-friendly and one that is wasteful of energy. The photos illustrate.

The first picture is of the floor register commonly found in the west. They have been traditionally located right in front of windows to offset the cool air coming off of the window. With today's windows this problem is virtually non-existent but old habits are hard to break.

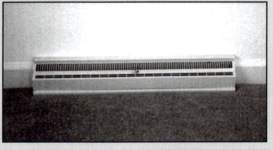

Furniture is often placed directly over the register resulting in a very inefficient delivery of the hot or cold air.

The register in the third photo, a type that is not often seen in the western part of the country, permits furniture to be placed in front of the window without blocking the register.

The last photo is where a register was built into a wall. This avoids problems of being walked on and of furniture being on top of it. But, when it's in an outside wall like this, there will be heat loss because the duct cannot be properly insulated against the cold that's there.

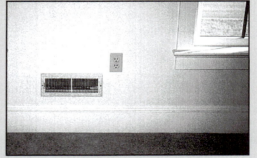

A cold-air return in a traffic area, above, (really user-unfriendly) and another one, right, in the wall where people won't *be walking (much better). These are among the things that many HVAC designers and builders don't think about. Generally, it's whatever is easiest.*

When you are considering an existing house look at the registers. You generally won't be able to have them changed, but it'll give you some idea of what you'd be facing when it comes to putting furniture in the rooms.

You will see cold air returns in upstairs hallways and bridges—areas where people could be walking in bare feet. These are large registers and clearly neither the mechanical subcontractor nor the builder care about this—it's a sort of standard thing to do. Wooden grills on the registers are bad

enough but metal ones are worse. With a little forethought they can, and should be, mounted in an adjacent wall.

Registers are not designed to take foot traffic nor are feet designed to walk on registers. When heating registers are put in front of outside sliding doors the builder must coordinate the work of the mechanical sub and the door installer, otherwise there's a good chance the register will be installed in front of the sliding part of the door. When it ends up where it will be walked on, it's just wrong.

Toe-kick registers

In kitchens and bathrooms with cabinets, the registers may be placed in the toe kick region at the base of the cabinets. This has several aesthetic and functional advantages over floor registers:

⇨ Nothing dropped on the floor will get into the register or duct work. (Ever go searching for something, like a dropped ring, down a heating duct?)

⇨ Mopping a floor can be done without concern that mop water will get into the register or ducts.

⇨ The registers cannot be walked on, a relief for people who may go around their kitchens or bathrooms in bare feet.

⇨ If you live where there is a potential of pipes freezing in outside walls, they are protected by this register arrangement because the inside of the cabinet and the pipes are kept warm by the duct under it.

In yet another example of a builder not paying attention, the cabinet installer forgot to cut the toe-kick register into the base of the kitchen cabinet in our house. When cold weather came, we noticed that the kitchen was the coldest room in the house and there was no way enough heat could be forced in to make it comfortable without overheating everything else.

BAD REGISTER LOCATIONS

The locations of registers are an integral part of the design of the HVAC system. In most cases they serve that purpose very well but sometimes you will see them in locations which ignore the home user. This may be just bad work by the installer or the house designer may not have left a suitable spot and the installer had no other choice.

Registers should NEVER be in outside walls where they let cold into the house for no good reason.

And they should not be where people will be walking on them.

In front of an entry door.   *In front of a shower door.*

Stairs where people walk.

In a kitchen where people walk.

Look where your foot is when you're here.

In the center of a walk-in closet!

Then one day, while looking at houses, I noticed a register in the toe space under a kitchen sink. Sure enough, back home I found the cabinet area under the sink was toasty warm but the heat had no way to get out. After a discussion with the builder, the cabinet installer was called back to finish his job, a hole was cut, the register was put into place, and the problem was solved. (Where was the builder to let this happen? And nothing would have happened if I hadn't been looking at houses. **Caveat emptor.**)

A toe-kick register is a user-friendly alternative to one in the floor.

In some areas there is an effort underway to tighten up houses by requiring that all heating / cooling air be passed through metal ducts rather than using wood framing elements and cabinets to provide for the heated / cooled air. If toe-kick registers are to remain (and they are a very user-friendly option) they will have to be brought out to the front of the cabinet in a special piece of duct work and not rely on the space under the cabinet to take care of the transmission.

The fix is wrong. If the house is built and insulated properly, there would be no heat loss this way. Such is bureaucracy.

Builder's dirt in the registers

There is a further problem with floor registers—construction dirt and debris. The mechanical subcontractor installs the heating ducts at a time when much of the house is unfinished. To prevent rain and dirt from getting into the ducts, a good mechanical subcontractor seals them immediately at the time of installation. When the outer shell of the house is completed, unless forbidden by code, the builder takes the covers off of the boots leaving them wide open, and turns the furnace on to dry out the house. (A boot is the piece of metal shaped to connect to the round heating duct on one end and to hold the register grill at the other.) Then come the wallboard, floor coverings, finish carpentering, interior finishing, wallpapering and painting. From all of this a significant amount of debris, dirt, and dust fall into the open boots and lies there in wait for you, the new owner, when you move in.

The worst is the dust from wallboard work. This is very fine and will be in the house forever unless you get a special set of furnace filters. We were in our new house for almost two years with this coating of fine dust always present. Different filters caught most of it.

When the builder uses the furnace for warming and drying the house during the latter phases of construction, he may do one of several things:

➪ Nothing. This is the easy way out.

➪ Clean out the ducts before turning the property over to the buyer. This won't get it all because it simply isn't possible to get high-power vacuum hoses through the whole ducting system. (I got a whole handful of debris from a duct that the builder paid to have vacuumed—but never checked to see if it had been done right.)

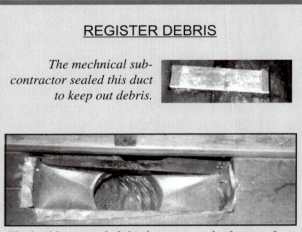

REGISTER DEBRIS

The mechnical sub-contractor sealed this duct to keep out debris.

The builder unsealed this boot to use the furnace for heating and drying out the house. He didn't re-cover it. (The boot is the piece you see here that connects to the duct and holds the register.)

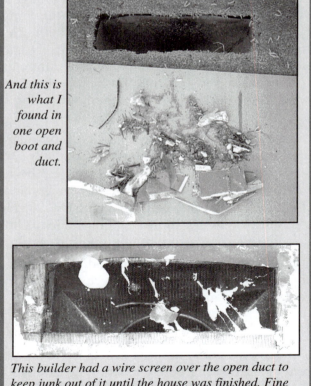

And this is what I found in one open boot and duct.

This builder had a wire screen over the open duct to keep junk out of it until the house was finished. Fine for large stuff but no good for small debris and dust.

⇨ Not open the ducts until construction is complete. With this approach a portable propane heater is used to heat and dry out the house. One builder I know also uses a dehumidifier to remove moisture.

⇨ Buy a set of special air filters to go over the open registers that lets the heat out but does not let debris into the duct. These filters are removed and thrown away after the construction work has been completed and the floor covering installed. Or, put a wire mesh over the open boot as in the bottom photo. It'll keep out pieces of debis but not dust.

⇨ Put caps over the ends of the ducts or the boots whenever workers are in the house and run the furnace only when they are gone. If you are involved when the house is under construction, you may be able to arrange with the builder to do this yourself. It's one way to know it's done right.

In an older house, if you have a continuing dust problem, take a look in the ducts. You may be able to improve things by having the ducts vacuumed out. In any case, try some finer filters in the furnace.

Collapsed ducts

In one house, when I put my arm down to check the debris in the duct, I could hardly get my hand into the 4" duct. The flexible duct had been bent so much where it connected to the boot that it had collapsed, restricting the size of the opening. Whoever bought that house would have had a problem with his heating system. (I told the builder about it, so it should have been fixed before the new owners moved in.)

Note that collapsed ducts are not unusual. They shouldn't happen in a new house but they do. When you find one, there should be no problem having it fixed. And it's a good idea to check every one in your new home before moving in. For a pre-owned house, you might be sure the home inspector checks this out, it's not a usual thing on their list of things to do.

Master bedroom air return

Not all of houses have an air return in the master bedroom suite but it's a good idea to have one. It serves two purposes:

⇨ First, when the door of the suite is closed, the flow of air from the registers to the return will not be disrupted. It is not unusual to find that a master bedroom is comfortable when the hall door is open but gets too warm or cool, depending on the time of year, when the door is closed. With a return in the suite, this won't happen.

⇨ Second, it keeps a closed door, especially a double door, from rattling every time the furnace goes on or off. When the door is closed and there is no place for the air from the registers to go, the pressure will shove the door hard against the jam. When the furnace fan stops, the pressure is released. The result is a door that can make disturbing noises in the middle of the night. This can be helped by putting several little rubber stick-on bumpers on the door jam, the same type that are used on cabinets to keep them from banging. (This isn't a bad idea anyway; it makes it much easier to close a door quietly.)

House design vs. HVAC design

If yours is a big house and the heating and cooling equipment is far from some of the rooms, there may be no good way to get enough hot or cold air to them. A supplementary system for these rooms

is often a good idea but many designers and builders don't know or care about this; they leave it up to the HVAC contractor whose hands are tied by the time he is brought in—by price if not by the house's primary design.. If you have a say and if you have any doubts, you and your designer or builder should consult the HVAC contractor before the plans are finalized and before the final price is fixed.

If you can, for an older house, check out how even the temperatures are in different areas in the house. If you find parts of it are significantly different from others you may want to see why. It could make you change your mind about the house before you sink your money in it.

Zoning

Even with forced-air systems, it is possible to break the house into zones that are heated and cooled independently by using separate thermostats for each zone and having electrically controlled dampers in the ducts. A programmable control unit then controls the temperatures by zone. You can change the program according to the time of day and the day of the week.

The usual zoning arrangement is to control the upstairs and downstairs of a house separately. This leads to more comfort since upstairs get hotter both from the natural tendency for warm air to rise and from the sun beating on the roof. A zoning control system is more efficient and less costly than the alternative of two separate systems.

Zoning can also be applied to individual rooms, such as solariums, that have special heating and cooling requirements.

High-efficiency gas furnaces

High-efficiency furnaces extract up to 90 percent of the heating potential from the gas that is burned. But there is a precaution. In these units there is not enough heat left in the exhaust vent to keep moisture in the exhaust from condensing. This results in water collecting at the bottom of the vent which must be gotten rid of someplace. If planned for ahead of time, this need not result in an eyesore or an inconveniently placed drain pipe. If you are going to have one of these furnaces, talk to the builder and the HVAC subcontractor about the drain pipe before everything is literally poured in concrete.

Heat Pumps and Air Conditioners

There are two parts to an air conditioner, the compressor which is in the open air and the expander which is integral to the furnace. The compressor needs power. It compresses a refrigerant and that generates heat which is dissipated into the outside air. The compressed refrigerant is pumped through an insulated tube to the expander in the furnace unit where it expands and cools the surrounding air in the process. This is the air that is blown into the house. The expanded refrigerant is pumped back to the compressor and the cycle starts again.

If yours is a forced-air system and you want an air conditioner with it, either initially or in the future, or if you are going to use a heat pump, it's a good idea, if you can, to pick the location of the external unit before the house is built. And have the HVAC sub look at the plans to see what problems there may be in getting the wires and tubing between the outside and the inside units. Planning ahead can avoid headaches. Sometimes the only available space, by the time the system is actually installed, makes it an eyesore—which is something to consider when you are buying an already existing house.

"Air Conditioner Ready"

Some house ads read "air conditioner ready." This can mean one of several things:

⇨ The wiring and piping are in place ready for the air conditioner,

⇨ The wiring is in place, or

⇨ Only that the furnace has space for adding the expander coils.

Adding wiring, once the house is finished, is a fairly expensive proposition and may involve running the wiring in a conduit on the outside of the house. It's worthwhile, if there's a possibility of adding an air conditioner, to have the wiring done when the house is built—and good builders will do this. Depending on the house design, it may

The compessor part of an air conditioner sitting on its own concrete pad. The power comes via the switch box in the upper-left corner. The refrigerant tubes and the control wires go through a hole bored through the foundation (lower left). The black hose is the insulation on the tube carrying the compressed refrigerant. The unit was not a part of the original house design and it shows—but it works fine.

also be worthwhile to make the openings in the foundation or elsewhere for the pipes that go between the furnace location and the outside compressor.

Heat pumps

Heat pumps operate similarly to HVAC systems with separate heating and cooling units. The difference is that the outside unit generates heat in the winter as well as cooling in the summer.

In practice, heat pumps are generally more expensive to buy and less expensive to operate than separate heating and cooling units. In climates where the outside air temperature gets too low for efficient winter heat pumping, two options are available:

> ⇨ Use a gas, oil, or electric furnace as a backup or

> ⇨ Use the ground as the source of heat.

The latter arrangement, called "geothermal heating" is more expensive to install, but doesn't require as much backup heating. However, geothermal heating does involve underground piping and, if not installed properly or if there is a failure with time, it can be a relatively expensive fix involving tearing up large segments of your yard .

Heat pump sizes and costs depend on the size of the house, its insulation and the location. This is for a mid-size house (approx. 2000 square feet) in a mild climate.

People who use heat pumps report another concern—houses with pumps respond to temperature changes slowly. This is because the amount of heat they can pump is limited. With modern, well-insulated houses, heat pumps keep up with day-to-day temperature changes quite well. But if you are away from home with the heat pump turned down or off, you can expect it will take longer to get the house back to normal temperature than it would with a separate furnace or air conditioner.

Non-Forced-Air Systems

Since only forced-air systems can be used for cooling, manufacturers of non-forced systems will tell you how to have air conditioning at a lesser cost than a full-blown forced-air heating and cooling system. If you see one of these arrangements, consider it carefully for convenience, comfort, cost, and resaleability. Non-forced-air systems can do a good job of heating on a room-by-room basis and, if this is important to you, one of them may be the way to go. (As explained earlier, you can accomplish much the same thing with a forced air system using "zoning.")

Hot-water baseboard

With a hot water system, the "furnace" is a water heater from which hot water is piped to the various rooms in the house. Baseboard heaters are basically fins attached to pipes that are stretched along the baseboards on several sides of the room. Thermostats control small pumps and each room can have its own thermostat so that only the rooms in use need to be heated. The basic energy source is usually gas or oil.

The possibility of damage to the room and its contents (and it does happen) from one of these springing a leak may give you second thoughts about using this technique.

Radiant floor heat

These systems use hot water in plastic pipes laid in a special solid matrix under the floor covering. In other ways they are similar to a hot water baseboard system. A claim is made that this system heats rooms more evenly than forced air systems. This is probably true. However, it also radiates heat under furniture where it is not needed or wanted.

A potentially more severe problem with this system is repair. If a pipe springs a leak (and it isn't clear why it ever should), it is necessary to take up the floor covering (rug, hardwood, linoleum, or tile) to expose the matrix which is then dug out to get to the pipe. As was discussed in Chapter 6, plastic pipe, such as polybutylene, cannot be cemented. To repair it, enough has to be exposed to permit two mechanical connectors and a replacement piece of pipe to be joined together. While this shouldn't have to be done very often, even once in the lifetime of the system is a significantly bigger undertaking than the repair of any of the other systems.

Electric baseboard

With this arrangement, as with hot-water systems, each room has its own thermostat that controls the electric baseboard heating elements in it.

Wall heaters

With these systems, the heaters are built into the wall. Fans blow the heated air out into the room. Depending on the system, each room may have its own heater or it may depend on air movement to heat several rooms from a centrally located unit.

Thermostats

Several types of thermostats are available. The simplest has a single setting for controlling the heater. You turn it down at night and you turn it up in the morning. At the other extreme is a computer-controlled unit that resets the operating temperature several times a day with different settings for weekdays and weekends. As a minimum, it is a good idea to use a unit that includes a clock that lowers and raises the thermostat setting at preset times. This will result in a more comfortable house and in savings in heating and air-conditioning operating costs. These are called "setback" thermostats and are an energy code requirement in some states.

If you have trouble setting up your VCR, you should probably avoid the digital units, particularly those that include a lot of functions—they can be tedious to set. It's worthwhile to visit your local heating supply company or home improvement store to get a look at different types of thermostats.

Seeing your thermostat

For a mechanically adjustable thermostat, insist on one that lets you easily see its settings and then coordinate the locations of thermostat and lights. If you choose a unit with digital readouts, don't forget that you will need light to see the digital display and you will also need light to see the keyboard when the thermostat is being programmed. This ability to see the thermostat is one of the things you should note when looking at existing homes.

For new construction or a remodel where the thermostat is involved, let the builder know the type of thermostat you want and that you want it to be lit, either internally or by a nearby light.

Thermostat location

The thermostat can sense the temperature only where it's located, so it should be placed where you want to control the temperature most closely.

It should not be near a heat register because the furnace will cycle on and off more often than you would want. Since most heat registers are around outside walls, putting the thermostat in the center of the house usually works best. Normal practice is to put them more or less in the flow of air toward a return register.

Thermostats should be installed where average people can see the settings comfortably with little stooping or standing on their toes.

For an existing house, check that the thermostat is appropriately located and that there is a light that lets you see the readings and the controls. If there isn't light where it should be, be prepared to wrestle with another minor irritation if you buy the house.

Chapter 8

Fireplaces and Stoves

Look for your choices, pick the best one, then go with it.

Pat Riley, basketball coach, speaker (1945?-   )

In this chapter:
The several options for fireplaces and stoves are discussed along with the impacts of building and energy codes that can limit what you can have. The key factors of pilot lights and of efficiency are reviewed in detail along with their impacts on the cost of operation.

Except in rural areas you don't see stacks of wood piled around the house as winter sets in. Smoke from chimneys is mostly something from pictures and paintings of the past. Stoves are still used as room heaters but they burn pellets or gas instead of wood or coal. And fireplaces used for heating don't burn wood but gas, with efficiencies that are surprisingly close to those of central heating systems.

Note. "Stove" as used here refers to units used primarily for heating, not cooking. Kitchen stoves are discussed in Part III.

Stove or Fireplace?

Usually we think of a fireplace as a unit built into a wall of a room and a stove as a free-standing unit with a stovepipe to the outside. It used to be that we had our stack of wood in the backyard and one of the chores was to bring the wood into the house as needed for burning. Then came the fireplace logs made of compressed wood particles, available at the grocery store instead of having them hauled from the hillside where the trees had been cut down and dried. And finally the ubiquitous use of natural gas, first for cooking and HVAC systems, then for fireplaces and heating stoves.

When you start looking at the options available today you'll find that the difference between stoves and fireplaces has blurred. It is often a matter of appearance, not one of function. Yes, a fireplace is built into the wall of a room and a stove is free-standing. But the way they work and their venting arrangements are virtually identical. (A vent is the pipe that carries burnt fuel gasses outside.)

And you can find fireplaces that are mounted inside a room, against the wall, or in a corner, as well as in the wall. Then there are look-through fireplaces in the wall between rooms and, finally, one manufacturer, at least, offers a see-through fireplace to go in an outside wall between a room and the deck or patio. And there are ventless fireplaces which dump their burnt gasses back into the room; efficient, yes, but...(more below).

If you have one of the old-fashioned, wood-burning fireplaces in your house or you are considering an existing house which has one, you can update it by getting a high-efficiency "insert" which fits into an existing brick and mortar fireplace and then burns gas.

A fireplace can be used between two rooms to give ambiance to both.

Considerations

With a fireplace or stove, here are five things to take into consideration:

⇨ Warmth. Stoves, particularly, are still used as the primary source of heat for a specific room. The HVAC system, if there is one, keeps the rest of the house at a different temperature.

⇨ Efficiency. In today's sensitivity to energy use, does it get a maximum of heat from each unit of fuel that's burned?

⇨ Ambiance. Most people enjoy sitting in front of a fireplace and watching the flames flickering while being warmed. It is a feeling of yesteryear, a getting away from the problems of the moment. Some newer stoves have transparent sides so that much the same effect is possible with them.

⇨ Ease of operation. Does it go on or off with a single push of a switch or remote control button?

⇨ Emergency operation. Does it continue to operate in the case of an electric power failure? This can be important since HVAC systems depend on the availability of electricity to operate fans and blowers. Most modern stoves and fireplaces meet this criterion of operating without electricity.

⇨ Safety. Units in new homes can be expected to be in accord with current building codes where safety should not be a problem. However, in older homes this may not be true and it may not be feasible to remodel and install the kind of unit you'd like to have.

Fuel

Three types of fuel are common:

⇨ Gas. In both stoves and fireplaces

⇨ Wood. In both stoves and fireplaces

⇨ Pellets. In stoves.

Efficiency

Efficiencies—how much of the potential heat in the fuel is used to heat the room—vary widely. State code bodies also vary widely in what they say about fireplaces and stoves, resulting in significant differences about what may acceptable where you live.

Fireboxes

There are three distinctly different firebox arrangements for stoves and fireplaces, two of which we have had with us for centuries and one which is relatively new—brought on by the emphasis on energy efficiency.

⇨ No vent. With this arrangement whatever products, smoke and gasses, are generated by the burning go right back into the space where the unit is. High efficiency but...more later.

⇨ Type "B" or Top vent. This is the old "standard" stove and fireplace arrangement that's been used forever, from caves to today. There is a flue or chimney to take the smoke and fumes out of the house. Combustion air (the air that a fire needs) comes from the room. Efficiencies vary widely.

⇨ Direct vent. This unit has become increasingly popular as environmental concerns about tight houses and efficiency have increased. The combustion air and the exhaust are completely separated from the air in the house. Efficiencies are comparable to those of a modern HVAC system. This is the unit seen extensively in new construction.

Detailed information on what's available and the terminology used with fireplaces and stoves can be found at the HearthNet website[8C].

What's included here

Several different versions of fireplaces and stoves are discussed below in more detail using the above considerations. This should give you a good feeling for knowing what you'd like when looking at houses or considering a remodel.

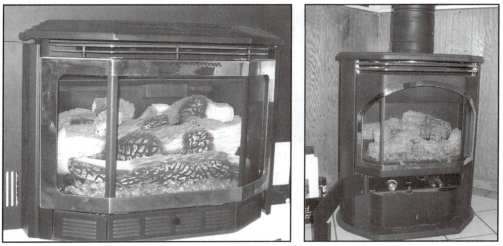

A modern-day gas fireplace (left) and gas stove (right) both use direct-vent technology. The controls make it possible to shut the pilots off during the summer and relight them for the season when the unit is needed. (The door on the stove is open here to show the controls.)

What we don't touch on are older units, like stoves that burn oil or kerosene. While still in use, it is suggested that you go to the Internet to see what info may be available[8E, 8F].

Operation

Fireplaces and stoves depend totally on convection to get rid of the burned gasses. Convection is the movement caused when air of different temperatures are mixed together. Hot air is lighter in weight and will rise while cooler, heavier air sinks. When a fire is burning, the smoke or burned gasses will go to the top of the firebox and up the exhaust vent or stove pipe and, in the process, draw heavier, cooler air into the firebox.

The operational basic concept is simple: when the fireplace or stove is operating, air is mixed with the fuel and burns, giving off heat which is then transferred into the room.

When I was growing up we had a wood stove in our living room. In cold weather we put newspaper, kindling and wood into the stove and, after opening the front and stovepipe dampers to let air through, we'd start the fire by lighting the newspaper. When the fire got going the dampers were closed both to slow down the size of the flame (by restricting air flow) and to keep the heat in the room instead of having it go up the pipe.

The physics haven't changed. The fuel needs combustion air to burn and we want to get all of the heat out of it we can—with one possible exception, discussed below.

But much else has changed. Today the trend is towards fireplaces that burn gas rather than wood although solid fuels are often used in space heaters. By keeping the combustion air separated from the room air the efficiencies far exceed those which were possible even a few decades ago. And there is no problem with smoke or exhaust gasses getting back into the house.

Another thing that is different, and is a driving force in the changes, is the need for energy saving. Since there is a finite supply of both gas and wood, we must be prudent in how they are used. From this comes building and energy codes which dictate not only how we must insulate our homes but also how we keep from burning them down or asphyxiating ourselves

Which Vent-Type?

The pros and cons of the three different firebox configurations are discussed here.

No-vent

As the name implies, this gas heating unit has no vent or flue to take the burnt gasses out of the house.

It used to be that portable gas heaters were used to take the chill off of a room on cold winter mornings. Gas was piped to the rooms where it might be used and the heater hose was connected when it was wanted. This device was 100 percent efficient—since there was no vent, all of the heat from the burning gas stayed in the room. Such devices are no longer used because they are dangerous: it is easy to catch something on fire if it gets too close to the open flame and, if misadjusted, it can lead to the formation of carbon monoxide. But they are 100% efficient!

The unvented gas fireplace is the equivalent device available today. Burned gas is returned to the room and no heat escapes.

If for some reason the level of oxygen drops too low, there would be additional combustion products besides the normal carbon dioxide and water vapor. Some of these are potentially toxic and it is a requirement that these no-vent units be equipped with oxygen-deprivation sensors that will turn the fireplace off before any damage is done.

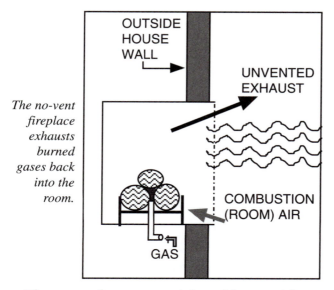

The no-vent fireplace exhausts burned gases back into the room.

There are three potential problems with an unvented fireplace:

⇨ The combustion products from the burning gas go right back into the room the same as with the old-time room heater. These will be primarily carbon dioxide and water vapor but that's not all—there are other products coming from minute amounts of impurities in the gas. With vented fireplaces and stoves these are taken outside but with the unvented units they are dumped back into your house. They may not be dangerous or presumably codes wouldn't allow them. But they do depend on the purity of the gas and accurate adjustment of the fireplace to keep unwanted combustion particles (greasy soot) and water vapor from messing up your drapes, furniture and carpet. Gas stoves do the same thing but with significantly lesser amounts of exhaust.

⇨ In a tightly sealed house there may be no way for replacement oxygen to get in,

which means the fireplace will turn itself off after it has been burning long enough to affect the oxygen level. While safe, a fireplace that turns itself off may not be to your liking. And, of course, the safety of the device depends totally on the oxygen-deprivation sensor *never* failing.

⇨ Water vapor is a normal product of burning gas and, in past years, you'd never notice it. Now with tight houses, if there is a mold or fungus problem, the additional water is going to make it worse. As to how much worse—who knows?

The efficiency is the plus side of unvented units but, in today's houses, even that is tainted. The units burn the oxygen that's in the room/house, the same oxygen we need to breathe. In very tight houses it will be necessary to replace this oxygen to keep the units going; in other words to let in outside air which is unheated and there goes the 100% (or 99.8%) efficiency. How serious all this is seems to depend on to whom you are talking.

When you visit the web trying to get more useful information, you'll run into a problem. There are two schools of thought:

⇨ Those who say that the no-vent concept is great—they tell you to look at the energy savings they represent. They also down play any dangers from the units as being so small as to be irrelevant. This school *makes* no-vent fireplaces. They do have some pretty impressive groups on their side, however.[8G]

⇨ And those that put down no-vent fireplaces...guess who they are? Those who don't make them, of course.[8H] Although permitted by building codes in many places in the US, they are not in Canada.

If you think you might want one of these, understand the turmoil that's going on about them.

There is yet another side to this story. Neighbors unwittingly bought a house with two of these no-vent fireplaces. After they moved in they realized what they had. Six years later, they hadn't turned them on because they had become well aware of the potential problems. If you get a house with such a fireplace, be sure you understand that you may be making your house harder to sell when the time comes because knowledgeable people simply may not want any part of a no-vent fireplace.

Type B (aka top-vent)

This is, by far, the type of stove and fireplace most commonly used in our country—although not in new construction. They come in several different configurations, but the basic facts are that they take heated air from the room and exhaust it up the vent—whether the fireplace is lit or not! They do not go with the tight-house concept.

There are two problems with top-vent units that direct vents do not have:

⇨ They cannot be used in a tightly sealed house.

⇨ Unless used with a damper, they lose heated room air continuously, whether lit or not. Dampers can be a different problem as discussed later.

For convection to work with top-vent units there must be a supply of air coming into the firebox: air that gets hot in the combustion process and then goes

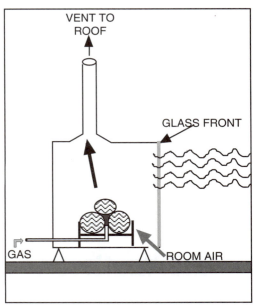

Heated room air is continuously lost in a top-vent (type-B vent) fireplace or stove.

up the vent. If there is no "spare" air, there is no convection and the fireplace or stove doesn't work. In a tightly sealed house this could be the case.

The fireplace could get its combustion air from, say, the crawl space, so that it always has a supply of air for the convection process to work. But, unless it's a sealed firebox—in which case it would be a direct-vent unit—it is not sealed off from room air. Now, when there is no fire, the outside air can come directly through the firebox and into the room—and who wants outside air coming out of their unlit fireplace?

This problem is exacerbated when a kitchen or bath exhaust fan is working. It, too, needs to get

This is below the firebox in a top-vent gas fireplace showing the aluminum duct where heated room air is lost 24/7. It is not allowed in new construction today.

its air from someplace and it'll pull it down the stove or fireplace vent as well as from anyplace else that isn't sealed.

We've seen that a top-vent unit won't work well in a tightly sealed house. However, if it is not well-sealed, it opens the door for the other problem with top-vent units. There is absolutely nothing to prevent heated room air from escaping—continuously!

The top-vent gas fireplace in my house gets its air through a four-inch duct under the firebox. The duct could have been connected to get the combustion air from the crawl space under the house but it wasn't. To see just how much heated room air might be going out through the fireplace, I put a lighted butane BBQ lighter in front of the duct opening. (The fireplace was off.) There was a good flow of air—the flame was bent sideways. When the same thing was done with a breeze blowing outside (which causes suction), the rush of air into the duct blew out the butane lighter instantly. And this is all my heated room air! And it goes on and on! The gas company would love it if they weren't so energy conscious.

While not a way to measure how many BTUs the fireplace loses, it does show that this isn't the way to go. It's similar to leaving a four-inch hole in the ceiling. And note that **any** flue in an open firebox without a closed damper—whether stove, wood-burning fireplace or gas fireplace—will do exactly the same thing.

The rated efficiencies of top-vent fireplaces and stoves do not take this loss of heated room air into account. But it's there, it's real, and it costs money. (Isn't there always a caveat that nobody tells you about? It's no different here.)

There's another problem with dampers in gas fireplaces to the extent that some state codes forbid them. This is discussed in more detail later.

Direct vent

Direct-vent fireplaces and stoves are sealed so that none of the combustion gas gets into the house. The only interaction between the room and the combustion air is the transfer of heat from the firebox to the room.

The direct-vent stove or fireplace uses convection to avoid the need for a fan in getting rid of the combustion gasses. The rising of the heated air in one pipe pulls <u>outside</u> air into the firebox through the other one. Anything that restricts the air flow will lower the efficiency of the unit so it is important that the pipes be straight and the shorter the better.

The original direct-vent fireplace or stove used concentric pipes and had to be mounted in an outside wall. Neither the masonry nor the metal used in fireboxes is a good insulator. To avoid heat loss from fireplaces on outside walls, the back sides should be enclosed in an insulated chase. But the chase doesn't have to be two stories high as you'll find on some houses (photos later).

Then came a fireplace which, while on a outside wall, is mounted so that most of the unit is

This direct-vent fireplace extends into the living room and does not need a chase. Only the vent extends outside the house.

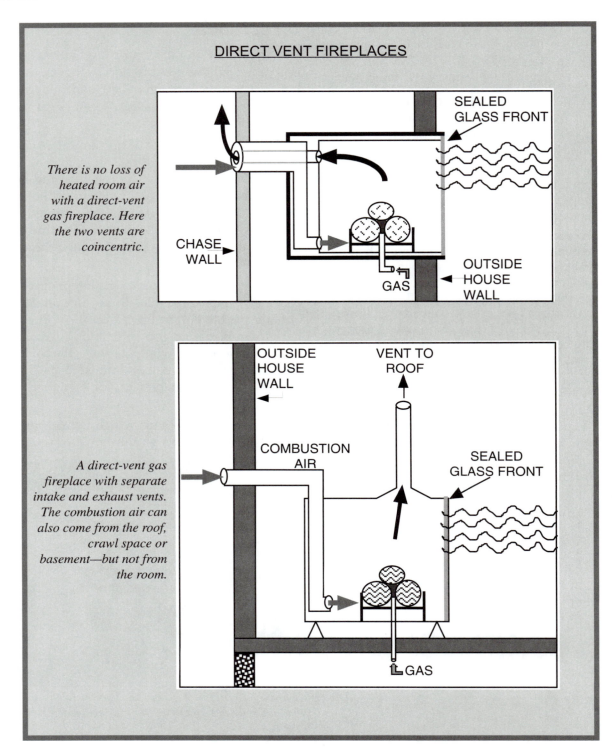

DIRECT VENT FIREPLACES

There is no loss of heated room air with a direct-vent gas fireplace. Here the two vents are coincentric.

SEALED GLASS FRONT

CHASE WALL

OUTSIDE HOUSE WALL

GAS

A direct-vent gas fireplace with separate intake and exhaust vents. The combustion air can also come from the roof, crawl space or basement—but not from the room.

OUTSIDE HOUSE WALL

VENT TO ROOF

COMBUSTION AIR

SEALED GLASS FRONT

GAS

The concentric vents on the top of a direct-vent stove. Hot exhaust air inside, cool intake air outside.

Concentric vents and caps used with direct-vent fireplaces. Note the "HOT" warning on both of the caps. They can be a hazard for small children.

inside the room and only the vent cap is outside. Corner fireplaces use this technique.

But outside walls aren't always where people want their fireplace or stove. Now stoves and fireplaces are available where the concentric pipe connection is on the top of the unit so it can be run straight up through the roof. Other units have separate connections for the air intake and the exhaust. With these arrangements there are no restrictions on the location of a direct-vent stove or fireplace—except, maybe, one due to the length of the exhaust duct. You'll have to check that out with the supplier. But remember, the longer these runs, the slower the air and exhaust products will move and the less efficient the unit will be.

Chases on two-story houses are often made to look like chimneys...which they are not. (*See* the photos on the next page.) These are strictly for looks and whether they add to the attractiveness of a house is matter of personal taste. While usu-

ally on the side or the back of a house, vents are where the fireplace is and sometimes this is on the front and we are not used to seeing things like this there. They are particularly noticeable when the house is a dark color because the vent caps are sheet metal which is very obvious against dark siding. The caps can be painted, using stove paint because of the heat involved, but often it's not done, leaving an eyesore. But, then, that is all aesthetics, not function.

Pilot Lights

With pilot lights, gas stoves and fireplaces can be turned on and off with a switch or remote control—matches or lighters aren't needed. The pilot is an integral part of the design because the heat from the pilot light is used to thermoelectrically generate the power needed to turn the gas on and off from the switch. This ability to operate without external electricity is one of the attractive features of these units—they don't depend on electric power and will continue to operate even with a power outage. They are used on no-vent, top-vent and direct-vent units.

A single on-off switch for a fireplace.

Here the flame is controlled by a thethermostat (top right) and the fan is controlled by the switch below it.

CHASES

The purpose of a chase is to protect the part of the fireplace that sticks out into the weather. When made to simulate chimneys they are purely window dressing - that is, an aesthetic feature.

Chase for a no-vent fireplace. There is no vent.

Chimney-like chase for a direct-vent fireplace. Note the vent.

This "different" chase is from the design of a well-known, respected designer. The vent on the front of the house is at an interesting location.

Two simple, utilitarian chases.

A chase stuccoed to match the house decor.

Vents for direct-vent fireplaces without chases.

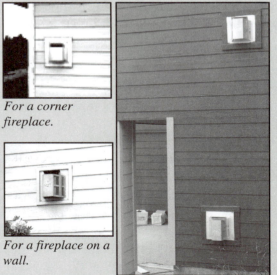

For a corner fireplace.

For a fireplace on a wall.

Note that the pilot light in your gas water heater also burns continuously but that the burner gas is controlled by the temperature of the water, not by a switch or remote control.

During the summer, when you're not going to be using the fireplace, a continuously burning pilot is a waste of energy and that costs money. But you don't want a unit that requires electricity to ignite the gas because one of the features of a gas unit is that you can use it for heat in an emergency when the power is off. What you'll find in modern-day fireplaces and stoves is a way "to have your cake and eat it too."

The controls on these units let you:

⇨ Turn the pilot off during the summer and relight it when cooler weather returns. It needs electricity to do this but this isn't an emergency situation.

⇨ Operate the unit in the winter without needing electricity.

They are a part of the continuing improvements in technology that make life more comfortable while using less and less energy.

When you are looking at an existing house, you can usually tell if there is a pilot light in one of three ways:

⇨ You may be able to see it burning in the fireplace.

In this new upscale home there is a gas turnoff in the floor. Different strokes for...

⇨ If there is a switch for turning the fireplace on and off, there will be a pilot.

⇨ If there is a gas turnoff in the floor or wall, there is no pilot.

Fans (Gas Units)

While, in gas fireplaces, blowers are not used to move combustion air, they are often used to help get the heat from the firebox into the room. These switches may include speed controls for the fan. They may be located with the switch that controls the fire or they may be separate. While fireplaces work just fine without them, as they must do when there is a power failure, they do move heat more effectively than radiation alone.

Dampers (Wood-Burning Units)

In wood-burning fireplaces and stoves, dampers are used to manually control the amount of air flow into and out of the firebox. By reducing the air flow, the fire is made smaller and the fuel lasts longer. And, of course, to keep the warmed room air in the house, the damper needs to be closed when the stove/fireplace is not in use.

The next step in convenience is the fireplace with gas piped to it to be used as a starter instead of newspaper and kindling. With these fireplaces, you put in the wood you want to burn, open the damper, turn on the gas with a manual valve, and light the gas. When the logs are burning well, you turn off the gas and adjust the damper in the flue to optimize the heat your wood fire generates. Hopefully, when the wood is all burned up you remember to close the damper to keep your heated room air from escaping up the chimney. And, just as hopefully, you did already remember to turn off the gas.

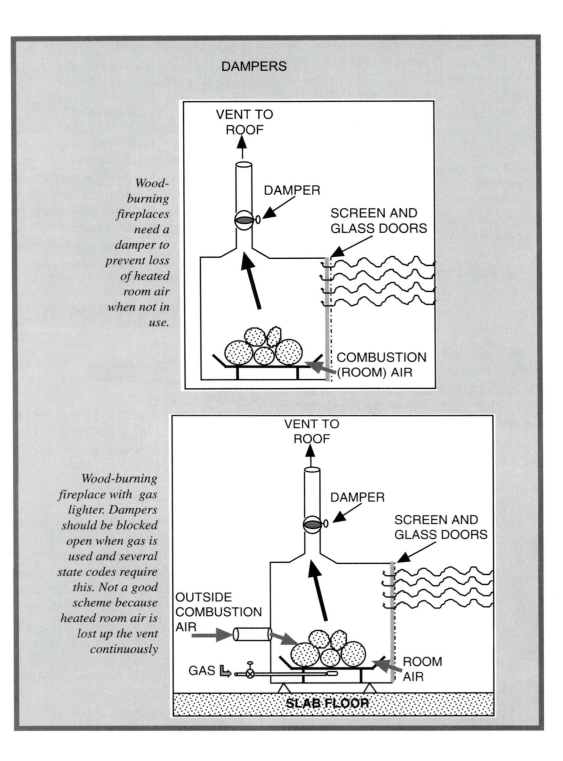

DAMPERS

VENT TO ROOF

DAMPER

SCREEN AND GLASS DOORS

COMBUSTION (ROOM) AIR

Wood-burning fireplaces need a damper to prevent loss of heated room air when not in use.

VENT TO ROOF

DAMPER

SCREEN AND GLASS DOORS

OUTSIDE COMBUSTION AIR

GAS

ROOM AIR

SLAB FLOOR

Wood-burning fireplace with gas lighter. Dampers should be blocked open when gas is used and several state codes require this. Not a good scheme because heated room air is lost up the vent continuously

In the 1980s this was the latest thing. But there were problems. If it was turned on without being lit and the damper was closed, the gas would escape into the room and could lead to an explosion.

It's a scary feeling, to walk into your family room or living room and smell gas and then remember that you forgot to turn it off. You hold your breath, turn off the gas and open the windows--- hoping the whole time that it won't catch on fire.

This led to the requirement by some states that when gas is piped to a wood-burning fireplace the damper must be blocked open. This, in turn, leads to the continuous loss of heated room air up the chimney 24/7, which is very much anti-energy saving.

This brought about the demise of gas-lighters in fireplaces. You seldom see them in today's new homes.

The open damper is a relatively recent requirement. Our southern California house had a gas lighter but the damper wasn't blocked. We tried to remember to close it when the fire wasn't burning—and to open it before turning the gas on. We had no problems, but the changed codes are obviously appropriate.

If you want a wood-burning fireplace or gas logs, the blocked-open damper will cost you money. Even if there is gas in the house for heating or cooking, don't be in a hurry to have it piped to the fireplace either for gas logs or for use as a gas lighter because that will mean an open damper forever. If it can be accommodated, a direct-vent gas insert is a good solution. They are more expensive and will probably never pay for themselves but they are safer and they are energy saving—and make the house more saleable when the time comes—to say nothing about the convenience of gas.

Inserts

Manually controlled pilots in top-vent fireplaces were all we had for many years. If you see one in a house, remember that it's something you'll be dealing with as long as you live there. And it's not necessary. A direct-vent insert can be put in place so you can "have your cake and eat it, too". You might want to consider it in an existing house.

With these units the combustion air and the exhaust air are carried in two parallel vents, rather than in concentric ones. This is necessary because the vents generally must be made with flexible tubes so they can be bent and run up the old chimney. Note, too, that this means that the old chimney must be big enough to let the vents go through. A single 5" or 6" vent won't support a direct-vent unit. A type-B unit with its inherent inefficiencies, however, can be used if you are looking to change from wood-burning to gas.

Efficiency

The efficiency of a heating device is the ratio of the actual heat generated to the available heat from

A gas-fireplace insert with the side doors opened to show the controls on either side of the firebox.

the fuel. Efficiencies are averaged over a year's time using standardized methods. Potential heat that isn't used goes up the vent pipe and is lost. We see efficiency ratings on gas heating units—water heaters, stoves, furnaces, and fireplaces. Ratings typically run around 85 to 90% for furnaces and upward from 55% for fireplaces and stoves. Efficiency ratings for oil-burning units are comparable.

Chapter 9

Doors

In this chapter:

Three rules for the appropriate use of doors are given and explained.

Photos show many good and bad ways to use doors. The several types of doors are described along with their appropriate applications.

Bad door use in existing houses can sometimes be easily corrected, sometimes it cannot. With new construction, better door use can usually be implemented as the house is built.

One of the more obvious signs of a poor house design is to find doors that are used inappropriately: hinged doors that should be pocket doors, doors that cover light switches, doors that bang into other doors, doors that block doorways. Better ways to use the doors in a house is the subject here.

Our Rules for Doors

Unsuitable use of doors is one of the most irritating, least excusable, and *potentially hazardous* of home design sins. We key the discussions to these three rules for using doors.

Our three door rules:

(1) A door should never open across another door of any type.

(2) Any door that may normally be left open should never be in the way when it *is* open.

(3) A door should never swing where someone is apt to be standing or sitting.

Some door arrangements can violate more than one of these rules. In the following discussions you can see again that it's just common sense. If one of these arrangements is in the plan or house you want, see if you can't do something to improve the situation before you make a commitment. Easy fixes are not always possible.

And what great candidates for change when you're remodeling.

Then there's the sidle toilet. This is discussed in detail in Chapter 20 but in a tight-quarters situation someone using a toilet can be hit by a door that's being opened. It shouldn't happen but it does.

The pay off for watching where doors swing will be a more user-friendly home.

Rule 1.

A door should never open across another door of any type

Consider Photo 1 on the next page. If you're coming out of the walk-in closet when someone is coming into the bedroom, there will be a collision of doors. To avoid this, sometimes builders will swing the closet door inside and then when you come out of the closet as some one else is coming into the bedroom, you'll get the door in your face (or whatever part of your body is pointed that way). Avoid combinations like these. (In practice, if you had a house with this in it, you could swing the door from the hall on the other side which would improve the situation—but not cure it.)

Extend this rule to include closet, cabinet, and appliance doors as well. While these doors are normally closed, having to close a room door before opening a closet or an appliance door just doesn't make good sense. (The general problem with laundries is discussed in Chapter 21.)

In one custom house I visited, the door from the master bedroom into the vanity opens right across the door into the room where the toilet is. So to get to the toilet, you go from the bedroom into the vanity, then you must close the door you just came through so you can open the door to get to the toilet. Wanna' try this in the middle of the night?

Rule 1. A door should never open across another door of any type.

Here are several examples of the ways in which designers and builders ignore the practicality of what they design and build.

In Photo 1, if someone is in the closet with the door (the one on the right) open, anyone trying to come into the room will cause the two doors to bang into each other.

Photo 2 is similar, except that the entry is a double door with the normally-used door being the one that's open in the photo. Here the two doors are virtually hitting each other.

Photos 3 and 4 are of an entry door opening across closets that have bifold doors. In 3 the bifold door (on the left) will prevent the entry door from opening or closing, depending on where it is. In 4, the bifold door simply must be almost closed to make it possible to use the entry door at all.

Photo 5 is similar to Photo 1 except that, during the tour of homes where this was taken, the door into the bathroom (behind) was removed and the rope strung across it to keep people from using the bathroom. There was a second effect, one that you should try to look for when you're touring houses. When a door has been removed, check carefully where the door will swing when it is in place. Here it will go across the guest closet door, the one on the right. With the door gone its user-unfriendliness isn't obvious.

Rule 2.
Any door that may normally be left open should never be in the way when it is open.

Perhaps the most obvious application of Rule 2 is to walk-in closets where you shouldn't have to close the door to get at your clothes. And, of course, a door opening across another door (Rule 1) will usually result in an open door that will be in the way sooner or later.

Sometimes hinging a door on the other side will improve on or eliminate the problem, but thinking through things like this is not high on the priority list of altogether too many de-signers, builders or their carpenters. And as long as buyers don't know the difference, nothing's going to change—it's another thing for you to watch for when you're home look-ing. One consolation: it's something that can often be changed later.

Still another application of Rule 2 deals with external doors. If hinged doors are in-stalled to swing out, there will be no place for a screen door because the main door will be right in the way. (This is discussed in more detail below.)

Rule 2. Any door that may normally be left open should never be in the way when it *is* open.

Walk-in closets are where open doors are often in the way.

Photo 1 in a model is of a closet without clothes where clearly the door would have to be closed to reach any clothes hung on the rods behind it. In this closet you must go in then close the door to get to your clothes.

Photo 2 has clothes in place. Same problem.

The earlier caution about doors which were taken off of their hinges in models shows up in photos 3 and 4. Such an arrangement may make it easier for people to walk through the houses but they also hide the distinct inconvenience that such closets have. Photo 3 shows a closet from the bedroom and Photo 4 from inside the closet. Almost surely these doors were taken off so people wouldn't see the way they block the insides of the closets.

Pocket doors are a decidely better choice as shown in the last two pictures. But they have to be used with caution, too, as discussed in the text.

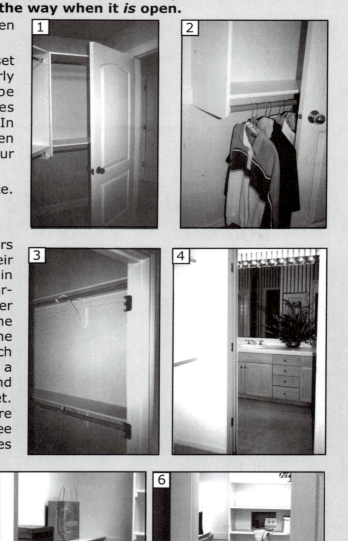

Rule 3.
A door should never swing where someone is apt to be standing or sitting.

In far too many cases you'll see doors that are dangerous to use because there's apt to be someone on the other side.

In a laundry anyone doing the washing and leaning over the washer or tub is vulnerable to being hit by the door from the garage. What to do about this is discussed in Chapter 21.

In the other example, the usefulness of the breakfast bar can be degraded by an in-swinging door. The doors in Photos 1 and 4 (opposite) would be lot less objectionable if they were hinged on the other side. Sometimes a sliding door would be far better if it can be used in a particular wall.

The use of a door with glass from the garage in Photo 6 is a splendid idea. It let's you see if someone is at the laundry tub before you crash them. (But before you have this done, be sure to check building codes which may require a solid-core door between the house and the garage for fire-safety reasons.)

Besides the baths and laundries of Photos 5 and 6, there are entry doors that open across stairs which will block the stairs as long as the door is open. This is particularly annoying when you come in the front door with something to carry upstairs.

Rule 3. A door should never swing where it might hit someone.

Photos 1, 2 and 3 show the common ways to swing doors into a kitchen nook. In 1 and 3 the doors hit the chairs but not in 2. It's the homeowner, not the designer or builder who finds this out.

Photo 4 is a door swinging into the breakfast bar. In this case there was lots of room to move the door over where this wouldn't happen.

But eating areas aren't the only place. Photo 5 is a door opening into a vanity area and if you're standing there it's "ouch" time. And you can't wash your hands without closing the door! Just bad.

The glass in the door gives someone at the laundry tub a chance in Photo 6. An unusual user-friendly plus.

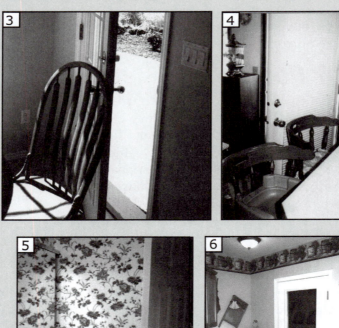

Types of Doors

Several different types of doors are commonly used in today's houses:

⇨ Hinged doors. The most common type, they are used everywhere, including places where they shouldn't be.

⇨ Sliding glass doors. Used for entering and exiting the house.

⇨ Sliding wooden doors. Used as closet doors. Sometimes with mirrors.

⇨ Pocket doors. Used as interior doors where hinged doors would get in the way.

⇨ Bifold doors. Used primarily for closets. May be louvered. The doors themselves may be mirrors.

Exterior Doors

Entry doors are usually decorative with wood being the most popular material. However, wood is disadvantageous in three ways: it can warp, finishes deteriorate rapidly when exposed to weather, and it is not a good thermal insulator. If appearance is not a prime consideration, you might want to consider exterior metal doors. These are a metal sheath over a foam interior. They transmit less heat than wooden doors and have better lasting finishes. Vinyl doors that simulate wood are available and are also foam-filled.

Note that, unlike interior doors discussed below, exterior doors are never hollow core for two reasons:

⇨ Solid-core doors provide better insulation than do hollow-core doors.

⇨ Most building codes require that solid-core doors be used between the house and the garage because they are better fire blocks. (This may be a prob-

lem for the scheme in Photo 6 on the previous page.)

Exterior doors that swing out are potential security problems because the hinge pins are on the outside where they can be easily removed. Special hinges are available to overcome the security problem but:

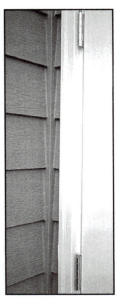

Exterior doors that swing out have several disadvantages.

⇨ If you want a screen with these doors, it would have to swing inside,

⇨ There's no place for a storm door and

⇨ Fire officials deplore doors that swing out and in some jurisdictions they are forbidden by code in new homes. When firemen have to get into a burning house with locked doors, they must break in. It's much easier to push a door in when it is hinged on the inside.

It's just better to avoid doors that swing out.

Even the best of insulated exterior sliding glass doors passes much more heat than an insulated door without glass. Given the large amount of glass in sliding doors, they will always be a major source of heat loss. Use them sparingly, even those with the best insulation properties. And don't forget to watch carefully where a heat register is placed in front of a double sliding glass door (*see* Chapter 7).

Locks for sliding doors that provide a reasonable amount of security are available but don't usually come with the house. It's a good idea to use them.

Entries

Door sidelights have become very popular as a way to make entries lighter and more attractive. These narrow vertical panels of glass on one or both sides of the door are often decorative, intended to give the entry a touch of luxury. They also provide an easy way for burglars to break in and unlock the door.

In bigger homes you'll often see double entry doors. These, too, are security problems because they are much more easily entered by a good push from a shoulder. Again, an alarm system is suggested. The normal way doors are mounted can

ENTRY DOORS

Glass sidelights are a nicety that are easy for someone to break and then reach the door locks from the outside. And, unless curtains are used, they are an open view into the interior of your home. They almost make an alarm system a necessity. (Consider using glass or acrylic blocks here. They let in light, keep your privacy and are not subject to security problems.)

Double entrance doors with glass in them look great. They are also attractive to burglars. Better have an alarm system.

make them relatively easy to be broken by a solid shove. What to do about the security aspects of entry doors is discussed in Chapter 11.

Unless planned carefully, sidelights can also cause problems with the light switch location—as was pointed out in Chapter 5. The entry door is always in a load-bearing wall and framers tend to fill the area around the door and the sidelights with studs, leaving no place for the switches. This should all be figured out ahead of time.

Another sometimes-heard objection to entry door sidelights is that someone can see into the house. The windows are so small that putting an attractive blind or curtain over them is difficult but, without something, you lose your privacy at night. To let light in during the day while avoiding this fishbowl aspect of door sidelights, some builders use glass bricks or acrylic blocks instead of window panes. You may want to give some thought to the advantages of using other than easily broken sidelights. Or seriously consider having an alarm system. Or both.

The kitchen - when you have a choice

A door that opens into a kitchen nook often needs special attention. There is usually little room in the nook for a swinging door so builders will swing the door outside—which, as noted above, needs special care if it is not to be a security problem. Further, this arrangement leaves no place for a screen door.

The lesser of the evils is a sliding glass door that, even with its heat loss, is the more user-friendly answer. Another solution could be to have the outside door open into the family room adjacent to the nook. The disadvantage to this is that the outside door then opens directly into a carpeted area—which isn't good for carpets.

KITCHEN DOORS

Outside doors that open directly onto carpeting make it difficult to keep the carpet clean.

This door cannot have a screen. Hinged outside doors should swing inside or be avoided entirely.

If the nook can be made big enough that an in-swinging door doesn't get in the way, the problem is solved. Otherwise there will be an inevitable compromise, usually ending up with a slider.

Interior Doors

Since insulation value and security are of no relevance, interior doors are chosen for their appearance and it is generally desirable that they be compatible with the cabinets—a consideration when you are looking at the patterns and finishes of doors and cabinets.

Interior doors are usually hollow core. In a hollow-core door a frame of wood goes around the outside edge of the door and across the center. This is covered by a veneer of wood, molded hardboard, or vinyl. The center piece is used to mount the door latch. The rest of the interior of the door has a honeycomb of material to support the outside veneer.

A flat-surface and a raised-panel interior door.

Interior doors may be painted or finished to match the woodwork in the house. They may be a raised panel design or a single solid surface. The single surface doors are usually a hardwood veneer intended for staining and lacquer or varnish. Raised panel doors come in several different styles in wood and simulated wood hardboard or vinyl surfaces.

Hardboard raised panel doors can be painted or finished to look stained. White hardboard with white painted molding is a common finish although some builders choose a mixture of white doors and natural woodwork or vice-versa.

Bifold Doors

Bifold doors are often used in preference to sliding or hinged doors, particularly for closets. They have advantages and disadvantages.

Even when open, bifolds always block part of the doorway and can be a real annoyance when installed in closets that aren't walk-in. Another disturbing characteristic of double bifold doors is that when you close one side the other side often pops open. This is, at least in part, because as you close one door, air pressure builds up in the closet that forces the other door to open. Louvered bifolds can alleviate this annoyance but don't put them on laundries.

Some designs in starter homes have the laundry room next to the kitchen with bifold doors to close off the laundry. You'll have a serious noise problem unless sound insulation is used around the laundry and the doors close snugly. Louvered doors cannot shut out the sound.

There are right and wrong ways to have mirrors on bifolds. The right way is to get doors which are basically mirrors with metal frames. The wrong way is to put mirrors on wooden doors because the hardware is not designed for this heavy combination and it may not last.

Bifold doors are often used for closets.

Pocket doors

Pocket doors need different considerations. The pocket must be deep enough for the door to be pushed all the way in. Nothing else can go into the wall where the pocket is— no wiring, outlets, switches, or plumbing. This sometimes means that the

Pocket doors are usually the better way to go for doors that are normally left open.

pocket door may not be possible even when it otherwise makes the most sense.

Any place where a hinged door would be in the way when left open should be considered for a pocket door. Walk-in closets are good examples as discussed earlier. The door into the toilet/bath

A hinged door should NOT be used in this situation because there's no place to swing it. A pocket door or nor door at all, as here, are better solutions.

part of a master bedroom suite is another place where a pocket door may be better. Still another is a walk-in pantry.

Although hinged doors are frequently used between dining rooms and kitchens, they shouldn't be because, when open, they take valuable wall space if swung into the dining room or they block counters if swung into the kitchen. They can also interfere with refrigerators. A pocket door, or even no door at all, is a better option.

For a custom house look at your floor plan carefully to see where pocket doors, rather than hinged doors, should be used. Replacing a hinged door with a pocket door on a floor plan may not be easy when the walls beside the hinged door mount the room light switch, an outlet, or contain water pipes (like to a shower head). It may take some rearranging to use the pocket door, such as putting the shower head at the other end of the shower, moving the light switch to the other side of the doorway, etc. If you can eliminate an inappropriately hinged door, however, it will be worth it.

And there was the building designer who got a call from the electrician wiring a house to say that there was a pocket door in the wall where the designer had an outlet. *Caveat emptor!*

Doorstops

There are two types of doorstops:

 ⇨ Screw-in which may be mounted in a baseboard, in the door, or even in an overhead beam.

 ⇨ Hinge mounted.

Screw in

Doorstops that screw into moldings won't work when they are very close to the floor because the door can slide over the top of the stops. This happens when moldings are not high enough to let the doorstops be mounted higher.

A screw-in door stop. Good—if they're not put where there'll be foot traffic.

Hinge mounted

The one place with any strength inside a hollow-core door is across the door center. Inside the door at that point is a block of wood (the rail) for mounting the door latch. When a door is mounted with three hinges, and the center one is used for a hinge-mounted doorstop, the stop hits the door over this block. When the stop is placed on the top or bottom hinge where there is no block inside the door, the stop can make a hole in the thin veneer.

A hinge-mounted door stop. Good—if they are used correctly.

When visiting in an area where interior hollow-core doors are mounted by two hinges, not three, my hosts showed me what happened within a week after they moved into their new house. A gust of wind caught the guest-closet door and the doorstop punched a hole through the thin veneer of the door. Someone should have been more careful. But who?

Not the home user. The builder screwed up. Our house has the same kind of doors and doorstops. But we'll never have this problem because our doors are all mounted with three hinges, not two, and the stops are on the center hinges where the cross piece is located. A hinge-mounted door stop should be mounted on the top hinge only after careful checking.

Often, a hinge-mounted doorstop is put on upside down. When it's installed correctly (as in the photo), the stop hits the door and the door trim

squarely but, when it is wrong, it hits at an angle and can put undue stress on the hinge.

It is good practice to use hinge-mounted door-stops only where there is no alternative because they are much more likely to cause damage to hinges.

Double doors

Designers and builders use double doors as entries into houses, master bedrooms, and dens to give a touch of luxury to a floor plan. After all, if your house is big enough to use double doors then it's obviously in the luxury class. Well, maybe.

In one unfortunate master bedroom in a custom house that was proudly on display by the designer and the owner,

⇨ one of the doors opens across another door and

⇨ the light switch for the room is behind the door that normally opens.

The location of light switches is a particular problem with double doors. When you have to take more than one step to reach a light switch after entering the room through a double door, you need a better arrangement. And, as discussed in Chapter 5, light switches should never be behind a door.

With double doors the light switch is most accessible when it's on the wall just past the end of the door normally used for going in and out. Therefore, be sure the finish carpenter knows which door will normally be used as the entry and which will normally be fixed. Or check out an existing door and see if you want it changed. Sometimes they can be.

Doors and furniture

Double doors, when opened, sometimes occupy wall space where you intended to place furniture.

Our Oregon home had double doors between the master bedroom and the vanity area. The designer's floor plan showed these doors opening into the vanity area—one door blocking the doorway into the toilet/shower room and the other door blocking light switches. The builder properly decided that the doors should swing into the bedroom—where they blocked two walls from having

Originally there were double doors in this archway. There shouldn't have been—they were very much in the way.

furniture on them. After living in the house for several months I removed both doors, leaving a totally acceptable archway and a much better furniture arrangement.

The problem with hinged doors interfering with furniture placement can also occur with single doors. Sometimes the solution may be a pocket door, as mentioned earlier, while in other cases simply hinging the door from the other side may solve the problem.

At times you may be forced to accept a compromise in door location:

⇨ For a new house take a good look at the floor plan to prevent door problems before your house is built.

⇨ For the times when you cannot change the floor plan, maybe you can have some influence on the type of door that's used or where it's hung.

⇨ In an existing house, usually it's not the most important user-unfriendly item, but it can add to your negative or positive assessment of the house. Or it may be relatively easy to fix as in the photo.

⇨ Remodeling often gives you an opportunity to fix a problem that came with the house. And do be careful to not make a bad situation even worse by not understanding the right and bad ways to use doors.

Internet Resources

The websites of national door manufacturers are not referenced in the text of this chapter. They are in the list of Internet Resources for Chapter 9. User friendliness is not a criterion for them. How they may make your house look is up to you. These sites are given for your further perusal if you want to get an idea of what the manufacturers think is important for you to know about their products.

Chapter 10

Windows

Truth is such a great thing, it is delightful to tell it.

Emily Dickenson, American lyric poet (1830-1886)

In this chapter:

It is pointed out that aesthetics are probably more important than energy in the minds of homebuyers, that windows are a resale consideration and that they are an important part of how a house looks.

Windows are increasingly important in today's efforts to save energy. The characteristics to look for are discussed along with other features that should be considered.

Energy saving is an integral part of the design and construction of today's houses. And a very important part of that energy savings has to do with the number and types of windows that are used. In this chapter we discuss the relationship between energy and windows as well as form and function.

I've tried to present the somewhat technical information in a user-friendly way. In the rest of the book, I've stayed away from anything that isn't self-evident, that isn't simple common sense. But in our energy-conserving environment, I felt it wouldn't be right to ignore the driving force that determines the window options available for today's homes.

A bit of semantics to start with. One dictionary defines "fenestration" as an architectural term dealing with the way in which windows in a building are arranged. In the building business it is a general term that covers anything dealing with glass; doors with glass in them, windows and skylights. We won't use the term here, but, if you do see it, you'll know it's a word used by specialists, although not generally by the home buying public. You'll be as up to speed as most of those who do use it.

WINDOWS AND CURB APPEAL

Windows are a major factor in how a house looks. The right windows are also important for other reasons. Here are some examples.

In the Colonial style, along with all of its related designs, windows are entirely functional—to see out of. There is no attempt to make them energy conserving other than in the type of glass that is used.

At the other side of the country there is a significant awareness of the need for energy conservation. Note how the windows are recessed into the thick walls to avoid summer heating from direct sun rays.

Windows are used for curb appeal in this Pennsylvania modular home. Sun protection is given on some of the windows but their sizes and locations are generally a compromise between form (how it looks) and function (letting light into the rooms). Any energy conservation is totally a function of the kind of glass that is used.

This Colorado "green" home faces south and its windows are all designed to absorb as much sun heat as possible. It is a complete departure from the curb appeal importance given to most homes.

In this Oregon home, glass is used as an important part of the front facade of the house. The fading problems with ultra-violet sun rays are accentuated by having a part of the window so high that they are difficult and expensive to drape. Summer cooling is also a problem with these large south-facing windows.

A contemporary California home uses windows to decorate as well as to be functional. Note the two windows closest to the street. These are in the garage—form not function! The roof overhangs on this west-facing house protects the windows from the early afternoon sun.

Another term that may be new to you— and this *is* one you're likely to run across. "Single-" or "double-glazed" windows. These are what most of us call single- or double-paned windows. That's what we'll call them here.

Windows and Aesthetics

You know the real estate agent's expression "curb appeal." It's the impression prospective buyers have when they are taken to look at a house that's for sale. Windows make up a big part of that impression. They should fit in with the overall style of the house and they should make the house look inviting—a place that gives you a feeling of being lived in. And, it's different strokes for different folks—some like the large and multitudinous windows found in many of today's designs while others are happier with the conservative approach with more modest sizes and numbers of windows. The two previous pages have photos of a number of distinctly different house styles.

Inside the house, windows, probably more than any other feature, control the ambiance of a room. Correct windows are vital parts of how you will enjoy living in the house and, later on, of the resale value of the house.

Double-pane windows are made with and without a decorative grid between the panes. This grid makes the windows appear to be made of a number of pieces of glass when, in fact, they are not. More and more of these windows use vinyl-clad frames for its better insulation. The vinyl is usually white but colors are available. (Anything other than white can limit your choice of house colors.)

Enough of aesthetics and ambiance. These are correctly left to architects and designers and are not the thrust of this book. But there is, as always, some give and take between form and function, between how windows look in a house and their costs in terms of energy and dollars.

Windows and Safety

Small windows high on bedroom walls were common in houses many years ago but are not found today. Stories of people being trapped in their bedrooms in a fire, because the windows were too small or too high, caused codes to be changed. And, even if not forbidden by building codes, common sense would dictate a safer design.

Today, bedroom windows must be large enough and low enough to get out of in an emergency. And there must be such a window in every bedroom in the house. (Codes spell all of this out in inches and millimeters.)

You might think that building codes would change little from year to year. Not so— particularly in the energy area where continuing improvements in materials make greater energy savings possible. One of those areas is windows. And well it should be because glass represents the biggest single source of heat loss in most homes built today.

And, if you live in hurricane or tornado country, there is another consideration — how well the windows withstand the high winds and the debris that the winds may be carrying. This has led to the development of windows which are not all glass but have a layer of tough plastic in them which can withstand the beating that windows take during such a storm[10A].

Window Construction

Windows are made of glass which is made of silica, the same thing that sand is made of—right? Well, yes. But there's a lot more to today's windows than that. The use of single-pane windows has disappeared from new homes, at least those made in conformance with today's energy codes. (And, if you run across a new home with single-

Chapter 10. Windows   139

pane windows, run the other way. That builder is both ignorant and without care. He doesn't build the kind of house you'd want to live in.)

Double-pane windows have these five things going for them:

- ⇨ They make a house more comfortable.
- ⇨ They don't weep or sweat (at least they shouldn't).
- ⇨ They save energy in heating and cooling.
- ⇨ Saving energy saves money.
- ⇨ They make the house more saleable.

The downside is that they are more expensive initially. Note the word "initially." They can pay for themselves in a relatively short time from the energy they save.

In the remodeling area, changing the windows will also often pay for itself relatively quickly.

There are three mechanisms by which heat goes through a window:

- ⇨ Radiation. This is heat you can "feel," like the sun's rays or when you hold your hands in front of a burning fireplace. This heat (infrared) goes through the window like visible light does.
- ⇨ Conduction. This is the heat a solid material carries from one place to another, like from one side of a window pane to the other.
- ⇨ Convection. This the heat that is carried by air (or any gas) from one place to another. Heat is carried by convection (air or gas movement) between the panes of glass in a double-pane window.

Modern window technology tackles all three of these to keep energy costs down.

The panes may be *low-e* (low-emissivity) glass. This involves a special manufacturing process that reduces the ability of the glass to pass certain heat rays (as well as ultraviolet that we'll discuss later) while still letting us see through the window. The idea of low-e glass is to let the direct sun's rays through for heating help in winter while stopping other heat rays so that the warmth generated in the house can't get out. In summer you have to depend on trees, drapes, shades, and roof overhangs to keep out the direct rays from the sun.

Conduction through the glass itself is a fact of life, but the materials around the edges of the window also conduct heat. This source of heat loss is tackled by using materials to mount the glass that are not good conductors—vinyl, for example. Wood and aluminum are also used. (Note how aesthetics get into the act here, too.)

The transfer of heat by convection between the panes of glass is inhibited by filling the space with a gas that doesn't do a good job at convection. Argon is the most commonly used but you may find other more exotic gasses. (A vacuum would stop convection entirely but it's not a practical solution.)

Putting argon between the panes of glass poses another problem—how to keep it there. In truth you can't, at least not with cost-effective manufacturing techniques. In time it will leak out, being replaced with plain old air. When this happens the window will become a poorer insulator. And, if the air has moisture in it, you may find condensation between the panes of glass.

At that point you'll have three choices:

- ⇨ If the window is covered by a lifetime warranty, get the manufacturer to replace it,
- ⇨ Replace it at your own expense, or
- ⇨ Live with it.

Windows and Energy Codes

Windows are rated by a standardized process resulting in a "U" rating. This is a number that is always a decimal fraction smaller than 1. The smaller the number the better the window in terms of energy conservation. Good windows will have a U-rating of less than 0.5. Better ones get down to 0.4 with manufacturers striving to get to 0.3. But note: a U-rating of 0.3 (very expensive) is not even twice as good as a rating of 0.5 (low cost). To spend a lot of money for a specially low-rated window is probably not effective in terms of either comfort (you'll never notice the difference) or energy savings (it may take a lifetime to recoup the additional cost).

You may not have the choice, however, depending on where you live. In states where the idea of energy savings has a bureaucratic stronghold, there is continual pressure to reduce energy usage—even when it is not cost-effective. If you live in one of these areas (as I do) you may find low-e, low U-rated windows are required to meet energy code requirements. Because in most houses, windows account for more heat transfer between inside and outside than walls, floors, ceilings, or doors, some codes restrict the amount of glass, including skylights, you can put in your house. If you have these kinds of restrictions, some floor plans cannot be used.

On the other hand, these same codes may take into account that winter sun can be used to help heat the house and give "credit" for south-facing windows to reduce the amount of insulation you must have.

But don't be dismayed even if they cost more, because these double-paned windows make a house a whole lot more comfortable than the ones many of us were brought up in.

Windows and Fading

In southern California our house had a large west facing living room with the window glass in two tiers. We put drapes on the lower tier but, because of the irregular shape, had difficulty getting coverings for the upper ones. We did add a plastic coating which was supposed to cut down both the sun's heat rays and the ultraviolet—the part that does the fading. We thought it did a good job until we moved and found the original color of the carpet every place where furniture had covered the floor. The part of the carpet where the sun could get to it was several shades lighter.

Today's low-e glass may be better than the plastic sheet but probably not much. It cuts out only a little over half of the ultraviolet. So, by all means, plan on trees, drapes, blinds, or whatever you can scrape up to keep the sun from beating into your house—unless, of course, you don't mind multi-shaded furniture and carpet. And feel good about it—you're not only saving your furniture and carpet, you're lowering the cooling bill too.

Windows and Decorating

When windows are selected for their appearance, whether from the inside or the outside of

Because they are hard to decorate, windows high on a wall can be serious sun problems

the house, don't forget energy loss and fading—to say nothing about privacy.

Large windows will lose more energy than smaller ones with a resulting increase in heating and/or cooling bills. The more of the window you can cover with drapes when the outside temperature is too hot or too cold, the more comfortable the house and the lower your energy bills will be.

It can be expensive to get coverings for the upper parts of the two-story high windows found in many modern home designs. And, of course, ultraviolet rays don't care if they come in through a round, trapezoidal, or triangular window above a more conventional lower one—they'll still cause fading.

Window Ratings

With the introduction of low-emissivity glass in 1979, another great improvement in homes and in the saving of energy was under way[10B]. Since then we have had more thermally designed window frames and, of course, double-glazing.

You may well see a rating sticker on windows or in advertisements. The National Fenestration Rating Coalition (NFRC)[10C] is an organization supported by window manufacturers that uses standardized procedures to rate windows in their abilities to insulate homes.

Note that the effort is focussed specifically on insulating the inside air from that outside. Other factors of importance to the homeowner, such as stopping ultraviolet light, are not emphasized.

The two energy performance factors which are rated:

⇨ U-factor, discussed earlier. 0.5 means an R-rating of 2.0, which isn't so good, but ratings much better than this start raising the price.

⇨ Solar Heat Gain Coefficient (SHGC) which is a measure of the infrared that goes through the window, i.e., of how much of the sun's heat rays get passed. It is of particular interest when air conditioning is a factor. Ideally, this number would be 0. In practice, the lower the number the better, with 1.0 meaning that all of the sun's heat rays get through.

In addition to these factors the NFRC also rates windows for:

⇨ Transmittance (VT) which measures how much visible light comes through the window. This is important because it would otherwise be possible to darken a window significantly and get good U- and SGHC-ratings and at the same time not being able to see through the window. 100% transmittance indicates all of the visible light gets through. 0 would indicate a totally opaque one. Obviously, the higher the better as long as U- and SGHC-ratings are also good.

⇨ Air Leakage (AL) measures how much air infiltrates through and around the window. Since heat (or cooling) can be lost through such air, it is an important practical factor even though it is not measured by the U- and the SHGC-ratings. (Note that manufacturers are not required to report on this rating. It is obviously a caution flag if they don't.) The lower the AL, the less air passes through cracks in the window assembly.

⇨ Condensation Resistance (CR) measures the ability of a product to resist the formation of condensation on the interior surface. The higher the CR rating (maximum 100), the better that product is at resisting condensation formation. (Like AL, manufacturers are not required to report on this rating.)

And, finally, another factor which is being studied by the NFRC, and which is of particular interest to the homeowner is ultraviolet-light protection. This, as noted above, is what fades your carpeting and upholstery. When it is available, this rating will be of significant interest.

Skylights

Most of today's house designs include skylights. They are used where windows would be inconvenient (as in small bathrooms), where windows aren't possible (as in an interior room that has no outside wall), or where they let in light while still maintaining privacy. There are penalties to pay when skylights are used. As windows, they are poor insulators. In general, it's not possible to shade them from the hot afternoon sun.

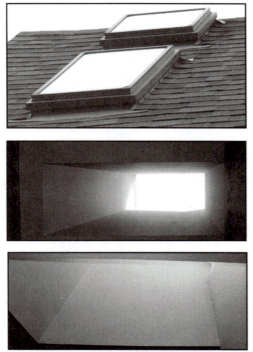

Skylights offer a way to get outside light into windowless rooms.

When this is a problem, skylights will need to be made from tinted or low-e glass and/or they'll need some kind of interior blinds.

Where skylights are used in rooms like bathrooms that do not have vaulted ceilings, there is a shaft or "well" that brings the light down from the roof-mounted skylight. This well is often bigger at the bottom than the top thus spreading the light over a larger area in the room. These shafts are also heat traps when the summer sun shines on the skylight. And it significantly heats up the rooms where such a skylight is installed.

Skylights range from one to four feet on a side. Think carefully before using the smaller sizes. Many people don't like their penny-scrimping appearance.

When choosing skylights for a well that can trap a lot of heat, get types that can be opened to let accumulated hot air escape during hot weather. Either that or get blinds that can be closed when summer comes along.

Tubular Skylights (a.k.a. Light Funnels)

Another technique for homes are metal tubes that funnel light from the roof down into a room. A small glass or plastic dome is mounted on the roof with appropriately shaped reflectors to capture the sunlight. At the bottom end a diffuser spreads the light around in the room. They are designed to mount between existing structural members making them attractive for additions to existing houses where the original plans could have had a skylight but did not.

The light that is delivered into the room is *not* the same as you get from a regular skylight but rather has a distinctly cold metallic cast—which is not surprising since it depends on the reflection off of the aluminum that makes up the unit. For new construction the tubes are less expensive than skylights with their wells. But, because of the cold, unconventional color of the light, they detract from the saleability of the house for many buyers. They are probably best left to remodeling when there is a crying need for more light in a room.

Window Woodwrap

In some parts of the country, window openings are usually encased ("wrapped") in wood while in others builders offer it as an option. In Arizona, California and other areas with southwestern architecture, the usual approach is to provide just a wooden sill or even no sill at all; the opening is simply handled as a continuation of the wallboard. These regional differences can be explained by the weather differences in combination with older single-pane windows. In climates with damper, colder winters old windows wept or sweat and wallboard or plaster was unsuitable around them..

Where today's codes require double-pane windows that don't sweat (or at least not much), the functional need for woodwrap has been eliminated everywhere. Aesthetically, woodwrap has a richer, more finished appearance than does wallboard around a window and this has helped to

Windows may completely wrapped like this one (left), they may have only a wooden sill (right) or be completely finished only with plaster (no wood at all).

keep its popularity in areas with more traditional architecture. When it is used it is usually finished to match the other woodwork.

Woodwrap is an expensive proposition. For example, a tract builder in Tacoma, Washington offered this amenity as an option for the whole house with a $2000 price tag on it! You might give some thought to whether you really need it, particularly if you plan to paint the wood white against a white wall and then cover it with a valance and drapes so that only the sill shows. (With double-pane windows, this whole discussion is about aesthetics.)

Energy Savings Programs

Windows are a key element in any energy savings program, both in terms of the heat which passes through them and in terms of how well they are sealed to prevent heat loss through their mountings. These programs tell you how to have your house built or how to remedy an existing house to make them more energy savings.

Energy Star[10E]

The Environmental Protection Agency's program: "ENERGY STAR is a government-backed program helping businesses and individuals protect the environment through superior energy efficiency." Their claim is that "Just one ENERGY STAR qualified new home can keep 4,500 pounds of greenhouse gases out of our air each year."

For more information, you should see the Energy Star website[10E].

Freedom Seal[10G]

From their website:

"The FREEDOM Project Alliance is a group of industry leaders with a common vision:

To build 2,000,000 new homes nationwide

by 2012 that are:

* Energy Efficient
* Healthier
* Stronger/Safer
* Environmentally Friendly
* Technologically Savvy and
* Cost Less to Own"

It is suggested that you visit their website to find out more.

One of the more intriguing claims is that you can get a lower interest rate on a home built to meet the Freedom Seal requirements.

The argument for the Freedom Seal approach is that, because the houses are better houses, they are worth more money than they would otherwise be. Therefore the affiliated lender(s) will lend money on them at a lower rate. Or, alternatively, for the same monthly payment, you can get a bigger loan and, hence, a bigger house.

There is nothing to indicate that you can't shop for your loan and do as good or better than you would get from a Freedom Seal lender. It might be safe to assume that they are "upfront" mortgage lenders, i.e., that they don't tell you something when you're inquiring about rates and then when closing time comes you find that there are a bunch more charges that weren't discussed before. Or they may not be so upfront, the Freedom Seal site doesn't get into this at all.

So, even if you might otherwise be interested, be careful. The companies which make up the organization are all for-profits—with which there is nothing wrong. But *caveat emptor* is still a good process for a buyer to follow. And if you're buying an existing house, spec or production, that has this seal, maintain your care. It is a promotional scheme which looks good on the surface. Whether it is good for you is your decision.

Commentary

These programs achieve the greater energy savings by having good wall insulation, using more efficient windows and then sealing the house to prevent the loss of conditioned air to the outside. They have means of checking how well the house is sealed by putting it under pressure and seeing how much air is lost. This sounds good on the surface but there are concerns - some of which they address. When a house is sealed too tightly, moisture and odors can accumulate, something that is not wanted. To alleviate this problem various techniques are used, including the dependence on kitchen and bathroom exhaust fans and their vents to let the unwanted products out. There are three problems here:

⇨ Bathroom vents, particularly, are, more often than not, completely useless as discussed in Chapter 20.

⇨ If the house is, indeed, tightly sealed, an air-to-air heat exchanger is needed to move inside air out and outside air in to keep the inside air healthy. But the inside air is conditioned air (heated or cooled) so that this process uses energy not only to move the air but to remove the heat from the outgoing air and to put this heat into the incoming air. Just what this does to the overall efficiency is not clear. And, of course, the amount of humidity must be controlled for comfort and health reasons. It is a complex process that must continue year around.

⇨ To upgrade an existing house can be expensive:

• All joints involving floors, walls, ceiling and, particularly, windows, must be sealed.

• If you have an older fireplace, it will have to be replaced with a direct vent one and the whole installation must be sealed.

- All exhaust fans must be checked and probably replaced to keep unwanted air movement through them, in or out, when they're not in use.

The drive toward more energy efficient houses is commendable. As time goes on it will be interesting to see how well the concept works out.

Chapter 11

Security Considerations

> *No outward doors of a man's house can in general be broken open to execute any civil process; though in criminal cases the public safety supersedes the private.*
>
> Sir William Blackstone, English jurist (1723-1780)

In this chapter:
Several different aspects of making your home more secure are discussed here. It is useful to note that many of them do not involve a security system at all—just common sense things that make it more difficult for someone to break and enter.

While we may bemoan the circumstances and societal failures that are responsible, residential burglary is a fact of life. This chapter discusses some of the things you can do to cut down on the susceptibility of your home to break-ins. The most obvious is an expensive alarm system that includes sensors that trigger whenever there's an unauthorized entry. But there are other small, inexpensive things you or the builder can and should do that will help. These are appropriate even with an alarm system.

Securing Doors

Deadbolts are put into new houses routinely. They operate by moving a heavy piece of metal (the bolt) from the door through a hole in a metal striker plate fastened to the inside of the door frame. If this plate is not well secured, a hard shove on the door will break the plate loose and the whole door swings wide open. Unless instructed to do otherwise, the carpenter who installs the striker plates will often use short screws that extend only into the door frame. He should use much longer screws (2-1/2 inch minimum) to get all the way into the wall studs behind the frame.

Door hinges should also be mounted with screws that reach into the studs behind the door frame. This isn't usually done. Both the striker plate and the hinge screws will be stronger if the gaps between the frame and the studs are snugly shimmed. To beef up the door installation even more, horizontal blocking should be used between the studs on either side of the door. These recommendations are courtesy of the Portland, Oregon, Police Department.

With external doors, the screws that hold striker plates and those that hold hinges should be longer than those that are normally used in order to reach through the door trim and into the studs behind.

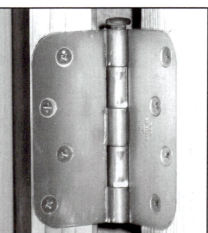

You should insist on having doors put in right. It doesn't cost much at the time of installation but it virtually eliminates one method of easy access for burglars.

You can and should put in the longer screws if they are not put in the house initially but, once the wallboard is in place, you cannot do the shimming or blocking that makes them stronger. It's better if the installation is done properly.

Glass In and Around the Entry Door

The utilitarian purpose of door sidelights is to provide illumination in the entry hall or foyer during the daylight hours. Decorators, suppliers, and builders have seized on this need to make them a decorative and attractive part of the entry way. Unfortunately they ignore how easy they have made it for people to break into our houses.

Beware of glass either in the door itself or in the sidelights beside the door. These features make it possible for the burglar to break the glass and reach in and open the door from the inside. You

Sidelights are attractive but...

Sidelights also make it easy to break in. (This happened when the owners were on vacation.)

could stop this by using deadbolts that require a key to open from the inside. However, this is dangerous if there's a fire and someone is inside the building. (And it's not permitted by building codes.) The safest approach is to not put glass where it'll let someone get in the house easily. And, for the sidelights, this can usually be accomplished without significantly degrading the appearance of the entry.

This problem doesn't exist for double doors because the deadbolt can't be reached from any sidelight location. For single entry doors, one of two things can be done—and this should happen at the house design stage. For a single sidelight, either put it on the hinge side of the door or space it far enough away that the deadbolt cannot be reached from the sidelight. For two sidelights, space both of them, or at least the one on the deadbolt side of the door, away from the deadbolt. Note that this approach does something else, too; it leaves a place close to the door for the entry light switches—they don't have to be several feet away on the other side of the sidelights as you'll see in many of today's houses and as was discussed in

Chapter 5. The Rule 3 discussion there shows a photograph of a good way to do it.

Alternatively use glass that cannot be broken enough to let a hand in. Glass with wire embedded is one way. Or use glass bricks. While this makes it so you can't see who's at the door (and vice versa), it does let light into the entry way.

And don't forget the door itself. Many doors include decorative glass inserts; some decorators feel that the more ostentatious the house the fancier the front door needs to be. When these inserts are within easy reach of the deadbolt, the situation is akin to that of close-in sidelights: the door can easily be opened once the glass is broken. When the glass is higher up on the door it's no longer a means of easy entry.

Some pictures of what you don't want to have are in Chapter 9 in the section on Exterior Doors.

Garage Sidedoor

When there is a sidedoor in the garage, the door hinges and the deadbolt striker plate should be mounted with long screws as discussed earlier.

Garage sidedoors with windows are security concerns for two reasons:

⇨ They let people look into the garage from outside and

⇨ They can be broken to get at the locks on the inside of the door.

Since the sidedoor is almost never on the street side of the house, it is a more attractive target than the sidelights on the entry door, for example. For these reasons, it is strongly suggested that the sidedoor not have glass. If you feel you really need the light such a window lets in, then use a heavy metal mesh to prevent someone from reaching their hand through the door after the glass is broken. Or get an alarm system.

The same considerations apply to any windows in the garage that are large enough for someone to crawl through.

Garage Door Openers

When you are going to be gone for an extended period, it is a good idea to make your garage doors inoperative. Four ways for doing this:

⇨ Have a separate wall switch in the garage that turns the power on and off to the openers. This is the most convenient way to control the doors. It needs to be done when the house is wired.

⇨ Have the electrician put the door openers on their own circuit in the circuit-breaker box. Then turn off the breaker to disable the doors. (This assumes the circuit-breaker box is not accessible from outside the house.)

⇨ Get a cord with a switch in it and put this between the outlet and the power to the openers. Let the cord hang down so the switch is convenient.

⇨ Unplug the power to the openers when you are gone. This is the least convenient, particularly when it requires a ladder to reach the plugs.

These two switches by the door into the house from the garage are both used for security options. The "LIGHT" turns the security lights on and off, the "DOOR" switch is used to control the power to the garage door opener.

Security Lights

When the house is being built, it's relatively easy to have wiring installed for security lights around your home. Where there are no street lights, it's convenient for guests at night to have a light that's turned on with an infrared sensor in front of the house. It's also a way of dissuading unwanted visitors.

You can have such lights installed by the builder or simply have the wiring put in place so you can mount the lights and sensors at your convenience. A switch is needed someplace, usually in the garage, that can disconnect these lights. As an alternative, have them on their own electrical circuit so that they can be turned off from the circuit-breaker box.

Depending on the layout, it may be possible to add these lights to an existing house. It's usually a good idea if you can.

Between the House and the Garage

In some areas (the Puget Sound is one), it is common to not include a deadbolt or any other kind of lock on the door between the garage and the house. While it is true that once someone gets into your garage it is easier to break into the house, a lock on this door will make it more difficult and will make the house more secure. If you find a house that doesn't have a lock on this door, then it's suggested that one be installed, preferably a deadbolt.

This is one of several things in this chapter that you can do or have done at any time.

Alarm Systems

The photos show a door sensor and a motion detector from a modern wireless alarm system. (Wireless in that there are no wires between the sensors and the control panel.) An appropriately designed, installed and used alarm system automatically detects any undesired entries or persons moving around in the house. They are tied to the telephone lines and can alert law enforcement to the situation.

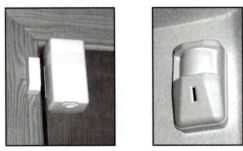

Wireless door sensor (left) and motion detector (right) of a modern internal home alarm system (control panel below).

These may be wired systems but the ease with which a wireless system can be installed without worrying about wires makes it a good choice even for a new home.

But, improperly used, they will set off false alarms which, in quantity, would overload law enforcement. For this reason, in many jurisdictions, you are allowed only one or two false alarms per year and you get whacked a pretty sizeable charge for each one after that. Used with a reasonable amount of care, this won't happen and the system can offer a peace of mind you can't get any other way.

Many systems have one or more smoke detectors tied to them which will call the fire department if you're not home when smoke is present. Comforting, yes, but the same concerns about false alarms occur here.

And there are "panic" buttons which can be actuated manually to get emergency help. It's easier than dialing 911 and may be the only option available at a given moment such as a medical emergency.

Remote controls usually go with these systems so you can turn them on and off when you're not next to the control panel. Very convenient for the bedridden or when you're coming or going in your car.

Three companies who have websites that explain their systems are found at references [11A, 11B & 11C].

Surveillance Systems

These systems use cameras to watch chosen locations on your property. Generally these are wired systems and should be planned for ahead, probably when the house is built, but they can be added later at a greater cost. They are particularly convenient if you want to see who's at the door or want to be able to keep track of the baby in its crib without frequent trips to the bedroom. They are often part of the overall wiring system for the house discussed in Chapter 5. Or they may be wireless which means they can be added anytime.

Fire Safety

Smoke detectors are a code requirement for safety reasons. These are usually installed in the bedroom wing of the house because of the concern of fires trapping people in their beds. Don't hesitate to install extra detectors in rooms with tall vaulted ceilings. The tendency of heat to rise can make these detectors more effective in some cases than those in bedroom halls.

Some jurisdictions have a code requirement for automatic fire sprinklers in two-story houses. Others have special requirements for houses abutting open areas where grass or other wild fires can be a hazard.

Chapter 10 noted that there are code requirements on bedroom windows to make it possible to escape in case of fire.

Chapter 12

Other Whole-House Items

> *Both tears and sweat are salty, but they render a different result. Tears will get you sympathy; sweat will get you change.*
>
> Jesse Jackson, minister and politician (1941...)

In this chapter:

A number of critical decisions in making a house involve the choices of materials. Some general considerations start this chapter. These are followed by discussions of interior items including finishes, wallboard, baseboard moldings, floors, ceilings, and sound insulation.

Knowing about these is helpful both in the design and construction of a home and in choosing an existing one.

Materials

Suppliers of materials for new homes are in a highly competitive environment and are always using new ideas and technology to come up with something that is different, attractive, saleable, and profitable.

As the consumer, it's hard for you to know when it's appropriate to opt for the latest thing and when it's prudent to stick to the traditional. Home building is a very conservative business and change comes slowly because no one wants to or can afford to be the guinea pig. Yet, at the same time, better products are continually coming into the market—products that could make a home a better, less expensive place to live.

In the area of energy savings, some of the decisions have been taken out of the builders' hands by changes in building codes. Walls must be well insulated and high-tech windows used to save energy. And, if there are earthquakes or hurricanes where the house is located, there are other sets of criteria that must be met. But oftentimes decisions must be made when what is really needed is the proverbial crystal ball.

If the new product is supposed to save money, balance this against the long-term cost if it proves to have a limited life. Some examples that come to mind:

⇨ A composite house siding made by Louisiana Pacific (LP) was supposed to be the answer to the dwindling supply and increasing costs of traditional siding materials. Yet in a few years of actual usage, the siding turned out to not last. The result was a significant loss to Louisiana Pacific and to we home owners who happened to have had it on our homes. They settled a class-action suit to reimburse people who had to have it replaced.

⇨ Some twenty years ago a cultured marble countertop with integral basins was a way to get a low-cost, handsome bathroom vanity. But after a few years the surface of the basins developed tiny cracks caused by the repetitive temperature changes of hot and cold water. In this case there was no Louisiana Pacific to fall back on and the home owners bore the cost of replacing the counters and sinks. (There is now better quality control on these items which the indus-

try says has solved the problem, but *see* Chapter 19 for other solutions.)

⇨ Polybutylene water pipe for inside homes offers a number of advantages as discussed in Chapter 6. But it wasn't always so. The connectors used when PB was first introduced didn't hold up with time to the dismay of the manufacturer and home owners. Again, it took time to find the problem and fix it.

Steel framing to replace the traditional wood construction has some obvious advantages in terms of stability—no warping, shrinking, termites, rotting, or fire. It's installed price is about the same. What most of us don't know are the potential disadvantages nor are we likely to find out from the suppliers and builders of traditional materials. Are today's tighter houses, for example, likely to keep the moisture content high in the walls resulting in life-shortening rust? Of course, a part of this involves how the exterior of the house is applied. If there's no place for moisture to build up, there's no problem, but more than one house has had serious problems when a material has not been used correctly.

Tighter homes, ones with lesser amounts of external air penetration, can cause dry rot in framing timbers or rusting of steel framing if care isn't taken. They can also result in severe health prob-

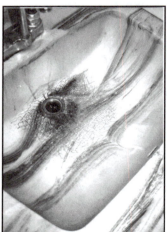

Cultured marble has improved significantly since this basin was installed.

A steel-framed house. The only wood here is around doors and windows and on the roof.

lems. These problems have been accentuated by the use of non-breathing exterior materials such as synthetic stucco (EIFS)[12B]. Some say that EIFS is OK when it's installed properly but the standards seem to be hard to nail down (*see* the discussion in Chapter 23). In your house you be the judge, but there are many exterior materials that don't have this problem. Dry rot takes several years to manifest itself by which time the responsible parties are likely to have disappeared - or are protected by mandatory arbitration clauses which put the homeowner in a no-win situation.

Low-emissivity glass for windows is now an energy code requirement in many areas (*see* Chapter 10). But at what point are further improvements no longer cost effective? And to whom do we turn to find out?

So, unless your crystal ball is working well, you'll find yourself in the position of making decisions about products that you know little about and what you can find out may be only part of the facts. Here are a couple of ideas:

⇨ Try to find actual experiences people have had in their homes. If it's a new product, find a reputable supplier who has competing products and *try* to get an honest appraisal of the situation. (The quartz resin composite sink mentioned in Chapter 13 is such a product. It appears to be an excellent option, but is slow getting general acceptance.)

⇨ If the new product is supposed to save money, get some quotes for the new one versus an old one and see if there is actually that much difference in the installed cost. To say a product is half the cost but to not include the additional shop or installation costs associated with it isn't the whole story. A competitive bid will give a much better price comparison. Then you can make a better

assessment of initial cost saving versus any long-term risk.

Finishes

Lighter colors do give a more open feeling to a room and a house, in fact one of the things that a seller should do according to an article in the Washington Post is paint everything light to make the house more saleable. But there is a richness to dark woods that is also attractive. In the never-ending chase to have the "latest" thing, the swing from dark to light and back is a cycle that goes on and on. It's a matter of aesthetics and it's all up to you.

Local tradition and custom are strong factors that apply to decorative wood in the house: baseboard moldings, crown moldings, wainscot, doors, and windows.

White or near white paint does make a room feel brighter and more open. This trend to white also extends to countertops. It's the safe thing for builders to use because almost nobody objects—we've become accustomed to seeing white everywhere in homes. But too much white may remind you of a doctor's office, a hospital, or a service station washroom. A popular compromise is to stain the woodwork a light shade and paint the walls white.

The decision whether to paint or to stain and lacquer is very much one of personal preference keeping in mind that a light color is supposed to make a room look bigger—something to remember for resale time.

Walls

Gypsum wallboard is the most commonly used interior wall material. The sheets are nailed, glued, and/or screwed to wall studs and ceiling joists. There are gaps where edges of the board meet and there are other irregularities at corners. These are all covered by a thin paper tape and a plaster-like "mud" and then made as smooth as the craftsman deems necessary.

Outside wallboard corners may be square or rounded. Generally rounded corners will be a little more costly, but are preferred by many people because of the softer feel they give to a house. But there are other aspects, too:

⇨ With time, the square corners in traffic areas can be expected to have the paint knocked off and will need touch up.

⇨ It is difficult to make a straight neat-appearing rounded corner if the walls that meet are different colors.

Square wallboard corners are much more likely to need a coat of paint earlier than rounded ones. Rounded corners, however, are more expensive initially. They need more attention from both the wallboard installer and the finish carpenter. It's not a matter of cut and nail.

Finishing the wallboard

In some areas wallboard is simply smoothed and painted and in others it is finished by texturing. This is the process of putting mud on the wall in an uneven pattern. A common finish is called orange peel because of the look of the texture. Ceilings generally have a deeper pattern. A builder can show you different wallboard textures or you can shop for the ones you like best.

Building codes may require that walls be sealed to make them vapor proof. There are several ways to do this but one is to use a special paint. If you choose this technique, you'll need to choose your wall colors from the paints that have this property.

Make sure that the board used on ceilings is designed for ceilings; wallboard should not be used. Ceiling board is stiffer and won't sag between joists.

Wallpaper

If you plan on having a wall papered, two things are important:

⇨ Don't let the wallboard people texture the wall. Be sure that someone marks the wall in big red letters to keep this from happening.

⇨ The corner where the wall meets the ceiling should be straight and even. If the corner is uneven, it is virtually impossible for the wallpaper installer to make the paper look straight across the top of the wall. You may see some examples of this while you're house looking.

Baseboard Molding
Wooden baseboards

There's no reason you shouldn't have a decorative molding of reasonable size or to not have any at all.

⇨ In some areas the baseboard moldings in tract houses are just plain 1/2 X 3 inch boards, sometimes with a 45-degree. bevel along the top edge and sometimes not. They are painted, not stained. They look cheap and detract significantly from the appearance of the house.

⇨ In other tracts, builders put in baseboard moldings that are too small, some no bigger than 3/8 X 1-1/2 inches. More than one model was seen where the door slid over the top of a doorstop because there was no place to mount the doorstop high enough to catch the door.

No baseboard at all

Builders, when they build houses for someone else, are constrained by their agreement with the buyer or, if it's a spec house, by their estimate of what will sell best. When they build a house for themselves, they are freer to do what they like best. One thing is to eliminate baseboard molding in the carpeted areas of the house. This requires that the wallboard be finished all the way to the floor. It also requires the use of hinge-mounted doorstops because there's no molding into which to screw the normal doorstop. And this, in turn, also means that hollow-core doors must be mounted with three hinges, as is explained in Chapter 9.

The carpet covers the area where the wallboard meets the floor, creating a clean, crisp appearance. It's certainly a better looking finish than those seen in most tract houses which look as if the builders picked up old boards from the scrap heap to use for baseboard moldings. Eliminating baseboard molding also eliminates the problem of getting a good finish on it.

Rubber mop boards

In some tracts builders have reverted to an earlier practice of putting rubber mop boards in kitchens, bathrooms, and laundries. Many years ago when a mop consisted of many sloppy twisted pieces of rope-like cotton, rubber mop boards were necessary to protect the bases of cupboards from excess mop water. This gave rise to the use of the 3- to 4-inch rubber mop boards. Today's mops don't do this and wooden baseboards with a rea-

sonable finish are fine. However, if you feel more comfortable with the utilitarian rubber mop boards, they are still out there.

Rounded wallboard corners

Rounded wallboard corners pose a problem for the finish carpenter. The molding should follow the walls smoothly around the corner, but this obviously won't happen. The usual solution is to cut a small piece of molding with 45-degree mitered ends and glue it in place across the corners. Gaps will still be noticeable in unpainted molding but if the molding is to be painted, the gaps can be caulked, resulting in a finished appearance.

Small pieces of wood carved to match the baseboard and curved to go around rounded wallboard corners are available, at least for some types of molding. If matched to the molding reasonably well, they may be more attractive than a straight piece at 45 degrees—it's personal preferences again.

With rounded corners and painted moldings, there is still another option; the moldings are simply mitered and cut so that they meet squarely at the corner. This leaves a space between the molding and the rounded wallboard corner. This is filled and painted over. The advantage is the lower cost for the finish carpenter work. The approach is useful only with painted molding although some low-end builders will do the same thing with wood finish moldings by filling the gap and painting it to try to match the wallboard.

Vinyl moldings are available in wood finishes and are used in some low-end houses. If you are trying to save every penny, you may want to take a look at them.

Gaps

For new construction, if you can, check the workmanship after framing and again after wallboard installation to see that walls are truly straight at the bottom where the molding goes. Where they are not, you'll have small but noticeable gaps between the molding and the wallboard. If there are problems, the builder should have them fixed before the finish carpenter starts work on the baseboards.

When care isn't taken in the framing, it can leave gaps like this between the wallboard and the molding. It's a sign of poor quality control by the builder.

If the molding is stained and lacquered, gaps along the baseboard will be clearly visible. They can be fixed but it may involve the wallboard mudder, the finish carpenter, and the painter. And, if the builder has to pay for it, he'll no doubt argue with you about whether it's necessary.

When the baseboard molding is painted, there is a much better chance of getting a finish job that doesn't draw attention to itself. The finish carpenter or painter can caulk the gaps and paint over them. The imperfections will still be there but will be covered up.

Functionally the whole thing may not seem worth getting into an argument about. But it's an aesthetic thing that will be there forever. And it's another of the myriad of little things that can ultimately impact on a buyer when you're ready to move on---and you would have to live with it until that happens.

Floors

The common materials used for floors are:

⇨ Carpet,

⇨ Vinyl (linoleum),

⇨ Wood,

⇨ Ceramic tile,

⇨ Stone, and

⇨ Laminates (often known as Pergo, one of the suppliers).

With any of these it usually doesn't pay to buy the cheapest thing around because it won't last.

We consider each of these, good and not-so-good points and their applications. On the Armstrong[12F] website you'll find a fairly detailed comparisons among vinyl sheets, vinyl tiles, ceramic tiles, laminates, linoleum and hardwood floors. The ifloor website[12L] describes laminate, hardwood, bamboo and cork floors with their pros and cons.

Carpet

Carpet is laid on a pad which, in turn, is laid on a subfloor. Where two pieces of carpet come together there is a seam. While ideally the seam wouldn't show, in practice it almost always does—but it shouldn't be an eyesore.

There are many, many kinds of materials used for carpeting, some softer and more luxurious and others very utilitarian. Some are made to take a lot of foot traffic, others won't. And there are many colors and patterns. What you have in your house will be a matter of taste and cost. Time spent in a carpet store talking to the clerk to get an idea of price vs. wearability vs. appearance is time well spent.

Carpet is used in every room in the house except the kitchen and, while it's done, the appropriateness in bathrooms is questionable.

Cleaning spills or stains from carpet is not always a simple matter of wiping it up because, depending on the material, carpets usually absorb whatever gets on them. The commonly used materials are:

⇨ Nylon

⇨ Polyester

⇨ Polypropylene (Olefin)

⇨ Wool

⇨ Blends, usually of wool and one of the synthetics.

More information on these can be found at the Mohawk carpet website[12D.] The Carpet and Rug Institute website[12E] includes discussions about where to use different carpet materials and on cleaning them.

And there is always the question of the materials used in the padding and the carpet itself because they may off-gas(give off gas) after installation and can cause health problems. This, of course, becomes more and more important as our houses are made tighter. Some people have found it necessary to move back out of a new house and move air through the house for days or even weeks until the level of toxins has abated.

Vinyl

While true "linoleum" is available, most of today's flooring of this type is made of vinyl. It comes in many grades, in sheets and in tiles. The better grades are virtually indestructible, resisting scratching, dents and water spills.

A very user-friendly characteristic of floors covered with vinyl is that it gives a little when standing or walking on it so that the home user won't suffer the same stress on feet and legs as happens with the harder materials. Similarly, dropping a cup or glass on this surface is much less likely to

break than with most of the other floor coverings used in kitchens.

The installation of a vinyl floor covering is relatively easy to do, particularly with tiles. And with the tile you can make patterns to give the floor an individual look.

Maintenance is simple, just keep it clean with an occasional damp mopping .

Vinyl tile flooring is suitable for use anywhere but most commonly is found in kitchens, bathrooms and entries where its water resistance is used to advantage.

Linoleum is like a less sturdy vinyl. It is composed of materials that were available in the last half of the 19th century. While still around, it is more expensive than vinyl and is less durable.

Wood [12C,12G, 12I]

While wood floors in houses have been used for centuries, today's floors are made to last longer and have appearance values unknown in the past.

The wood may be just the surface on a plywood sheet, it may be in the form of tiles, strips or more traditional planks. The surface itself is protected with modern-day materials which make it more resistant to stains and scratches as well as easier to maintain. Yet one of the continuing problems with wood is that it does scratch more easily than vinyl, ceramic, stone or laminate.

From the Wood Floors On Line website[12H], surfaces available using domestic woods include: "Ash - Beech - Birch - Cherry - Douglas Fir - Heart Pine - Hickory Pecan Maple (Hard) - Mesquite - Red Oak - Walnut - White Oak - Yellow Pine".

The same website lists many more imported species that are available including bamboo[12J] and cork[12I] which have touters of their own.

Bamboo is, botanically, a reed. Pieces of it are laminated together to give a wood-like surface.

Cork is more resilient than other wood products and would get away from the foot and leg tiring problem in kitchen applications. It does not absorb water and will not rot (else how could it be used in wine bottles?) It is also more sound absorbing than other woods. Cork is used not only for surface applications but also for the underlayment of other floors where its imperviousness to water makes it attractive.

Wood colors range from very light to almost black. It comes pre-finished or unfinished. In the latter case a urethane surface is added by the in-

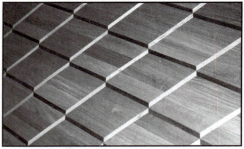

An idea of what can be done with wood (or laminate). This parquet floor is in the entry hall of an upscale home. Regardless of its appearance, this is a flat, horizontal surface.

staller. It is suggested that you visit website references[12G] and [12K] to get a deeper insight into the subject.

While wood floor suppliers would have you believe that these floors are as economical as others, this is simply not so. Generally, you can ex-

A kitchen floor made up of hardwood strips. It is impressive.

pect to pay significantly more for wood than for carpet. On the other hand, wood will probably outlast carpet in most areas of the house although it may need resurfacing periodically.

In kitchens and bathrooms where there is more expected exposure to moisture than elsewhere in the house, wood, other than perhaps cork, probably is not the best bet. It'll simply take more maintenance than vinyl or laminates and be significantly more expensive. If you're willing to do that maintenance and like the appearance of wood, it's a choice you can make.

Ceramic and stone tile

Ceramic tile may have a hard, impenetrable, glazed surface or it may semi-glazed. Stone tiles are usually more porous than ceramic.

In some parts of the country these materials are the regional choice for kitchens and bathrooms, particularly where they can be laid directly on a slab floor. They have a hard, non-resilient finish which makes standing on them for a period of time quite tiring. It also is "sayonara" to anything breakable that gets dropped on it.

They are generally water resistant except for the grout. While a glazed ceramic surface does not stain, the grout does and maintenance that keeps the grout sealed is required if it is not to discolor with time and stains. Similarly stone tile is subject to staining if it is not properly sealed.

Too often this is something the homeowner finds out about when it's too late. Builders should warn people buying houses about the need for maintenance of grout, on counters, walls, and floors—but, in my experience, they don't. We all learn it the hard way.

Tiles must be laid on a rigid subfloor and right here is another potential problem. If the subfloor is a slab, any crack in the slab will also cause the tile to crack unless special precautions are used when it is laid.

I had this happen in a bathroom in our southern California home. The slab evidently cracked because right across the floor of the bathroom was an obvious crack. Whoever laid that tile didn't do a good job. Since this happened a couple of years after we accepted the house, there was nothing that could be done. I assume it's still that way.

Another common use of tile that should have "caution" all over it is in entry halls. Run-of-the-mill ceramic or stone tile entry ways can cause accidents when someone with wet shoes comes into the house. The usual glaze on tiles is smooth

This entry tile is very slippery when wet. Discovered the hard way.

and slippery when wet. Tiles used for entries should be not be slippery when wet—they probably should be unglazed.

To test a tile's suitability for your entry way, take a pair of rubber-soled shoes, put some water on the tile, and test the traction. For a new entry, the people at the tile store should be able to advise you on the best purchase.

The reason for saying "should" is that we have slippery tile in our entry—purchased before I wrote the book, obviously. I'm still thankful that when I found out the hard way, like landing on my backside, how slippery it is that I didn't break something. But it scared me, as it would anyone.

In any case, if you are planning tile (ceramic or stone) in the entry, be sure to have a large absorbent rug at the door which will catch most of the water that may be tracked in. It may help prevent an accident.

Of course, the same precautions should be taken in a bath room. While it probably should

not be used there because of the potential for slipperiness, nonetheless tile is put in homes for its eye-catching beauty. Don't let it be a type that is dangerous when wet. And be ready to provide something to stand on—tile and stone floors can feel pretty cold to bare feet.

Laminates

"Pergo" is often used to describe this material, just as "Formica" is used as a generic name for laminate countertops. (It is not surprising to find that Formica, Inc. is one of the suppliers of laminate flooring.)

Like laminate countertops, this flooring is a made of several thin layers of different materials cemeted together to give a tough, long-lasting floor. It is available to simulate about any wood material, color or pattern.

The ifloor.com page[12M] has a detailed description of the material and how to use it. A page on that site[12K] lists 20 different suppliers and a different page compares them in quality and price[12N].

It is generally impervious to water, making it suitable for kitchens and bathrooms as well as other places in the house where the hardwood appearance is wanted.

It is often used in existing houses and is usually installed without having to remove the original floor (other than carpet, of course). This makes it an attractive material for remodeling.

Subfloors

If you choose a flooring that has to be nailed down, make sure it's nailed to plywood rather than particleboard. Particleboard won't hold nails and the flooring will loosen with usage.

Unless special precautions are taken, unyielding materials, like ceramic tile, marble, and other stone, will come loose or crack. These materials should be laid on a very solid base. Most subfloors don't meet this requirement. With post-and-beam construction and its 2-inch deck under the flooring, the deck lumber can be expected to dry out, warping in the process. Further, changes in temperature and humidity will cause the boards to move.

Floor joists made of sawn or dimensioned lumber are subject to the same drying and warping. Composite ("silent floor") joists are more stable over time but are still subject to changes in temperature and humidity.

To get the necessary rigidity, special treatment under ceramic tile or stone should be used. This may consist of a concrete-like foundation or mud, thick plywood, or backer board made of concrete mortar with fiberglass mesh reinforcing. Ceramic tile or stone should not be laid on particleboard or interior grade plywood that is not stable with changes in humidity. Two things can happen;

> ⇨ The movement of the subfloor will cause the tile to crack, at least in the grout areas and

> ⇨ With cracks, any water on the floor will get through to the subfloor, making an ideal place for mold growth and rot.

If plywood is used, it should be exterior grade measuring at least 3/4 inches thick. Backer boards are typically 3/8 or 7/16 inches thick and do a better job.

Kitchen

What to put on kitchen floors is largely a matter of regional preference and personal taste. A reader in western Kentucky relates that ceramic tile kitchen floors are the regional choice—linoleum (vinyl) is considered tacky. The same thing was seen in the San Francisco Bay area. From a strictly functional viewpoint tile is a poor choice.

> ⇨ It is potentially slippery,

> ⇨ It is subject to scratches and grout stains,

> ⇨ It is harder on the feet,

> ⇨ It's hardness means that objects dropped on it are more likely to break than on vinyl, linoleum, cork or wood, and

> ⇨ Because of its unevenness, it is a problem for furniture when used where there is a table, chairs or stools. Later we discuss the problem of floor under eating bars which should be spill resistant. When that floor is tile it's more difficult to keep the stool or chair from rocking.

A California reader objects to vinyl or linoleum for the very reason that others find it attractive, it is noticeably softer than tile or wood. Because of this, it is subject to damage when abused—like improperly dragging a heavy object such as a refrigerator across it. Modern-day vinyls are sturdy and do not require the maintenance they did decades ago. One website suggests using a piece of 1/4-inch Masonite under anything heavy that must be moved across it. With a modicum of care, like sweeping and occasional mopping, vinyl should last many, many years—as will tile, laminates and today's hardwoods.

Hardwood floors are an in between. They are not as hard on the feet as tile nor on objects dropped on them. And they will stand more abuse than vinyl because when you drag that refrigerator across it the scratches can be taken out of the surface— it doesn't have to be replaced. But it's still a good idea to put the Masonite piece under that refrigerator.

What you choose is, obviously, a personal preference. And, if you don't like what's there, it can always be changed.

Flooring summary

Any comparison of different types of flooring is, of necessity, broad-sweeping. It cannot take into account the quality of any particular brand nor how it is installed. With this in mind, you may find the following useful:

- ➪ Vinyl - relatively easy to damage or scratch, resistant to moisture and staining, easy to maintain, expensive to repair, least expensive to buy.

- ➪ Wood - somewhat easy to damage or scratch, moisture absorbent, subject to staining, average maintenance difficulty, average ease of repair, more expensive than vinyl.

- ➪ Laminate - good resistance to damage or scratching, good moisture resistance, easy to maintain, more difficult to repair and more expensive than vinyl.

- ➪ Ceramic - most resistant to damage or scratching, best resistance to moisture and staining, easy to maintain, repairable, among the more expensive materials.

The US Floor Source website[120] includes a detailed comparison table as well as descriptive information about each of the types of flooring.

Squeaky floors

Squeaky floors are a source of irritation. Often there's little that can be done about them—not, at least, at a reasonable cost. And they are a real turn off for potential buyers at resale time.

Particleboard is usually used under carpeting. It expands and shrinks with temperature and humidity so, if it is laid without adequate space between pieces, squeaks can occur when pieces of the particleboard expand and rub together when they're walked on. This is something that is hard to write into specifications but if you're having a house

built and don't see small spaces between boards before the carpet pad is laid, don't hesitate to speak up. And in an existing house check it out, walk everywhere. If you hear squeaks, decide if it's something you want to live with. It's unlikely you'll be able to change it.

Squeaky floors can also develop as the lumber in a house dries. Unless it is kiln dried, lumber shrinks and/or warps with time, leaving a gap between the beam or floor joist and the deck or subfloor just above it. When someone walks on it, the floor or subfloor will give and move up and down on its nails. The rubbing on the nails can cause squeaks. This doesn't usually happen until the house is a year old or more. With a new house, you are on your own unless you have an agreement with the builder that he's responsible for more than the year of the normal move-in warranty. The best insurance is to take all the reasonable steps you can to eliminate the sources of the squeaks during construction.

You may not be as lucky as a neighbor who, after about nine months in his new house, couldn't walk in his bedroom or dining room without squeaking. In his case the problem was covered by his 1-year warranty. The carpet had to be pulled back and the subfloor re-nailed. A few months later and any squeak fixing would have been on the owner's nickel.

Not all floors will have squeaks. With slab floors, for example, there's nothing to squeak. The squeak mechanisms for post-and-beam construction are different than for floors that use joists.

With post and beam

This has been the most common crawl-space construction used in the western states. Typically four-inch wide beams are spaced on four-foot centers and supported every eight feet by posts that rest on concrete piers under the house. Two-inch lumber, typically 2 X 8 inches, is then laid across the beams to form the deck on which the house is built. Plywood, particleboard, or tile backer board is laid on the deck as the subfloor that holds the carpet, vinyl, or other flooring surface.

There are a number of places where squeaks can develop. An obvious one is where the deck is nailed to the beams. As the beams dry and warp, or as the deck lumber warps, nails will pull up and then squeak when someone walks on the floor above. Warping of the deck lumber can cause the subflooring nails to pull loose, another place for squeaks. Ideally, kiln-dried lumber will be used. If not, and you have a squeak problem, do the best possible job of fastening the deck pieces down, using screws or lots and lots of nails.

With floor joists

Some construction uses floor joists with much longer spans than are feasible with beams. Joists are used on second floors, in houses with basements, and as an alternative to concrete piers and posts. Joists may be either sawn lumber or they may be manufactured joists made like I-beams in which multiple pieces of wood are glued together to form the joists. These are lighter, stronger, and longer than a single piece of sawn lumber. As the price of sawn lumber increases, these manufactured joists become more attractive economically. Joists are typically installed on 16-inch centers and plywood is laid across them as the subfloor. Gluing the subfloor to the joists eliminates one possible source of squeaks.

These manufactured joists are advertised as the way to have a silent floor. Since they're made with dried wood, as is the plywood on top of them, there's nothing to dry out and warp, hence nothing to cause squeaks. But there are other sources of squeaks with these floors. Joists are held in place with specially-shaped metal hangers. If a joist is not properly fastened, walking on the floor above can cause the joist to move in the hanger, causing the squeak.

A 'silent' floor joist.

With a new house, talk to your builder about the use of silent joists versus those made with sawn lumber. Or check to see what's under a house you may be considering. (Slab floors are no problem but squeaky floors can happen in any house that has an upstairs.) Where the span is long, the manufactured joists may be the only choice. If manufactured joists are not used, then consider having the subfloor fastened down with screws rather than nails.

Ceilings

This section is about an aesthetic factor having little to do with function but it does have to do with resale values. The living and dining room ceilings in many of today's houses are either two stories tall or they are vaulted These ceilings are all high and give a feeling of airiness. But watch out for ceilings in other rooms. Large rooms need high ceilings or they will seem oppressive.

⇨ One house I visited is on a hillside lot with a nice view of the city. The great room has a ceiling that is 7-feet, 9-inches high. It has a feeling of being even less than that. It gives a feeling of being closed in. The builder had trouble selling the house. That low ceiling in a big room was a real turnoff.

⇨ On the other side of the coin is a house with a small living room about 10 x 12 feet but with a 10-foot ceiling. The high ceiling actually makes the room feel even smaller than it is. It pays to have the ceiling height in keeping with the size of the room.

Note that "8-foot" ceilings are frequently a few inches lower than this. Builders do this to save on studs that come in 8- and 10-foot lengths. When 8-foot studs are used, the inside of the room is several inches smaller.

Attic Storage

Crawling around the lumber in the trusses in our attic getting things out and putting them away every year at Christmas time reminds me again about the importance of having suitable attic storage space. If you plan on attic storage, this is certainly one place that, given the opportunity, you should be more than willing to spend a few dollars to have it done right.

For attic storage you should:

⇨ See that the attic area is stick framed or that special attic trusses are used to leave a maximum of open area.

⇨ See that any attic insulation is roll or batting (not blown in)—at least in the part of the attic you'll want to use for storage.

⇨ Spell out how much and what type of attic flooring is to be used. (3/4 inch plywood or a dense particleboard is fine.)

⇨ Spell out the means of access you want, such as a door off of an upstairs hall or bedroom or a pull-down ladder in the garage. (Don't skimp on the size of the opening, you'll want to be able to get both a big box and yourself through it at the same time.)

⇨ Use screw-in bare-light sockets mounted to a rafter—they are entirely adequate

for attic lighting. The switch for the lights should be mounted at the entry to the storage area.

In areas with slab floors it isn't possible to put heating ducts under the house in the basement or crawl space and the furnace is usually put in the attic. This means that ready access to the attic will have been built in. It's then up to you to have adequate lighting and flooring in place for the storage area. If it's a new house, having the builder do this as the house is being built is a much easier approach. But don't forget to have suitable framing in the attic so you can get around. This may become even more important if you decide to add an air conditioner later. There not only must be room in the furnace for the expander, it must also be possible for the HVAC people to connect the necessary wires and tubes to the outside condenser.

Quiet Please!

When we bought our new house, we didn't notice that the location for the entertainment center in the family room would be just a four-inch wall away from the head of the bed in the master bedroom. Going to bed early means using ear plugs.

Besides the obvious need to sound insulate bedrooms from adjacent family rooms, it's also a good idea to put sound insulation in the walls around bathrooms so that you or your guests are not awakened by early risers or middle-of-the-night users.

Laundry room walls are also good places for sound insulation, especially if the laundry is close to an area where people are likely to be when the machines are operating.

Sound insulation is relatively inexpensive to install before wallboard is put in place. It's better to think ahead than to consider a retrofit. While it's possible to insulate the walls after construction, it is much better to have it done when the house is being built. The following techniques, used in apartments and zero-lot-line houses, can be used to significantly reduce the noise level inside a house.

Sound goes through walls in two different ways:

⇨ Through the space between studs.

⇨ Through the wooden studs themselves.

Between studs

Often simply filling the space between studs with sound insulation provides enough sound reduction. This is controlled by filling the space with fiberglass batting similar to that used for thermal insulation in exterior walls except there is no moisture barrier.

For an existing house this will require tearing the wallboard off one side of the wall in order to install the batting. This approach also lets you add resilient channels or soundboard to one side of the wall to reduce the noise transmitted by the studs themselves. Blown-in insulation can be used but requires making holes in the walls that must be closed and painted after the work is done.

Through the studs

The sound transmitted by studs is in the lower-frequency ranges and is often heard as a series of thuds. When this is or could be a problem it must be tackled in addition to filling the spaces between the studs.

There are three methods to reduce the sound carried this way. All three separate the wallboard from the studs and all result in thicker walls:

⇨ Double studs

⇨ Resilient channels

⇨ Soundboard

Double studs

A staggered double row breaks the path through the studs. All spaces can be filled with fiberglass batting.

Resilient channels

These are special U-shaped metal strips that are laid horizontally across the studs. The wallboard is screwed to these strips. Fiberglass batting is still needed for the space between studs. Using the channels on both sides of the wall obviously improves the performance.

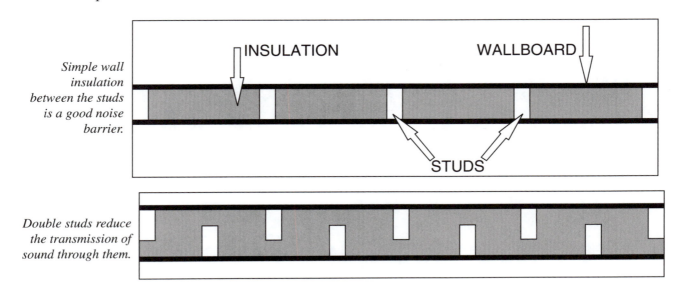

Simple wall insulation between the studs is a good noise barrier.

INSULATION   WALLBOARD

STUDS

Double studs reduce the transmission of sound through them.

Soundboard

Soundboard goes between the studs and the wallboard, is relatively inexpensive and comes in 4-feet x 8-feet sheets. It provides sound insulation for the whole wall including the studs. It, too, can be used on both sides of the wall. Fiberglass batting will provide additional sound deadening.

Other techniques

Special acoustic wall framing is available which is specifically designed to reduce sound transmission.[12A]

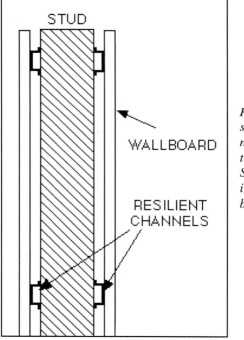

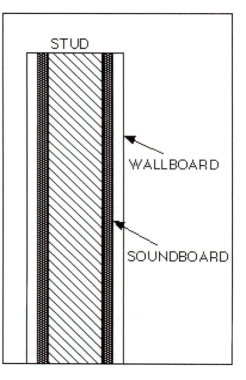

Resilent channels and soundboard reduce the noise transmitted through the studs. Soundboard also helps insulate the space between studs.

SECTION III

The Kitchen

> *If you want a golden rule that will fit everything, this is it: Have nothing in your houses that you do not know to be useful or believe to be beautiful.*
>
> William Morris, British industrialist and philanthropist (1877-1963)

The kitchen receives what may seem to be a disproportionate amount of attention in this book simply because it is the room about which far more decisions have to be made than any other.

Yet it is all rather simple. First there are the basic user-friendly rules. As with other parts of the house, they are all just common sense. You don't need to be a kitchen designer with years of experience to understand them. But do be careful—user-friendly design is not a major concern of architects, building designers, or kitchen designers as you can see when you look in magazines and books on kitchens, at design catalogs, websites, and at existing houses.

It is the room in the home where more work is done than all the rest put together. The emphasis should be on user-friendliness—minimizing the amount of effort needed in the kitchen and making it a more enjoyable place in which to work and live. Armed with this information, you can make the informed decisions that are right for your lifestyle.

Kitchens are areas of inevitable compromise. They must fit with the rest of the house and there are often conflicting objectives—aesthetic, as well as functional and, of course, cost. A nice view, a special decor, or the desire for a large informal gathering area with the kitchen at the center—these are a few of the possible criteria that come into play.

In Section III you will find discussions of the various parts of the kitchen—appliances, cabinets, counters, etc.—in terms of some of their characteristics and good and not-so-good ways to use them. The last chapter in this part puts it all together with discussions about basic kitchen layouts, pointing out good features and potential problems. It's work, but that's what makes dreams come true.

There are a number of website locations where you can get information about kitchen designs and what to put in them. In general, we don't disagree with what they say---except for one thing. They largely ignore the homeuser and the amount of work that must be expended day in and day out. Here we consider unnecessary steps every bit as or more important than the style and color of the cabinets, for example. How you respond to looks and user friendliness is your personal decision.

If you're buying a home that already exists, use the information here to help you make the best selection for you. If your new home is in a tract and hasn't yet been built, you have a good chance of making improvements---not in the basic layout but in the materials that are put into the kitchen.

When you have more complete say in the total design, whether a new home or the remodel of an old one, use it to your advantage. Make form follow function. Generally you'll find that you can have both if you plan ahead. And don't let the designer or architect try to tell you that it's OK to have the refrigerator on the far side of the kitchen, where you have to walk around an island to get to it. (We use this example because a reader of *Built It Right*! did just that. She got the kitchen she knew was right---and educated the architect about user friendliness in the process.)

One of the references is to a very informative website on kitchens[13B]. Use the info there to get ideas about your new kitchen, the pictures are beautiful. They present some very relevant ideas about what to put into your kitchen as well as what's popular in kitchens today.

Chapter 13

Sinks and Countertops

If you think you can, you can. And if you think you can't, you're right.

Mary Kay Ash. American entrepreneur (1918-2001)

In this chapter:
In this chapter we look at a number of different materials that are available for kitchen countertops and how sinks can mount in them. Materials used for counters are laminates (popularly known by the trade name Formica), ceramic tile, solid surface (such as Corian), natural stone (usually granite), and engineered stone. There are functional, aesthetic, and cost distinctions among them.

This chapter was written to describe the different kitchen countertops and sinks that you may see when looking at houses and to give you some insight into their pros and cons. If you're buying a yet-to-be-built home you may have some options in getting the countertop that you really want. And don't forget your local home improvement stores and demo kitchens in material supply houses; they'll have choices and ways of doing things you may not see in model houses. They'll also give you a better idea of the costs for the different materials and mountings.

Regional Differences

Regional perceptions about the different countertop materials vary widely. In some areas ceramic tile is the most commonly used material, laminates are considered "cheap," and solid surface materials are too expensive except, perhaps, in very high-end homes. In other parts of the country laminate is the material of choice for most people, with tile being saved for "show" places and solid surface for luxury homes. Or there may be a mix, with tile on islands that have cooktops and with laminate in the rest of the kitchen. Stone is often used instead of ceramic tile for cooktops and work areas.

And now we are getting a wide variety of manufactured stone materials.

Countertops

While what you get in your kitchen is very much a matter of personal choice, there are significant functional and aesthetic differences among the different materials. Here are some things to consider in deciding which is for you:

- ⇨ Appearance.
- ⇨ Cost.
- ⇨ Resistance to day-to-day wear.
- ⇨ Resistance to cutting, scratching, and staining.
- ⇨ Resistance to heat.
- ⇨ Hardness. A hard surface resists cutting, scratching, and wear but will crack or chip if mistreated. Hard surfaces are more likely to cause breakage to glass or china objects dropped on them.
- ⇨ Sink mounting. When sinks are mounted flat with the counter surface or below it, debris can be wiped directly into the sink.
- ⇨ Day-to-day maintenance.
- ⇨ Repairability.
- ⇨ Water lip. A lip along the front edge of the countertop that keeps minor spills from running on the floor.

Tried and true countertop materials include plastic laminates, tile, stone, and solid surface.

A new face in the lineup, introduced in this (the 21st) century, is engineered stone (quartz) which yields countertops with the advantages of both solid surface and stone. It is tops in cost, however.

An interior decorator website[13c] lists the different materials with a two or three sentence description of each.

Laminates, a.k.a. Formica

The least expensive countertops are the laminates. (Sometimes called "Formica" after one of the manufacturers.) These are made of a thin, hard, tough plastic sheet that is glued (laminated) to a piece of backing material, usually particleboard, for strength and mountability.

There are two major advantages to laminates:

- ⇨ They are the least expensive of the countertop options and
- ⇨ They are highly resistant to staining.

Laminates are not as hard as tile or stone. This is a disadvantage in that they are easier to scratch, cut or burn, but an advantage because dishes or glasses dropped on a laminate counter are not as likely to break.

Neither tile-in nor undermount sinks can be used with laminates.

Laminates are relatively easy to clean but scratches will hold dirt. They are easily scorched with hot frying pans, cigarettes or even candles. They cannot be repaired except by replacing a section of the counter.

Seams in laminates are usually obvious.

Improperly manufactured laminate counters may separate from their underlying material making a lump in the surface. This should not occur but does.

Laminates come in many colors with and without patterns. There are two basically different ways to make back splashes and counter fronts:

- ⇨ The countertop, the back splash, and the counter front are formed from a single piece of material. There is a raised lip at the front edge of the countertop.
- ⇨ Only flat pieces are used, with the back splash, the countertop and the front edge being separate pieces.

Aesthetically, the one-piece counter is plain and utilitarian while using three-pieces allows for a much greater variety in design and appearance.

One-piece countertops

From the user's point of view, having the back splash and the lip made as a single piece with the counter has two distinct advantages:

⇨ There is no seam where the top meets the back splash nor where it meets the front piece and

⇨ The front lip helps keep spills from running on the floor.

There is also a disadvantage. At inside corners of a 24" counter there will be a 45-degree seam that is 34 inches long, going from the corner at the front of the counter to the back corner of the back splash. Laminate seams are always utilitarian and this long seam is not a thing of beauty. Further, it takes special machinery to do a precise job of making this kind of countertop and not all fabricators have it. It's a tricky business, at best.

Three-piece countertops

The inside corner problem can be avoided when the countertop is made with three flat pieces of laminate: the countertop proper, the back splash, and the front. When a large sheet of material is used it is possible to include both sides of the corner in a single piece. Often this avoids seams altogether and, in any case, the long corner seam is eliminated. Virtually anyone can make counters in this way and a lot of fabricators do. Tile can be used for the back splash to add a little

A simple three-piece laminate counter with no surface seams. The backsplash and the edge are separate pieces of laminate. There is no front lip.

A tile backsplash is a nice touch for a laminate countertop. But note the discrepancy between the sizes of the tiles and the tile top-edge pieces. It doesn't have to be this way. A lot of us find the resulting dissymetry unattractive.

variety. Other times wood is used for the same purpose. Counter fronts may be laminate or wood. To break the monotony, front edges may be beveled and faced with either the laminate or with wood. The variations seem to be limited only by the imaginations of the counter makers.

Note, however, that the three-piece laminate counter does not have the option of a lip on the front. Again there is a trade-off between form and function.

The wood and laminate front edge of this three-piece laminate counter makes it more appealing—and makes it possible to avoid the corner seam which is so often seen when a single laminate piece is used.

Ceramic tile

Ceramic tiles come in many sizes, shapes, colors, and grades. In some places tile has developed a reputation for being difficult to maintain and is seldom used even in upscale homes. This undeserved reputation comes from ignorance. I should know, I was one of the uninformed.

Our last three homes had ceramic-tile kitchen countertops. We had no problems with either stains or pot marks with the first two. In the third we couldn't understand why the tile stained and why metal pots and pans made marks on the tile. It was while doing research for **Build It Right!** that I learned that matte finish tile is susceptible to staining and to pot marks. When I took another look at our kitchen tile, the light dawned—our kitchen counter tiles have a matte, not glossy, finish. We like the looks of the matte finish—but we're paying the price for it.

This is another place where you'll have to choose between aesthetics and function. My suggestion: if glossy surfaces turn you off, find a laminate or solid surface counter. Either that or be prepared to put up with stains on the matte tile surface from such things as fruit juices or wine (they will come out with bleach) and expect to live with putting a cloth on the countertop before you set anything on it that can make marks.

Glossy surfaces show scratches easier than matte finishes. The impact of this can be reduced by sticking to light colors in which the scratches and abrasions are not so obvious.

Tiles are laid by gluing them to the underlying material with spaces left between them. These spaces are then filled with grout. Unlike the tile surface, grout is a relatively porous material and absorbs stains readily. This problem is handled in three steps:

  ⇨ Have the tiles set as close together as possible, making a grout line which is in the order of one-sixteenth inch wide. Even if stained it's not as obvious.

  ⇨ Choose a darker grout—it won't show the stains as much.

  ⇨ Use sealer on the grout. Depending on the type of sealer (and how much you pay for it) sealing may last up to 10 years. (Don't use a surface sealer, it may make the grout look shiny like the tile, but it doesn't penetrate and will need frequent reapplication.)

Tiles are resistant to knife cuts (the usual result will be to dull the knife) but it is possible to scratch the hard surface. This is repaired by replacing the tile. Be sure to have a small supply of every kind of tile piece you have in your house so that it can be replaced if needed. Also keep a record of the manufacturer and color of the grout. Thoughtful tile installers will leave some pieces of each tile shape.

Tile surfaces are harder than laminates or solid surface materials. They have virtually no give so that a glass or a dish dropped on them will break easier than with other counters, except stone.

As discussed earlier, tile counters lend themselves to mounting the kitchen sink on top of, level with, or under the countertop.

A front edge tile (called a "V cap" because of its shape) is available that has a raised lip to stop water from running off.

Aesthetics

Sometimes the back splash will use a special decorative tile with a pattern to give the counter a more appealing look. Patterns can also be made with ceramic tile by installing them at 45 degrees to give a different-looking surface. This ability to have patterns in the overall tiled surface as well as in individual tiles is one of the attractions of this material.

Did you ever notice tile installations where the tile pieces along the edges are a different length than the rest so that there are two sets of grout

CERAMIC-TILE COUNTER

Ceramic-tile counters offer a wide range of asethetic looks. There are also functional considerations. It's classic form vs. function. Here are a few examples.

This countertop has a V cap with its lip to keep incidental spills from running off onto the floor. Note that the tile is set at 45°, another way to give it some individuality.

This island counter with the sink and dishwasher does not have a lip. It uses a patterned tile which gets away from the "all the same" look.

A larger tile with a wood front instead of a V cap gives this counter its own distinctive character. The use of wood instead of a V cap may be aesthetically pleasing but is functionally a negative.The matte finish on this tile is more susceptible to marking and staining than a gloss finish would be.

Another case of a special effort to make a distincively different counter-sink combination. The under-mount sink is a plus, the lack of a V cap and its lip is not. These compromises are ones you'll want to remember when looking at counter materials and designs.

lines, one for the edges and a different one for the rest of the counter? (*See* the earlier photo of a tile back splash with a laminate counter.) This doesn't have to be. It's just thoughtless, sloppy work.

Counters usually use the same tile for the back splash. Rounded pieces can give a finished look to the top row. Tiles come in many different sizes, with 4-1/4 and 6-inch square tiles being common. If you have a back splash with 4-1/4 inch tiles, it is not unusual for the installer to finish it off with 6-inch rounded trim pieces. This results in the two sets of grout lines. This has been done so often that some people don't object to the appearance— but to many of us it is very unprofessional. If trim pieces are available the same size as the tile, they should be used, otherwise cut them so that the grout lines line up in a neat and orderly fashion.

In one unfinished house I visited, an installer was putting tile in a tub surround and the edge pieces weren't lining up with the tile. In this case the tile was 6x8 inches and the edge pieces were 6 inches long. However, the way the tile was laid, the 6-inch edge pieces were finishing the 8 inch side of the tile! When I asked if he didn't think it would make a nicer looking job with the grout lines lined up, he said that, no, he liked the random appearance of the two sets of grout lines!

To each his own, but if you want your tile job to look as if the tile and the trim pieces came from the same place and if you have a say, it is suggested that you make this desire known to the builder and the tile installer. Be sure, too, that tiles and trim pieces of the same size are available in the tile pattern you select. It's a good investment to have it done right.

Workmanship

Good and bad workmanship in tile installations is usually obvious; tiles don't lie flat, grout lines aren't straight, etc. Proper edge-cutting is another indication of the quality of the work. Inevitably there will be places where the installer will have

This arrangement of tile and backsplash is amateurish.

This counter was the result of good planning. With the tile laid at 45°, the backsplash is set vertically and the electrical boxes don't overlap the backsplash.

Here is a clean, neat appearance that is quite user friendly—a tile-in sink of the same color as the counter. Note how the corner is handled.

to cut a piece of tile or trim to make it fit the available space. These cuts, whether made with a saw or made by scribing and snapping (breaking) the tile will leave edges that are sharp and, sometimes, rough. A tile-cutting saw makes cleaner cuts than does a snap cutter.

These edges can be smoothed and rounded by using fine sandpaper or a grind stone. The color of a piece of ceramic tile is in the surface glaze so that, when the glaze and the body are distinctly different colors, rounding the edges too much lets the underlying color show through. This should never be a problem if a saw is used to cut the tile. Rounding is then only necessary to smooth the sharp edge—and not to smooth away chips.

Another sign of poor workmanship—or rather poor job management by the builder—is to have an electrical box partly overlapping the backsplash tile. It should be totally inside the tile area or totally outside of it. To do otherwise is not necessary and there's no reason you should have it in your home. (This is a matter of looks, it'll work fine either way—or maybe such mundane things don't bother you.)

Maintenance

Sealers to protect grout from staining have to be renewed periodically. In looking at grout colors, remember that light-colored grouts are more likely to show stains and discoloration than darker ones. Your supplier should tell you this, but it's sometimes overlooked. If it can be worked into your decor, choose a darker grout color because it's easier to maintain.

This is an area where improvements are always being made. Check with a competent tile supplier to see if there may be a grout available that is inherently resistant to staining.

Tile won't burn but care should be exercised about putting something very hot on it because it can crack from thermal stress.

Stone

Because of its hardness granite is the usual stone for kitchen countertops. Since the material is the same color all the way through, it is possible to work out surface scratches or even shallow chips. But it is not maintenance free.

Granite is a granular rock, containing feldspar, quartz, mica and traces of other components. It is the most common igneous rock in the earth, forming deep below the surface when magma congeals. It has been mined for centuries and today's raw material comes from all parts of the world.

This is granite, a ubiquitous material and major constituent of mountains all over the earth.

The various trace elements in granite give it its colors and the size of the granules give it its texture. One manufacturer's website shows 43 different patterns[13A].

Thickness varies, generally it is between 3/4" and 1-1/2". The thinner pieces require a board under them for support.

Granite is available either in tiles or in slabs suitable for an entire countertop. The tiles are typically larger than ceramic, 12" square being common. The large pieces may go to 62" x 102" or even larger. Thus the laminate counter shown in a earlier photo could, for example, also be made of stone. But it would be noticeably more expensive.

Space between pieces of stone may be very thin or wider like that used with ceramic tile. With the wider spacings, the stone tiles are beveled on the edges to mate with the grout; with the thin spacings they are square edged and the grout is the same depth as the tile. But they must be laid with care otherwise there will be noticeable edges where adjoining tiles meet. Nothing is rounded and you can really feel it.

Because the color and patterns of granite are not just on the surface it is possible to shape the edges. This is particularly useful around edges of an undermount sink and no special edge pieces are needed as they are with ceramic tile. Pieces of granite can be cut and shaped to give the edge of a counter a wide variety of looks.

Generally, the stone tile pieces are handled just as ceramic tile is, the installation being done by countertop installers who mount them just as they would ceramic tile. The larger pieces, those which make up an entire counter, must be cut to fit. The holes for sink mounts are generally cut on site. This is done by a company who specializes in this work. Unlike laminate which can be cut with a hand saw, stone requires a special tool to cut the much harder material.

As noted, granite is a mixture of minerals molded deep in the earth when hot magma cools under extreme pressure. This process leaves tiny empty pores in the material which leaves it vulnerable to staining. When red wine, for example, gets into the pores it dries leaving a visible residue which can only be avoided by using a special sealer. This sealer must be applied about once a year[13O]. Otherwise granite makes an excellent countertop in terms of ruggedness, hardness and durability.

Engineered stone

To make a material which has the advantages of granite but which does not stain, a new type of stone, this one man-made, became available in the 1990s. It is termed "engineered stone" or simply "quartz". The quartz mineral is found in veins large and small in the earth but its structure does not let it be mined and cut into slabs as would be needed for countertops. (A quartz vein, incidentally, is a place where gold may be found in tiny flecks.)

For engineered stone, quartz is taken from the earth in whatever size is convenient. At the processing plant it is crushed into very small grains, mixed with a polyester or acrylic resin base and colors as wanted and then molded into the slab size that is wanted. When it is hardened, the resultant material has the hardness of the quartz, which is itself harder than granite. It is non-porous, does not stain and is highly heat resistant. Other stone granules can be added to give the appearance of granite of various shades.

In home use it is impervious to everything, making an ideal material for countertops. A detailed description of how it is made is found at the Verona-Legacy website[13G].

Engineered stone is touted for its looks, having a brilliance in depth that is not seen in other materials. It can be combined with solid-surface materials such as sinks or can be used to make attractive patterns in countertops.

Dark granite or engineered stone makes a spectacular counter. This one, unfortunately, got saddled with a drop-in sink.

STONE COUNTERS

While more expensive, stone has some definite functional advantages over ceramic tile. Here are some examples:

An expanse of granite does look handsome. Note the gloss finish which you may not care for. The straight front edge is one of many that are available for stone counters.

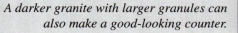

A darker granite with larger granules can also make a good-looking counter.

Here a backsplash and ledge of the same granite behind the counter gives this counter an elegant look.

Like the others here, this counter has an undermount sink. While this is as it should be, it doesn't always happen. And note that the lip on the front edge of the counter is not a characteristic of stone counters.

Its drawback is price, generally the tops in the hierarchy of countertop materials. As it becomes better known and competition grows, it is expected that the costs will come down.

It is sold in the US as Zodiaq by Dupont[13E], Silestone by Consentino US[13D], Legacy by Verona Marble Co.[13G], Caesarstone by Caesarstone US[13F] and probably others.

Solid-surface materials

There are a number of different countertop materials in the solid-surface category, Corian being the best known. These surfaces are two to three times more expensive than ceramic tile. Solid-surface countertops have a smooth surface that is almost impervious. It is stain resistant and it doesn't have grout to keep clean. Properly made seams are virtually invisible. Sinks of the same material are available that can be mounted under the countertop, so that they seem all one piece. These are known as an "integral" sink

Solid-surface materials have the same consistency throughout. They are a cast resin that may be polyester or acrylic or a combination of both, giving somewhat different properties to the resulting materials. Generally all-acrylic counters, like Corian, are more durable and a little more expensive.

Descriptive websites include Dupont's Corian[13I], Avonite[13J], Swanstone[13K], Formica's Solid Surface[13H], Wilsonart[13L], and Quarry Stone[13M].

Maintenance

The durability of solid surface is excellent. Burns can be polished out as can cuts or scratches.

Some solid-surface counters come in a matte surface while others are glossy. Glossy surfaces will show minor scratches more than matte finishes, but these can be buffed out. It does mean more maintenance, however.

Uses

Because the joints can be buffed smooth, two pieces can be directly abutted to make invisible, waterproof seams. It is this property that makes it possible to cut out damaged material and replace it with the repair being almost invisible. It can also be seamed with other materials such as wood, brass, etc. It's the material of choice for kitchen countertops—or any other application that requires a tough smooth surface that is visually appealing.

The primary drawback to solid-surface countertops is the price, but if you can afford them, they're both elegant and utilitarian. They are used in kitchens because their greater resistance to cuts and scratches and their repairability make them more attractive than other materials. Solid surface materials are shipped by the manufacturer, usually in flat sheets, to fabricators. The extensive seaming, cutting, and grinding operations needed to make them into counters are done locally.

Solid surfacing veneer (SSV)

A relatively recent innovation (mid 1990s) was solid surfacing veneer made by Wilsonart. Older solid surface materials are one-half inch thick, solid all the way through. The all-acrylic solid surfacing veneer is one-eighth inch thick and is laminated on top of a different, far less expensive sheet material, like particleboard, for strength and rigidity. The combination has the advantages of the solid surface material in appearance and maintainability but at a significantly lower cost. SSV counters are, however, still a little more expensive than tile. When their maintainability and repairability are considered they are an attractive alternative.

Solid surface sinks of the same material as the SSV are available but their cost detracts from their attractiveness. Because of the weight of cast iron undermount sinks, they are difficult to put under

SOLID-SURFACE COUNTERS

Solid-surface materials can be used to make just about any kind of imaginable countertop. Here are a few:

A plain white truly functional countertop. Like the others shown here it has no lip to catch spills—but it could.

Here the tile backsplash adds interest to the otherwise plain countertop. The grout lines in the tile pieces are somewhat random which adds distinction for those who don't like things all lined up.

One of the attractive properties of solid-surface materials is the ease with which craftsmen can join pieces of different colors and patterns to create unique and interesting countertops. Here this property was used in the area behind the sink to avoid a plain-looking counter.

Here the flexibility of the material was used to create a geometric pattern in the main part of the counter.

an SSV countertop. However, there is no obvious reason that lighter weight and less expensive sinks, like stainless steel or quartz resin composite, could not be mounted under an SSV counter to make a handsome, functional, and relatively inexpensive combination.

The availability of veneers for laminating brings the advantages of solid-surface material within just about anyone's reach. As this material is becoming more widely used, we are seeing a variety of both aesthetic and functional options. You can expect to find them in both older and new homes.

Interiors and Sources describes SSV on its website[13Q]. Olympic Countertops, a countertop manufacturer in Washington state, has some nice pictures on its website showing what can be done with SSV[13P].

Breakfast Bars

Many kitchen designs include an island or a peninsula that separates the kitchen from the family room or the breakfast nook. This island or peninsula is often designed to double as an eating bar. When you see such a plan be sure that the countertop extends out far enough to let someone sit there (12 inches is a minimum, more is better).

If the cooktop is also on the same counter as the breakfast bar be especially careful that there is a way to prevent a person sitting at the bar from getting burned by something on the cooktop. (*See* the warnings in the section on islands in Chapter 18.)

Sinks

Popular sinks and how they are mounted also vary by region. In some areas you'll find mostly cast iron drop-in or steel self-rimming sinks sitting on laminate counters while in others tile-in or undermount mounting is used almost exclusively. Regardless of the regional differences, some sinks and their mountings make life just plain easier in a kitchen.

Sink materials

These five different materials are used in kitchen sinks:

- ⇨ Cast iron,
- ⇨ Porcelain,
- ⇨ Stainless steel,
- ⇨ Solid surface, and a
- ⇨ Quartz resin compound.

Cast iron

This is the most common. Its enamel coating is hard and resists scratching and staining. As the surface becomes abraded with use, it becomes harder to keep clean and gives the sink a finite life. Items dropped into the sink can chip away the enamel, leaving an unattractive black spot from the cast iron underneath. The heavy weight of a cast-iron sink can be a problem in some mountings.

Available styles are made for drop-in, tile-in, or undermount mounting.

Porcelain

The major objection to porcelain sinks is their relative fragility. They can shatter when something heavy is dropped in them.

Stainless steel

This common sink material obviously doesn't chip or stain. Its brightly polished surface does become scratched and less attractive with age. Where water is hard and a drop dries, the inevitable spotting shows up on any dark surface but especially on steel. Aesthetics are another objection to stainless sinks—some people just don't like them.

They are used for both drop-in and undermount mounting.

Solid surface

The advantages of solid surface materials apply to sinks as well as countertops. These sinks are mounted under the countertop and, when properly made, the countertop and sink look like a single piece. They can be aesthetically pleasing and functionally top notch. While resistant to staining, the sinks can be scoured if necessary. Similarly, scratches can be burnished out because the material is the same throughout the whole sink body, not just on the surface. The major consideration is the cost.

Solid surface sinks are designed for mounting under a solid surface or engineered-stone counter.

Quartz resin composite

Quartz resin composite sinks are made by a number of manufacturers and are available in designs which range from plain old sinks to the exotic. The material is a mixture of quartz and a resin. Granite is sometimes used instead of quartz. Like the solid surface materials, composite sinks are the same throughout. The material is hard and has the appearance of an enameled sink but, because there is no surface coating, it does not chip off. It is warranted against staining by most manufacturers. Scratches and tough stains can be rubbed out. Sinks made of this material are much lighter in weight than cast iron and some brands and styles are price competitive with cast iron.

Composite sinks have been used in Europe and have been available in the United States for over fifteen years. Like everything else in home building they have been slow to gain popular acceptance. They are available for both drop-in and undermount mounting.

Mountings

There are three ways a sink can be mounted in a countertop: drop-in, tile-in, and undermount. In every case the sink is supported at its edges.

Drop-in or top-mount

These sinks are mounted by cutting a hole in the countertop and dropping the sink in from above. The edge or rim of the sink sits on top of the counter. This rim may be up to half an inch high in the case of cast iron or it may be the thin rim of a stainless steel sink.

Because it sits on top of the counter, the rim is in the way when wiping or drying the countertop. Further, the joint where the lip or rim meets the countertop often requires special attention to keep clean.

Drop-in is the most common type of mounting, not because it's the best or makes the least work in the kitchen, but because it's the only way that sinks can be mounted on laminate, the least expensive countertop material.

One counter manufacturer told me that he has developed a means of mounting a sink under a laminate counter. I haven't seen one and remain skeptical—particularly about how well such a combination will withstand the test of time.

Drop-in sinks are also used on tile and solid surface counters even though more user-friendly mounting, like tile-in or undermount, could be used. This appears to be a matter of regional preference—and not to the advantage of the home user. It's as if builders and buyers got together and agreed that that's what people are going to buy and forget function.

Tile-in

This technique is useful only with tile counters—ceramic or stone. The sink is made with a special rim which is rectangular and not rounded at the edges. The top surface of the sink is level with the tile making it a continuation of the countertop. The interface between the sink and counter is the line of grout around the edge of the sink.

The result is a countertop and sink combination which is easy to keep clean. The counter can

DROP-IN or TOP-MOUNT SINKS

These sinks are common, found in every kind of countertop. Unfortunately, while inexpensive and easy to install, they are not user-friendly. After you've lived with a tile-in, undermount or integral kitchen sink, you'll never be happy about having one of these.

A drop-in cast iron sink on a laminate countertop. Simple,inexpensive and user-<u>unfriendly</u>.

Here a stainless-steel sink has been dropped in on a laminate counter. The rim or lip still gets in the way when wiping the counter and is a dirt catcher where it sits on the countertop. (Don't use stainless if you have hard water, you'll have spots everyplace a drop of water dries on it.}

Another drop-in cast-iron sink, this time on a ceramic-tile counter. Its dark color gives a more dramatic appearance but it's still a pain in the neck when you'd like to wipe something off of the countertop into the sink. And don't try this either if you have hard water. This dark sink will have the same spot problem as stainless steel.

A stone tile countertop with a stainless-steel sink. Again, there's that rim which makes it difficult to wipe cleanups directly into the sink.

be wiped directly into the sink without fighting the rim of a drop-in sink.

If you dislike ceramic tile counters in general, consider stone which can also be used with tile-in sinks. Either way, day-to-day work in the kitchen is less onerous than with a drop-in sink.

The next two pages are of photos of tile-in and undermount sinks.

Undermount

There are three ways a sink can be mounted under the counter, all involving how the sink and the countertop are joined together.

> ➪ With a tile counter, special quarter-round tiles are used at the edges where the sink and counter meet. These provide a smooth transition from the top of the counter to the sink edge under it.

> ➪ When solid-surface material is used in both the sink and the countertop, the interface between the two materials is at the underside of the counter where it meets the top of the sink. Properly made, there is no visible line and there is nothing to get in the way when cleaning.

> ➪ When a different sink material is used under a solid-surface or stone counter, another technique may be used. The edge of the counter sticks out past the inner edge of the sink so that the sink is recessed slightly back under the countertop. Again there is nothing in the way when cleaning.

I find it disheartening to walk into a model or show home and see a drop-in sink on a solid-surface counter. Whoever makes that decision does it from ignorance, not because of the cost—after all, when there's a solid-surface counter, expense cannot be a major consideration. And this is always done in upscale houses where you'd think that someone involved in the process would see how incongruous it is.

Sink replacement

At some point sinks may have to be replaced and this should be no particular problem—if they were installed properly. Drop-in sinks come out from the top. A tile-in sink also comes out from the top with the line of grout around the edge of sink providing the breaking point between tile and sink.

An undermount sink should be installed with clips holding the sink to the countertop above it. The sink is removed by undoing the clips and lowering the sink into the cabinet space below. With a

An undermount vegetable sink. Attractive and, definitely user-friendly.

ceramic tile counter, salvaging the quarter-round tile pieces around the top of the sink will be touch and go.

Accessory mounting

You may want to mount a soap dispenser, a filtered water tap, an instant hot water spigot or a disposal switch in your sink. For cast-iron sinks you are better off if you think ahead and get a sink with the holes cast in it. Holes can be drilled in cast-iron sinks but it's a tricky business in the presence of the hard enamel surface.

Stainless, solid surface, and composite sinks can be cleanly drilled for accessories when you want to add them. Granite and engineered stone can also be drilled but with more care than the softer materials.

TILE-IN SINKS

When the sink is mounted even with the counter instead of on top of it, it makes cleaning the countertop a much easier chore. Note that these cannot be used with a laminate countertop.

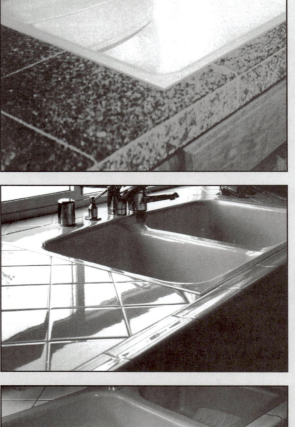

This white sink is tiled into the stone-tile countertop, where it makes a nice-looking and practical arrangement.

Here the sink is the same color as the ceramic tile, a nice coordinated touch. And easy to use!

A darker colored sink is used with a white ceramic tile. The folks who had this in their house when they bought it have since replaced it with a dark stone-tile counter and a color coordinated tiled-in sink. It's both attractive and functional.

UNDERMOUNT SINKS

These sinks are mounted under the countertop so there is no rim or lip to be in the way when the counter is being cleaned. Like tile-in, these cannot be used with laminate tops.

An undercounter sink in a ceramic-tile counter. Note the small quarter-round pieces that complete the transition from countertop to sink. As is usual, there is no symmetry between the two sets of grout lines.

The stainless-steel sink does not need the quarter-round pieces because the stone can be cut and polished to match exactly with the top of the sink.

Another stainless-steel sink mounted under a stone counter top.

Disposal Switch

The garbage disposal, of course, mounts in the sink. It has been traditionally turned on and off using a wall switch mounted above the backsplash on the same side of the sink as the dishwasher. Relatively new on the scene is the "air switch" which mounts *in* the countertop. The disposal is turned on by pushing the switch and then turned off by pushing it again.

The button that's mounted on the sink may be either chrome or white to match the decor. The button is not connected directly to an electrical switch, rather there is an air tube (smaller than a pencil) that runs from the counter-mounted button to the switch which is mounted under the counter. Pushing the button sends a pulse of air to the switch. This way there is no danger to either you or to the switch if water gets onto the button—as it certainly will considering where it's mounted.

Whether it's more user-friendly than a wall-mounted toggle switch is something that could be argued for a long time. But it is different and it *is* more modern.

This "air switch" button operates the disposal. It is mounted on the counter close to the disposal.

Chapter 14

Dishwashers

The first step toward change is awareness. The second step is acceptance.

Nathaniel Branden, author and philosopher (1930-   )

In this chapter:

Putting the appliances in a kitchen where they are handiest and where they'll cause the least work is the thrust of this part of the book. Dishwasher placement is one of the things which, if done unthinkingly, is often the cause of much muttering by anyone who works in the kitchen.

This chapter considers good and bad places for them and explains what to look for and why.

The most important thing about dishwashers is how well they do their job and you can find out about that from your local appliance dealer and from *Consumer's Reports*. Our concern here is where the dishwasher should be located to minimize the work you have to do to use it.

The issue is not trivial. Sometimes an otherwise desirable home plan has no suitable place for the dishwasher—whose location is one of the key elements in a good kitchen design. How the dishwasher location interacts with the overall kitchen layout is discussed in Chapter 18.

Location

The requirements for the dishwasher location are few and simple—but, oh so important for that design that minimizes the effort needed to load and unload it. Its relation to the sink and to the cupboards are the focus here, along with ways in which a poorly placed dishwasher can be a real day-to-day pain in the neck.

Location considerations turn around three criteria:

⇨ The dishwasher should be easy to load,

⇨ The dishwasher should be easy to unload into convenient cabinets, and

⇨ There should be plenty of room in front of an open dishwasher door.

Loading

While modern dishwashers do not require as much rinsing and scraping as was necessary with older units, scraping and/or rinsing at the sink is still needed for some dishes, pans, etc. before they are put into the dishwasher. Most folks are careful not to overload the dishwasher with debris which the disposal is better equipped to handle.

Therefore, when we want to make it easy to load the dishwasher, we need to put it right next to the sink. A person using the dishwasher should be able to stand in front of the sink and load the dishwasher without taking steps in the process.

Unloading

When it is unloaded, where the contents go will, of course, depend on how the homeuser arranged the cupboards, cabinets and shelves. The dishwasher should be located so that dishes, etc., can be moved from the dishwasher to the storage areas with a minimum of steps—typically one step will do for the items that are used daily, dishes and glasses.

In particular, it should not be necessary to have to close the dishwasher door to access storage areas either above or below the counter. (This happens when the dishwasher is in a corner as we'll discuss later in the chapter.)

Open door

When the dishwasher door is open and there are cabinets too close in front of the dishwasher, it can make it difficult or impossible to get around the door. The aisle between the dishwasher and whatever is in front of it should be wide enough to avoid this problem.

Another problem, when the dishwasher door is open, occurs when there isn't room to open the door on the cabinet across from it. When this cabinet is a storage place for pots and pans, it's just plain unfriendly.

Drawings and Photos

With a few basic ideas of what needs to be done, it isn't difficult to design kitchens that will be easy to use, ones without the really user-unfriendly characteristics that are seen in so many house.

Designing a home is a lot of work and the chief concerns of the designer are to make one that is safe for the occupants, which meet the requirements of the building codes and which is economical to build and to live in. With the concentration in those directions, it is not surprising that a kitchen where the homeuser has to do extra work is not a major concern of either the designer or the builder.

Dishwashers and sinks at 45° work out fine if they aren't too close together or too far apart. With the cupboards right there, too, this one is great. (More discussion later.)

GOOD DISHWASHER LOCATIONS

These dishwashers are located where they can be loaded and unloaded without taking needless steps. These aren't the only ways that the dishwasher location can be a real plus. They are here to give you a few examples of what can be done.

This sink is in front of window, a nice location, and the dishwasher is right next to it, comfortably away from any corner.

With the sink on a peninsula, there is a danger of either separating the dishwasher from the cupboards or of putting it in a corner. This was nicely done here so neither happened. Good job.

Another good job where the sink and dishwasher are on a peninsula. Note that access to the upper cupboards is different, but good. It does take care to avoid some of the user-unfriendly things discussed in this chapter.

(Actually the builder's wife designed this kitchen. She'd had the homemaking experience to know what she was doing.)

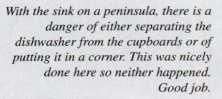

But how much work you have to do should be a concern of yours. Each of the ways a dishwasher location can cause extra steps is discussed here. The graphics illustrate the points.

Separation between Sink and Dishwasher

The separation between the sink and the dishwasher is important for two reasons:

⇨ The potential of dripping water on the floor when loading the dishwasher and

⇨ The number of steps you need to take in the process.

With today's dishwashers, dishes do not need to be rinsed as in the past; just scraping will do. But for many of us, "scraping" means rinsing them off into the disposal without doing a thorough job—we don't want stuff drying on the dishes or silverware. And the dish is wet either way.

Besides this, when the dishwasher is separated from the sink by more than about a foot, you have to take at least one extra step to put dishes into the dishwasher. This, coupled with dishes that may be wet even when scraped, argues that the dishwasher should be right next to the sink. All in all, it's just more convenient to have it there.

Some how-to design books state emphatically that a right-handed person will find a dishwasher easier to load if it is to the left of the sink. (*I personally have had both kinds of kitchen layouts and cannot see what possible difference it makes.*) Check this out for yourself and, everything else being equal, put

the dishwasher to the left of the sink but don't make it an imperative in your layout.

And be sure the side where the disposal is to be located is on the same side as the dishwasher. Or at least consider it...that's the way that makes less work.

There are several ways where you'll find the sink and dishwasher are too far apart:

⇨ They are in the same counter but, for reasons best known to the designer and builder, a cupboard is placed between them.

⇨ They are in cupboards which are at 90° to each other so that the dishwasher must be in either a corner or well separated from the sink.

⇨ They are in cupboards which are at 45° to each other and the dishwasher is placed well way from the sink.

Keeping the dishwasher close to the sink is another thing that the designer and builder often do not think about.

The worst dishwasher location I have ever seen. I still find it hard to believe that someone would do this. But that stone counter does look nice, doesn't it?

If you have the choice, with a non-symmetric sink match it to the dishwasher location.

DISHWASHERS SEPARATED FROM THE SINK

When you have to take steps to get dishes from the sink to the dishwasher, there's something wrong.

Look at these examples.

When dishwashers and sink are in counters at a 45° angle, you need a little room between them. But this is way too much. It'll just make extra, unnecessary work.

Dishwashers in counters that are at 90° to the sink are always bad news. This will result in extra steps and drips on the floor.

Different, huh? These two 45° bends in the counter do a real job of separating the sink and the dishwasher. It makes you wonder if the designer and the builder had ever seen what is to be done in cleaning up after a meal, doesn't it?

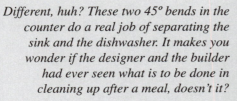

Dishwashers in Corners

When the dishwasher is in a corner, the open dishwasher door blocks access to base cabinets and makes access to upper cabinets either difficult or impossible. When you do not have easy access to *all* cabinet doors you'll end up unloading the dishwasher onto the counter, closing the dishwasher door, and then putting the dishes away. This extra handling is not only more work, but is a good way to chip dishes and glasses.

The problem occurs most often when the sink is at the end of the a narrow U-shaped kitchen. In any case, there must be a convenient amount of space between the side of the dishwasher and the closest cupboard so you have a comfortable place to stand while moving dishes from the dishwasher to the cupboards. To reach upper cupboards, two feet beside the dishwasher is a good target. For lower cupboards, you need room to get the doors open as a minimum and then be comfortable in putting things away. (Pull-out shelves are a big help here.)

Seriously consider rejecting an arrangement where there is no room to stand beside both sides of the dishwasher or if it isn't possible to open cabinet doors when the dishwasher door is open.

The disaster at the end of a U-shaped kitchen. An open dishwasher door will block access to the lower cupboards on the right and will keep you from reaching any of the upper cabinets in the corner.

You'll find dishwasher-in-the-corner problems in three different counter configurations:

⇨ When the dishwasher is in the same counter as the sink. Here it's simply a matter of getting the sink and dishwasher away from any cabinet corner.

⇨ When the dishwasher is in a counter that is at 90° to the sink's counter. There's virtually no way that a dishwasher located in such a counter can be user-friendly. It's simply a situation you should avoid.

⇨ When the dishwasher is in a counter that's at 45° to the sink's counter. Such an arrangement can be good or bad.

The photos on the next page show a number of different user-unfriendly dishwasher locations involving corners or a 90° counter. In every case these dishwashers will make more work, either because they make it impossible to get into cabinets when the doors are open or they make take you extra steps to unload the unit—or both.

Pictures 1, 2, and 3 show dishwashers in the same counter as the sink. These are bad enough because, even though it will be easy to load the dishwasher, unloading it will be a totally different issue, particularly into both upper and lower cupboards in the corners.

Pictures 4 and 5 are of dishwashers in the right-angle counter, where loading will mean dripping on the floor as well as having to turn and twist with each item going from the sink to the dishwasher.

But Pictures 6 and 7... dishwashers in the corner of a 90° counter. What absurdities! With the door open it keeps you from standing in front of about half the sink, it blocks the lower corner cabinet entirely and will make it virtually impossible to reach any upper cabinets behind it in the corner.

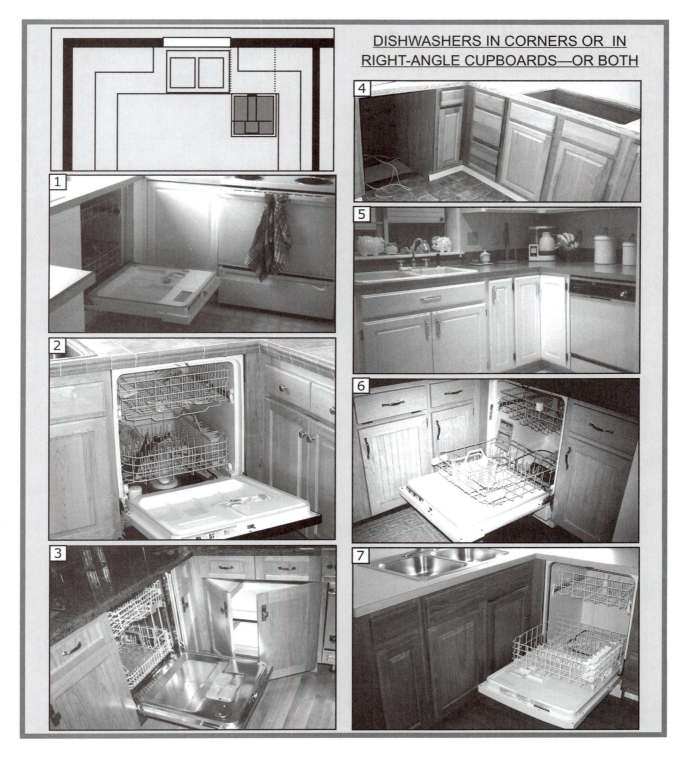

DISHWASHERS IN CORNERS OR IN RIGHT-ANGLE CUPBOARDS—OR BOTH

45-Degree Sinks

Anyone working in the kitchen appreciates lots of windows and light around the sink and the adjacent work areas. When the layout of the house permits, having the sink at 45° across a corner with windows on two sides is attractive and makes life in the kitchen more pleasant. There are a couple of precautions, however:

⇨ When the sink is set at 45 degrees across a corner, be careful not to have the dishwasher too close to the sink. If there is no space at all, an open dishwasher door will create a narrow corner in front of the sink that makes it difficult for you to even turn when you're loading the dishwasher. A spacing of 6 to 12 inches will solve the problem. Don't go more than 12 inches or it'll mean steps and dripping when loading the dishwasher. A picture earlier in the chapter shows how it should be done.

⇨ When a single door is used on the cabinet under the sink, the door should be hinged on the *same* side as the dishwasher, otherwise you will not be able to get under the sink with the dishwasher door open. Double cabinet doors, of course, do not have this problem.

The pictures on the next page show good, indifferent and bad.

Too close

The diagram is of a dishwasher right next to the sink and as you can see in Picture 1 there is simply not enough room to comfortably stand in front of the sink with the dishwasher door open.

Picture 2 shows a different problem. When the dishwasher door is open you cannot get under the sink to get soap or anything else. If the door were hinged on the other side it would be better but the door would then be between you and the open dishwasher. A pair of smaller cabinet doors as shown in Picture 3 is a better arrangement.

Good

The arrangement in Picture 3 is really what you'd like to have with possibly one exception. There is just enough separation between sink and dishwasher so that standing there when loading the dishwasher will be comfortable and you won't be dripping on the floor with wet dishes.

The exception is that the cabinet space between the sink and the dishwasher appears to be wasted. This would be a great place for a vertical cupboard to store trays and flat pans.

Well...

The arrangement in Picture 4 is marginal for two reasons:

⇨ The space between the dishwasher and the sink could be smaller which means that, while you can probably move wet dishes without taking a step, you will need something on the floor to catch the dripping. (And you'll need a flooring that can stand being damp over a period of time.)

⇨ There is no cupboard close to the dishwasher which means unloading it will be a bigger job than most people would like.

Finally

The last picture (Picture 5) is what happens when the designer is more interested in looks than in utility. The dishwasher is clearly too far from the sink and, while there is lots of light from the windows, putting dishes away will not be much fun with the lack of cupboards in the vicinity.

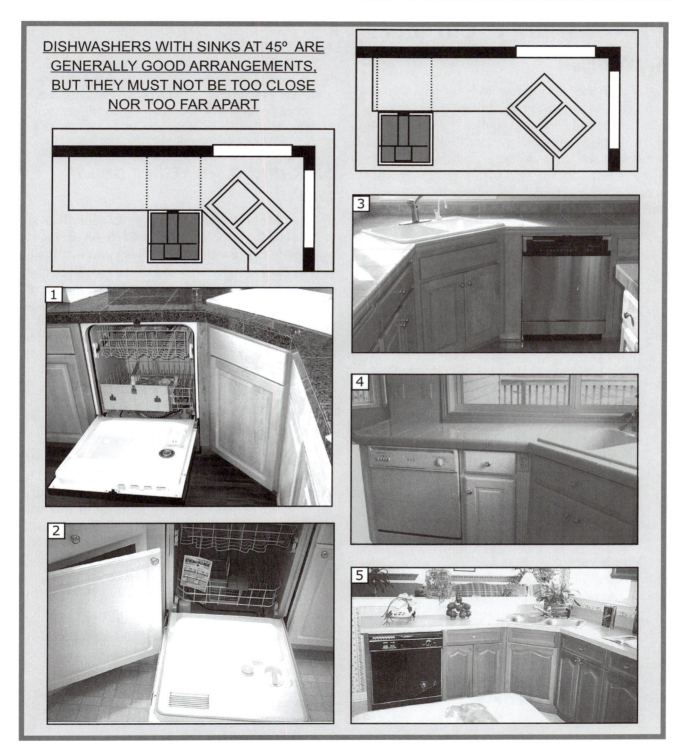

DISHWASHERS WITH SINKS AT 45º ARE GENERALLY GOOD ARRANGEMENTS, BUT THEY MUST NOT BE TOO CLOSE NOR TOO FAR APART

Dishwashers & Cabinets

Separation

One of the more annoying things a designer can do is to separate the cabinets from the dishwasher so that steps are required as each item is put away. Sometimes there is a single upper cabinet above the dishwasher and, in other designs, there is none at all. Two different arrangements account for most kitchens where this separation occurs:

> ➪ In one, there is a big window with the sink centered on the window and the dishwasher is placed on the side of the sink away from the cabinets. Sometimes this is needed to keep the dishwasher out of a corner and in others it's just a plain bad design. (As in Picture 1 on the next page.)

> ➪ In the second arrangement the sink and dishwasher are placed on a peninsula where a person using the sink can look across the family room or breakfast nook to a view or onto a golf course. (As in Picture 2.) There are better ways to take advantage of the view. If you don't want to take many extra steps unloading your dishwasher, avoid sinks and dishwashers on peninsulas unless there are cabinets over the peninsula.

A more subtly unfriendly arrangement is seen more often. Here there is only a single cupboard above the dishwasher. (Picture 3.) This is far better than none but still not enough to hold the dishes, glassware, cookware and silver used daily in a household. You'd like to have them all where you can reach them while standing beside the dishwasher when you're unloading it. In other words, most of the time it would be nice to un-load the dishwasher without having to haul things across the kitchen.

I was most impressed when visiting the home of a stepson and watching him standing beside the dishwasher and unloading it into the cupboards and cabinets that were right there. No steps. I haven't forgotten how friendly that arrangement can be. May you be so lucky.

Sink and dishwasher on an island

Another arrangement that is occasionally seen is to have the sink and dishwasher on an island where the cupboards and cabinets you want to be able to reach are right behind the island. Then dirty dishes are put on the island, processed in the sink and put into the dishwasher without a lot of steps. To unload the dishwasher, it's simply a matter of standing in one place, reaching down to get the dishes and turning to put them away behind you. No steps. (Picture 4.)

Space in Front of Dishwashers

Open dishwasher doors stick out 24 inches into the aisle. At least 18 inches should be left to get by the open door, more if possible. This means a minimum of 42 inches clearance in front of the dishwasher, preferably 48 inches. An island that's too close is the usual reason for this problem. (*See* Picture 5 and the drawing.)

A Note

Chapter 18 ties together the information in this chapter with that of the chapters in Section III to help you in your kitchen decisions.

THE LOCATION SHOULD MAKE IT EASY TO UNLOAD THE DISHWASHER.

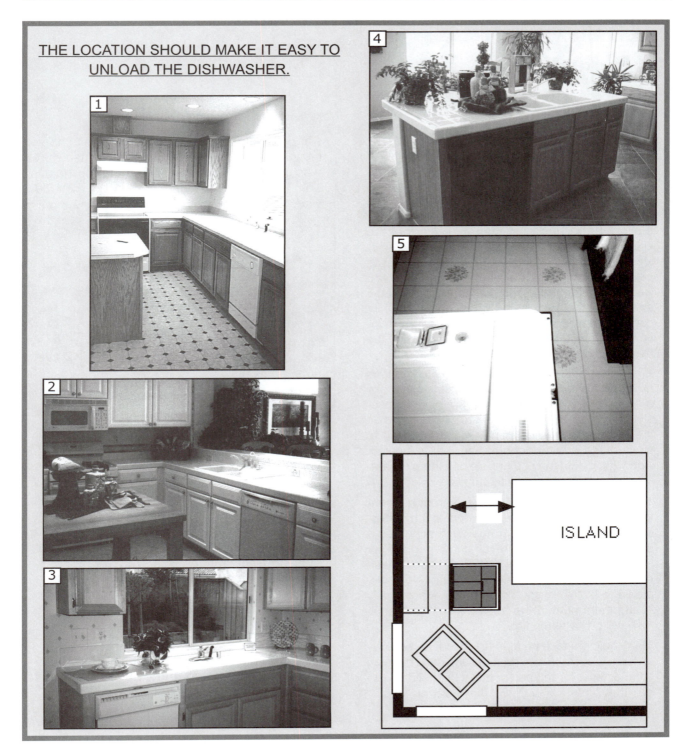

A Reflection

Dishwashers are an excellent example of the kinds of things you need to be alert for when you're considering a home. Certainly the designers, builders and salespeople know, or should know, that many dishwasher locations are inconvenient at best. (I'm reminded of an experience I had during a tour of homes several years ago. It was a spec house and the builder was at the house. After I had toured it, I stopped to talk to him. He asked me what I thought and I hesitated then told him that the kitchen layout had a shortcoming, the dishwasher was in a corner. He didn't have a clue what I was talking about. When I explained how difficult it would be to put dishes into the cupboards behind and above the dishwasher, I could see the light come on. It was something no one had ever mentioned before. I didn't follow up, I don't know if the next house he built was like this or not.)

The problem is that, like so many other things around a home, the builder's objective is to make a house that is saleable at as low a price as possible so it'll sell quickly. In their efforts to focus on these aspects they don't pay much attention to such things as where the dishwasher is located. And why should they? If people buy them regardless, there's no incentive to change.

You and I aren't going to stop this from happening. We can, however, make a dent in it by refusing to buy a house which has such things as a dishwasher located where it'll cause more work for anyone working in the kitchen. And don't hesitate to let the salesperson know what your displeasure is. When you do that, you're potentially hitting them right in the bank account and, that, they will pay attention to.

Many builders take pride in their work and *do* pay attention. But there are enough who don't that you should never forget, and don't let the builders forget, that it's YOUR MONEY that's paying for it.

MY FRUSTRATION

I had completely finished writing this chapter when I happened to look in a house that was under construction in my neighborhood. This is picture of what I saw. After over 10

Sink will go here   *Dishwasher goes here*

years of preaching about user friendliness and dishwashers in corners AND to this builder...it is throughly disgusting and discouraging about how little some designers and builders think about the homeuser—except for his money, of course.

This house's builder is a "master builder" and makes a good living at it. He is disdainful of anyone outside of his industry who suggests things could be better. The homeuser isn't his concern, the profit he makes is.

I'll keep trying...you do too. When they realize they're losing money because of this attitude, they'll change. Let's do it.

Chapter 15

Refrigerators

> *Nobody can do it for you.*
>
> Ralph Cordiner, CEO General Electric (1900- ?   )

In this chapter:

The refrigerator—and where it is placed —is another of the user-friendly considerations in a home's kitchen.

Here we look at the kinds and sizes of refrigerators and why location is so important. Illustrations are used to make it as easy we can for you to be able to look at a plan or to walk into a house and say "Aha, that's a good one" or "Look at that. It must have been designed by a man."

The location of the refrigerator in the kitchen is an important consideration in a user-friendly home because you should:

⇨ Not have to take unnecessary steps because of where it is.

⇨ Be able to open all the doors far enough that shelves and internal bins and trays can be pulled all the way out.

⇨ Not have to walk around an open door.

⇨ Be able to stand in front of the refrigerator, take things out of it and have a landing area on which to set them without moving your feet.

In many kitchens the refrigerator location does not meet these criteria, at least not for all refrigerator configurations. Refrigerators are not a minor cost item and when the day comes for you to sell the house, you will find people who will object to having to buy a new refrigerator if they buy your house. Which is why it is important to have a refrigerator location that is suitable for any refrigerator. And don't forget that you may want to update your own refrigerator someday and it should be feasible to change, for example, from a top-freezer or a bottom-freezer to a side-by-side model, or from a deep model to a thin one.

These considerations are the subject of this chapter. We start with a review of refrigerator configurations and sizes.

Considerations

There are several interrelated factors to consider with refrigerators in kitchens,

⇨ The refrigerator itself:

- size, both inside and outside
- the configuration—top freezer, side-by-side, or bottom freezer.
- how the doors swing

⇨ Its location:

- corners limit door opening
- convenient landing areas
- closeness to sink work area

Built-ins are usually side-by-side units but they may have separate freezers that are similar to the pull-out freezer of a bottom-freezer refrigerator.

A note re pictures: there are several pictures in this chapter showing good and bad ways to install refrigerators. Chapter 18 has more in conjunction with the rest of the kitchen.

Refrigerators sizes

When looking at refrigerators in appliance and home-improvement stores, one gets the definite impression that manufacturers try to outdo each other to make a unit that is a different size than any that has existed before. Finding the one to suit your needs will be a challenge.

As a point of reference, the dimensions given here are of ones we found. There are undoubtedly units beyond these but it is a starting place in getting the idea of what's out there.

⇨ Compact. Usually used for a bar which is not convenient to the main unit.

⇨ Small, "small dwelling" or "apartment". Usually about 14 cubic feet but may be down to 10.

⇨ Thin or "counter depth". Range from 18 to 24.6 cubic feet.

⇨ Deeper. Up to 29 cubic feet.

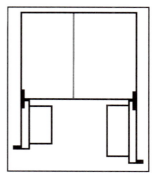

In this side-by-side example, the outside of the open doors line up with the outside of the box itself. This is the usual arrangement.

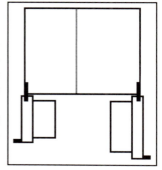

Some units are made larger by simply using thicker doors. The outsides of the open doors are wider than the box. Used with top- and bottom-freezer models also.

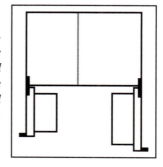

With a thin or counter-deep refrigerator the body isn't as deep and the internal space is smaller. Used with all models.

Heights range up to 72" with most of the full-size units being over 68". The higher units are used when the object is more interior space but they do make it more difficult for most people to see what's on that top shelf (or in the freezer if it's a top-freezer model.)

The height is important when you're looking at houses and want to keep your present refrigerator or when considering a new home or remodel and want to specify the size of the opening.

Colors

There are four common colors for refrigerators:

➪ White, the ubiquitous one,

➪ Bisque,

➪ Black,

➪ Stainless steel (*see* comments re this material in Chapter 18).

You may find combinations with one color on the body of the unit and a different one on the doors.

Shelving & bins

Wire and glass are two types of shelvingused in refrigerators,. The wire is needed in some units to have an open air flow to and from the condenser where it is cooled. It is another of the decisions that will help you decide which unit to get.

Shelves will sometimes be adjustable heightwise, sometimes not. Another functional consideration.

Bins at the bottom of the unit are meant to keep foods in them at a constant temperature. They are often marked for vegetable, meat, etc.

You should be able to get the bottom bin completely out of the unit so you can clean the bottom of the unit. This is true in both the food part of the refrigerator and in the bottom of the freezer for a side-by-side unit. When you're looking at units and you're not sure if those bins come out, check it for yourself.

Ice & water

Most side-by-side units have ice and water available through the front door. It is one of the attractive features of this configuration.

Bottom-freezers may or may not include icemakers. If they don't, you can usually get them as an add-on unit. They go inside the freezer unit and take away from the space there.

Filtered, chilled water is another add-on that you may be able to get for top-freezer and bottom-freezer units. Check it out when you're considering a unit.

Before the appearance of the side-by-side refrigerator, ice was always made in trays placed in the freezer, frozen and removed as needed. They are not very convenient but do get the job done. When there is no built-in ice freezer, it is still a way to go.

Doors

Doors have small shelves mounted on them which are considered part of the storage area. They can cause problems in some arrangements.

When doors don't open fully because of walls adjacent to a refrigerator, the shelves on the doors will be in the way when you need to pull out bins or shelves. And this limits access to what's inside. It also means that bins and shelves cannot be removed for cleaning because they hit the shelving on the doors. (Some units are made so that the door shelving doesn't interfere with the interior shelves or bins. They are usually inflexible in where shelves and bins can go. But it is a way out in an "emergency" such as having a house where the refrigerator is in a corner.)

In top-freezer and bottom-freezer models with doors you'll find that doors most often open on the right side of the unit. With some, the hinges are on the left side and with still others the hinges can be moved. In some kitchen arrangements you may need to be sure you get one that opens on the side that it needs to be on or one whose hinges can be moved. Otherwise you may find yourself walking around a door every time you use it. Side-by-side units have different considerations as discussed later.

Energy Star

The last site on our Internet Reference list for this chapter is the U.S. Environmental Protection Agency's Energy Star site[15H]. Here you'll find the criteria that a manufacturer must use to qualify. They say,

> ENERGY STAR qualified refrigerators require about half as much energy as a 10-year old models(sic). ENERGY STAR qualified refrigerators provide energy savings without sacrificing the features you want.

Since most, but not all, of refrigerators sold today meet the Energy Star criteria, you'll want to keep this in mind, too, when considering a unit.

Top-Freezer Models

In top-freezer models the freezer compartment is behind a hinged door the full width of the refrigerator. Both the freezer and fresh food doors swing from the same side. With deeper units, access to foods at the back of the freezer compart-

ment is not convenient both because it is at the top of the unit and of the shelf depth. If they have the size wanted, thin models are better where this may not be a problem.

An apartment-size, top-freezer refrigerator.

Another concern is that the bottom of the fresh food compartment may be so low that it becomes inconvenient to get anything from that part of the refrigerator, usually the vegetable bins. (A concern with side-by-side units as well.)

Bottom-Freezer Models

In bottom-mount models the freezer is under the fresh food section. It may be:

⇨ a full-width hinged door where, again, access to frozen foods is not very convenient or

⇨ a pull-out unit the full width of the refrigerator—the usual bottom-mount arrangement.

Our concerns here are the problems that can occur when the opening of doors is restricted—

A refrigerator with a top-freezer.

A refrigerator with a bottom-mount freezer.

both top-mount and bottom-mount models with doors have the same potential.

Side-by-Side Models

Generally, side-by-side are more expensive than top- or bottom-freezer units of the same sizes. The availability of cold water and ice through the door is an attractive feature and, when the frozen food is in bins that can be pulled out for access, side-by-side units are also more convenient to use—if they're located properly.

A large side-by-side refrigerator.

Refrigerator Location

There are three primary concerns in locating the refrigerator in the kitchen. They are summarized here and discussed in detail in Chapter 18 in conjunction with the layout of the rest of the kitchen:

⇨ **There should never be anything next to any refrigerator that restricts how far any door can open.** The usual culprit, altogether too common, is a corner.

⇨ There should be a landing area convenient to the refrigerator to set things going into or coming our of the unit.

⇨ The distance between the sink work area and the refrigerator should be a minimum with nothing such as an island in between.

The next two pages are pictures of refrigerators in houses and commentary about each of them.

Landing Areas

When you are standing in front of the refrigerator and putting things into or taking them out of it, you need a "landing area" that is within easy reach . The place to set things that works equally well for all types of units is counter space directly in front of the unit. For top-freezer models, counter space next to the latch side of the refrigerator also provides a good landing area.

To reach a landing area you should not have to reach around an open door and it's more convenient if you don't have to reach across the closed door of a side-by-side unit. From this we come to these conclusions:

⇨ It is better to have a landing area right in front of the refrigerator. This works well for any type of unit.

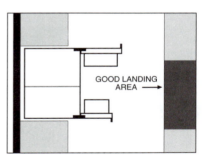

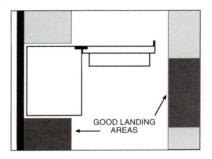

A good landing area makes it easier to use a refrigerator.

REFRIGERATORS IN CORNERS

Putting the refrigerator in a corner will cause a problem (with the exception of a short stub wall beside the refrigerator sometimes used for cosmetic reasons). When the doors won't open more than straight out (90°), you can pull any internal bins or shelves only part way out. (It's a real pain, we've got one.)

The graphics (opposite) deal with refrigerators in corners. As you can see there are a number of subleties—things which it is a good idea to remember when you're considering a house.

Photo 1

The corner location in this photo is a very common one you'll see in both plans and existing houses. As you can see from the drawings, it will always be a problem regardless of the refrigerator configuration.

Photo 2

In a model or open house this built-in refrigerator looks benign enough—until you try to open the right-hand door.

Photo 3

Here you see how the door on the fresh food side can open only straight out. Any shelves or drawers inside cannot be pulled out because of the storage units on the door. A corner is simply no place to have any refrigerator.

Photo 4

When the wall is on the left side of the refrigerator, the problem is with the freezer compartment door. (This is my house, it was one of the driving considerations that led to "Build It Right!")

Photo 5

When it's tucked into a corner with the counter instead of the door, it's no better. The freezer door won't open past 90° and it also blocks the lower cabinets so that they are virtually inaccessible.

Photo 6

Here you can see the refrigerator sticking out into the doorway. For a side-by-side this would be OK functionally—if you don't mind something blocking the door. For a top- or bottom-freezer, like this one, it won't work. (Doorways are typically 30" or 32" wide. Refrigerator doors are 31" to 34". The door will hit the jamb on the other side of the doorway.)

REFRIGERATORS IN CORNERS

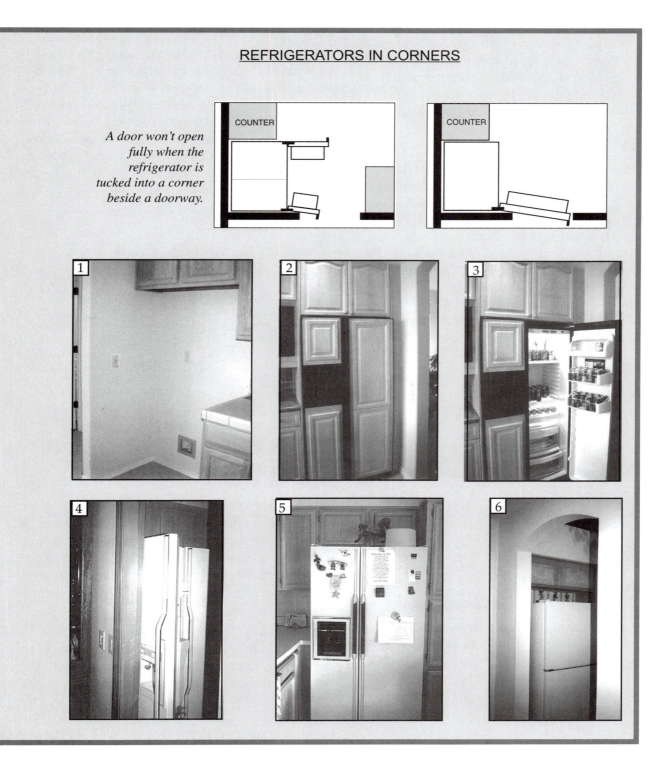

A door won't open fully when the refrigerator is tucked into a corner beside a doorway.

⇨ If the kitchen layout doesn't permit a landing area in front, a top-freezer or bottom-freezer unit will be more convenient to work with. (Of course you have to trade this off against the overall convenience of the side-by-side unit.)

Screening walls

When a refrigerator is turned so that its side is beside the doorway, a screening wall is sometimes added beside it to give a more finished appearance. It is strictly cosmetic but, if not done properly, it *can* interfere with function. If the wall is too long it will stop a door from opening. And particular care needs to be exercised if one of the thin models *may* be used because the wall may have been designed for a regular model and will be too long for the thin unit. A good length for the screening wall beside a refrigerator is 25 inches.

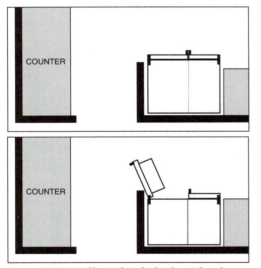

A screening wall used to hide the side of a regular refrigerator (top) may not be suitable for a thin one (bottom).

Door clearance

When an island or other counter is too close to the front of a refrigerator, it forces the use of a side-by-side model with its smaller doors. This is generally not a good design because not everyone will be happy about this constraint when resale time comes. A good distance is at least 64 inches from the wall behind the refrigerator to the island or counter in front of it. Of course, this distance can be less for a thin side-by-side.

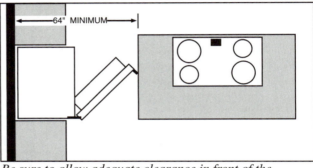

Be sure to allow adequate clearance in front of the refrigerator.

Other Things to Watch For

Height

Take care to check out the height of the space for the refrigerator. As noted earlier, there is a wide range of heights, even for comparably sized units. If the cabinets are made for a 66-3/4" high refrigerator then there will be real problems if someone comes along with a 70-1/2" unit.

Water

Most plumbers use a small recessed metal or plastic box behind the refrigerator in which to terminate the pipe for the refrigerator's ice-maker water. This makes the connection more or less inside the wall but in one tract I visited the connector for the water is in front of the wall so that the refrigerator had to be put several unnecessary and wasted inches farther out into the room. Be sure to insist on the recessed arrangement. (You can see one in Photo #1 on page 205.)

Refrigerator depth

It is common practice in kitchen floor plans to show the refrigerator about the same depth as the adjacent counters. This can be misleading since refrigerators are frequently much deeper than the 24 or 25 inches of a counter. For a 27 cu. ft. unit,

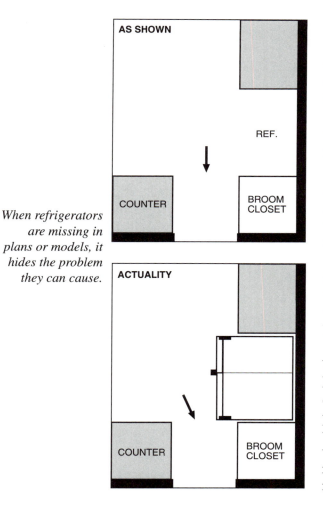

When refrigerators are missing in plans or models, it hides the problem they can cause.

the overall depth (not including the door handles) is well over 31 inches, almost 8 inches in front of the counter. Sometimes this causes no problems but in others the refrigerator may be in the way or it may look out of place. Or a door may hit a counter, particularly with a top-freezer or bottom-freezer unit.

Use your measuring tape when looking at models and your ruler when checking plans. (If plans don't have dimensions, remember that standard counters are 24 inches deep.)

Re Internet References

The list Internet references for this chapter are for your convenience. These sites are of manufacturers or sellers of refrigerators. **We do not endorse any site nor the products they're selling there**.

To help you in using the sites, we have a few comments to make, some general, some specific to the site **at the time we visited it**.

The Sears' site[15A] was by far the most useful for someone trying to find a refrigerator to fit the dimensions which exist in a kitchen. The utility of the site is enhanced because of the number of manufacturer's they stock—nine at the time of our visit. To get to the refrigerator page, use the URL given in the references then in the "Appliances" category click on "Refrigeration." There you'll find a list of criteria, including sizes, which will help you narrow down your options.

Like Sears, Lowe's is a retailer carrying a number of brands. Unfortunately, on their site[15G], they haven't chosen to even give you the dimensions of the units which makes it virtually useless when you're looking for a refrigerator. (At the time we visited their site there was evidently something wrong with their server. We were unable to get more details than those given in their general listings.)

Five other sites are manufacturers [15B, 15C, 15D, 15E, 15F]. None of them enable you to sort or choose a unit by size. And some don't even give the sizes.

One last note. When you're considering how large a refrigerator your kitchen can accomodate or when you're trying to figure out how much space to leave for your refrigerator, remember that the heat that it takes from inside the unit must go someplace. There are coils at the bottom of the unit that are cooled by air that naturally moves past them. Leave a little space on both sides of the unit to allow this natural convection to happen. Crowded up against a wall isn't good.

And, above all, get a unit or choose a space that is user-friendly. Unopenable doors are for the ignorant—don't be one.

Chapter 16

Cabinets

[Common sense] is the best sense I know of.

Lord Chesterfield, British statesman, diplomat and wit (1694 - 1773)

In this chapter:

Cabinets are an important part of how a kitchen looks and, of course, of how user-friendly it is. Here we look at a number of the functional aspects, things which people often don't think about when they're deciding what's good and not so good for cabinets in the home they'll be living in. (And, surprise, there are a few aesthetic things here, too.)

As you go through the chapter you'll see a wide variety of cabinets, both in looks and in function. We picture a number of them to give you some idea of what's available. And, please, remember that these here are not, by any matter of means, all that you may or can find.

There are a number of manufacturers of pre-manufactured cabinets (ones made in a factory, not in the local cabinetmaker's shop) and theirs is a highly competitive business with all of them striving to get a bigger share of the on-going market for cabinets. And there are the made-to-order cabinets done by local tradesmen who often have some pet ideas of their own—or who have to design and make a cabinet to fit an unusual kitchen layout.

Cabinets come in a wide variety of looks. They are the dominant feature of a kitchen and set the tone for the whole house. Functionally, there are two different cabinet styles, face-frame and European or box. Both are discussed below in detail..

With these go a wide variety of door hinges which have both functional and aesthetic differences. These all become an integral part of how the kitchen works and looks.

Among the things you'll want to watch for:

⇨ The convenience of the storage space. Space which is hard to reach or which has the potential for gouging your arm is not that useful.

Display rooms at cabinetmakers and kitchen centers are good places to look at examples of cabinet styles and exteriors.

⇨ The usable storage space. All cabinet and hinge arrangements have space which cannot be used. Some are much worse than others.

⇨ The finish on the surfaces. This is a longevity consideration as well as one of looks.

Cabinet Styles

There are two distinctly differ-ent cabinet styles:

⇨ Western or face-frame. In these cabinets the frame mounts on the front or face of the cabinet box. This is both a functional and an aesthetic consider-ation. These are the more

Hinges mount on the frame of face-frame cabinet.

common ones you'll see in newer homes as well as older ones.

⇨ European, frameless, box or full-overlay. The frame on the front is absent in these cabinets so that the open cabinet looks like a box from the front. The hinges mount on the inside of the cabinet in

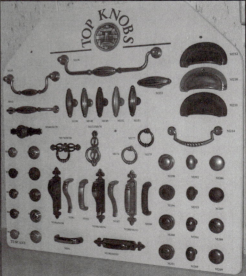

The Euro-style hinge is mounted on the inside of the box cabinet. Like other simple hidden hinges, the doors open only about 110º, as shown here.

The variety of door and drawer pulls is even greater than of cabinet exteriors. From a display by Top Knobs.

lieu of the face frame. This is a relatively newcomer to the cabinet scene and won't be found in older homes.

Exteriors

Cabinet exteriors offer many choices. The first decision a buyer has to make is whether to get a wood (natural) finish or a painted one. If a wood finish is chosen, you need to choose the type of wood as well as the finish color. Generally, cabinets throughout the house are given the same finish but it is a matter of personal preference. Then there is the question of design, raised surface or flat. The options seem endless. But these are generally aesthetic decisions.

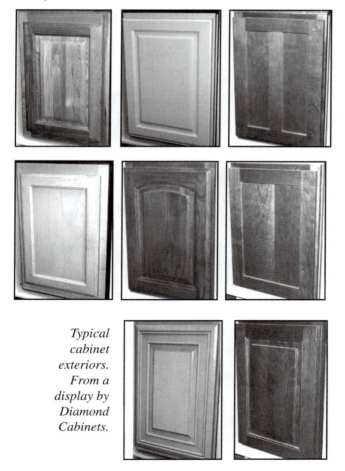

Typical cabinet exteriors. From a display by Diamond Cabinets.

Cabinet exteriors range from plain to decorative. To open the doors you may prefer finger grooves, which get soiled and may need refinishing sooner or later, or you can choose from a variety of hardware pulls.

Cabinet hinges

Today most cabinets, both face-frame and European, use hidden hinges where the hinge isn't visible when the door is closed. Not that many years ago cabinets were all face-frame and the part of the hinge that mounted to the face frame was clearly visible when the door was closed. This visible part of the hinge was made decorative and, in its own way, added to the character of the kitchen. The choice of styles for hinges is tremendous[16A] with wide differences both in looks and in how they mount.

Most of the variations in hinges today are in those used on face-frame cabinets. These are virtually all hidden hinges as you can see if you go to a show room where you simply do not see a hinge in sight. From your perspective as the home user, there are three important factors:

⇨ Opening. Unlike the older visible hinges, doors using the standard hidden hinge do not open wide, the doors going only slightly past straight out. There are hidden hinges for special applications that do open farther than this but they are complex both in appearance and operation and they are significantly more expensive.

⇨ Clearance. Hinges, by their nature, are visible in the opening when the door is open. The apperance of some of them are worse than others while one, in particular, sticks into the cabinet space so as to be a physical peril to the person using the cabinet. More on this one later.

⇨ <u>Self-closing</u>. A characteristic of hinges that you may not think of is that some of them are "self-closing"—they close the door for you. With these you simply close the door most of the way and the hinge takes over. For most people this is an appreciated nicety. Don't get any other kind.

The following discussions look at, first, face-frame cabinets with their several hinge variations and then at the European-style or full-overlay cabinet.

Face-Frame Cabinets

The face-frame on a western-style cabinet is clearly visible around the top and side edges of closed doors. When two cupboards are adjacent, a common face-frame piece is used. The width of the face frame varies from one cabinet to another, depending upon the design and manufacturer.

A face-frame cabinet with visible hinges. This one has pull-out shelves. Note the spacing, the face frame, between the doors on adjacent cupboards.

Hinge options

Types of hinges for face-frame cabinets include:

⇨ Traditional visible hinge. Doors open a full 180°.

⇨ Small hidden hinge. Doors open just a little pass straight out.

⇨ Larger hidden hinge. A user-unfriendly adaptation of the hinge used on European cabinets. Doors open just a little past straight out.

⇨ Knife hinge. A hidden hinge that gets away from a major disadvantage of other hidden hinges. It lets the door open a full 180°.

⇨ Soss hinge[16I]. Seldom used for kitchen cabinets, it is a hidden hinge that truly disappears when the door is closed. It, too, lets the door open a full 180°.

Cabinets with traditional hinges

With western- style cabinets, traditional hinge units are visible from the front of the cabinet along the edges of the doors. These hinges are made of thin pieces of metal that mount to the door and to the side of the face frame. Doors open a full 180 degrees and, when open, the cabinet opening is obstructed only by the face frame and the thin metal of the hinge mounting

One of the hundreds of variations of traditional hinges for face-frame cabinets.

The space just behind the face frame is useful for storage when shelves don't pull out. With pull-out shelves, however, this space is lost because shelves must be narrower than the inside of the face frame.

Hinges derived from the European hinge

Most new face-frame cabinets use hidden hinges. This is an anesthetic consideration—they certainly don't work any better than the older, traditional ones. And cabinetmakers like them, too. With the older hinges care has to be taken in mounting the hinge on the door and the cabinet so the door closes squarely. The newer hinges have adjustments that make it easier and quicker to make the cabinet and to mount the doors.

With these hinges the door part of the hinge fits into a round shallow hole (the "cup") cut into the inside of the door.

The hinge pin, the pin around which the door rotates, is inside the cup. As a result of this construction:

⇨ Doors don't open much past straight out (95 to 115 degrees), and

⇨ When open, the inside edge of an open door may not clear the cabinet opening very effectively reducing the effective width even more.

There is another drawback to all hinges which do not open much past straight out—whether used in box or face-frame cabinets. Even a cursory examination shows that, when they are open as far as they'll go, there's so much leverage at the outside edge of a door that a small child could ruin a door by pushing it. An adult who accidently bumps an open door can also cause damage. For cabinets above a kitchen counter this is more of a nuisance than a problem, but for base cabinets, pantries, or broom closet doors that go all the way to the floor, it is always a concern, particularly with a growing family.

The smaller hinge

This is the one you'll usually see in showrooms and is the one used by makers of pre-manufactured cabinets. By clamping onto the face frame (some versions have two mounting screws, some one), it does not intrude into the storage space.

This hinge clamps on the face frame and is not in the way when the door is open.

A somewhat different smaller hinge (below) has more adjustability and makes it easier for the cabinetmaker to do his job of getting things lined up. This hinge does stick back into the storage area about 1/4-inch which is not enough to be a concern.

Another small hinge which is easier to adjust than the one above.

The larger hinge

The larger European hinge adaption for face-frame cabinets also mounts on the face frame but it sticks way back into the storage space. The real disaster occurs when it's used on a corner cabinet. This, of necessity, results in having to mount the hinge on the edge of the cabinet frame. Now the hinge juts back into an otherwise wide open cabinet space inviting you to gouge your hand or arm if you're trying to get something out of the end of the cabinet.

A European style hinge mounted on a face frame. The end of the hinge sticks back into the cabinet.

One way around the gouge danger is to put a piece of lumber in the cabinet on which to mount the hinges. Now the gouge threat is gone but that part of the cabinet is blocked from view and made virtually useless. And the shelf must be made narrower...something that in itself is not advantageous.

One of the problems with the European-style hinge when it's used on face-frame corner cabinets is that it sticks back in the way—with or without a board to mount it on.

There are two reasons that this hinge is often used...or misused:

➪ The two parts of the hinge, the part that is screwed to the door and the part that's screwed to the cabinet snap together making it easier to remove the doors during installation. (But how many times a year do *you* remove your cabinet doors?)

➪ The hinge is easily adjusted after installation: up-down, right-left, and in-out.

It's easy to see why cabinetmakers love them—and who cares about the homeuser who has to dodge around them?

And don't you believe it when, as one builder who had put these in the house he was selling, told me, "You should like these because they're stronger." Stronger, yes, but who needs it? He just got them cheaper.

Why?

You may ask why these hinges, used in this obviously inappropriate way, are found in so many houses? It comes from the way a house is built. Neither the designer nor the builder is a cabinet designer. His job is to choose a plan—or take one a customer has chosen—and see that it gets built. He subcontracts virtually all of the actual work, framing, plumbing, HVAC, etc., and, of course, the cabinet work. He chooses a cabinetmaker who is trustworthy and does good work at a reasonable price. Then, once he's chosen the subcontractor, he trusts him to do a good job. Watching the kind of hinge that is used in the cabinets is not on the builder's list of concerns.

The subcontractor is then free to chose the hinge that works best for him, one that's easy to install and adjust. And, if his customer, the builder, is satisfied, he has no incentive to change anything. Other cabinetmakers, seeing what satisfies builders, then do the same thing and a custom is established.

Earlier it was commented that *none* of the cabinets of the dozens found in home-improvement local showrooms, like Lowe's and Home Depot, used this inappropriate hinge. These are all pre-manufactured cabinets and those manufacturers are looking for the lowest price, acceptable product. Their business is, in its own way, much more competitive than the subcontractors working for a builder. If the pre-manufactured cabinetmaker doesn't make it with the home-improvement store customer, he's out of business. If the homebuilder has ill-advised hinges in his cabinets: (1) he'll probably sell the house anyway, it's not a make or break thing and (2) potential customers are unlikely to tell him or his sales agents that they don't like the hinges—if they even know that things could be better. In the overall it is, indeed, a relatively small thing—until they get into your house, of course.

The knife hinge

Used only on face-frame cabinets, the knife hinge has a notch cut in the edge of the door where the hinge is. This arrangement lets the door open fully while still being hidden. (In some cabinets with these hinges, the notch *is* visible from the front. Done properly, it should not be.) This hinge

is invisible, it lets the door open fully, and it does not take up valuable space that may be needed for pull out shelves in deep cabinets. Because of its construction it looks

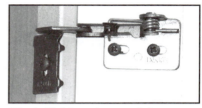

The knife hinge is one of the original hidden hinges for face-frame cabinets. It is disliked by cabinetmakers and is no longer popular.

flimsy (particularly when compared with the Mac-truck appearance of the European hinge) and cheap. Hence there is resistance to using it in expensive cabinets—even though it has functional advantages. (*And a cabinetmaker told me he hates them because they are very difficult to install.*)

The Soss hinge

Used in commercial applications (*I saw my first one on a cruise ship*) this hidden hinge for face-frame applications

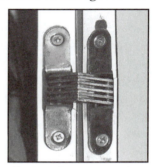

The Soss hinge is another truly hidden hinge that lets doors open 180°.

allows the door to open a full 180°[16H]. It is meant for cabinets in which the closed door and the frame

A face-frame cabinet with hidden hinges and pull-out shelves. This is as far open as these doors go. Note the phony "center mullion" connected to the left-hand door. This is strictly a matter of looks. The doors could have been made wide enough to meet without the pseudo-mullion. Our guess—this is probably a cost-driven approach.

are flush, i.e., where the door does not close over the frame. This is a concept that is totally different than we see in today's cabinets and cupboards. It is used significantly more outside of the U.S. than in. It is more expensive than the other styles of hinges. And any misalignment is clearly evident.

European-Style, a.k.a. Box or Full-Overlay Cabinets

Without the face frame on which to mount doors, the box cabinet differs in several ways from the face-frame design. Doors are mounted with hinges that mount directly to the insides of the cabinet behind the doors. The hinges are hidden and the doors don't swing clear of the cabinet opening. This is a potential problem for pull-out shelves—the same as with face-frame cabinets with hidden hinges.

With box cabinets the doors must be adjusted carefully both for proper operation and for appearance. (With the doors right next to each other on both sides any misalignment is obvious.) Adjustment is accomplished by using a hinge that mounts on the inside of the cabinet wall and is easily adjustable sideways, in-out, and up-down. This is the European-style hinge.

The hinge sticks back about two inches into the cabinet with feet that mount to the wall. While invisible when the doors are closed, they are large and obvious when the doors are open.

Having the door hinge like this is necessary so adjacent doors on a cabinet don't hit each other (remember that without a face frame, doors on adjacent cupboards are themselves right next to each other).

Because the hinge mounts on the inside of the cabinet wall and open doors and hinges do not clear the opening, pull-out shelves in European-style cabinets have the same problem as face-frame cabinets—the useful shelf width is a little less than the inside width of the cabinet.

When you're deciding about cabinets, remember that "new" and "in" aren't necessarily better. The older face-frame cabinets may well be the best for you—they are certainly more traditional. When used with pull-out shelves, a cabinet with a

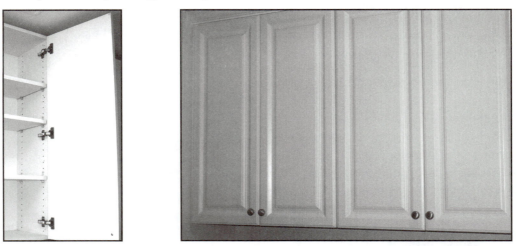

Box cabinets are characterized by the absence of a face frame. The hinge is fastened to the inside wall of the cabinet. Doors on adjacent cabinets do not need a space between them. They are almost touching. The lack of face frame also gives a clearer access to anything on the end of a shelf.

minimum-width face frame is optimal for maximizing the available space. Unfortunately, they will give your house a dated look, something that may be a problem when it's time to sell it—or who knows what the "in" thing will be then?

There are "double-jointed" versions of this hinge that do let doors open all the way. These are larger and even less attractive than the normal European-style hinge—but they are hidden (as

This more complex hinge available for European-style cabinets allows doors to open a full 180°. They are also used where there are lazy Susans.

long as the doors are closed) and they do let the doors swing open. Because they are more complex they are also more expensive. They are used in places where there are special requirements, such as corner openings for lazy Susans.

Center Mullions

Some cabinets have a piece of wood, called a center mullion (pronounced "mull yun"), mounted vertically up the center of the front opening. The cabinet doors close against this mullion. This design is deadly to the use of pull-out shelves because it means you end up with two much smaller shelves. The mullions are in the way even without pull outs. Except in very wide cabinets, center mullions are used for cosmetic, not practical, reasons. If you're planning on pull-out shelves either initially or you plan to add them in the future, DO NOT choose a cabinet design with a center mullion.

A center mullion is used with the style of face-frame cabinets whose double doors don't meet.

Other designs handle wider openings without a mullion.

Center mullions don't go with pull-out shelves. A builder who knows his stuff simply wouldn't let the cabinetmaker put this in his house.

Corner Cabinets

In corners of kitchen cabinets there will often be locations where fixed shelves leave areas that are almost inaccessible. There are four options:

⇨ Live with it (and watch out for the ugly Euro-style hinges discussed earlier).

⇨ Backside doors.

⇨ Lazy Susans.

⇨ Big doors.

Backside doors

When the backside of the corner cabinet is accessible it may be possible to put a cabinet door there so that things stored in the corner can be reached. This area is not as convenient to the kitchen's working area but it's a whole lot better than a deep corner. It is a place to store things you don't have to get to very often.

This backside door makes the corner accessible. Useful for storage of items not needed on a daily basis.

Lazy Susans

While more expensive than fixed shelves, lazy Susans end up providing more useful shelf space. They are available for below- the-counter cabinets in a number of different styles. (*See* photos on the next page.)

A potential problem with lazy Susans is that if something falls off of the back of a shelf it becomes necessary to empty the bottom shelf to be able to reach back in there and retrieve the fallen item. A well-made lazy Susan has a curved piece of wood behind it that eliminates the empty space where things could drop. It is a highly desirable feature for both 90° and 45° corners.

A lazy Susan in an upper corner cabinet. It's small and that top shelf is a long reach from the floor—but it's still more accessible than without the lazy Susan.

Lazy Susans can also be used in the upper cabinets in kitchens although they're not as popular because the shelves aren't as deep and there is less need for a shelf that turns.

Big doors

An alternative to a lazy Susan in the corner is to have a door that is hinged in the middle with one half of the door along each side of the corner. It's like the door in the right-hand lazy Susans in the photos opposite except that the door is bigger. The door then opens up nicely to give reasonable access to the shelves all the way back into the corner. The advantages here are:

⇨ No space is lost from putting a round peg (the lazy Susan) into a square hole (the cabinet corner). All the space can be used albeit that an item farthest from the door is not as accessible as it would be with a lazy Susan. (There is 20 percent less room on a lazy Susan than on a shelf using the same space.)

⇨ There is no problem with things falling off behind the lazy Susan.

⇨ It's less expensive.

The disadvantage is what led to the lazy Susan in the first place, it's just a long reach to the back of under-the-counter shelves.

And don't forget that to use this approach, it is necessary that the opening be large when the doors

LAZY SUSANS

Lazy Susans bring accessibility to corner cupboards. Here are four different implementations.

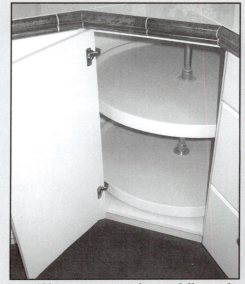

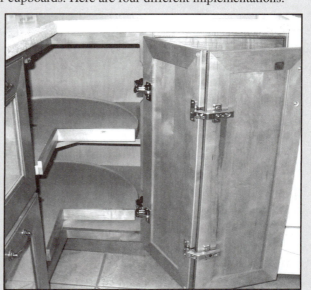

In a 45° corner you can have a full-round lazy Susan with a single door.

In a 90° corner this choice is a 3/4-round lazy Susan. This takes a two-part, folding door.

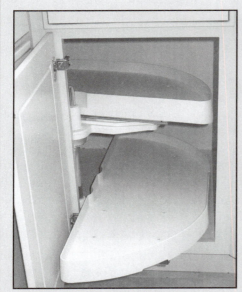

When there is a single door to access the 90° corner, you only get a 1/2- round lazy Susan

Like the one above except that there is a curved wall behind the lazy Susan that keeps things from falling off.

are opened (larger than needed with a lazy Susan). A single door on one side of the corner won't do it. There are attractive arrangements where the door and the shelves inside are curved and no special hinges are required to open the door fully.

Be careful of door arrangements, whether for lazy Susans or just shelves in the corner, which involve two separate doors rather than one hinged one. While less expensive, these require that you open and close both doors one after the other. They are not as convenient.

Soffits

Should the cabinets go all the way to the ceiling? If not, should the space above them (the soffits) be boxed in? There are several things to consider:

➪ Some folks like to have the space above the cabinets as a place to display knick-

These soffits are open, ready to be used or left open.

Here the soffit is used to show off whatever the homeowner wants.

These soffits were closed in. No dust catchers here.

knacks. Others consider it a dust catcher and prefer that soffits be boxed in.

➪ When the soffits are boxed in, differently colored paint or wall paper is sometimes used on the wallboard above the cabinets to add a decorative or festive touch to the kitchen.

➪ A consideration with cabinets that go to the ceiling, i.e. no soffits, is that the top shelves are useful only for storing things you almost never need, because you have to use a chair or a ladder to get to them.

➪ Don't forget the vent for the stovetop exhaust fan. If the exhaust system is an updraft unit, it usually vents through a duct going up through the ceiling. This duct work will need to be covered up, either by boxing it in or hiding it with tall cabinets. If the system vents through a wall, there is obviously no duct that needs covering up. (But as a matter of good practice, ducts should be straight without bends to go through walls. *See* Chapter 17.)

Tall Cabinet Doors

Here's a word of caution about very tall cabinets: wood warps and twists. Cabinet doors are no exception and, when they're warped, they are apt to rattle or bang when you close them—and gaping doors are not attractive either. Tall doors are more likely to do this than shorter ones. This problem has been seen in many tracts as well as in custom and spec homes in all price ranges.

Some cabinet manufacturers add stiffeners to the inside of tall cabinet doors. These will reduce warping but not twisting. Catches can help keep the door straight when it's closed.

By making this tall cabinet door of serveral pieces of wood, it is less likely to warp. Look closely and you can see the magnetic catches at top and bottom. These, together with four self-closing hinges which close the door firmly, insure it doesn't gape when it's shut.

Cabinet Interiors

Particleboard

Particleboard is used in lower-end cabinets. If the cabinets are not to be painted, two options are available:

➤ A wood grain is printed on the surface.

➤ A thin layer of wood is laminated to the particleboard. For painted cabinets this isn't necessary and the paint is applied directly to the particleboard.

Most people cover particleboard shelves with a thin plastic sheet or even vinyl linoleum to give a surface that can be easily cleaned and maintained. With better-quality cabinets this isn't necessary.

A precaution with particleboard. It will absorb water and disintegrate. This is a particular problem under sinks but may also happen over time when undried glasses and dishes are set on it if there is no protective covering.

Melamine[16J]

Plastic laminate (melamine) is popular for the insides of cabinets and drawers because of its resistance to wear and its ease of cleaning. The basic plastic is the same material used in laminate countertops and is glued directly onto the particleboard.

Some cabinetmakers will paint the shelf edges which doesn't do a particularly good job of covering the particleboard. Others use a vinyl strip that's attached to the shelf.

Usually the plastic laminate is white but colors and even patterns are available. Besides the tough, easy-to-clean aspects of plastic laminate, it is popular with cabinetmakers because it is less expensive than wood and doesn't have to be finished as wood does.

The edges of melamine-clad shelves and interiors should be smooth and clean. In cheap cabinets the edges may look like they had been cut with a hatchet.

Wood

Finished wood is found in better cabinets and drawer interiors. Good finishes on interior wood surfaces can be quite durable while poor finishes will stain, become dirty, and be difficult to keep clean. Well-made and finished wooden interiors will always have a richness in appearance that's not possible with plastic.

Backs

How the backs of cabinets are handled speaks loads about their quality. Cheap cabinets won't have a back. They'll have nailing strips for screwing to the wall and that's all. The wallboard behind the cabinets is exposed and the whole arrangement looks like it is—cheap. Better cabinets will be backed with the same material as the rest of the interior: wood or melamine. Look for the joints where the cabinet back and the sides meet. In well-made cabinets this joint will be smooth and tight. Sloppily-made cabinets may show definite, unattractive gaps.

Mountings

The nailing strip used to hang cabinets from a back wall is typically wood, plywood, or melamine-coated particle board. In good cabinets the material will have the same surface as the cabinet back and walls so that it matches the rest of the cabinet interior. Particularly for the melamine-coated particle board, this may result in a visible unfinished edge on the nailing strip that should be covered or painted to match the melamine but sometimes is not. The mounting screws used in better cabinets are not visible but are covered by special plastic buttons. (These are inexpensive and easy to use. Good cabinetmakers put them in place when the cabinets are installed. The who-cares installers don't bother. Actually it's something you can do yourself but shouldn't have to.)

Shelves

In pantries and in other cabinets, shelves may be adjustable up and down, they may be pull out, or they may be fixed in place. When shelves are deep, typically 22 to 24 inches, articles in the back of them are difficult to reach. In these cases, pull-out shelves make a lot of sense. And shelves that are adjustable up and down, whether pull-out or not, also make a lot of sense. (It's not hard to make pull-out shelves adjustable but to cabinetmakers they're an additional cost item.)

Fixed shelves

In some parts of the country you'll find it's common practice to make the shelf in lower cupboards some 6 inches shallower than the depth of the cabi-

net. The front of the shelf is then that much back from the front. This makes things at the back of the cabinet easier to reach on both shelves. The down side is that there is just plain less storage area on that shelf.

Recessed shelves, like this one, make the cabinet have a lot less storage area.

In the earlier discussion about the European hinge used on face-frame cabinets a photo was shown where the hinge is mounted on a piece of board that sticks back into the cabinet, requiring a recessed shelf, wanted or not.

Pull-out shelves

The amount of actual storage space is reduced when shelves are made pull-out because of the room taken by the slide hardware. However, the increased accessibility to the back of deep shelves will usually more than make up for the reduction in shelf width. To say nothing of the convenience.

And of course, there should be no center mullions when there are pull-out shelves.

Watch for pull-out shelves in which the front of the hardware used with pull-out shelf hardware is not covered. Regardless of how careful you are, sooner or later someone will pull out a shelf without fully opening the cabinet doors. When the front of the pull-out sliders is left uncovered, this will re-

Where an improperly made sliding drawer gouged the door.

sult in gouging the interior finish of a partly-opened door. Some cabinetmakers put a piece of plastic in front of the hardware so that the plastic hits the door first, virtually eliminating the problem. The usual arrangement has the front of the shelf extending out to cover the hardware. But some custom cabinetmakers aren't up to speed on these things. (This problem was seen on both coasts. It's not common but it does happen.)

The simplest pull-out design is just the shelf with slides mounted on each side. These have no sides or backs. Then there are those with fronts, sides, and backs several inches high, looking more like a parts bin in a hardware store than a shelf. These are sometimes called trays or baskets. Unless someone is expected to slam them around, there seems little reason for other than minimal front, side and back pieces, if any at all. Such pieces take away from the space available for storage as well as add to the cost. But, again, personal preference should be the determining factor. If you have a choice, get what satisfies you.

This pull-out shelf was added by the home user. Note that the original up-down shelf adjustments have been utilized. Note, too, that the shelf only has a front on it, no sides and no back. This works just fine.

While pull-out shelves can usually be added to an existing cabinet, this is not always the case. In some house designs the cabinets are irregularly shaped, making pull-out shelves impossible. Since these are usually deep cupboards, the homeusers are forever saddled with a large amount of virtually unusable cabinet space.

Drawers

Because cabinet drawers by themselves are similar to uncovered boxes, they are often referred to as drawer boxes.

The sides of drawer boxes may be connected to the fronts and backs of the drawers in two different ways. In one, the pieces are dovetailed, i.e., they are cut and grooved so that they intermesh at the corners. In the other, the pieces are simply

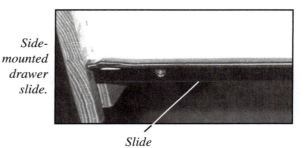

Side-mounted drawer slide.

Slide

butted and then stapled, nailed, or screwed. In all cases the pieces are glued. Dovetailing is "better" in that it has a more hand-crafted look and is more expensive. Because of the glue, both approaches are more than sturdy enough for cabinet drawers. In upscale houses, expect dovetailed drawer boxes; in starter homes expect stapled pieces. It's a matter of cost and taste. Utility doesn't enter into it. (Dove tailing is used only with wood, not with melamine or particleboard.)

Older drawers will use slides mounted on the sides of the drawer. These are quite visible when the drawer is opened. These usually have a "bump" next to the front of the drawer. Which is the equivalent of the self-closing spring on hinges—when you push the drawer almost all of the way closed, it'll finish the closing itself.

Sometimes you may find a single slide centered under the drawer. This is less expensive and usually doesn't operate quite as smoothly as the side-mounted slides.

A newcomer on the scene is a more sophisticated bottom slide which closes the front of the drawer squarely with the front of the cabinet even though the drawer itself or the cabinet may not be square. It's a cabinetmaker's helper.

No Slammers

Or they might be called "slam away." There are a number of little gadgets on the market that make it so you cannot slam a cabinet door. They catch the door just before it hits the face frame and makes it close gently. Similar items are also used on drawers so you cannot slam them shut.

Recycling Bins

A trend in cabinetry for our environmentally conscious society is to have built-in recycling bins. They are a convenient amenity if you have room. And should be put reasonably close to the working area around the sink. A person shouldn't have to walk across the room to use it.

These little extras may appeal to you. Inevitably they will be extra maintenance with time.

Finger Grooves or Knobs?

One of the more annoying things seen in kitchens with wall ovens—microwave or thermal—is that the doors on the cabinets just above the ovens come down too far. When knobs or handles

To get the cabinets open, you need space for fingers between this oven and the cabinet doors.

are used, this is no problem. When the design uses finger grooves and the doors are too close to the oven, it is annoyingly difficult to get the doors open. The cabinet design should take into account that the top of the oven typically sticks out several inches in front of the cabinet doors so that there must be enough space between door and oven to comfortably insert one's fingers—or use knobs.

Grooves on a door under a kitchen sink are likely to be used by wet fingers from time to time. This can ultimately damage the finish on the door.

Another place that finger grooves are very inconvenient is a bottom drawer where the grooves are only a few inches off of the floor. And cabinet doors above refrigerators are always hard to reach. Knobs or handles are a lot more convenient.

The cost of putting knobs on drawers and cabinet doors is small. The inconvenience of not having them goes on a long time. They are always a safe bet if they go with the cabinet style.

Cabinet Bases

Here's an aesthetic item. Watch out for custom cabinets in which the base, the part of the cabinet that sits on the floor, isn't mitered at the corners. The base is generally 3/4" plywood with a hardwood surface. From the front of the cabinet unmitered corners look fine but, if the cabinet is where it can be seen from the end, the view is of the edge of a piece of plywood, not the hardwood surface. Fortunately this sloppy piece of work isn't common but, if you see it, you'll know that it's not like it could or should be.

Custom versus Pre-Manufactured Cabinets

In many ways the differentiation between custom and pre-manufactured cabinets has blurred brought on, in part, by the flexibility of manufacturers to customize their products. They have a very wide range of styles and exteriors to choose from and, when you add to this the ability to make them in almost every conceivable size, they're now found in every part of the home-building market. Among their websites:

⇨ Diamond Cabinets[16B]

⇨ KraftMaid[16C]

⇨ Medallion Cabinetry[16D]

⇨ Edgewater Cabinets[16E]

⇨ Aristocraft Cabinetry[16F]

⇨ Canyon Creek Cabinet Company[16G]

There are some things they don't do, some of the unusual and exotic arrangements seen in design magazines, for instance. That's left up to the local cabinetmaker who works with the designer and builder to accomplish eye-catching combinations.

But today's electronic technology has significantly blurred the differences. First, the manufacturers of pre-manufactured cabinets do not sell directly to the builder. As do other suppliers, they work through subcontractors who integrate the cabinets with the rest of the kitchen—the counters, the exhaust systems, etc. And you'll find them at kitchen centers, both local ones and the "big-box" ones like Lowe's and Home Depot.

Note the parallel between the manufacturing of cabinets and of homes and their components in the controlled environment of a factory. It's all part of bringing the whole building industry into the 21st century. Expect to see more and more of it as time goes by.

Local cabinetmakers may do all of the detailed work themselves but often their main job is to do the integration, working with builders of all sizes to meet their needs while using pre-manufactured cabinets extensively.

Or the local company will build the cabinets from scratch, doing it as inexpensively as they can, in order to get the job. This, along with builders who don't know or don't care, is what leads to such things as the "gouging" European-style hinges seen in so many new homes but not in pre-manufactured cabinets.

There is one important area where the quality that comes from the pre-manufacturers is significantly better than you can get from locally built cabinets—the finish. To bake the lacquer into a hard durable surface requires factory equipment and, with it, an OSHA-conforming working environment which most local cabinetmakers do not have. Instead they do the finishing work on site as the cabinets are installed. The result simply doesn't match up. You won't see this at first, but you will a few years downstream.

This leads to the next question. If you are in the position of making the decision of where to get your cabinets—a remodel, for example, where should you go? Since you have control, it is suggested that you lean toward pre-manufactured cabinets simply because they are probably better made and no more expensive than custom ones. But, you ask, should I go to one of the home-improvement stores where they have an extensive display of different styles and manufacturers or would I be better off at a local kitchen center or even at a local cabinetmaker's shop, one who deals in pre-manufactured cabinets?

Unless you've had a significant amount of experience in cabinet design and installation, it is suggested that you go where you are likely to get the best advice from someone who's been around the business for some time. Yes, all of them will probably use the same computer programs to help in the selection and to get installation instructions. But not all will have had that most-useful, hands-on experience. It's an important decision.

And, above all, be careful. The computer-aided design (CAD) programs will help them arrange their choices into the available spaces. You come in with your requirements and leave a half hour or so later with a completed kitchen design and a price for the cabinets. But, as you can see from the photos in this chapter, there are still decisions that have to be made that impact on the functionality of the kitchen. It's right here where you need to be involved. Once it's been built, it'll be expensive to change. It's still *Caveat Emptor*.

Chapter 17

Kitchen Exhaust Systems

When you come to a fork in the road, take it.

Yogi Berra, baseball player & manager (1925-)

In this chapter:

It may seem a waste to dedicate a whole chapter to the kitchen exhaust but, as you'll see, there are enough potential problems to make it worth taking the time to see what's out there and to note the ones you'd rather not have.

Exhaust systems, which are used to rid the house of steam, smoke, fumes, and odors, frequently exist because of a code requirement and/or because of a conception by the buying public that they should be there. Unfortunately, too often in both kitchens and bathrooms, exhaust systems are often ineffective in performing the function for which they were intended.

Cooktops are almost always equipped with a means for collecting the smoke, odors, and steam generated at the stove and exhausting it into the outside air. Occasionally you'll see a house without a kitchen exhaust system or it'll be in the ceiling many feet away from the cooktop—where it is useless.

Our thrust here is to help you understand what's going on. You'll be exposed to "cubic feet per minute" and why it's not everything by a long ways in getting rid of whatever comes off of the stove. And you'll have a better feeling for why exhaust systems are so noisy and what can be done about it.

Basic Vent Types

Kitchen exhaust systems may be:

⇨ Underline: Updraft where the smoke, et al, are pulled by a fan upward from the cooktop and exhausted. The fan and hood may be:

  ° A part of a microwave oven,

  ° Wall-mounted units that are integrated into the cabinets,

  ° Mounted in a special cabinet over the cooktop, or

  ° Suspended from the ceiling, often by the exhaust pipe itself.

⇨ Downdraft where the exhaust products are pulled sideways off of the cooktop and exhausted downward and outside.

Each of these is discussed in this chapter.

Rating Criteria

Two criteria of interest used to rate exhaust systems are:

⇨ How much air does it move? (And be careful here. Volume isn't everything.)

⇨ How noisy is it?

Air Volume

First a technical thing:

CFM stands for Cubic Feet per Minute. It is used as a measure to compare different fans in their abilities to move air.

In new homes you can often look under the hood and see the actual CFM rating. Typical updraft fans are rated at around 180 to 200 CFM. This appears to be reasonable for daily use. You can get bigger, more expensive (and noisier) fans. Downdraft ratings are from 300 to 500 CFM, although at least one manufacturer offers a unit that moves upwards of 1000 CFM. (For comparison, the rating of the fan in a forced air heating system in a 2000 square-foot house is typically about 1350 CFM.)

A word of caution—in today's tightly sealed homes very large fans have been known to pull soot down out of a chimney and spread it around in front of a fireplace.

The amount of air a fan can move is directly related to the "back pressure" or resistance that it sees. If there were no ducting at all, the fans would do a much better job of air movement than they can in real life. The size of duct, the length of the run and the number of elbows all add to the back pressure. In this respect, downdraft units—mounted on islands or peninsulas where the ducts must bend at least once—are inherently less efficient than an updraft unit with a straight duct. (Which is part of the reason downdraft systems need bigger fans.) For the maximum utility with the least noise it is important that duct runs be kept straight and as short as is feasible. Every bend will mean less air but no less noise.

But note. What we're really interested in is how much of the smoke, air-borne grease, cooking smells and heated air are gotten rid of. The system must collect those first and it's only then that the CFMs matter.

Noise

People don't use their kitchen exhaust systems as much as they should because of the noise they make. Unless the smoke rising up from the cooktop is severe, the fans are usually not turned on and, with time, the grease and smells, which could be exhausted outside, end up in drapes, carpets, furniture and on walls. A system that has the least noise for a given amount of air will be the most effective because it will be used more.

There are four things that can help in keeping the noise down:

⇨ It is a general rule of hydraulic engineering that, for maximum effectiveness, you avoid bends and length in a pipe carrying a fluid. Air is a fluid and, we repeat, *an exhaust system vent pipe should be as short and straight as possible.* When it is not, it takes a bigger fan to get the air through and a bigger fan means more noise—and more money.

⇨ Have the fan toward the exhaust end of the vent pipe, getting it away from the kitchen. The attic is a good location. But it is necessary to have access to the fan for cleaning and maintenance. Because of the cost, this is not commonly done.

⇨ Use a fan design that moves more air with less noise. A "squirrel cage" design does this but is more expensive.

⇨ Use a larger than standard-sized exhaust pipe. (The noise of air rushing through a pipe is related to the speed of the air and a larger vent pipe means lower air speed.) Making a larger vent pipe may require a modification of the hood itself but may be worth it.

Careful design is imperative for effective operation. To exhaust the same amount of air, a better installation means the fan can be run at a lower speed, and hence lower noise, than in a carelessly installed unit. If you're getting a new custom house you should talk to your designer about this so that he makes special provision for the exhaust vent pipe if that's appropriate. Then, when the time comes, make sure the subcontractor who is installing the exhaust system knows exactly what you want.

I watched as a neighbor's house was being built. The exhaust fan had been completely ignored during framing and when the time came to install the vent pipe, the only option was out the back of the house. The fan doesn't work well and the outside flap is noisy. It really does need to be planned for.

If you look at exhaust system specs, you'll find that the noise is specified in terms of "sones", a term from physics[17E]. Fans are rated from less than one sone to over four, which is a ratio of over 100 to 1. You'll find 1 sone is not bad, but 4 is pretty darn loud. Unfortunately, the low end of the range goes with small and not-so-effective fans. **Which is why fans come with speed switches, so we can adjust them for the best compromise between controlling noise and air flow—even though "the best" may be pretty sad.**

A rheostat for controlling the fan speed makes more sense than a simple hi-lo switch arrangement. This gives you the capability to adjust the fan speed to fit the job while keeping the noise to a minimum. Alternately, a three-speed fan is simpler to operate than a rheostat, albeit a little less flexible.

Wall-Mounted Systems
Updraft fans

UPDRAFT FANS WILL BE EFFECTIVE ONLY FOR THE STOVE BURNERS THAT ARE DIRECTLY UNDER THE HOOD OR MICROWAVE OVEN.

One way to get a feeling for this is to look at just how fast a fan makes the air move. With a typical fan (200 CFM), the average speed of the air moving across the bottom of a standard hood is 0.6 miles per hour! This is the gentlest of breezes. So it's not surprising that the hood is effective only for things that rise up into it by themselves. Which is why the exhaust fan on a microwave oven or hood is not effective for the front burners of a cooktop or range under it. Using a

300 CFM fan obviously helps, but 1.5 times 0.6 mph is still less than 1 mph.

These fans may be part of the microwave oven (located at the bottom of the oven) or they may be part of a hood. Because a hood sticks out farther than a microwave oven does, the hood is more effective in catching the smoke and steam from the front burners of a cooktop than a fan in a microwave oven can be.

Fans in microwave ovens are not going to do a complete job. You can see this for yourself if you have one or visit someone who has. Boil some wa-

This unit sticks out over more of the stovetop and should do a better job on the front burners.

ter and turn the fan on. When the pot is on a front burner, most of the steam goes into the room but, when it is on a back burner, most of the steam will be captured. While cabinet-mounted hoods are better than microwave ovens, they do not usually cover the entire cooktop and are only partially effective on the front burners.

The exhaust in the usual microwave oven works OK—for the back burners.

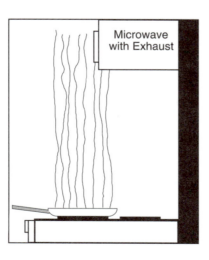

Cooktop and hood are a better combination than most microwave oven exhausts.

An upscale burnished-metal updraft hood. (In a penthouse in the Donald Trump World Tower, New York.)

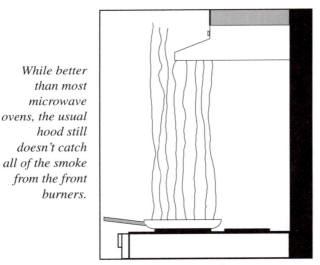

While better than most microwave ovens, the usual hood still doesn't catch all of the smoke from the front burners.

A wall behind the cooktop will help keep stray air movement from taking the smoke or steam away from the hood. When there is no wall, the venting problem is even more difficult. This is the case for islands and peninsulas.

Ductless exhaust

Did you ever note the grill work across the top of a wall-mounted microwave oven? (*See* the upper left photo on the opposite page.) Or that there

is no grill in one meant to sit on a counter? Wall-mounted units with fans are the ones with the grill. But, you may wonder, if they exhaust into a pipe that goes outside, why is there a grill? It's because they are made so they may exhaust *either* outside or back into the kitchen!

"Ductless," "recirculating," "no vent," or "no duct" is a nice way of saying that whatever the fan picks up from the stove will be passed through an internal filter and dumped back into the room. When it's not vented outside, the exhaust system does very little good. When the heated air, smoke, fumes, and steam coming up from the stove are run through the filter, it removes only a little of the smoke and fumes and none of the water vapor or hot air. In short, it is about as close to useless as you're going to find. A magazine article rated this arrangement as "five percent effective."

The usual place where you'll see a ductless or re-circulating exhaust system is in a microwave oven. But, they aren't the only place. National manufacturers of kitchen exhaust systems make

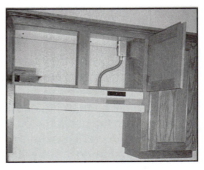

Here are a hood and a microwave oven without evident vents. IF there is one that goes directly outside through the wall of the house, fine. But don't get one that exhausts back into the room.

updraft units that aren't a part of a microwave oven but which are intended to be used in a ductless mode.

Finding these ductless systems is easy. If the power is on, simply turn the fan on and use your hand to feel if the air comes back into the room from the louvered area at the top of the microwave or hood. If it does, you're looking at a ductless exhaust. You can open up the cupboard above the microwave to check if there's duct work there. (It'll usually be boxed in if it is.) If it is there, fine. If not, you've probably got a ductless exhaust, although it is possible to vent the exhaust directly through the back wall without any duct work showing in the cabinet above the unit. To be sure, check it with the power turned on—or look outside where the vent would be.

Ductless systems are also available for downdraft units. They won't be effective there, either.

One of the most annoying things about these systems, aside from their uselessness, is that they often blow the air back into the room at just about head height. Having a blast of whatever is coming from the stove blowing in your face is not very friendly.

One woman told me how, when she remodeled her house, not knowing better, she had a microwave oven with a ductless exhaust fan installed. With the combination of air blowing in her face and the overall uselessness of the unit, she opens a window next to the stove when she needs to have smoke exhausted. Most of us don't have windows close to the cooktop, nor do we feel like pouring money down a rat hole to get a useless piece of machinery.

Another housewife's comment was, "I hate it." She is saddled with a ductless exhaust in a house bought when *she* didn't know better.

Manufacturers don't recommend the use of ductless units if there is any way to duct them outside. But, as one customer representative said on the telephone, "They're better than nothing." Well— maybe. They're used in new houses, not because there's no other choice, but so the builder can save a few dollars. They add glitz by paying attention to customer's expectations but there's no substance.

I've even seen them in a new home where the stove and the ductless unit is on an outside wall where ducting it outside would have been a trivial job! Surely this wasn't a matter of saving a few bucks...it was a matter of ignorance.

Or how about the house built by a national production builder in Aurora, CO where the run of duct to an outside wall would have been short and straight, about 8 feet at most. Ignorance? No, save a few bucks and as long as people buy it, why not? **Caveat Emptor.**

These ductless vents can get into new houses because:

⇨ The builder doesn't know better, or

⇨ The builder is trying to save a few bucks on the duct work, and/or

⇨ The builder is an area where the practice is to use the ductless fan when the hood isn't on an outside wall and he's following local custom.

In any case, the use of these arrangements is one more user-unfriendly thing you're likely to find in a house.

Separate from Kitchen Cabinets

On islands or peninsulas where there are no cabinets over or around the cooktop there are two options for the exhaust system:

⇨ Downdraft.

⇨ A hood over the cooktop suspended from the ceiling or in its own special cabinet.

Downdraft fans

Downdraft fans must pull the smoke and exhaust fumes sideways across the stovetop. This is not nearly as efficient as catching what rises into it so that downdraft units must use bigger fans and move a larger amount of air. Because of this, the efficiencies of downdraft exhaust systems are more sensitive to the length of the exhaust vent and to bends in it. Further, the nature of the system requires at least one bend. Which also means a bigger fan is needed and is one reason why downdraft systems are generally noisy.

If the kitchen has a slab floor, the vent pipe requires special attention. It must be approved to run under the slab using PVC or other plastic pipe. And it must have someplace to go which isn't always easy from under a slab. (All of which is a major reason downdraft units are seldom used with slab floors.) Crawl space or basement is the usual routing for the vent pipe. (Or directly out a wall if the kitchen arrangement permits.)

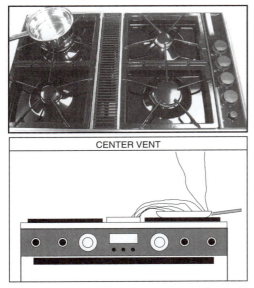

CENTER VENT

With a center-vent downdraft exhaust smoke and/or fumes from pans and pots on the stovetop are pulled sideways to the grill, then exhausted. It takes a lot of air movement to make this happen effectively.

There are two kinds of downdraft systems: one where the exhaust intake is on the same level as the burners, usually between them (center vent), and one where the exhaust intake is across the back of the cooktop (back or rear vent). This may be fixed in place or it may be raised up and down as needed. The back vent is separate from the stovetop itself and is a bit spendy.

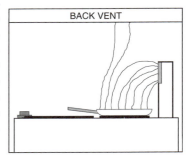

BACK VENT

A back-vent downdraft unit. When in use it sucks smoke and fumes off of pans on the cooktop to the baffle at the back where it is pulled down into the vent. When not in use the baffle can be lowered.

It was enlightening to actually watch an exhaust fan do its job when barbecuing on an island grill with a center-vent downdraft unit. When the air in the room was quiet, the fan got rid of most of the smoke, but not all. However, there was a ceiling fan about 12 feet away in the kitchen nook and, when this fan was on, the effectiveness of the downdraft fan was clearly very poor.

A similar test was carried out with an updraft fan over a peninsula cooktop. The hood apparently protected the cooktop to a large extent from effects of the ceiling fan. There wasn't a noticeable difference when the ceiling fan was on or off.

Downdraft systems with the exhaust in the center between burners will be even less effective in venting steam from a tall pot of boiling water, such as is used to cook pasta. The back vent units work better on the back burners, but the inability of the fan to pull steam and smoke sideways from the space over the cooktop will always be a limitation—particularly for the front burners.

Fan in separate hood

For an island or peninsula with no cabinets over it there are two ways to have an updraft exhaust system :

⇨ Mount a large hood similar to those used in restaurant kitchens over the cooktop. This is a very effective proven system whose main drawback is looks. When it's made of copper and kept clean even the looks are OK, particularly in a country-style house. (Don't forget lights. This type of hood may not have the built-in lights we are used to.)

⇨ Have the hood built into a set of cupboards. By "hiding" the hood in the

cabinet, both aesthetics and functionality are served. The next photo shows what one builder did using a hood specifically designed for this type of application. Note that this is probably not feasible with a vaulted ceiling.

Hoods which hang from the ceiling are large and eye-catching. Look for these in upscale houses and on the manufacturers' websites[17A, 17B, 17C].

An updraft system over an island cooktop. This hood has its own set of cabinets.

An updraft system over an island cooktop. Spectacular and effective. (In passing, note the paucity of landing area around the stove—not an exhaust problem but not user-friendly either.)

Other exhaust system considerations

The height of an exhaust system above the cooktop is important. The lower the exhaust system, the better. But too low will put the hood or microwave oven in the way for cooking. Too high will make the exhaust system even more sensitive to extraneous air movement. A suggested compromise is 24 inches for hoods that stick out in front and 21 inches for microwave ovens. (24 inches would put the bottom of a microwave oven just five feet above the floor, making it difficult for a short person to see inside.)

A common complaint about exhaust hoods is the appearance. There are two designs that address this. Both use movable parts that are brought into use only when needed. One is a simple flap that is pulled out from the front of the hood to try to increase the effective size of the hood.

In the other design, the part that pulls out is much more than just a flap. It is the full depth of the hood and includes a part of the exhaust system filter. When it is not in use, the movable part is back even with the front of the adjoining cabinets. The front of the hood may be glass, black or white enamel to match the stove, or the same wood used in the cabinets. The unappealing appearance associated with hoods is gone.

The entire under surface of the hood is covered with filters. Lights, which are an integral part of the hoods, are above the filters so that they must shine through to illuminate the stove top. The manufacturer[17A] offers these in versions with 300 and 400 CFM, both of which are larger, noisier, and more effective than most updraft exhaust systems.

But note that to effectively use these hoods it does take a manual operation on the part of the user, something which needs to be done infrequently in most home kitchens. It's just easier with a fixed hood to use the back burners for the times when the exhaust system is needed.

Keeping It One Way

With an exhaust system, there should be a flap in the duct that prevents outside air from coming into the house when the fan is off.

With a vertical exhaust vent, the flap is normally in the hood, right in the kitchen. If this flap sticks open, it lets cold air into the kitchen and makes a startling noise when it finally closes. If possible, check the action of this flap before the hood is installed or when you're looking at a house. It should firmly return to the closed position when the fan is turned off. If you run into the problem while the first year's warranty is in effect, the builder should have it fixed.

We have this problem in our house. We try to remember to check the flap by putting a hand under the fan in the hood. If we feel cold air, a solid thump on the hood will usually close it. The flap sticks open when the exhaust fan has been run or when a strong wind causes suction up the pipe. Obviously it is better, if you can, to avoid getting a hood with a temperamental flap.

With a horizontal vent pipe, the flap is outside the house at the end of the pipe to keep rain and cold air out. This flap rattles and can be quite noisy when the wind blows. For this reason, don't use such an arrangement if there is any reasonable way to have a vertical vent. Unfortunately, for downdraft systems there is no choice.

Relying on these flaps to open and close with air flow is counter to the tight-house, energy efficient concept. A strong wind will cause the flap to open and your warm heated air is sucked outside at a good rate. I haven't run across a system where this problem is avoided, i.e., where the flap opens when the fan is on but is held firmly closed when it is off. If you find one, give it some serious thought.

Chapter 18

Kitchen Layouts

If a man knows not what harbor he seeks, any wind is the right wind.

Seneca, Roman philosopher, statesman, and playwright (4 BC?–AD 65)

In this chapter:
Whether working with plans or looking at models, it is very useful to recognize the basic kitchen designs and the pros and cons of each. It makes it easier to decide how well a particular arrangement will work for you and whether it is appropriate to the house you're considering.

Kitchen Design Basics

In today's open floor plans the family or great room and kitchen are often more like one room than two. And certainly a breakfast nook is an integral part of most kitchens.

Other than how it fits into the whole house, there are only a few basic common-sense constraints on good kitchen design:

⇨ Dishwashers should be close to the sink, close to cupboards, never in a corner, and not in the way when its door is open.

⇨ Refrigerators should be located where all doors can be fully opened. (No wall next to a refrigerator door hinge.)

⇨ The kitchen should not be a traffic path from one part of the house to another.

⇨ The *walking* distances from the sink to the cooktop, to the refrigerator and to the microwave oven should be kept short.

⇨ There should be landing areas—places to set things—convenient to the cooktop, microwave oven, wall ovens, refrigerators, and cabinet-type pantries.

Overall Considerations

Before going into discussions of actual kitchen layouts, we will review a number of the requirements for the various parts of the kitchen.

The breakfast eating area

Three different breakfast eating areas are found in homes today:

⇨ a breakfast nook,

⇨ as part of an adjacent great room and/or,

⇨ an eating bar.

If there is a breakfast nook is it large enough for table, chairs, and still have room to walk behind the chairs? For room to get behind people seated at a table, you need 36 inches between the edge of the table and the wall.

Doors that swing into the kitchen nook were discussed in Chapter 9. Here's another one that will restrict the usefulness of the room.

If there is a kitchen eating bar, is it convenient? If such a bar is the only eating area, you might well reconsider the whole design. Many folks prefer a sit-down table for family meals.

The pantry

Both walk-in and cabinet pantries are seen in today's houses. There are advantages and disadvantages to each.

Walk-in pantries

Walk-in pantries should be convenient to the kitchen working area. Take a hard look at any walk-in pantries to figure out just how utilitarian they will be. Pay particular attention to how much useful shelf space there is. Also, make sure that, when a person opens the pantry door, the door doesn't block access to shelves. Doors that open into the pantry often do this.

With walk-in pantries, there should be a light inside and the switch should be placed in a user-friendly place—outside, *next to the latch side of the door*, is fine. As with other light-switch locations, the thing to be careful of is not to have the switch where it is:

⇨ not expected,

⇨ behind a door or

⇨ inside the pantry hidden under a shelf where you fumble to find it even when you know it's there.

Hence the suggestion that it is better to have the switch outside than to have it inside in a bad place.

When looking at houses, don't forget to check that the light in the pantry is indeed there. In one set of tract models I saw, there was no light

A walk-in pantry. The light swutch is inside, maybe not the best spot. And see the comments in the text re the use of wire shelving.

and the kitchen light didn't shine into it. You wouldn't usually notice it in daylight but after you moved in you would need a flashlight to find things.

When there is a corner where cabinets meet, putting the pantry at 45° across the corner is a functional way to avoid otherwise difficult-to-access corner cabinets. (As in the photo on page 237.)

While they *may* be okay in closets, the wire shelving seen in pantries in numerous tract houses in all price ranges has its drawbacks. Small bottles and packages should sit level which they won't do on the wire. Wood does a better job.

To me this is another good example of the builder leaving it up to the cabinet maker and the cabinet maker going the low-cost way—to the detriment of the eventual home user.

Cabinet pantries

Cabinet-type pantries are usually a continuation of the cabinets in the kitchen and have the same depth as the under-counter cabinets, that is, about two feet. There are two distinctively different types of pantries that are made as a part of the kitchen cabinets: those with horizontal shelves and those with tall hinged vertical panels.

Horizontal shelves should be pull out, otherwise the back half won't be useful unless you enjoy unloading the front part of

A cabinet pantry with pull-out shelves.

the shelf to get to something in the back. Alternatively, the cabinet can be made wider and not deep. Bi-fold doors were used in the following photo to keep door sizes smaller.

In the other type of cabinet pantry, narrow shelves are mounted on the back of the door, on both sides of hinged vertical panels and across the

An unusual cabinet pantry. Note the relatively shallow shelves, making stored items easier to find.

back of the pantry. Access is by opening the door and swinging the vertical panel to readily reach a stored item. Because of their cost, don't expect to see these in tract models. You will pay extra to get them.

Eating bars

You might come across a potential floor covering problem when a peninsula or island eating bar separates the kitchen and family room. Many builders put the family-room carpeting all the way to the bar. Since food and drink spills can ruin carpeting, the kitchen floor covering should be extended to cover the area under the bar.

Another problem you may catch is an eating bar so narrow that there's not room enough in

Carpeting under an eating bar is just nonsensical. The kitchen floor should be extended into that area.

You may need to use plastic under the chairs when it wasn't done right the first time.

An overhang that is just not big enough.

places for plates, glasses, etc. This happens when a sink or a cooktop on the eating bar takes room away from the eating area.

The sink makes the left half of this bar useless—stools or not.

Then there are eating bars which you'd almost never use because there's not enough overhang for a person to sit under, whether on a stool or a chair. The overhang should be a minimum of 14", but 18" is better.

These narrow overhangs often happen when the countertop is simply too narrow to allow for the cabinets under it and the overhang on the opposite side. Designers do these things when they're worried about fitting everything into a room. User-friendliness takes thinking and planning.

Finally, watch out where there's a cooktop that may be so close to the eating area as to present a danger to someone using the bar for eating. While potentially more of a problem when small children are in the family, it's just good practice to make a home user-friendly for everyone. Some-

times builders will put the eating area on a level which is below that of the cooktop. Burners, upsets, or spattering food stuffs make these disasters-waiting-to-happen. Not only is there the danger from spattering grease, but scalding water from pots and tea kettles is an ever-present danger to someone at the eating bar.

Maybe I'm a safety nut but when I see an eating bar and a cooktop on the same counter it waves a red flag at me. The potential for injury, particularly to children, is too great.

Take a close look at something like this yourself to be sure it satisfies your ideas of safety.

Islands

Islands are an integral part of many kitchen designs. When we put an island in a kitchen, we may take away the room for the family table but add a significant amount of working counter area as well as cabinets under the island.

There are several ways this island area can be used—and misused:

⇨ **Don't** make that most common energy-consuming error—your *personal* energy that is—don't put the refrigerator across the room from the sink on the far side of the island. Islands are great but not between sink and cooktop or sink and refrigerator.

⇨ A real plus for an island is that it automatically becomes a landing area allowing you to efficiently use any type of refrigerator.

⇨ When the island abuts the breakfast nook, the family room or great room, one side of the island can be—and often is—used as an eating bar.

⇨ As discussed earlier, if the cooktop is in the island, it will have to use either a downdraft exhaust system or, preferably, a ceiling-mounted updraft hood, either of which adds cost to the kitchen.

⇨ There should be enough room in front of the appliances to be able to open their doors without causing problems. Our recommendation is 48" between a counter and the island.

⇨ If the sink and dishwasher are in the island, the dishwasher should be on the side of the sink closest to the majority of the upper cabinets. This puts the open dishwasher door near the cabinets, making a more efficient arrangement.

⇨ Having doors on both sides of the island base cabinets insures that things will always be accessible. Pull-out shelves are usually a good idea—but this can't be done with a downdraft cooktop on the island.

I 'll always remember a house I saw in a special "Showcase of Homes" sponsored by a prominent building designer. The house itself was his own new home and one assumes that it represented his best effort. It had a U-shaped kitchen with a large island and...you guessed it...the island was between the refrigerator and the sink work area. It will always be a reminder to me about how insensitive designers and architects can be to the functional aspects of their designs.

Appliance considerations

A word of caution. Stainless steel has become a fashionable trend for the fronts of refrigerators, stoves, and dishwashers. Here's what cleaning person Nikki had to say,

"Stainless steel is very hard to clean. It takes a special cleanser that leaves an oily film on the surface. Smudges and children's fingerprints are a real pain."

Add to this what cleaning person Judy says,

"I hate them."

There is an alternative. It is vinyl-coated metal (VCM), a surface that is a plastic coat over bare metal. It doesn't shine quite the way that stainless does but it doesn't smudge as easily and it's much easier to clean. Or you can go with colored surfaces which are often textured for appearance.

A double dishwasher, one of the many appliances available with metallic front surfaces.

Stoves, cooktops and ovens

The configuration of the stove's cooktop and oven or ovens are decided as a part of the house design. If you have the option, you will need to decide if the stove is to operate with gas or electricity and then select manufacturers and model numbers.

An alternative to the standard thermal oven is a convection oven. If there are two ovens, having one convection is a good choice.

Microwave ovens

Be careful when comparing houses that you don't overlook the microwave oven. In an effort to keep the basic price of a model down, many builders will not include the microwave even though they know that buyers will want one. The worst part of this practice is that they also leave out a reasonable place to put it when you move in.

If the microwave oven is mounted in the same cabinet as the thermal oven, be careful to follow the manufacturer's instructions. Most of them insist that there be a way to protect the microwave oven from the heat rising from the thermal oven. In particular that there be a space between the two with vents that allows the heat to escape before it affects the microwave oven.

And putting a microwave oven on a counter is a real waste of often-precious space. For a new house it's not a bad idea to try to visualize the kitchen with the microwave oven in it and see if the builder will accomodate you and how much it's going to cost.

And don't forget that microwave oven doors always hinge on the left side so the landing area for it should be to the right of the unit. Or have a shelf right under it which can be used to set things on.

Oven door clearance

There should be 48 inches of clearance in front of a thermal oven so someone can comfortably stand in front of the open door and take out a roasting pan. Most oven doors stick out 24 inches. A person leaning over to take something out of the oven needs at least another 24 inches or a total of 48 inches. If you are going to be using the smaller ovens with 21 inches doors, you can cut the 48 inches to 45 inches. When you don't have this clearance, you have to take pans out of the oven from the side which puts you in danger of burning yourself. Caution: this argument applies to ovens that are a part of a range as well as to cabinet-mounted units.

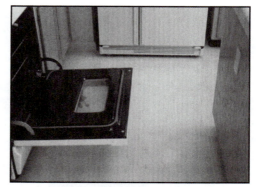

There is about 18" in front of this open oven door. It is enough to get by, it is not enough to let you stand in front of the oven and pull out a roasting pan.

Oven height

Be careful how high both thermal and microwave ovens are above the floor because these vary widely from one builder to another. The height of thermal ovens should not make it difficult for a short person to get a hot roasting pan out of an oven.

This seems obvious, yet I have seen ovens so high that you would need to be well over six feet tall to use them comfortably. In one case it was in a custom house and I can only assume that the new owner was a very tall person. In another case it was in a spec house and it was hard to understand the logic.

If you are tall and want an oven way up there, be well aware that when it comes to resale time you will really restrict the number of potential buyers. Better you should lean over a little bit to see in the oven and not seriously lower the value of your property.

If the microwave is over the burners, then it should be as low as possible while still leaving room to work on the cooktop. Check it out for yourself, but having the bottom of the microwave oven about 21 inches above the cooktop is about as low as it should be even though this is still uncomfortably high for short people.

When the bottom of a wall-mounted micro-wave oven is in the order of 48 inches above the floor it is convenient for everyone.

Corner sink

If the kitchen is on a corner of the house and the sink is in that corner, it can double the amount of window area in front of the sink without sepa-rating the cabinets

A cornersink is an attractive way to brighten up the sink area during the day.

from the dishwasher. It is useful for all but the in-line and the galley layouts. The cautions about dishwasher location were covered in Chapter 14.

Power and light

General kitchen lighting

If the kitchen has a flat ceiling there are several useful lighting options. This is a place where re-gional differences are noticeable; fluorescent pan-els are popular in some areas while floodlights are usual in others. Track lighting can also be used but many people object to the aesthetics.

If you see a vaulted ceiling in the kitchen, re-member that it will restrict the kind of general lighting that can be used. Fluorescent panels, for ex-ample, won't do as good a job when mounted on a sloping ceiling. And re-cessed lighting systems must be designed carefully to make sure the lights point downward and that the cov-erage is uniform.

Ceiling-mounted flood lights are a good choice in a kitchen.

If you have the option, choose what you want but make sure there is enough light where its needed. In looking at an existing house, take a hard look at how evenly the light is distributed. If you can, do this at night.

An attractive scheme was seen in the kitchen of one up-scale house that has a large deco-rative translucent panel with a skylight above it in the center of the room. After sundown fluorescent lights mounted in the well of the skylight are used to continue the effects of the decorative panel.

Light for the cooktop

If there is an island with a downdraft exhaust system, check that there is good lighting for the cooktop because there may be no special light for the island unless you ask for it. Sometimes a sky-light is used to provide light during the day, but night can be another problem.

Light for the sink

Most layouts, other than sinks on islands, have a window in front of the sink. Large windows make the kitchen feel more open but take away wall space that might be better used for cabinets. It's a matter of personal preference.

Just when you think you've seen it all, along comes another one. This was in an above-av-erage-price spec house being shown as a part of a tour. The sink was on the side of a U-shaped kitchen but not facing a window. And there was no light over or around it! Whoever bought that house has a problem.

Light at night for the sink work area is usually as simple as installing a light when the house is built. But sometimes it is forgotten. One attrac-tive, but different, arrangement has been seen in a few model homes. Watch for this one.

The sink is in front of a tall window that goes to the ceiling. The ceiling has several feet of glass that comes down to the tops of the windows, giv-ing a solarium effect. During the day, all that light and airiness is appealing. But at night there is no provision for lighting the sink and surrounding countertop!

If you run across this arrangement in a house design, be sure you figure out a way to get light around the sink or forget it. If you decide to go ahead anyway, don't forget to check the orientation of the kitchen relative to the sun, because, since there is no obvious way to put shades on these windows, it will be a problem for south- or west-facing kitchens particularly on summer afternoons.

Counter lighting

Cabinets often shade portions of the counter work areas from the regular kitchen lighting. While small fluorescent fixtures can be hung under the cabinets at any time, it is better if they are wired in place so you don't have cords running around to the nearest outlet. This lighting is another inexpensive functional feature that will make working in the kitchen easier.

The breakfast nook

Light in the breakfast nook is usually provided by a small chandelier or some kind of hanging fixture. If you prefer a ceiling fan in place of the chandelier or may want to change it later, be careful. When the chandelier is installed, its mounting should be made strong enough to hold a ceiling fan.And there should be a 3-wire cable run to the switch location (unless you want to be forever looking for the remote control if you go that way instead). Depending on the exact layout of the nook, carefully check the placement of the overhead fixture. You may

A ridiculous kitchen chandelier's swag. A good example of what happens when nobody's thinking ahead about where the light should be.

find that the chandelier isn't centered over the table and it may not be that easy to change. Chandeliers can be swagged but ceiling fans present more of a problem to move.

(A "swagged" ceiling fixture is one where the electrical box is mounted in one place and the fixture hangs from another. A loop of wire and chain, the swag, is then necessary between the electrical box and the top of the chain holding the fixture. The photo shows one way it should *not* be done.)

Some builders solve the question of where to put the chandelier by lighting the nook with can lights. This is okay as long as no one ever wants a ceiling fan. In any case, make sure there are enough lights (which builders don't always do).

Air switch for the disposal[18A]

Now being seen in more new houses, you may want to consider a different switch for controlling the disposal. The standard has been a switch mounted on the wall behind the sink. The "newest" thing is an air switch where the control is simply a

This air switch, mounted on the counter behind the sink, is used to control the disposal.

button mounted in the counter itself right alongside the water controls and whatever else that may be mounted there. It doesn't work better. It may be a little more convenient. It is discussed in more detail at the end of Chapter 13.

Instant hot water

Depending on the layout of the house, the kitchen sink may be many feet away from the hot water tank so that you run gallons and gallons of water down the drain several times a day before hot water reaches the kitchen from the water heater. You may decide that in these days of water shortages it would be not only convenient but also socially responsible to have an instant hot water unit.

There are two different types of these tanks as discussed in Chapter 6.

Be sure there is an outlet under the sink where the instant hot water unit can be plugged in and be sure that the power to it is on all the time and is not switched on and off by the disposal switch.

Outlet under the kitchen sink

Where the builder is trying to save pennies, he may not put an outlet under the sink at all. The disposal and the dishwasher are permanently wired in place. If left to the electrician, this may be what happens because it's the least expensive. But if any work ever has to be done on one of them or if either must be replaced, it requires both an electrician and a plumber. Thinking ahead will come up with a better scheme. (In many areas this practice is not allowed by today's building codes.)

A better arrangement is have a split-wired dual outlet in the back wall under the kitchen sink. One half of the outlet is wired to the garbage disposal's on-off switch and the other half has power all the time. There are two ways this outlet is used:

⇨ Sometimes the dishwasher is wired permanently to the house wiring which leaves the "hot" half of the outlet available for an instant hot water unit.

⇨ In other regions the dishwasher plugs into this "hot" side of the outlet. This is the preferable way. It means the electrician is not needed when work has to be done on the dishwasher. But it leaves no place to get power for an instant hot water unit—unless a second outlet is available.

So when the wiring is installed, it is better if there is a switched outlet for the disposal and an unswitched one for the instant hot water. Note that the cost of putting this outlet in place initially is low. To have it done later could be expensive.

(Don't try to use the line to the dishwasher as the source of power for the instant hot water. The dishwasher takes 15 amperes and is on a 15- or 20-ampere circuit. If you add the instant hot water unit (about 6 amperes when it is on), you can

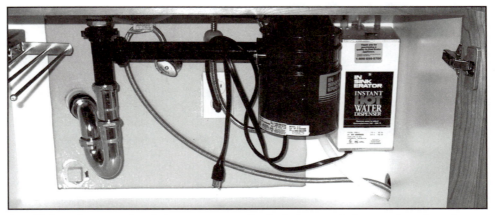

A well-thought-out under-sink arrangement. On the left are rods for towels and wash cloths for dishes. On the right of the disposal is the instant hot water unit. The switch part of the air switch used for disposal control is in the center behind the pipe. Hoses to and from the dishwasher go through the hole on the lower right.

overload the circuit. The electrician should save you from this problem by providing a 25- or 30-ampere circuit, but sometimes they'll take the easiest approach.)

Work Areas

Most kitchen work generally occurs in a few areas, the primary one being around the kitchen sink. Secondary areas include the cooktop, the ovens, the refrigerator and a secondary sink (if there is one) suitable for rinsing food items. Note that the dishwasher is not mentioned separately because it is (or should be) next to the primary sink.

The primary area

You need counter space for preparing foods, you need a place to soak bowls and pans after they're used, and you need water handy for rinsing your hands and utensils. After the meal you need a place to set dirty dishes before they're readied for the dishwasher. Watch in your own kitchen and you'll find that it is the area around the sink where most of the work is done.

You need at least a couple of feet of counter space on both sides of the sink. And you need plenty of light. Many kitchen layouts have the sink in front of a window both for light and to break the monotony of a bare wall. And the larger the window the better—except for one consideration. Upper cabinet space close to the dishwasher is usually at a premium and you can't put cabinets where you have a window. Since the dishwasher should be next to the sink, modest window sizes are appropriate.

Putting the sink in a 45° corner is a way around this, there is then both light and work space, and if properly done, cabinets for storing dishes and glasses close to the dishwasher.

Secondary areas

The counter next to the cooktop should be open for two reasons:

⇨ you need a place to set a hot pan off of the burners and

⇨ you don't want grease spattering on an area that is hard to clean.

You need places to set things going into or coming out of the refrigerator and the oven. These landing areas are usually present in a kitchen design but occasionally you'll see a problem, particularly with refrigerators, as was discussed in Chapter 15.

Islands and peninsulas

In all except the simplest in-line design, you will see islands and peninsulas used to add to the functionality of the kitchen. As a minimum they give additional counter and base-cabinet space. They are also used as:

⇨ Breakfast bars (discussed earlier).

⇨ Locations for cooktops (with downdraft exhausts).

⇨ Landing areas for refrigerators, making it suitable for both side-by-side and freezer over/under models.

⇨ Locations for sinks and dishwashers. For islands this location is usually fine but for peninsulas it generally is not.

Both islands and peninsulas are sometimes used as locations for the cooktop. As discussed earlier in the chapter, there are safety concerns when there are eating bars on the same counter.

A general drawback to both islands and peninsulas is that the additional cabinet space they provide is only below the counter. It makes for a more open kitchen but the above-the-counter space for dishware and glasses may be missing.

Outlets in islands and peninsulas

Building codes require that there be at least one outlet in an island or peninsula. Careless, unthinking electricians will sometimes put these in the side of a beautiful hardwood cabinet where they stick out like a sore thumb. Alternatively, outlets can be completely hidden by mounting them face downward under the overhang of the countertop—but this may not be possible with some kinds of countertops. If you can, insist on having a say in precisely where any outlets are placed.

Islands

Having the sink and dishwasher located on an island can work out great because to unload the dishwasher it becomes possible to simply move the dishes to the cupboard without taking a step. This, of course, requires that the cupboards be located directly in front of the dishwasher and that the aisle between them be relatively narrow. (But not too narrow.)

Properly placed and equipped islands make very convenient work areas. When there is a sink on the island, it is a good place to fix foods that need washing in preparation, things like fresh vegetables and salads. Be sure there is suitable room around such a sink to do this. The fact that the island is the usual landing area for the refrigerator makes this a nice arrangement.

A potential problem with islands in the middle of the kitchen is that they may be obstacles that require walking around when moving from one side of the kitchen to the other.

With islands, which are generally three or four feet wide, access to the backs of the cabinet shelves can be almost impossible. With these wider cabinets, doors on both sides can make the space more useful—or use deep pull out shelves.

As discussed below, an island is sometimes used instead of a set of cabinets and counter to make up the second side of a galley kitchen.

Something to check when there's an island in the kitchen is that the aisles between counters and the island are wide enough to let doors open and people work there.

Peninsulas

As discussed earlier in Chapter 13, having the sink and dishwasher on a peninsula generally has one of these unfriendly aspects:

⇨ The dishwasher may be in a corner (not a 45° one) or

⇨ It may be well-separated from the cupboards.

This nice granite counter with sink and dishwasher exemplifies the problem of putting them on a peninsula. The cupboards are several steps away from the dishwasher making unloading the dishwasher a bigger chore than it should be. That corner back there will also be an access problem. On the other hand, the eating bar behind the sink is very convenient.

Where the peninsula meets the counter there is yet another corner in the cabinetry which, in turn, means accessibility problems. A lazy Susan is one answer. Another is to put an access door on the "back" side of the peninsula which makes it possible to get to the back of what would otherwise be a pretty useless corner.

Peninsulas come in all sizes from the short just-one-cupboard long to ones that extend a long ways across the kitchen.

The kitchen triangle

Kitchen designers have made a big thing of the kitchen triangle—the triangle formed by the sink, the refrigerator, and the stove. In book racks at home-improvement stores you'll find a bundle of how-to books, many of them dealing with how to design kitchens and bathrooms. Watch out! Too often these books have little to do with a user-friendly home; the designs are not for the convenience of the people who will be living in them—the stress is on how it looks, not how it works. Remember? It's the pretty pictures that sell these magazines and books, not the quality of the designs.

The stress on the triangle is hard to understand. To be sure, the number of steps from the sink work area to the refrigerator is important and so is the spacing between sink and cooktop. But the distance from the refrigerator to the cooktop is almost trivial because so seldom do foods go directly from the refrigerator to the stove without a stop-over at the sink work area—for unwrapping, if nothing else. (This isn't the case in restaurants where large amounts of food are prepared for the stove and stored in the refrigerator ahead of meal time and, when an order comes, it *does* go directly from the refrigerator to the grill. But a restaurant is not the same as the family home.)

And little is said about the microwave oven as a part of the work pattern. While some people do not use the microwave as much as others, for most of today's on-the-run or quick-and-easy meal preparers having the microwave close to the sink's work area is very useful. This is a positive aspect of having the microwave over the cooktop.

And nothing is said about another step-causing part of many layouts—the distance from the dishwasher to the cupboards.

It is suggested that you don't worry about how far the refrigerator is from the cook top but concentrate on the distances between:

- ➪ the sink and the cooktop,
- ➪ the sink and the refrigerator,
- ➪ the sink and the microwave
- ➪ the sink and the cupboards.

The greater the distances, the more steps it takes every time you use the kitchen, so see that they're short. Measure off for yourself the difference it would make whether you have to go, say, 4 feet from the sink to the cooktop against what it's like if they're 6 feet apart. Remember these are distances you walk again and again and, if there's an island in the way, it's *you* that has to go around it.

And don't be like a double-page ad that GE ran in national magazines in 2002. It shows Donald Trump in a kitchen in a penthouse in his Trump World Towers in New York City. Clearly the sink and its work area are on one side of the room and the cooktop and refrigerator are on the other. And there's a nice big island in between! About as unfriendly as you can get.

I had the opportunity to visit the Trump World Towers and to see a couple of the penthouses but not the one in the GE ad—I would have remembered that!

Summarizing what to look for in a good, user-friendly kitchen design:

- ➪ Sink—closeness to cupboards. Good-sized work area.
- ➪ Dishwasher—adjacent to sink, closeness to cupboards for dishes, glassware and silverware. Not in a corner. Room in front.
- ➪ Refrigerator—closeness to sink area. Convenient landing area(s).

▷ Stovetop—closeness to sink area and with its own work area. Closeness to cupboards with pots and pans.

▷ Microwave oven—closeness to sink area. Convenient landing area on the right side.

▷ Thermal oven(s)—convenient landing area. Space in front. Reasonably close to the sink work area.

It is interesting to note that last three of the criteria can be satisfied with a microwave oven and the exhaust fan over a range that includes the thermal oven as well as the cooktop. There are two drawbacks:

▷ The exhaust fan in the microwave oven isn't usually as effective as a stand-alone fan—but some are better than others, look for those whose hood sticks well out over the stovetop and

▷ The heights of these ovens are inevitably compromises—you want it lower to make it more effective as an exhaust system while at the same time you need room to work at the stove.

The right choice is an individual one depending on a person's family status, likes and dislikes, and finanacial situation.

Aisles

The width of aisles in a kitchen is always a compromise between making them narrow to keep down steps and making them wide enough to let doors open and still have room to get around. The photos on the next page show several not so user-friendly arrangements. They typify the kinds of problems that occur when aisles are too narrow.

And don't forget the concern with oven doors discussed earlier where a minimum aisle width of 48" was recommended.

You'll see some aisles later in the chapter which, if they were narrower, would cut down on the number of steps that are needed in daily kitchen work.

Basic Layouts

Because of the complexities of kitchen design, the basic layout should be a high priority consideration in deciding what you want in your home.

The fundamentals are the same for all layouts—convenient arrangements that include the sink, dishwasher, refrigerator, stove and ovens, their work areas, and the cabinets and counters. Because every designer wants to be different and how to do this is an arena that's rife with innovation, you'll see virtually an unlimited number of designs, all different, some being obviously a lot of work to use and others where it would be a pleasure.

While almost every kitchen is unique, they are all some form of one of these layouts:

▷ In-line,

▷ U-shaped,

▷ Galley or corridor, or

▷ L-shaped.

Many kitchen layouts are combinations. For example, a galley may be two parallel counters or it may be one set of cupboads with a parallel island to form the corridor. And the other layouts are similar, bend a counter 45° or 90° or add an island or a peninsula and you have that desired difference. Islands may be simple, square with the rest of the kitchen, or angled. Or they may be curved, taking up a large area in the kitchen.

But our stress here is on the user-friendly aspects, i.e., on the criteria listed above. We include a number of photos of different kitchens with commentary, pointing out good, bad and could-be-bet-

SOME AISLES THAT DON'T MAKE IT

The top photo shows a disaster of a kitchen design. The aisle is so small that neither the refrigerator nor the dishwasher doors could be opened and still get by them. The working area by the sink is away from the stove, meaning another couple of steps when taking something to or from the stove. At least the island makes a good landing area for the refrigerator.

Note, too, the floor register right where people will be walking. (See Chapter 7 re this unnecessary unfriendliness.)

In the next photo we have another dishwasher with three serious problems: (1) it's too far from the sink, (2) it's too far from most of the cupboards and (3) it's too close to the island in front of it.

The last two photos are examples of what can happen when the aisle in front of a dishwasher isn't wide enough. In the left, you'd have a real problem unloading anything from the dishwasher into the opposite cupboad. In both of them, there would be a problem getting past the open door.

ter. The effort here is to help you become aware of what to look for before you make a commitment, not have to figure out what should have been after it's too late.

In-line, the simplest of all

Although almost never done in the U.S. (which is why we used our South American photo below), there is nothing wrong with putting all appliances and counters in a straight line. Ideally the sink would be between the range and the refrigerator (which they didn't do in the Santiago photo). Since there's no landing area in front, only top-freezer or bottom-freezer refrigerators should be used. And there will be a refrigerator door-in-the-corner problem.

The primary design consideration is to have a good sink working area while keeping the range and the refrigerator close to the sink (to minimize steps).

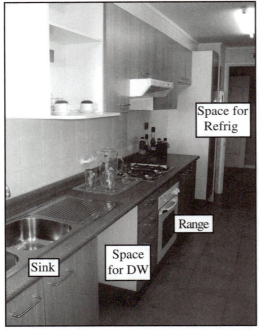

An in-line kitchen in a condo in Santiago, Chile.

Because it's the main work area, the space in front of the counter should not be a major traffic arterial. This can be a serious problem in a small house and is one of the potential disadvantages of the in-line layout—the other being the scarcity of walls for cabinets.

Sometimes an island is put in front of the in-line counter, in effect making it the galley design discussed next.

And you thought a galley was on a ship!

In today's homes the galley or corridor kitchen is usually a countertop and set of cupboards on one side and an island on the other. Instead of a counter with upper cabinets, using an island preserves the openness between the kitchen and an adjoining family room. (*See* the photos on the next page.)

Generally either the sink/dishwasher or the stovetop will be on the island so they are across from each other.

If the "aisle" is not too wide, it is an efficient kitchen design, efficient in that most of the work can be done with very few steps—everything is right at your fingertips. But it can be cozy when there are two people in this kitchen.

The layout precautions are pretty standard. Be sure there is enough space between the counters for open appliance doors—48 inches is a recommended. If the sink is on the island, keeping the island close to this minimum puts the dishwasher close to the cupboards for easier unloading. If the stovetop is on the island, making the aisle a little wider will make it easier for two people to work in the kitchen at the same time.

In the photos note the door at the end of the kitchen, presumably into the dining room. If this were a wall instead, we would have a U-shaped

GALLEY KITCHENS

Here the "galley" is made up of an island on one side and a counter on the other. But the cupboards on the back right of the photos would suggest these are really L-shaped kitchens with islands. The family rooms are on the right side of the island in the photos.

A good layout except that there is 6 feet between the counter and the island with the sink. This means: (a) there is no convenient landing area for the side-by-side refrigerator, (b) the dishwasher is a long ways from the cabinets that hold dishes, and (c) since all microwave oven doors hinge on the left side, it means walking around the door everytime you want to use it.

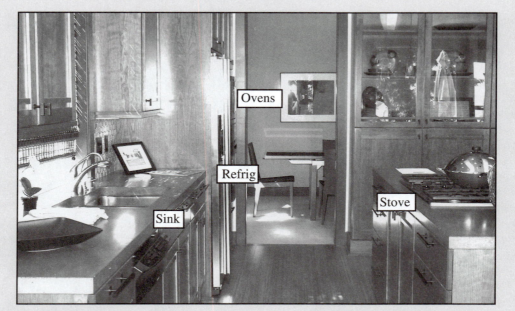

Here the distance from the island to the wall cabinets is 4 feet. Now the island makes a good landing area for the refrigerator and the dishwasher is close to the cabinets. You'll still have to walk around the microwave oven door whenever you use it.

Do not have a narrow U-shaped kitchen with the sink at the end. Either the dishwasher is in a corner, above, or it is separated from the sink.

The U-shaped kitchen

The U-shaped kitchen, with cupboards on three sides, is probably the most common kitchen configuration.

When the sink is placed on the side of a narrow U-shaped kitchen (rather that at the end) you have an efficient arrangement, similar to a galley kitchen.

When the sink is at one end of a narrow U, however, it is an arrangement that is *not* satisfactory because there is no suitable place for the dishwasher—separated from the sink or in a corner.

When the U is wider, there is more flexibility in sink and dishwasher placement and there is room for more than one person to work in the kitchen at a time. It is often used with an island. The open end of the U is also a good place for the kitchen table if there is no separate nook.

kitchen or you could call it an L-shaped layout with an island. Either way its user-friendliness is unchanged.

This high-end L-shaped user-friendly kitchen has the sink and dishwasher on the island. The stove with its big hood is in the 45° corner with landing areas on either side. The landing areas for the refrigerator are on the end of the island and on the counter beside the freezer door. The microwave oven is in the cabinet to the left of the picture as are the cabinets for dishes. And note the raised cabinet with the dishwasher. This has two pluses: it makes it easier to reach the lower shelf when loading and unloading and it makes the top of its cabinet a handy work area.

U-SHAPED KITCHENS

A different U-shaped design with three visible 45° corners. The user-unfriendly part is that you have to go around the island when going between the sink and the refrigerator. Note the small sink on the island, it can be useful in preparing food stuffs.

An unfriendly U-shaped design with an island in the way. Even without the island, the stove and the sink shouldn't be so far apart in the first place.

(Below)
A wider U-shape with a center island which has the cooktop. If you could ignore the location of the ovens, this would be a nice arrangement.

With most of these kitchen arrangements there will be two corners that need lazy Susans to make them accessible. Or one of the corners can be the site of a door.

Oftentimes this arrangement or an L-shaped kitchen is used with the sink in a 45° corner of the kitchen, a nice way to get more light into the room.

The open side of the U-shaped kitchen may be used:

  ⇨ As the place for the kitchen table.

  ⇨ As a place for an island which, in turn, may have the sink or stove and/or an eating bar on it.

  ⇨ As a place for a peninsula extending from one of the cabinets on either side.

The L-shaped kitchen

The L-shaped kitchen has two counters at right-angles to each other rather than the three of the U-shaped kitchen.

With an L-shaped kitchen without an island, the refrigerator landing areas are still the adjacent counter(s). For a side-by-side unit, the lack of an area in front would make it inconvenient to use—which is why this arrangement usually includes an island. The island also makes suitable landing areas for the ovens if they are needed.

As can be seen from the photos, the L-shaped kitchen with island is usually a user-friendly design. The island can suitably include the stovetop or the sink and, of course, serve as an eating bar.

It is well to think carefully about this design if the kitchen is very large, it simply spreads things out too much, again making unnecessary steps.

Other Kitchen Help

We have a few websites which may be helpful to you if you're looking for info on some of the items that go into a kitchen. We are not, of course, recommending any of the products you may find. It's a place to start.

On-line pictures of many different kitchens with different motifs can be found at Kitchen.com[18F]. These should be very helpful in giving you some ideas of style and looks.

Faucets, sinks, disposals, and instant hot water dispensers are at[18B, 18C, 18D].

The National Kitchen and Bath Association[18E] stresses remodeling and using their members in your kitchen design.

Review

We've covered a wide range of kitchen topics in this Part III of the book. We summarize them here to be helpful to you when you're looking at kitchens in models, in existing houses, in floor plans and architectural drawings. Having a good idea of what you want and don't want before you have to start making decisions will make that process both more focussed and more satisfying.

  ⇨ Countertops—there is a wide variation in materials and their prices. Consider the durability, repairability, maintenance, suitability for undermount sinks, and flexibility in fitting into available space.

  ⇨ Sinks—the options are: drop in, tile in, undermount, and integral. Those without a lip that sits on the counter make it easier to clean up the kitchen.

  Some sink materials can be used with any option, others are limited.

  Sink location is an important consideration because it must be placed where it has a good work area and where the dishwasher can be located adjacent to it.

L-SHAPED KITCHENS ARE USUALLY USER-FRIENDLY DESIGNS

A generally user-friendly L-shaped kitchen with an island. The microwave oven is not in the photo. If it's to the right of the sink, fine. If not, it should be above the stovetop where the hood is now. Like other L-shaped kitchens, this one will require a lazy Susan in the corner, a usual characteristic with this design.

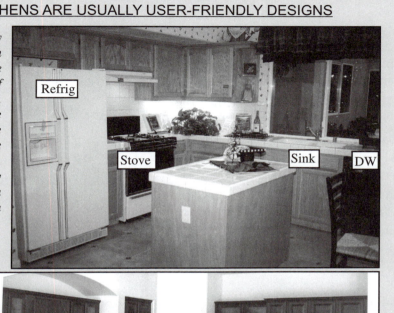

A large L-shaped kitchen with an island. The large amount of space between the island and the cabinets gives a commodious feeling but will make more kitchen steps than if the island were closer to the stove, refrigerator and the ovens. Here the island serves as an eating bar.

This L-shaped kitchen with an island is about as user-friendly as you'll see. The range is on an island with a hood. The microwave and refrigerator are across the aisle from it. Note the space between the dishwasher and the corner and also the generous quantity of cabinets.

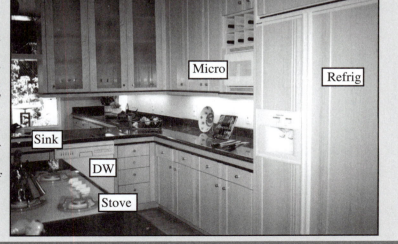

⇨ Dishwasher—location next to the sink, not in a corner and not too close to the sink with a 45° corner. It and the sink should be located where it is easy to unload the dishwasher directly into the cupboards with a minimum of steps.

There should be room to comfortably walk around an open dishwasher door.

⇨ Refrigerator—it's style and location should not block a door from opening fully.

It should have a landing area either in front or on the side(s) that have doors that open.

It should be convenient to a sink and work area where foods can be taken out to prepare them for the stove or the table.

⇨ Stovetop—exhaust systems are a major concern with stovetop locations. In general, updraft systems will be more effective than with downdraft units.

With updraft systems, the farther the hood extends over the burners, the more effective it will be.

With downdraft systems, whether center vent or back vent, expect steam and fumes from tall pots to escape into the room.

⇨ Microwave ovens—may include the exhaust fan for the stovetop under it. When located separately it should be near the sink work area.

⇨ Thermal ovens—may be a part of the range that also includes the stovetop or may be located in a separate cabinet, usually with the microwave oven.

The overall thrust has been to show those arrangements which make for an easy-to-use user-friendly kitchen, the things to do and those to avoid.

SECTION IV

The Rest of the House

There is no place more delightful than one's own fireside.
Cicero (Marcus Tullius Cicero), Roman statesman, lawyer and scholar. (106-43BC)

From Cicero's time to today, not much has changed in our perceptions of what our homes should do for us.

With the subject of the kitchen done, this part of the book looks at the rest of the rooms in the house. In Chapter 19 attention is paid to potential problems and how avoid them in bathrooms and then to bedrooms in Chapter 20.

The formal dining room is singled out because it is so often designed with little thought to what will be in it. And in Chapter 22 the laundry is not overlooked because it, too, needs more attention than it usually gets.

The garage can be a blessing or a curse and should not be forgotten when looking at how houses are laid out and built.

There are a number of tips in Chapter 23 on the little items outside the house that can make a big difference after you've moved in.

Chapter 19

Bathrooms

Nothing astonishes men so much as common sense and plain dealing.
Ralph Waldo Emerson, American poet (1803 - 1882)

In this chapter:
Bathrooms seem to be a place where building and interior designers spread their wings. Here we look at a number of different options and at the user-friendly and -unfriendly things you may find, all places where decisions will have to be made.

Bathrooms require critical decisions about lighting, windows, counters, sinks, vanities, tubs, showers, and switch locations. Wherever they are used with function, as well as looks, in mind, your new home will be the better for it. First we look at counters, what's used and how they vary from kitchen counters.

Counters

Counter heights

Counter heights for kitchens are pretty standard at around 36 inches. In bathrooms that may be used by children, it's common to put the counters lower, typically 32 inches. In the master bedroom vanity area, however, you'll find a variety of heights, the argument being that the higher counters are more comfortable for an adult and there's no reason to make them low enough for children. You may want to give some thought as to what would work best for you.

Countertop materials

Most of the countertop materials used in kitchens are also found in bathrooms. But there is one that is different. While not used in kitchens, cultured marble is found extensively in bathrooms.

These kitchen countertop materials, all described in Chapter 13, are also used in bathroom vanities:

  ➪ Laminate,

  ➪ Tile,

  ➪ Stone,

  ➪ Solid surface,

  ➪ Engineered stone, and

  ➪ Solid-surface veneer.

Solid-surface and engineered-stone counters are seldom in used bathrooms because their higher cost is not warranted—except, maybe, for their looks. The relatively new solid-surfacing veneer works fine in vanities and bathrooms.

Cultured marble

Cultured marble is a countertop material that is excellent and popular for vanities. It is not used in kitchens because of its relatively soft surface and somewhat higher cost than laminates.

"Cultured marble" is not what its name implies. It is a cast polymer which can have a marble-like appearance. It is manufactured by molding a mixture of finely ground limestone and polyester resin. The surface has a gel coat that makes it more impervious to water.

Materials other than limestone are sometimes used to get "cultured onyx" and "cultured granite." The resulting products are different in appearance and are a little more expensive then cultured marble, functionally they are much the same.

Cultured marble may be a single color but it can be made with a marbleized appearance that many people find elegant. A well-done cultured marble shower or tub surround, for example, can be quite handsome.

Cultured-marble countertops are usually made with the counter, backsplash, and the front face all molded in one piece. Sometimes a small lip on the front of the countertop keeps water from run-

ning onto the floor. The ends are separate pieces that are installed at the same time as the top. The material is rather heavy and there is a limit to the practical size of a single piece.

The basin may be integral with the countertop or it may be separate as discussed below.

The top surface is a gel coating that is about one-fiftieth of an inch thick and has a hardness that is between laminate and tile. Minor scratches in surfaces can be polished out by someone experienced in handling the material. Major damage to gel-coated cultured marble can also be repaired but the knowhow to do this is not widespread.

A caution: this material should not be scoured with any kind of abrasive, it will leave scratches in the surface that may not be removable. Nor should steel wool be used. It is interesting to note that, worldwide, many hotel and motel bathrooms use cultured marble which attests to its cost effectiveness, its suitability and its ruggedness as a vanity countertop.

Seams are an aestheticproblem. When two pieces directly abut one another there will be inevitable small differences in thickness that cannot be smoothed out because the gel coat surface is so thin. When seams do occur they always involve a

The kind of handsome vanity that can be achieved with cultured marble. This one was seen in a new condo in Santiago, Chile.

mastic that is usually quite evident. For the same reasons, gel-coated material isn't usually seamed directly with other materials.

With cultured marble, basins can be molded as one piece with the countertop making a smooth unified appearance. A disadvantage to this arrangement is that any problems in the basin will require that the whole countertop be replaced. Alternately, an undermount basin can be used as in the Santiago photo.

The International Cast Polymer Association (ICPA)[20A] is the trade organization for the cast polymer industry—including manufacturers of solid surface materials. A serious past problem with cultured marble was the inconsistency in quality and performance. In poorly made cultured marble, particularly for applications subject to hot water such as basins, tubs, and shower pans, the gel coat would crack or craze over a period of months or years. This gave the product a bad reputation that hurt the industry. Another place to get more information about cultured marble is columnist Tim Carter's website[20B] where he describes the material and how it can be used.

A cultured-marble countertop with integral basin. Note that the backsplash, countertop and basin are all one piece. There are no seams and no lip on the basin.

Relative costs

Laminate is the least expensive countertop and solid-surface the costliest. Tile, stone, solid-surfacing veneer, cultured marble and engineered stone are in between.

Basins

Basins may be:

- ⇨ Dropped in (also called "top mount"),
- ⇨ Integral with the counter (in the case of cultured marble or solid surface),
- ⇨ Mounted under the counter, or
- ⇨ Mounted on top of the counter, called "floation" by at least one manufacturer (this is a very recent "in" thing to call this user-unfriendly arrangement).

There are several pages of photos of these four different kinds of basins. They are here to:

- ⇨ More thoroughly illustrate the different kinds of basins.
- ⇨ To show the plethora of basins that are available—and these aren't all of them by any matter of means.
- ⇨ To show the good and not-so-good of the many different kinds of basins.

Besides these basins you may want to take a look at the website of Anawalt Ceramics a company that makes specialized basins, mostly ceramic[20D].

Drop-in basins (photos below and opposite)

There is the same objection to drop-in basins in the bathroom as in the kitchen: the basin lip sitting on top of the counter makes cleaning more difficult.

This lip on top of the counter may be even more objectionable in the vanity than in the kitchen where there is always a sponge or cloth around to pick up spills. In the vanity you probably have to go searching for something to clean up hair or beard trimmings that fall on the counter. How nice to be able to just brush them into the basin. Again, the voice of experience.

A laminate (left) and a tile counter with drop-in basins. These make it difficult to wipe anything from the counter into the sink.

DROP-IN BASINS ARE FOUND ON ALL TYPES OF COUNTERS

Some look utilitarian while others were obviously chosen for their distinct differences. Whether they are overly unfriendly is a personal choice between the form and the function.

Standard drop-in basin on laminate counter.

A metal basin dropped into a cultured-marble countertop. Different, huh?

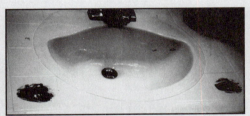

This child's bathroom counter has several decorative tiles in it. Note the different shape of the basin. It IS distinctive.

A ceramic "look at me" drop-in basin on a tile counter. More work at cleaning time.

This rectangular drop-in sink sits way above the counter. A real cleaning problem. AND, being in a corner like this makes it more inconvenient in day-to-day use.

A tile counter with built-in geometric patterns. Note the unusually wide decorative lip on the basin.

Integral basins (photos below and opposite)

When the basins are integral with a cultured-marble countertop, you save money, both for materials and installation. The disadvantage is that if you ever need to replace the basin, it's not straightforward—it usually involves the replacement of the entire countertop.

And there is another caution—when the drain pipe is installed into the bottom of the basin it must be done carefully, otherwise it may crack the gelatin coat on the cultured marble making it unattractive over time as it accumulates dirt. If this happens be sure to get in touch with the builder or

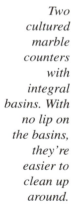

Two cultured marble counters with integral basins. With no lip on the basins, they're easier to clean up around.

whoever is responsible. You'll need a new counter with sink because they are all one unit.

Banjo counters

In the guest or hall bath, the countertop is sometimes extended out over the top of the adjacent toilet tank. While usually done with cultured marble, these banjo-shaped counters are sometimes used with other materials. It looks nice and adds a little counter space. But, if it is not to be an eventual maintenance headache, it takes a very low toilet tank. With standard tanks the counter makes it impossible to get inside them. Usually this won't be a problem for a few years until a valve needs replacing or a tangled chain needs attention. Then it will be necessary to move the whole toilet to be able to get inside the tank. This turns what should be a small chore for the homeowner into a major job where a plumber will be needed to reseat the toilet. *Caveat Emptor.*

A tile banjo countertop with drop-in basin. Doubly user-unfriendly.

A reader reports another potential problem with banjo counters...the ledge above the toilet is narrow and it is very easy to knock things from the counter into the toilet bowl. All in all it is a tradeoff between that little ledge of a counter and the problems it can cause.

CULTURED MARBLE MAKES INTEGRAL BASINS POSSIBLE

When basins and countertop are one piece, they are cost effective and there's no basin lip in the way when cleaning off the counter.

Here the flexibility of cultured marble is used to make a banjo counter (see text) and an integral basin in one piece—along with the backsplash.

Matching basins integral with a cultured-marble countertop. But note that this isn't a very user-friendly counter—it's too short, there simply isn't room enough on either end.

A more decorative integral basin in a cultured-marble counter. As above, the backsplash and the basins are all one piece with the counter.

Undercounter basins (photos next page)

In the usual case, undercounter basins are a little larger than the hole in the counter so that the edge of the counter sticks out over the basin.

H aving had a cultured-marble counter with a separate undercounter, cast-iron basin, I would recommend it as a way to get the advantages of the cultured marble counter without worrying about what the basin may look like after several years.

A more sophisticated version is to have the hole in the countertop contoured to the exact size of the basin underneath. This gives a very clean, smooth, and unified appearance to the counter and basins. This appearance is enhanced even more when the colors used in the counter are matched to the basin underneath.

How basins are mounted under the counter depends on the type of countertop material.

⇨ Laminate counters, as noted earlier, are not suitable for undercounter basins.

⇨ Tile presents a special problem. In some cases small pieces of quarter-round tile are cut and fit into the opening. With the small almost circular basins used in vanities, finishing pieces of tile must be made so short that they can give a busy unattractive look to the basin. With a relatively large basin and a very skilled

A circular basin under a tile counter.

artisan, it *is* possible to get a handsome undercounter mounting as in the photo.

I 've seen both. A poorly done basin in a tile countertop is ugly. A well done one will do justice to the finest vanity.

⇨ Stone counters, particularly marble with a suitably colored basin, make another attractive vanity. Because the color in stone is not just on the surface as it is with tile, it becomes possible to contour the stone countertop to match the shape of the basin resulting in a luxurious combination.

⇨ Solid-surfacing veneers require basins that are cemented directly to the veneer for a seamless interface. Cast iron sinks may be too heavy for this. Or the technique described in Chapter 13 can be used. It'll depend on how comfortable the countertop fabricator may be with it.

⇨ Cultured marble countertops are made with holes for the basins molded in them. The edges of the countertop around the holes are finished (gel-coated) and mounting tabs are molded into the underside of the countertop. These are used by the plumber when the counter is installed. The finished counter/basin is as useful as a single unit but if either needs to be replaced, it is significantly less costly than if they were one piece.

UNDERCOUNTER MOUNTS ARE EASIER TO USE

These are found under every counter type except laminate. User-friendliness isn't the question here, however. Cost and how they look are where the personal choices are made.

This counter features large tile and a geometrically-shaped undermount basin.

Beautiful marble and basin combo.

A square undermount basin in a tile counter. Note that the tile itself is the top edge for the basin.

A round basin in a cultured-marble counter. A good, user-friendly combination.

A square undermount basin in a cultured granite counter. The counter itself is the top edge for the basin.

When a solid-surface counter is used, this kind of user-friendly upscale basin arrangement becomes possible

On top-of-the-counter basins (photos opposite page)

In the relatively recent past we've seen the resurgence of basins sitting on top of counters. It's reminiscent of the old wash pan. Only instead of sitting there and needing emptying after use as happened decades ago, now they are tied to the plumbing and you simply pull the plug to empty. They are different and the latest but...user-friendliness isn't so obvious.

Pedestal wash basins

Half-baths with pedestal basins have become very chic in many parts of the country. But be sure to have a place where paper guest towels can be laid out because many people object to having to use a communal cloth towel, particularly in someone else's bathroom. The top of the toilet tank can be used in a pinch, but a small shelf close to the basin is better.

Because pedestal basins are small there is no place to put paper guest towels around them. A separate small counter is appropriate.

Vanity cabinets

Consider having pull-out shelves in vanity base cabinets. The bottoms of these cabinets are always close to 24 inches deep and the items at the backs are virtually inaccessible without pull-outs. When the pull-outs mount as close to the bottom of the cabinet as is possible you lose a little vertical height but gain considerably in overall utility. These

shelves can and should have high sides on them to contain the miscellany that'll be put in them. They are called "baskets" in the trade.

A pull-out shelf or basket at the bottom of this cabinet would make items in it much easier to get to.

Bathrooms

Bathrooms with two doors

Hall baths and guest baths are sometimes made with entry doors from the hall and/or one or two bedrooms. The bath may be divided into a room with vanity and two basins and a separate room for shower and toilet allowing two family members to use the bath at the same time.

When the dual basins, toilet, shower and/or tub are all in the same room it's not clear what the advantage is in having two basins because one person usually ties up the whole bathroom, although with small children it could be OK. Look at this arrangement carefully when you run across it to see if it fits your needs.

When checking out bathrooms, the obvious things to look for are tubs, showers, and the number and locations of wash basins. But there are other design considerations which we look at next.

COUNTERTOP BASINS ARE THE LATEST "IN" THING

They look "different" sitting up on top of whatever kind of counter they're mounted on. They are not user friendly; you simply cannot wipe anything from the counter into the basin. Then add to this that bumping them could break the basin itself or the plumbing which holds them in place. And this happens more often than bathroom designers or the manufacturers tell us about.

Auxiliary hot water

Small hot water heaters are available that mount under a vanity counter to provide hot water immediately. If you want one for a shower or tub, the heater will need to be bigger than one that furnishes water to basins only. As with other hot water heaters, you'll need gas or electricity brought to the heater's location and for gas a flue will be needed. The feasibility of doing this and the cost will depend on how big a heater you'll need and on the impact it may have on the rest of the house design.

Of course, recirculating hot water is another option. (*See* Chapter 6.)

Picture windows in bathrooms

A popular arrangement in master bathrooms is to put a big picture window right next to the bathtub. Or the tub may be in a corner so that there are windows on two sides. (*I even saw a large clear glass window on one side of a shower stall—on a golf course in California, of course!*) These windows give a feeling of openness and often provide a great view (both ways?). The question is, what kind of window treatment is appropriate? Sometimes it

When there's a great panorama and no houses close by, enjoy the openess.

is possible to reach the controls for the blinds without taking off your shoes and climbing through the tub but more often than not it is simply downright user-hostile.

Here are some options:

⇨ If you are on a hill and the view is of trees and distant panaroma, leave it uncovered—and feel fortunate!

⇨ Put permanent coverings over the windows to ensure privacy but you'll lose the openness that was so attractive at first.

⇨ Install mini-blinds that you have to climb into the tub to adjust. If you find the right adjustment that allows you to let in some light while preventing peeping toms even at night, then don't readjust the blinds.

⇨ Get blinds with motorized controls.

⇨ Use pleated cloth shades that close from the bottom up. Close them up far enough for privacy, but not so far that you block out all natural ligh—but you'll lose any view you might have.

⇨ In one expensive, single-story house I was in the builder handled this problem by building a six-foot fence a few feet out from the window. Again, no view.

Other ways to let in outside light include using smaller windows placed high up on the wall or replacing windows with glass blocks, stained glass windows, or frosted window panes. You may want to consider acrylic blocks, which are less expensive than glass blocks, for both the material and installation. These are available in translucent (not transparent) styles as well as several colors.

You can have light and a feeling of openness while maintaining privacy by having windows high up on the wall where they are met at the ceiling by skylights above the tub. If this appeals to

Glass block is good for light and privacy.

Towels IN the shower. It's hard to believe but it was real in this Florida tract.

you, be careful of the potential summer sun problem, particularly if the arrangement faces south or west.

Towel rods

Many modern-day bathrooms are open and commodious. There are mirrors, doors, a tub with its surround, and impressive amounts of glass. But in the process of putting all of this luxury into the bath, designers and builders sometimes leave no place for towel rods, again forgetting that "form follows function." Look carefully at the plans for the bathroom to be sure that there are places for towel rods, hopefully next to the shower, the tub, *and* the wash basins.

To me, it is not satisfactory to use the tub surround as the place to lay towels after bathing. They simply won't dry that way. It can be lived with. A little planning can avoid it.

This attractive vanity has no place for towels other than laying on the counter. Lousy planning.

Medicine cabinets

Medicine cabinets are not only utilitarian, they can also improve the appearance of a bathroom—but they are simply not used in some regions of the country. If you want one in your house and you live where they are not common, you may have to use extra care to be sure that your wants get translated into reality.

Medicine cabinets are usually mounted in walls between studs. There should be instructions for the framers to leave room between studs to mount one. And be sure there is nothing else between the studs, such as pipes or wiring. Don't plan on using an outside wall for the medicine cabinet, the insulation in the wall will prevent it.

An alternative to a medicine cabinet is to put a cabinet on the wall above the toilet. This option has a couple of disadvantages:

⇨ The toilet is in the way when you want to get into the cabinet and

⇨ If you accidentally drop something or brush it off of a shelf, it's likely to land in the water.

Whirlpool pump access

Whirlpool tubs can be expensive, and you probably won't recoup your costs when you sell the house. Before you spend extra money for one, it's a good idea to talk to a few people who have them and get their reactions. Some people swear by them but many more say they're never used.

One thing is for sure: if there's ever a serious problem with the plumbing associated with the pump and the jet, you'll have an expensive-to-fix problem ripping out the tub surround and skirt. As with other places where you might not be aware of them, small water leaks can cause serious rot and mold problems. While it doesn't happen often, the possibility is a negative side to whirlpool tubs.

Then there's the question of access to the electrical and plumbing installations that are needed to run the pump—and to fix it if it malfunctions.

Section P2720 of the 2000 International Residential Code (IRC) says, "**Access panel.** A door or panel of sufficient size shall be installed to provide access to the pump for repair and/or replacement."

Yet I've seen houses on both coasts where there is **no** access door or panel! And I've had a contractor's supply house tell me there is no requirement for it!!!

About as bad as no door or panel is to have one that's too small, in an inaccessible place, or located so far from the pump that it's useless.

The poor wording in the code (it doesn't say where the panel must be, just that it must be of sufficient size), the builder's inattention, and the lack of enforcement leave it very much up to the buyer to insist on something that's useful.

When the door or panel is put in place, there's no reason it has to be an eyesore, but it often is. The locations builders use for the access door are limited only by their imaginations. Both form and function are involved but there is absolutely no reason you can't have both.

There is another caution—oftentimes access doors are there just to satisfy the code requirements and the pump to which access is required is actually not reachable from the "door", to say

nothing about having enough room to work on the pump if it's ever necessary. If you have any questions, have a plumber or inspector take a look at it.

Options for the location of the access door include:

⇨ A panel on the side(the skirt) of the tub. An aesthetic consideration. If it looks as if the panel is an integral part of the tub skirt this can be unobtrusive. But it is also not acceptable if, inside, the pump is so far behind the access door that it cannot be reached.

⇨ In a room that backs up to the tub. Closets are the usual location for this option (good) but laundry rooms are also used.

⇨ An adjacent bedroom where it can be an eyesore. Builders sometimes put a grill from a cold air return register over the access door to give it the appearance of being a part of the heating system. It's ugly. There are better ways to handle the problem

⇨ In the room with the toilet. But be careful because it may be so crowded that it would become necessary to remove the toilet to work on the pump—a functional consideration—as in the lower left photo opposite.

⇨ In the inside of the end of the vanity cupboard that abuts the tub (see photo center left). Maybe it meets code but I can't imagine a plumber being able to get down there and reaching through that little hole to do anything. Aethestically great—it doesn't show with the cabinet door closed—but functionally pretty useless.

WHIRLPOOL TUB ACCESS DOORS

They come in all variations of being user-friendly, functional, attractive and ugly.

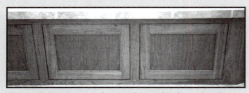

One of these panels on this whirlpool tub skirt opens up to allow access to the pump.

Another set of tub-skirt access panels. Funtional, yes, if you don't mind how it looks.

Outside access door on the deck. Convenient, efficient and not ugly.

This inaccessible hole under the vanity counter passed inspection!

Here the access is out of sight in a closet. Note that the door is bigger, making it more useful.

If access to the pump is required, the toilet would have to be unseated and moved—an expense you really don't need.

This access door is also under the vanity counter—but it's accessible.

⮑ An outside wall. This may be done even if it's on the second floor. Obviously good weatherproofing is required. It is, however, better than having an eyesore or an inaccessible arrangement in the bathroom.

Exhaust fans

Baths and showers should have exhaust fans even if not required by code. Fans can help reduce the amount of moisture which, in turn, helps control mildew and mold.

Most importantly, get fans that are large enough. Codes allow ventilation in bath and laundry rooms to be accomplished either using a window or an exhaust fan. Most of today's homes include the fan. This is a good idea, even if there is a window, because in the winter you'd probably rather not open it.

Unfortunately, most bathroom and laundry exhaust fans pay lip service to the code but don't do much for ventilation. A fan with a capacity of 60 cubic feet per minute (CFM) will usually meet code requirements. For the subcontractor the cost of such a fan is around $20. In a typical installation, a 4-inch flexible aluminum duct is tied to the fan to take the exhausted air outside the house as required by codes. At the lower end of the duct is a flap that keeps cold air from coming down the duct when the fan isn't operating. The fan must push air hard enough to open the flap then get the air up ten, twenty, or more feet of twisting, very rough duct. The $20 unit simply can't do this. And you get a useless exhaust fan.

Another place where fans are useless is in a modern open bath/shower that's an extension of the bedroom. Here the area to vent is much larger. Fans may meet the letter of the code. They can't possibly do anything more.

On top of all this, note that houses are being made tighter and tighter in an effort to reduce energy use. This means that the fan has to fight not only the exhaust ducting, it's also got to fight to get air into the house to blow out! Should the codes be changed? You bet! Then maybe we'd get our money's worth in at least this one small part of the house. And it's not just the $20—the ducting and the installation cost the builder and you several times that much for each and every bathroom and laundry. And all wasted!

Then you add to that the ever-increasing concern with molds—which must have moisture to exist. The efficacy of a fan in getting moisture from a shower outside quickly is a necessity in the fight.

I've developed a method of quickly and unobtrusively testing these exhaust fans where I tie a piece of thin thread on the end of a stick and hold it up to the fan. In only two different houses out of perhaps 100 did I find fans that moved the thread. But in most bathrooms and laundries it never wiggles; the fan moves no air at all, *none*.

Some building officials know this but the industry has been doing it this way for so long that no one has the guts to try to change it. And homeowners, nationwide, are getting ripped off by most of the industry including code officials as well as builders.

When visiting a model home, I used my thread trick to check a bathroom fan and to my surprise, the exhaust fan sucked the thread right up to the fan's grill. I commented about this to the salesperson who told me that the builder had found out about the problem when they left a fan on overnight to get rid of a smell in the bathroom. The next morning nothing had happened so they investigated. Now their exhaust systems use larger fans and short straight ducts to the outside.

What can you do about it?

⮑ New construction. Make a point with your builder that you want a fan that moves air. It can be done but it'll be up to you to insist. (The trick is to use short smooth ducting along with a bigger-than-code fan.)

⇨ Existing home. Check it out and see how much of an expense it would be to have it improved. Then decide if it's worth it.

⇨ Remodel. If the bathroom is a part of the remodel it should be relatively easy to make a bigger fan with better ducting a part of the job.

Heat

A heater in front of a shower or tub will make it more comfortable when towelling off. An overhead infrared lamp, a wall heater, or an electric baseboard heater all work. For a new house you should tell the builder the kinds of plain lights, lights with exhaust fans, heat lamps, and heaters you want. Fans, plain lights, heat lamps, and electric heaters should all have different switches, since not all of them are needed every time someone uses the room. And, if it matters to you, be specific about the exact locations of the elements and the wall switches that control them (*see* Chapter 5). The electrician will do the best he can but he can't read your mind.

If you're getting a house built or remodeled you have yet another option, you can use flooring that can be heated either electrically or with hot water. The cost of installation and running the system may exceed your budget for a nicety that only comes into play when you are barefoot in the bathroom. Again—your decision.

Then there's the toilet itself. You can now buy seats that are heated! They require a GFCI outlet (*see* Chapter 5) next to the toilet. Look at them at the Kohler website[20E].

Tubs

When you have a say, select a tub by manufacturer and model number—or let the builder do it for you and hope you end up with something you like in terms of style, material, and price. Your local plumbing supply store *should* be able to explain the pros and cons of the various available tubs, but not all of them can or will. It is probably prudent to visit more than one supply store and ask your questions. That way you stand a better chance of getting competent advice and of making the right decisions.

Some cultured-marble manufacturers make some really exotic appearing tubs that may appeal to you. These units are very heavy and the cost of shipping them is exorbitant but, if they are made locally, you may want to consider them. (If you buy one, be sure it's certified by the national cultured marble organization as explained above.)

Showers

While you're at the plumbing supply store, look at shower enclosures. Molded fiberglass units—both those with a gel coat surface and those made with acrylic—are popular. They present little chance for water to get into the wall, making it a good choice. Cultured marble is another option. Since it has no grout, cultured marble does not support mildew or mold growth, and its smooth surface is easy to keep clean. If you live in an area where cultured marble is not commonly seen in new houses, you may be surprised at how handsome it can look.

Ceramic tile is another popular shower enclosure. The drive toward tighter houses make it even more imperative that there be no water leakage to avoid molds. Shower stalls need to be watched in the damper climates. Be sure that tile, if used, is mounted on a stiff waterproof board.

All shower stalls should have a hand hold in them. You need something to hold onto while you're standing on one foot washing the bottom of the other one. Don't forget to insist on a slip-proof bottom in the shower!

When a shower head is placed through the shower-stall wall, it is not high enough for the average man to stand under without leaning over. It's usable, it's not friendly.

Most men wash their hair in the shower. The shower head should be high enough that they don't have to duck to get under it. This means putting the shower head in the wall above most manufactured shower stalls, i. e., well over six feet above the shower floor.

Can you sidle?

Many master suites have the toilet in its own small room or in a room with the shower. When the room is too small, you have to sidle in beside the toilet bowl to have enough room to close the door. When the same arrangement is shown in floor plans, sometimes the toilet bowl is not to scale so the problem isn't obvious. One option is to leave the door off altogether. Another is to use a pocket door if appropriate wall space is available, i.e., no wires and no plumbing.

Usually it's not hard to avoid the sidle toilet when you think of it at the planning stage. The photos on the opposite page show several ways that do the job. In an existing house it is something you have to decide whether or not you want to live with it.

Tub surround

Your choices for tub surrounds (the tub deck and the skirt in front) are ceramic tile, cultured marble, stone (marble), and, perhaps, solid-surfacing veneer. Don't consider plastic laminates, they make unattractive surrounds. Note that the material used for the tub deck may be different from the skirt but it's common to use the same material for the deck and vanity countertop. And, if you're using a whirlpool tub, don't forget the pump access discussed earlier.

There is another concern here—water. Not what's in the tub but the water that's splashed on the surround. Unless it is an impervious material like cultured marble or solid surface, water can seep through the surround material and be caught under it. This, in turn, can lead to wood rot and molds. If there is a tub surround, it should really be an impervious material, certainly not tile with its semi-porous grout.

The shoes were placed here to show where you'd have to stand to close the door.

SIDLE TOILETS AND WAYS TO AVOID THEM

When the room with the toilet is small, it takes care not to make it where you have to sidle in to be able shut the door. Here are two examples of what to watch out for and four examples of how to get around the problem even with a small room.

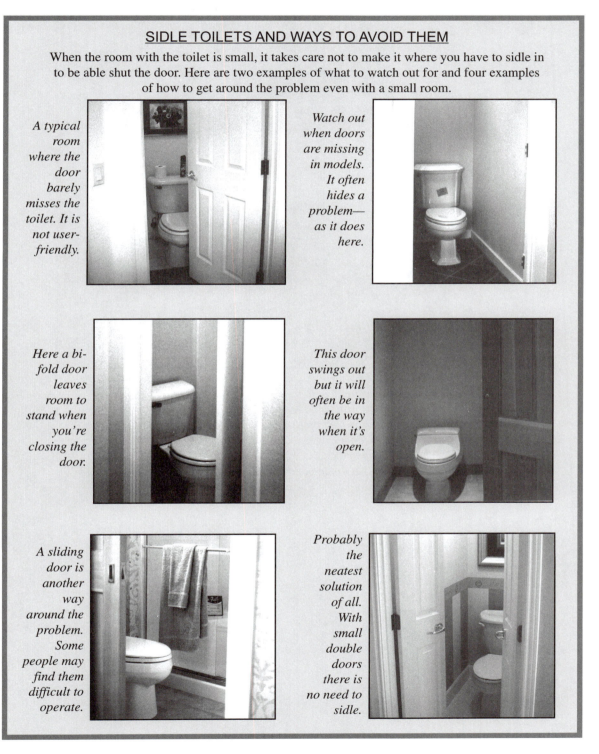

A typical room where the door barely misses the toilet. It is not user-friendly.

Watch out when doors are missing in models. It often hides a problem—as it does here.

Here a bi-fold door leaves room to stand when you're closing the door.

This door swings out but it will often be in the way when it's open.

A sliding door is another way around the problem. Some people may find them difficult to operate.

Probably the neatest solution of all. With small double doors there is no need to sidle.

An overview: *comments and questions re this nice bath. The tub deck and skirt use the same tile as the floor, a nice coordinated approach. But there are some questions. (1) Are the backerboards for both the floortile and the tub deck tile waterproof? If not, there is a definite potential for mold. (2) Why isn't there a towel rod instead of having the towels laying on the tub deck? Many people would like to be able to hang up the towel after drying with it. (3) Where's the pump access? If it's outside, fine, but if it's necessary to remove some of the tile work to get to the pump that's not so good and may not be code compliant.*

Chapter 20

Bedrooms

To repeat what others have said, requires education; to challenge it, requires brains.
Mary Pettibone Poole, humorist and philosopher (-?-)

In this chapter:
Bedrooms are, relatively speaking, among the easier design areas of a house. Yet, builders do things here that are not user-friendly and which will be major annoyances for the homeuser. That's what this chapter is about.

Even though we all know that a room needs to be big enough to hold the furniture that will be put in it, sometimes designers and builders overlook things that make it difficult to use a bedroom as we would like.

We look first at bedroom layouts and then at the closets that accompany them.

Bedrooms

The master is the largest of the several bedrooms and gets our first attention.

The master bedroom

Furniture placement

The master bedroom, like the dining room, is sometimes designed without any thought for placing furniture along the walls. A typical master bedroom suite consists of the bed, two night stands, a large dresser, and a chest or armoire. Besides these, there is often a TV stand or a wall unit for holding the TV, books, etc. When the designer includes several windows and unusual wall angles, there may be simply no place for the dresser—to say nothing of a chest or armoire.

In some larger homes, cabinets are a built-in part of the walk-in closet, obviating the need for spaces for a dresser and a chest or armoire. Or the chest or armoire, at least, are put into the closet, not because that's particularly desirable, but because it's the only place available.

Besides the bare necessities you will sometimes see master bedrooms that include a sitting area or an office.

When I walk into a model and see the bed at an angle across a corner of the room I always check to see if this is simply a dramatic decorating arrangement or if it's because there is no place else to put the bed and nightstands—it happens both ways. If you like this and there's room, that's fine, except don't unwittingly get caught with an unusual arrangement you can't change—in case you decide you want to later.

Window placement

Large windows on the south and west sides of the house can be sun problems in the summer. If possible, face any large windows east or north. Tall windows, of course, should not be in walls that may be needed for furniture.

Low windows mean that any mirrors on a dresser in front of them will block the view. This model had no dresser nor was there really a place for one.

Another consideration with large expanses of glass in a bedroom are the window coverings. In models where the emphasis is on the view, you'll find no coverings at all...while the house is being shown. After it's sold the problems of privacy and need to keep early morning summer sun out of the room come into play. You'll have to visualize what the room will look like with drapes or blinds.

Lighting

Here are some of the lighting arrangements you'll see in bedrooms:

⇨ No fixture. The power to an outlet is controlled by the room light switch and the light is provided by a plug-in lamp. This is the least expensive and is a common set-up in tracts where every dollar counts.

⇨ Room-center fixture. A ceiling fixture, usually small, is located in the center of the room. It is controlled by the room light switch. This is the usual arrangement in most bedrooms.

⇨ Recessed can lights in front of closets. One or more lights are placed in the ceiling to illuminate the room, particularly the closet. This is common outside of tracts.

⇨ A ceiling fanwith a light kit that is controlled by a wall switch or a remote controller.

This bedroom light is part of the ceiling fan unit.

⇨ Indirect ceiling lighting is sometimes used in large bedrooms with high ceilings to give a dramatic effect.

If the room-center fixture might be changed to a ceiling fan in the future, the mounting box should be strong enough to support the fan. Either a 3-wire conductor would be needed between the fixture and the wall switch location or the fan will need to be remotely operated. (*See* Chapter 5.)

Doors

Chapter 9 discussed a number of ways that room and closet doors can be unfriendly, including model houses with missing doors. When you're seriously looking at houses or plans, it would probably be a good idea to review that chapter.

Double entrance doors can cause the same problems in bedrooms as elsewhere: they can block light switches and take useful wall space that may be needed for furniture.

Other bedrooms

Smaller bedrooms do not, of course, need as much space for furniture, yet the need for a bed and a dresser is still there. Often times there should also be an area for a small desk to accommodate the child who needs a place to study.

Closets

If building designers spent as many hours doing housework in the houses they design as they spend in designing them, there are some things they'd be quick to change. The amount of closet space and closet design are two of them.

Walk-in closets

A discussion of the problems with walk-in closet doors is given in Chapter 9. Also see the photos there with the discussion of Rule 2.

A walk-in closet door at its worst. This door swings right where a nightstand would go—if there were room. (This is the master bedroom in a house the builder built for himself. Need I say more about planning ahead?)

Closets and accessibility

Closet sizes and types vary widely among houses and designs. The real caution here is to make sure that each closet is large enough and readily accessible. It's far too easy for designers to assign really unusable space as a closet. For example, when the door into a room is at 45° to the walls, it usually means that a closet will have a

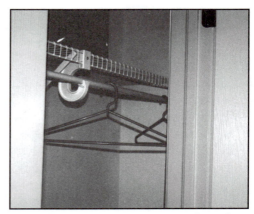

When door openings are not as wide as the closet, they severely restrict access.

deep inaccessible corner—which can be OK if there's enough usable space. It will depend on how you plan to use the room and whether the user needs a large amount of closet storage area.

Many closets that use sliding, hinged, or bifold doors are designed so that they are partly inaccessible! Even if not deliberate, it is *not* user-friendly. The problem is that the front open-

A double closet with inaccessible ends.

ings of the closets are too narrow. It's not unusual to see closets with over a foot of closet past the end of the door opening. Add 6 or 7 inches of an open bifold door in the front of the opening and you can have close to 18 inches of inaccessible closet on at least one end. Try getting a coat or dress out of the end of that closet and you'll be more than a little annoyed.

The problem arises because doors come in preset widths and these may not match the space the designer has available for the closet. Better planning should make it possible to have closets whose sizes match available doors. When looking at houses, keep an eye open for these designs. You'll be surprised at how many of them there are—it occurred in 25 percent of the houses in our floor plan review!

Closet interiors

It used to be that a closet had just a shelf and a pole for hanging clothes. Some still do but other, more useful, arrangements are seen today. These include built-in shelves for shoes or whatever else the home user may want.

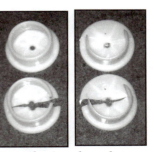

Some plastic pole sockets don't last. Before and after less than a year.

Poles may be two levels in height for greater utility.

Some builders use stiff vinyl-coated steel wire instead of shelves in closets. Again, these may or may not appeal to you. (But not in pantries, please— *see* Chapter 18.)

Here's a little problem, easy to fix when it arises, but annoying when it happens. In less than two years in our new home we had clothes dumped on the floor seven times by breaking pole sockets. Pole sockets are the plastic, wood, or metal pieces that hold the ends of the clothes rods or poles. Ours were a translucent white plastic that, over a short period of time, de-plasticized, lost their strength and split in two. If you find these in your house, keep your fingers crossed. If the first one breaks, bite the bullet and replace them all because it'll be just a matter of time until the rest go. (We've gone over to wooden sockets that won't de-plasticize.) If you can take care of this ahead of time, the problem won't arise.

Electrical Considerations

Electrical outlets in bedrooms are the same as elsewhere except for the need to carefully consider where furniture might go and be sure there are accessible outlets where they may be needed for lights, TV and computer

While not all bedrooms may have TVs, in today's houses it is usual enough that TV connectors are generally found in every bedroom. Again, it's location, location, location. It does little good to put a connector close to where the bed will be. A better location is across the room where the TV would be set in a wall unit of some kind. (If you or your spouse want a small TV beside the bed, than you'll need a TV connection there, too, of course.)

An electrical power outlet plate (right) and a standard TV coaxial connector along with two Cat. 5 connectors (keft) that can be used for telephone, televition and/or data connections. In a bedroom their locations are matters of concern.

Then, there is the computer. In a master bedroom this would usually be in a nook of some sort which is used for office space. In other bedrooms, there are two considerations:

⇨ The computer may sit on a desk in a child's room or

⇨ The room may be used as an office rather than a bedroom.

The location for the outlets for a computer connection should be such that the amount of cable needed to get to the computer will be relatively short. This is more of an aesthetic consideration than functional. A cable running around the room is not as clean an arrangement as when it is not. And there is less danger of snagging it with a foot or vacuum cleaner when it is short and behind furniture.

Chapter 21

The Living Areas

> *Truth is more of a stranger than fiction.*
>
> Mark Twain, humorist, writer and lecturer (1835-1910)

In this chapter:
Having gone through the kitchen, the bedrooms, and the baths we now look at the other parts of the houses that we live in.

The entry, hallways and stairs—areas of transition used for moving from one part of the house to another—have both aesthetic and functional aspects. The dining room and living room are not everyday rooms and do not exist in some plans. The family room and/or great room, on the other hand, are used daily. We look at these here. We save the laundry for the next chapter.

The Entry

Entry design, in general, focuses on how it looks. But there are a few functional aspects that shouldn't be overlooked. For example, there is the question of security and sidelights that was discussed in Chapter 11. Here are others.

The entry may be a separate room or it may be a part of a room which encompasses the living room, dining room, and/or family room. Stairs, if there are any, usually start from the entry. Although a large entry or foyer can add to the feeling of luxury in a house, it is an area that is not used that much. You may decide that you want one that is fairly small, saving the floor space for something more useful.

Occasionally a designer will forget to include a guest closet. That's usually not a good idea. When it *is* included, it should be close to the entry door.

The guest closet should not be blocked by the open entry door. It's just when people are coming or going that you need access to the closet.

This entry closet is commodious—right behind the open door. It is very inconvenient when guests are arrving or leaving.

Having a front door that opens across a staircase is almost as bad as one that blocks the guest closet. In general, you shouldn't have to close one door to open another or to use the stairs.

Be careful when there is a chandelier in the entry. Make sure there's a place to set a ladder to change light bulbs when needed. (*See* the later discussion re stairway lighting.) Entry lighting fixtures should be centered either on the entryway itself or on the front door.

Although they are not as popular today as in years past, the split-level entry home is still a useful concept, particularly on a hillside lot. People considering homes here need to take a careful look—before the house is built, if you can—at what visitors will see when they come in the front door.

Occasionally you'll go into such a house and, standing in the foyer, you look right into the hall bathroom at the head of the half flight that goes up. This isn't a functional thing and it may not bother you but it is a real turnoff to many people who feel that the view from the entry, or from any place in the living area of the home for that matter, should not include a bathroom. When you are considering floor plans, it pays, for resale consid-

erations, to avoid arrangements which may be aesthetically unappealing to some prospective customers.

Floor

Even without separate walls, the entry is usually an identifiable area. This is accomplished using a different floor covering than adjacent rooms or, as is commonly done in southwestern architecture, by making the entry raised, requiring a step down to the rest of the house. Floor coverings need to stand up to water and mud, so carpet is rarely used. The most common entry materials include hardwoods, vinyl, ceramic tile, laminates, and marble or other stone. For safety reasons, be sure the material isn't slippery when wet. Surprisingly, there are floor tiles that are like ice when your shoes are wet and, unhappily, some decorating and tile centers do not know or do not care about warning you of the potential danger. Or the builder may choose the tile without considering where it will be used. (*See* the discussion in Chapter 12.)

Hallways and Stairways

These two areas are among those that are non-living space. They are called "ways" for good reason. They are not intended to hold furniture nor are they areas where we spend any time. In more extravagant house designs they can be dramatic eye-catchers like a wide curving staircase or a bridge between two upstairs living or bedroom areas.

Hallways

Look carefully at model homes to get a feel for how wide you feel a hallway should be. A few inches can make a big difference in whether a hall feels comfortable or cramped. To many people hallways narrower than about 44 inches feel cheap and constraining.

One house where the hallway was particularly noticed is on a hillside and the bedrooms are on the open side of the lower story while the hall is on the uphill side. Even in daylight the hall tends to be dark. Some houses we've seen did not have enough light in that hallway.

People react to aesthetic things differently and what may be okay for you may not be for someone else. Things like a long, uninviting hallway will make some people turn away from the house without realizing why. (Remember Thoreau's quote from the Preface, "It's not what you look at that matters, it's what you see."?)

Lighting in hallways

Most of the time, light fixtures in halls are placed to provide general lighting, not where something specifically needs lighting. There should be hall lights where they're needed—specifically in front of closets and the thermostat.

This closet is dark. There should be a light in or in front of it.

Stairway lighting

Have you seen chandeliers that require scaffolding to change a light bulb because there's no place to set a standard ladder? *Caveat Emptor!* Look for these fixtures when you're visiting models and looking at floor plans. Consider these alternatives:

⇨ If there is a chandelier, the light bulbs should point downward so that they can be changed by a special tool on a pole.

⇨ Sconces along the staircase wall and/or on the landing to light the stairs.

⇨ Using several unobtrusive nightlight-type fixtures that are mounted in the wall a couple of feet above the treads in the stairwell. These units may be small (the size of a standard outlet cover plate) or they may be two or three times larger. They're installed flush with the staircase wall and have louvers in them to direct the light downward.

⇨ Have recessed can lights installed in the ceiling above the stairwell. This may be the least attractive solution because when you look up the stairs you look straight into the lights.

Chandeliers over stairs can be maintenance headaches.

There are special ladders where one side can be made shorter than the other which can be used under some circumstances. One manufacturer (Werner) calls them "articulated" ladders (type M1)[21B]. Little Giant simply calls theirs the "Little Giant System"[21A]. If you want to get into this yourself, the Werner ladders are carried at home improvement stores. You'll have to search for the

A Little Giant ladder seen at a home show. The adjustable legs and their feet are designed to stand on stairs for changing chandelier lights, for painting or whatever.

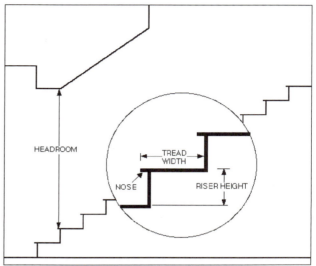

Stair design is important for code compliance, aesthetics, and ease of use.

Little Giant. In any case, depending on just where the light fixture is located, even these ladders may not make it possible to reach them. It's just good sense, if there is one of these overhead chandeliers, that they be the kind that let you change the bulbs using the specialized long pole.

Stairway design

Luxurious stairs are easy to climb but take a lot of floor space while steep stairs take less space and are more difficult to use. In some designs, stairs are too steep for comfort. Check one you may be considering to see how you react to it.

A good angle for the stairs is about 36 degrees with a riser height of $7\frac{1}{4}$ inches. Each step width should be close to $11\frac{1}{2}$ inches including a $1\frac{1}{2}$-inch nose.

Building codes usually require a minimum stair width of 36 inches. You will probably want more. Similarly, codes require a minimum head room of 6 ft.-8 in. Again you should consider more, say 7 feet, to give a more open feeling.

The Dining Room

In small starter houses the formal dining room is often omitted. The idea is that a young family has better uses for the space than for a room that

By eliminating the wall between the dining and living rooms there is plenty of room around chairs when people are sitting in them. The pillars are wholly decorative—but they do define the two rooms without the claustrophic effect of walls.

gets used infrequently and requires a significant outlay for furniture. If you decide to do without a dining room, be sure the eating area in the kitchen or great room is large enough to accommodate your family and guests.

Today's formal dining room isn't always a separate room. Often, it's an area in a great room set aside for the dining room furniture. Ways to set the area apart include using archways, partial walls, columns, changing the ceiling height or pitch, flow of a wall, the pattern in a heavily textured ceiling, and a different wall paper.

Room dimensions and furniture placement

Designers and builders hesitate to commit any more space to the formal dining room than they can get away with. Homebuyers recognize that dining rooms aren't used all that often, so they're torn between saving money and making the room big enough to accommodate a full-size set of dining room furniture. Unfortunately, the answer to this question in many of today's designs is to include a formal dining room in the floor plan but make it so small that it won't take a set of furniture.

When we moved into our semi--custom house in southern California, we had a separate formal dining room that barely held our dining room furniture. When we decided to replace our old furniture with a nicer set, there was no longer enough room. Whenever we entertained it was difficult to pull out the chairs far enough that people could sit down and almost impossible to get behind chairs with people sitting in them.

At least we could extend the table out into the family room to seat everyone when we hosted the family Thanksgiving dinner.

Our present dining room doesn't use much more floor space but it's open on two sides. What a difference. We have room behind the chairs and plenty of space to expand the table for large gatherings.

When deciding on the size of the dining room you need, it's a good idea to have room for a full-sized dining set in the future even if your present dinette set would fit now. Then, when you sell, you won't turn away buyers who want a bigger room.

Wall space in a dining room is a precious commodity. There should be room for a hutch or china cabinet. Some dining room sets include a server and there should also be room for that or a sideboard along a wall.

These dining rooms are too small. You should be able to comfortably get behind the chairs when people are sitting in them. You can't here.

Sometimes builders will build in the china cabinet so that you don't have to allow for it in the dining room layout. Take a careful look at such designs because it's easier to pay lip service to "built-in china cabinet" than it is to provide one that's large enough. *Caveat emptor.*

The table is usually put near the center of the room and the dining room arrangement should be able to accommodate extension of the table for large groups. This is often into an adjacent room or area.

A dining room table is typically about 42x72 inches. Another 36 inches of clear space on each side of the table is needed so that there is room to walk behind the chairs with people seated at the table.

Here there is a built-in china hutch which is a nice touch. Even so, there will be very little room to get between it and the chairs when people are sitting in them.

A typical china cabinet is 22 to 24 inches deep so that the minimum dining room width becomes 11 feet 4 inches. The popular 10 foot-wide dining room just isn't enough.

The length of the room without additional leaves in the table and with someone seated at each end of the table needs to be 12 feet. If there is no way to extend the table into an adjacent room or area, then the dining room should be 32 inches longer.

Any doors that extend into the area occupied by the table and chairs also need to be considered.

This is a lot of room for a small house. Clever combining of the dining room with an adjacent room can cut this down significantly without compromising the amount of room needed for the table and chairs. With dining rooms that have three or four walls, it is not possible to take advantage of the presence of the adjacent rooms.

Watch out for sunken living rooms. A dining room table cannot be extended in that direction. Unfortunately, it is easier to remember this *after* you've already moved into your new home.

A well-done dining room. There is room in front of the hutch for people to sit comfortably and still have room to walk behind them, the table can be expanded away from the window, the chandelier is in the center of the room, and is centered on the window.

The chandelier

One of the more disturbing things seen in many of today's houses is the inattention paid to how the furniture will look in the dining room. In particular, the chandelier should be centered over the table—to do otherwise is visually jarring. Unfortunately that is something which many times cannot be fixed after you move in. Planning is critical if you do not want to live with this aesthetic irritation.

Some contemporary home designs have forgone the traditional dining room chandelier in favor of recessed ceiling lights thus avoiding the

Here there are recessed ceiling lights and a chandelier. It is different. How much each contributes to the lighting was hard to figure out.

problems with chandelier location discussed here. (Other times recessed lights are used to augment the chandelier as in the photo.)

The chandelier and furniture

In all but extra wide dining rooms, when there is a china hutch on one wall the table must be centered between the hutch and the other side of the dining room. Then, to have the chandelier centered

Swagged chandeliers happen when neither the builder nor the electrician think about where the table is going to be.

above the table, it, too, must be offset relative to the sides of the room.

If the electrician has not been thinking ahead or you don't make a point of it, you'll end up swagging the chandelier as shown in the photo. Swagged fixtures are almost always the result of not thinking ahead. If you have the option, don't

make it necessary. Tell the builder what you want before the electrician does his thing. Or have the chandelier moved after you move in.

We were fortunate in our new home. We were able to get the electrician to come back and move the chandelier to where it is above the dining room table. It would have looked pretty bad if he hadn't.

In an existing house you may be able to do the same thing if there's room and if the new location can be achieved without a major redo of the wiring. And if there's a good place to put the electrical box for the chandelier.

Ceiling treatment

Be wary of special ceiling treatments such as coved, trayed, coffered, Pullman, a pattern in the ceiling texturing, or any other arrangement that is symmetrical around the center of the room. Aesthetically, these all dictate that the chandelier be centered in the pattern, i.e., at the room center. If the room isn't large enough to allow the table to also be centered, you'll have the problem discussed above, only this time you can't swag the chandelier to fix it—not if you want to keep the symmetrical arrangement that makes it seem so

As it should be, this chandelier is at the center of the contoured ceiling. Let's hope the center of the table can be there too.

elegant. These ceilings should only be used in wider dining rooms.

High ceilings

Many homes in the Southwest have a similar problem arising from the high ceilings used to get the open airy feeling in the architectural design. In this case the chain holding the chandelier is quite long and, visually, it becomes an important part of the dining room. Because it is so obvious, it needs to be symmetrical with the tall room walls. Putting it off center simply doesn't look right.

So, again, we have a chandelier which is centered between the walls—a fixture that should only be used with a dining room table that is also centered which, in turn, requires a wider room—or a built-in china cabinet.

Minimum room sizes

If there is no chandelier or if the chandelier can be hung off-center, room size requirements are:

⇨ With the hutch parallel with the table: 11 ft.-6 in. x 14 ft.-8 in.

⇨ With the hutch at the end of the table: 9 ft.-6 in. x 16 ft.-8 in.

If there is a special ceiling pattern or high parallel walls in the dining room, be sure your room is big enough to let you put a china hutch along one wall and still center the table under the chandelier.

Required room sizes then become:

⇨ With the hutch parallel with the table: 13 ft.-6 in. x 14 ft.-8 in.

⇨ With the hutch at the end of the table: 11 ft.-6 in. x 16 ft.-8 in.

Windows in dining rooms

Many floor plans have a window in the dining room. Be careful if it is close to being centered on the dining room table otherwise it will look as if the designers weren't talking to each other.

In one furnished model home the dining room table was parallel to the wall with the hutch. The chandelier was hung in the center of the room and a window was centered there too. The end of the table was close to the window. However, because of the china hutch, the table could not be placed

in the center of the room so that it was about a foot off from the chandelier and also about a foot off from the center of the window. The asymmetry of the table and the window was probably more visually irritating than the table and the chandelier.

In any case, be careful of arrangements like these. If there is a window in the dining room, take care that it is not located where it looks as if it were

Be careful of dining rooms like this one with the big window and the pillars and the openness. It looks great with the dinette set but the room is too small for a full-sized set of furniture.

meant to be centered on the table but never quite made it. This is, of course, a wholly aesthetic consideration and how important it may be to you is totally a personal decision.

The Living Room

Many of today's houses do not include a living room because, for a lot of us, there simply isn't that much need for it and we include its functions in a great room. Living rooms are usually arranged as a place for guests to sit and chat. Or maybe play bridge. If you have a piano, this is probably where it will be found.

So, when considering a house with a living room, you could ask yourself whether you will have enough or the right kind of furniture to take advantage of the space. Or, perhaps, whether you entertain with enough formality to make it a very useful space. There are other options in today's houses.

The Family Room

In today's living styles, the primary use for the family room is to house the TV and there should be a good place for it, either alone or in a wall unit.

If you are going to have a gas fireplace, the combination of the location and type of fireplace becomes important as discussed in Chapter 8. Besides that, you need to be careful where the fireplace is relative to the TV. The fireplace and the TV should be close enough to each other that the same furniture seating is used to enjoy both. But you don't want the TV where a window can cause a glare on the screen during the day. Again, these are not things you can put into feet and inches but for you to consider when your choosing your new home or remodeling your old one.

Ceiling fans are common in family rooms and the suggestions in Chapter 5 about running 3-wire power conductors or using a remote controller apply here also.

A nice galley kitchen with the great room on the left side of the eating bar. A modern, relaxing, comfortable arrangement.

The Great Room

Found in more and more homes, the great room takes on the functions of both the living room and the family room. It is the social center of the household often with one side open to the kitchen with a counter and breakfast bar in between. Rooms like the one shown in the above photo make for family togetherness as well as providing an relaxing, informal atmosphere when entertaining guests. The same precautions regarding TV and fireplace locations apply here as with the family room.

Chapter 22

Laundry

I do not think much of a man who is not wiser today than he was yesterday.
Abraham Lincoln, 16th president of the United States (1809–1865)

In this chapter:
Often given little heed, the location and layout of the laundry can make a big difference in the amount of work the homeuser does in this part of caring for the family needs.

Location

The laundry may be a simple niche off a hall-way, it may be a separate room including ironing board and broom closet, or it may be missing entirely with the washer and dryer in the garage. Whichever arrangement you consider, here are some things to keep in mind:

⇨ Washers and dryers are noisy. Consider the location carefully. Think about noise insulation and if the laundry room doors can be kept closed while the machines are in use. Louvered doors don't block noise but may be needed for air circulation.

⇨ Washer and dryer doors may open downward or they may be hinged on the side. Some allow the hinges to be moved to either side, others do not. If you have ones with side hinges that cannot be moved, try to locate them so their doors aren't in the way when moving clothes from the washer to the dryer—not like in the photo (next page).

⇨ The washer and dryer should be right next to each other. Separating them will mean extra steps.

⇨ If there is a laundry tub, it should be next to the washer. If there is a clothes-folding area, put it next to the dryer.

An impossible arrangement. Both doors should be hinged on the other side or the washer and drier should be switched. (What you don't see in model homes! No housewife would tolerate this.)

⇨ Figure out where the dryer vent exits from the house. As discussed below, it can be a shock to find it sticking out the front.

⇨ Be sure there is a light over the washer that illuminates the interior while you are leaning over it. This is a common

shortcoming, one that is alleviated by washers that are white inside although you can still leave a white sock or hankie in it. With the new front-load machines this can be a real problem.

When the laundry is in the hallway between the garage and the rest of the house, the door between the two is often a hip banger—someone coming from the garage into the laundry will push the door knob into the side of anyone working in laundry.

One way to avoid this is to have glass in the door so anyone coming into the laundry can see if there'd be a problem. (This was seen on an older house. You may want to check carefully to be sure this arrangement meets fire codes which usually insist on a solid-core door between the house and the garage.)

The problem can occur with the door at the other end of the laundry too where a pocket door might be used. Or just plain take the door off entirely if the noise wouldn't be a problem.

The next page shows three hip-banger laundry-room doors.

Don't have space between washer (on right) and dryer (on left). It'll just mean walking when you shouldn't have to.

There are several things here you'll want to avoid. a) The door will be a hip banger, b) the washer is separated from the utility tub, and c) there is no clothes rod to hang clothes taken out of the dryer.

HIP-BANGER LAUNDRY ROOM DOORS

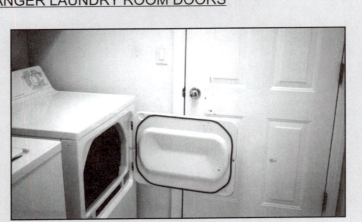

When you're leaning over the dryer to put stuff in or take it out and someone comes in from the garage...not very friendly, huh?

This photo is here to illustrate how sellers will "pretty up" a house and in so doing can distract you from the fact that this, too, will be a hip banger.

The door here is from an upstairs hall but the problem still remains—if you're leaning over in front of the dryer and somone opens the door, it hurts. Here the problem is less likely, however, because the door will probably be open when someone is in the laundry room.

LAUNDRY ROOM DOORS THAT AREN'T HIP BANGERS

If the laundry room is made large enough, opening the washer or dryer door will not interfere with the door from the garage. The space could be used for ironing but generally it's only purpose is to avoid hip banging.

This garage-laundry door eliminates the hip-banger problem. But it may be a fire-safety consideration.

Here a pocket door between the laundry and the hall avoids the problem.

No door at all into the laundry room is a good fix when noise wouldn't be a problem.

Laundries with corners

In general, avoid laundry rooms with the washer and dryer across one end and a counter along the side. These will leave an area under the counter that is inaccessible when the washer and dryer are in place. In the first photo, below, where the machines haven't been installed, it isn't so evident that:

⇨ The tub will be well separated from the washer (the connections for the dryer,

not the washer, are next to the counter) and

⇨ The space under the counter will be inaccessible when the dryer is in place. Watch for this in both models and plans; it isn't always obvious.

Front-Load Washers

The major manufacturers all have front-load washers available as well as the older top-load. These washers tumble water through the clothes rather than having an agitator that swishes them back and forth. This is said to be easier on the clothes and to use less energy. Whether they are more user-friendly is a matter of personal likes.

One of the on-going gripes about dryers, which are all front load, is their inconvenience because they are so close to the floor. When washers are also front-load, it becomes feasible to raise both of them up off the floor so the user doesn't have to stand on her head to see into the back of the dryer.

Corners like these in laundry rooms are inaccessible. And don't let the clothes basket fool you, when the dryer is in place the corner will be lost.

Another wasted inaccessible corner. Note, too, that the counter itself becomes useless as a work area because there's no room to get to it.

Front-load washer and dryer on raised platforms which make them easier to use. Definitely a user-friendly improvement.

The first time I saw an attempt at this was in a new home that a builder had made for himself, he built a platform under both of them for easier use.

Now there are platforms for the individual machines that do this. They can be installed either initially or later, the one proviso being that any shelves above the units aren't in the way.

Other Amenities

A well-designed laundry will have:

⇨ Cupboards near the washer for holding laundry materials (soap, bleach, softeners, etc.),

⇨ A short rod over the dryer for hanging clothes, and, if there's room,

⇨ A counter for folding clothes, and

⇨ An ironing board.

With a two-story house, here are arguments about the laundry room location:

⇨ If the laundry is on the first floor, a laundry chute will make it easier to get

A very unfriendly laundry seen in an upscale model home. There is no cupboard for soaps, bleaches, or anything else. There is no clothes rod and the laundry tub, if there is one, is well separated from the washer.

the clothes to the machines. Then you only have to carry the laundry back upstairs.

⇨ If it's on the second floor, it'll take fewer steps to collect the laundry and to put it away but it'll take more trips up and down the stairs while the washing is being done to take care of adding fabric softener if you want to, transferring the laundry from the washer to the dryer, and checking if things are dry.

⇨ There's something else to watch for when the laundry is on the second floor. Washing machines or the hoses feeding them have been known to malfunction and any 2nd-floor laundry should have a water catch pan under it. The pan is connected to the drain system so that no damage to the house results. It's just cautionary to insure that it is there. Many builders include this...but not all.

On this subject, I'll always remember a building designer's own new home that was on a tour and was praised as a model of excellence. The bedrooms were on the second floor and the laundry in the basement. There was no laundry chute! And this was not a cut-every-corner house, it had many upper-end design features. It's bad enough to have to carry laundered clothes up the stairs, but to carry them down, too? It was truly, as a woman real estate agent commented, a case of "it was built by men."

And, of course, if there's a laundry chute you can make an argument for an electric butler to carry the laundry both up and down.

As a Mud Room

If the laundry room doubles as a mud room, be sure of two things:

⇨ It should not be necessary to go through a room inside the house to get from outside to the mud room, and

⇨ There should be a place to put dirty, wet clothes and to clean up before going on into the house. This strongly suggests a utility tub in the laundry and room for a hamper.

Energy for the Dryer

Energy for the dryer is often a regional consideration; gas is the norm in some areas and electricity in others. Having both available in a laun-

With both gas and electricity available, this laundry can handle any dryer.

dry lets you choose the type of dryer you want and, with cost of electrical energy, this may be an economic nicety. It will also make the house more attractive to some buyers when the time comes.

Hint: When you're looking at houses where the washer and dryer aren't in place, you can tell where the dryer will be by looking for the exhaust vent, the 220V electrical outlet (the big one in the photo), and the gas pipe (if there is one).

The clothes rod, the towel rod and the tile backsplash give this laundry tub a user-friendly touch.

The Utility Tub

Many builders and designers do not include a laundry or utility tub in their houses and most homeusers need one. If there isn't one, you may be able to add it after you move in.

For pre-soaking especially dirty clothes, the tub is more convenient in the laundry. For cleaning tools and for cleanup after yard work and after play, the tub is better off in the garage. In the garage the faucet on the tub can also be used as a hose connection.

If there is a special heated "mud" room, that's an even better place for the utility tub.

The Dryer Vent

The dryer vent may, at first, seem like a trivial problem. *It isn't!* Unless having the dryer vent on the front of the house doesn't bother you, then pay close attention to where the laundry is located—there are both aesthetic and functional aspects.

Dryer vents involve important design considerations which are universally ignored—until maybe the building inspector catches up with it. He, however, is not concerned about how it looks, that's up to you.

This is the front of an expensive tour home. The dryer vent is the white cover in the circle. Can you imagine how the bushes will look as they get sprayed with lint day after day? To say nothing of the utilitarian look of steam coming out the front of the house into this upscale neighborhood.

There are two design facets to look for:

⇨ The vent outlet shouldn't be on the front of the house unless you want the surrounding shrubbery strewn with lint. The same consideration says not to vent it through the roof.

⇨ Make the vent pipe short and straight or it can seriously degrade the performance of the dryer or even cause the dryer motor to overheat and start a fire. And, if the air flow is reduced, lint can build up in the duct—another place for a fire to start. (Because of this, building codes spell out the maximum length of the duct.)

It is this potential of fire that has made code agencies take a hard look at dryer vents. The dryer, in effect, is a big blower that heats air and blows it through the clothes. The exhaust air is laden with moisture and with the fine lint that gets past the built-in lint screen. Anything that impedes the air flow degrades the performance of the dryer. The duct terminates outside so the moisture and lint don't mess up the house.

There should be a hood cap with a flap or some other way to prevent rodents and birds from getting into the duct. If a hood cap points downward it should be at least 12 inches above the ground for unimpeded flow.

For instance, section M1501 of the 2000 International Residential Code (IRC) said,

> "The maximum length of a clothes dryer exhaust shall not exceed 25 feet from the dryer location to the wall or roof termination. The maximum length shall be reduced by 2.5 feet for each 45-degree bend and 5 feet for each 90-degree bend. The maximum length of the exhaust duct does not include the transition duct."

(The transition duct is the connection from the dryer to the exhaust duct.) The code goes on to say that when the manufacturer and model of the dryer are known, the manufacturer's installation instructions may be followed for the allowable duct length.

When building inspectors take these words literally, they'll insist on using the code values unless the actual dryer is in place at the time of inspection (in which case they'll consider the manufacturer's instructions). If care is not taken and the dryer is located toward the front of the house, going out the front may be the only option.

When a building designer was told that he should have taken this into account his reaction was, "Now you're telling me I must design the house around the laundry room? No way!"

Yet that is exactly what must be done. It's another constraint that should have been in place for years. Be on the lookout for this, whether in an existing house or one that's yet to be built or re-modeled.

Whether in the wall or in the floor, insist that there is room around the end of the vent duct for the connection to the dryer.

We next consider some ways dryers can be vented. Note that in *every* case, the best arrangement is to have the dryer on an outside wall (not the front) and run the duct straight out from the back of the dryer.

Roof

Running the duct up through the roof has two drawbacks:

⇨ Steam and the lint that the filter in the dryer doesn't catch will go into the air above the house, both a short- and long-term appearance consideration. (Think about a house covered with a fine coat of lint.)

⇨ Birds think that this nice warm protected space at the top of the vent pipe is an ideal place to put their nest. It is absolutely necessary to use a type of vent cover that lets the dryer air out, keeps rain and snow out, and leaves no place for birds to build their nests.

Friends in Prescott Valley, AZ had this happen to them. They discovered the bird nest when the dryer didn't get clothes dry. (Fortunately it didn't cause a fire, it could have.) Their solution was to put the vent out through a wall into an area where they'd rather not have it, but what can you do?

Slab floor

When your house sits on a slab floor, the duct goes straight out through the wall or through the roof. To avoid the roof vent or running it through the garage, the dryer *must* be placed on an outside

wall. Be sure this isn't the front of the house. (It might be possible to run the duct between floors in a two-story house or through the attic and out a wall, but the length of the duct would be a concern—along with the additional cost.)

When the laundry is on the front of the house, you may have no choice but to exhaust the dryer on the front of the house with its aesthetic drawbacks.

Outside wall (basement or crawl space)

When the laundry is on an outside wall—but not the front of the house—vent it through the wall. If it is on the front of the house, run it down through the floor and then to the outside under the floor. For this, the dryer will have to sit out farther from the wall and the floor must have a hole cut in it, making it harder to install and keep tidy. The IRC code allows the total run to be 20 feet long (one 90-degree elbow). Look for this situation and where you can, you may want to rearrange the laundry to avoid putting the dryer where it would have to vent through the front outside wall.

Inside wall

The situation with a slab floor was described earlier. When there is a basement or crawl space then the situation is as above— either down through the floor, between floors, or through the attic as is appropriate.

Laundry in basement

The dryer should be on an outside wall where the vent duct can be run up the wall and outside.

Laundry in garage

The dryer should be on an outside wall or the duct will have to be run across the garage or up through the roof to get outside.

A heating contractor recently showed me a set of blueprints made for a custom house by a competent, well–respected designer. The laundry is a small room that sticks out into the 3-car garage and its floor is a continuation of the garage floor, i.e., it is a slab. It was not on a outside wall. The only places to take the exhaust duct were into the garage (unacceptable) or up through the roof (undesirable). (I didn't find out what happened. Suffice it to say that you can't be too careful—even the experts make boo-boos.)

Energy Savings

Energy Star

The Environmental Protection Agency qualifies some washers as energy savers. Their website[22A] says:

"Compared to a 10-year old model, an ENERGY STAR qualified washer can save up to $120 per year on your utility bills."

Energy Star washers are available in both top- and front-loading models.

Tax breaks

In some states the potential for energy and water savings with improved washer and dryer designs has led to the offer of a tax credit for the homeuser who installs them. You can check with you own state energy office to see what, if any, of this applies to you.

Chapter 23

Garage and Outside

> *Knowledge becomes wisdom only after it has been put to practical use.*
> ~ Source Unknown ~

In this chapter:
The house's garage and exterior are the subjects of this chapter.
Unlike the interior. functionality is involved in only a few of the
choices. Mostly it's a matter of cost versus looks.

This chapter is divided into two parts: the garage, which goes over several items to consider there, and the exterior that deals with a number of outside things that are too often overlooked when considering houses.

A. The Garage

Garage Design

Finishing (wallboard and painting) the inside of the garage is something for which there is no standard practice. For energy code and fire code reasons, common walls between the house and the garage will always be insulated and wallboard installed—as will the garage ceiling when it is also the floor of an upstairs room. Beyond that, you will find a wide variation in how things are done: what's insulated and to what R-value, and what's covered with wallboard and how it's finished. When you have a choice, these are among the decisions you'll be faced with making. For an existing house, if what is there doesn't suit you, most often it can be changed.

Garage doors (the big ones you open to drive your car through) may be metal, vinyl or wood. The metal and vinyl ones require less maintenance and last longer but are more expensive. Wooden doors that face the direction of the sun and of winter storms often are in need of a coat of paint after only a year or two.

A difference of two feet in width and/or length can easily make the difference between being crowded or having room to put in a work bench and storage cupboards. As a starting point consider that less than 22 X 22 feet will be a crowded double garage.

If there is a window in the garage, be sure that it is placed where it can't be used as easy access for burglars. Or, have bars put across it to block entry or make it of glass that cannot be broken for access. Such windows are usually on a side of the house that isn't readily visible from the street, making them favorite candidates for someone looking for the easiest way in. Chapter 11 includes a discussion of the security aspects of garage doors and windows.

Codes in some areas require that physical barriers be placed in front of the furnace and water heater to prevent a car from inadvertently running into them and starting a fire. Be sure any such barriers in your garage are firmly embedded in the concrete and are not just lip service to the code.

This pipe embedded in the garage floor is meant to keep cars from running into the water heater.

With new construction, if you want, the builder probably can change one double garage door to two singles or vice versa. Whether and how many garage door openers are to be included by the builder is an item that you should specify, otherwise you may not get any because for this, too, there is no standard.

Garage Wiring

If there is, or you are planning, an automatic sprinkler system for your yard, the usual place for the controller is in the garage. If the garage is finished, the wires from the controller should be placed in the walls before the wallboard is installed. If you want to add it later, then electrical conduit can be used to get the power to the controller location.

Check for outlets in the garage. Some houses are designed to have only the one required by the code. You will want at least one on each wall. These can all be on the same 15-ampere circuit and must be GFCI protected (*see* Chapter 5). If you have a freezer or other appliance in the garage, you should put it on a separate circuit so as not to reduce the available capacity in the other outlets. It is a good idea to GFCI protect this outlet, too, even though it may not be absolutely required by code. Whether it is a new house or you are improving an exiting one, it is appropriate to specify exactly what you want and not leave it up to the electrician and building inspector to do things right.

There should be power going to the outlet(s) for the garage door opener(s). Be sure to check because sometimes it's not included even when it's obviously necessary. It is convenient to have a switch in this line to be able to shut off the opener(s) when you are on vacation. (*See* Chapter 5.)

In an upscale tract in Montgomery county, Pennsylvania I saw what, to me, is a marketing outrage. Not only are there no garage door openers, there is no power wiring to where you would want to install them! It might have been an oversight, but that seems unlikely from the size of the tract and the evident experience of the builder. The unwary will get seduced by the low price on the houses only to find to their dismay that that low price vanishes when things like this—the wiring for the openers as well as the price of the openers themselves and their installation—are added on. Personally, if I were house hunting and ran across something like this, I'd get out of there so fast that the smooth-talking agent would wonder what happened.

Garage Lighting

In some places it is customary to put one light in the garage for each car that may be parked there. In others, one light is supposed to serve the whole garage. If you run into this latter, then increase the number of sockets so that, when the lights are on, there is a modicum of light even in the dark of night. You may want more than one per car stall or you may want the electrician to install fluorescent shop lights for you or at least put in suitable sockets so you can install them yourself. Generally, these can be added at any time, although it may look a little like an afterthought if it becomes necessary to put the wiring where it can be seen.

If you have ever come in the side garage door of your house at night and stumbled around to get to the light switch at the door into the house then you'll appreciate the suggestion that you have the garage lights wired with two switches in a 3-way operation, putting the second switch at the side door. (If it's too late for this, use a night light in the garage, it's a shin saver.) This, too, was discussed in Chapter 5.

Garage Sidedoor

Some designs have a garage sidedoor and others do not. There should be one unless the garage is dug back into a hillside so there's no place to put the door. There's no excuse for having to open the big garage door to get around to the side of the house. The door may be metal, vinyl or wood but, as with the big doors, metal or vinyl will last

longer and appearance is not critical. The door hinges and the dead-bolt striker plate should be mounted with long screws for security reasons as discussed in Chapter 11.

A sidedoor with a window in it is a further security consideration. If you are thinking of such a door or already have one, Chapter 11 is worth rechecking.

Garage Floor

With areas of concrete as large as a garage floor there will be cracking when the floor settles. To control where this cracking occurs, the concrete subcontractor puts dividers in the floor before the concrete is poured. These plastic dividers (about one-half inch thick and four inches high) are set on edge just below the surface of the concrete. If a trowel is used to make a line in the floor above each divider, the cracking, which will always hap-

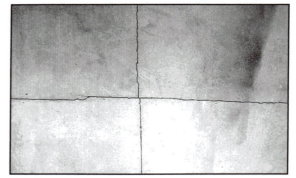

Heedless, sloppy work.

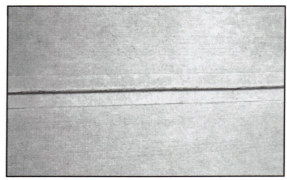

How it should be.

pen, will occur at the bottom of the trowel mark. When this mark is not put in the concrete, the cracking will be in a jagged unattractive line the length of the garage (*see* photo on the previous page). Besides its appearance, this is hard to keep clean. If the house is already finished, it's too late. Otherwise insist on proper finishing. And you'll need to be there when the concrete is being finished, otherwise, if it isn't done right, it's too late.

B. The Exterior

The areas outside the house we look at here involve both aesthetics and function:

⇨ The entryway. How it looks and how it works are usually both tied to the basic style of the house: Colonial, Victorian, Ranch, Craftsman, Tudor, etc.

⇨ The external materials. Again, these are often chosen for their looks as well as their utility.

⇨ Roofs.

⇨ Concrete.

⇨ Decks and patios.

⇨ Electrical considerations, outlets and lights.

⇨ Under the house. Basements, crawl spaces and slabs are areas where there are both good and bad ways to make them.

⇨ Attic. Whether used just for insulation, for storage or for rooms, be careful .

Entryways

There are two types of entryways you may want to avoid. One leaves the front door with no protection and the other puts the door at the end of a tunnel.

Protect the entry

Here are three reasons for having a roofed porch over the main door:

⇨ It provides a covered place:

° for guests to stand when they ring the door bell and

° for you when you're fumbling with your keys.

⇨ It keeps the sun and rain from quickly deteriorating the door itself.

⇨ It gives the house more curb appeal. A bare door does not exude a feeling of "welcome."

The covered porch is not a part of colonial and federal styles and it is also absent in some contemporary and Southwestern architectures. It is, again, a question of aesthetics versus function. If maintaining the façade is imperative, consider a vestibule where visitors can be out of the weather while not inside the house proper.

A bare door is not an inviting entry. Nor is it very friendly for the person waiting there in bad weather for someone to answer the door. Be sure the door itself can take the full brunt of the weather.

ENTRY DOORS - FORM OR FUNCTION - YOU DECIDE

Entry doors can have a big impact on how a house looks from the street and many entries are chosen with this in mind. Unfortunately this may overlook the need for functionality—this is where callers have to stand while they are waiting for the door to be answered. Here are a few of the virtually limitless number of entry door designs.

The point here is to not to forget that the door and its accoutrements do serve a purpose beyond making the home look attractive.

These single-floored homes, while of decidedly different architectual styles, all give callers some protection from the elements.

Two storied homes present different design problems. Whatever is done at the entry door must be a part of the overall façade. Unfortunately this, too often, leaves an unfriendly entry.

These two storied homes offer an entry where there is some protection from the elements, albeit not as much as you might like at times.

The effects of weathering were seen dramatically in a tract in Riverside, California, where, after only one winter, the finish on doors had broken down and the wood underneath was starting to come apart, particularly on the bottom third of the doors where they were exposed to both sun and rain. (Hopefully, the eventual owners got metal or vinyl front doors that stand up better to the weather.)

The tunnel

Ranch-style houses with the garage facing the street often put the door at the end of a long entryway that runs between the garage and a house wall. With roof overhangs, this arrangement can have all of the appeal of a dark tunnel.

The worst—an unprotected door at the end of a tunnel.

Exterior Materials

A first consideration in deciding what materials can be used on a house is in the CC&Rs. Many of them will spell out what is allowed and what is not. Even if they're decades old and out of date, they're still the law of the land where your lot is concerned. (Supplement D²³ᴬ is a tutorial on CC&Rs.)

The exterior material you have on your house will depend on your personal taste, cost, the general availability in your area, its suitability for your climate, its consistency with the house's architecture, its congruity with the neighborhood, and its longevity.

To a large extent the question, again, is a matter of aesthetics versus cost. Inevitably the most expensive is perceived as the most desirable, which may or may not be the case. But, when resale is an important consideration in your decisions, it becomes advisable to have a material that will make the house attractive to the greatest number of potential buyers.

Your builder or local building supply house will be able to tell you the available options and their relative costs. It isn't a bad idea to have some idea about these even when you're looking at existing tract and spec houses because it gives you a better feel of the quality of the house.

You'll find the use of actual wood is infrequent. Builders prefer vinyl or a composite board or hardboard that's made to look like wooden boards, shake, or siding. This material virtually eliminates the problems of warping and splitting that can raise havoc with boards and shake. In general, it is also less expensive.

Stone and brick are not used extensively in earthquake-prone areas as the primary exterior material because of the cost to reinforce them. (However, it is sometimes used as a decorative facing.)

When every effort is being made to keep costs down, one material may be used on the front of the house for appearance and a less expensive material for the sides and back. For example, many houses in northern California use a board-like hardboard material on the street side and stucco elsewhere. But in the Northeast, façades may be stone, stucco, brick, or vinyl siding depending on the architectural style being portrayed. Vinyl or composite hardboard is used extensively on sides and backs.

In the Southwest, stucco is used almost exclusively, with occasional wood, brick, or stone accents. In damper climates, some stucco is used but there is concern that it may develop cracks with time, letting water into the wall space that would never dry out.

One problem with stucco is that it stains easily. This was seen in a tract where the two-story houses had no rain gutters, very small eaves, and little landscaping. Water running off of the roofs splashed mud onto the stucco and permanently stained it. (The builder had gone bankrupt—imagine that!) It's important, particularly with stucco, to get gutters on the houses as soon as possible to prevent this from happening.

A material you may find is EIFS or synthetic stucco. On the surface it may look great. But it has been the cause of numerous law suits and homeowner dismay since its introduction several years ago. The problem is that it *is* waterproof and any water that gets into the wall behind it has no way to get out. Some houses have been built in ways that are supposed to avoid this problem but it's certainly an area to be super careful in. The National Association of Home Builder's website[23B] has a discussion about it. While intended for builders, it'll give you some idea of the problems.

Roofs

Styles

There are two basic roof styles:

    ⇨ Gable or triangular roof.

    ⇨ Hip roof.

Gable

The end of the house with a gable roof forms a triangle under the roof.

Hip

"Actually, you've seen it a million times, you just didn't know there's a name for it. A hip roof is gable roof with the ends brought together at the same pitch."[23D]

A house of many gables.

A hip roof with no gables.

Here, with dramatic effect, a few gables were added to a basic hip-roofed mansion.

Attic

Ventilation

Codes require that an attic be well-ventilated. And you want it, too. Roof vents are used to provide the means for hot summer air to escape and, in so doing, keep the house cooler. When a forced air heating system is used, there's another consideration—the heating/cooling ducts, though they are well-insulated, may pass through the attic with its cold winter temperatures and trapped summer heat. If the attic is not well-ventilated, the air in the duct will be heated in the summer, making it more expensive to keep the house cool.

There are two basically different approaches to attic ventilation:

    ⇨ Can vents spread across the roof just below the ridge or

⇨ Ridge vents where the vent is a continuous element that extends the length of the ridge.

Roof vents. The smaller ones let hot air escape and keep snow, rain, and birds out. They are an alternate to roof-ridge vents. The large white unit is an attic fan, turning on when the attic temperature gets too hot.

Hip roofs

The problem of venting is worse for hipped roofs. If your house uses roof-ridge venting, the shape of the roof means less ridge and less venting. If it uses can-type attic vents, there will be fewer of them when standard practices are followed. If your house has a hipped roof, you may want to consider adding more vents or an attic fan or two to keep the temperature down in the summer.

Rain gutters

Gutters should be included with the house when it's built, regardless of where you live. They are not used in some parts of the Northeast because of the perception that snow clogs them up and can cause water to come into the house. As explained below, this may be caused by inadequate overhangs on the house, gutters or not. If you feel more comfortable doing it, leave the gutters off, it's certainly less expensive.

In parts of the Southwest, builders rarely include rain gutters as a part of the houses they build—after all if there's virtually no rain, then why? In other areas no one even thinks about them because they're always included with the house. A set of gutters can run well over $1000, so don't

dismiss them as trivial when you buy in areas where they're not ordinarily included.

Gutters may be plastic, aluminum, or heavily galvanized and painted steel. They are available in two sizes; a larger one that completely covers a 6-inch fascia and a smaller one that covers part of the fascia. Another case of cost versus appearance.

A money-saving stratagem builders use in many places, when they do install gutters, is to just dump the water from the downspouts into the yard. Unless the soil is particularly porous, this will cause a muddy mess. It's not a big thing to have drain lines included if you have a downhill shot to the street. Having them is one less thing to worry about after you move in.

Of course, gutters are a continuing maintenance item because they do collect leaves and these can plug downspouts. There are special covers for gutters which are designed to let water into the gutter but keep the leaves out. How effective they are and what kind of maintenance problems they themselves cause is not discussed in the ads in the media.

Roofing materials

Commonly used roofing materials include:

⇨ Concrete, tile or shake

⇨ Composite, tile or shake

⇨ Clay tile

⇨ Cedar shake

⇨ Woodruf, a hardboard material that simulates shake. You won't find this in new homes but you might find it in older ones. WATCH OUT.

⇨ Composition roofing

⇨ Asphalt shingles

You'll usually get back some of the initial extra cost of nonflammable materials through lower insurance rates. This is something you will need to check. In general, the "carrots" for using concrete or composite tiles or shakes are fire resistance and near-zero maintenance costs.

Concrete tile

Concrete tile or concrete shake comes in many shapes and colors. It has the longest life of any of the materials. It is not damaged by weather or age but it can break when walked on. (It can also be broken by golf balls if you live on a golf course.) It is, obviously, fireproof. It is the most expensive roof, not only because of the cost of the material itself but, being concrete, it's heavy and may need a sturdier roof structure to support it. Its weight and the ease with which the pieces can be broken make it more difficult to install, all adding to the cost.

Composite tile or shake

This material looks like concrete but includes fiberglass or other strengtheners to reduce its fragility. It is lighter than concrete, making it less expensive to install.

Clay tile

Clay tile is a low-fired brick-like material. It is usually made in the form of a half of a red tile pipe. It has been used for several hundred years in southwestern architecture but has given way to its concrete counterpart because of its fragility. While clay is even more subject to damage from being walked on or hit with golf balls, it is less expensive than concrete.

Cedar shake

Split cedar shake has been a popular roofing material for a long time. It's perceived as being the luxury material in many areas. Unfortunately, the quality of available shake has declined. Now it's the shortest-lived modern-day roofing material except for the cheapest asphalt shingles. It requires more maintenance than any of the others. It's very flammable ("tinder box" is a term that is

often used) which results in higher fire insurance premiums. It's more expensive than other materials except concrete tile. Yet, in the Pacific Northwest it's still very popular. CC&Rs in many exclusive developments allow only cedar shake, concrete tile, or concrete shake roofs for appearance reasons. In these developments, cedar shake is seen much more often than concrete tile. Obviously, personal taste figures heavily in this matter. This is unfortunate because cedar shake is, by far, the worst buy in roofing materials available today.

Woodruf

A material with the trademark "Woodruf" was manufactured by the Masonite Corporation as an alternative to shake. It's a composite wood product with an appearance similar to shake, but more uniform. It was less expensive than shake and was often permitted where CC&Rs require shake or tile. The expected life of a roof of this material (15 years) is about the same as a cedar shake roof but not nearly as long as concrete tile or the better grades of composition roofing. It, too, will burn but not with the same vigor as cedar shake.

But it hasn't lived up to expectations with resulting law suits. Information re the settlement(s) can be found at[23C]. It's probably better to avoid it.

Composition roofing

Composition roofing is an improved, fiberglass-reinforced version of the old asphalt roofing that has been around for many years. It's a flat material that's installed very quickly using a staple gun. It comes in a number of colors and styles to match the house. It's less expensive than most other roofing materials and is available in a wide range of prices and guarantees (up to 40 years). It doesn't burn as readily as shake and walking on it does not harm it as it can other materials.

Asphalt shingles

Asphalt shingles are the least expensive material and are short-lived. They're seldom used on new homes.

Other considerations

Depending on where you live, the amount of sun radiation that the roof absorbs can be of concern. Light-colored materials will reflect more of the sun's rays while darker will absorb it. With today's insulation requirements this is not a matter of the same importance that it was in the past. Whether the problem is keeping cool in the summer or trying to keep down the heating costs in the winter will depend on where you are.

With a new home or a remodel, your builder can go over the costs of the various options with you. Whether you go with concrete tile for its durability, shake for its appearance, or composition roofing for its cost is a personal choice. But don't forget perceptions, because they can be very important when you are ready to sell your house.

In a tract near Sacramento, California it was noted that the first phase had cedar shake roofs, the second had composition roofing, and the newest phase used concrete shake. The builder explained that after the Oakland fire storm in the 1980s, nobody wanted anything to do with cedar shake and that composition roofing is simply not accepted, because it's viewed as a cheap material used mostly for replacing older asphalt roofs.

Unlike the rest of the country, the only places where composition roofing was seen on new houses in California were on the lowest-priced starter homes. Regional perceptions can be strong indeed, often flying in the face of good sense.

In some areas, the under sides of roof eave overhangs (soffits) are commonly left open and in others they're closed in. When vinyl siding is used, vinyl pieces are designed to close in the soffits. With other siding, soffits are closed in with plywood that is fitted under the overhanging roof beams. This improves the appearance since it gives a much smoother finish when someone looks up at the underside of the eaves. Closing in is much appreciated when you get around to repainting your house—a smooth surface is much easier to paint than one that's composed of overhanging room beams and the underside of the roof itself. It is a matter of local custom, cost, and your personal preference.

Looking up at a roof overhang showing the gutter (top) and an attic vent .

An overhang boxed-in with a solid piece of plywood covering the beam extensions. The vent is still here—even though it looks a little different.

Roof slope

The slope of the roof is measured in "pitch" using an expression such as 4/12 which means there is 4 inches of vertical rise for each 12 inches measured along the horizontal.

In today's houses there is less variation in the slope of roofs than in the past. There are two reasons for this:

⇨ Some roofing materials aren't guaranteed if the roof isn't steep enough and

⇨ Very steep roofs are not popular with builders because of safety concerns for installers. These concerns translate to higher costs for building steep roofs because of the care needed to prevent the roofers from falling and of the higher worker's insurance costs.

Overhang

Roof overhangs protect at least part of the house from the direct rays of the summer sun, helping to keep it cooler and provide some protection from rains. In snow climates, roof overhangs serve another important function: they help keep melting snow water from seeping into the house.

During cold weather, snow directly on the roof will be melted by the heat of the house under it. This water runs *under* the snow toward the eaves and gutter. When it comes out from under the snow at the edge of the room it will freeze. This can cause an ice dam at the roof edge backing up the water, causing the roof to leak. If there is inadequate overhang, this water goes into the house, otherwise it will just seep through the overhang. (Besides the overhang, further insurance against this type of leak is to have waterproof "ice guard" installed under the roofing just above the gutters. This material extends about three feet up from the gutters, preventing leaks caused by the ice dam.)

Roof overhangs are sometimes omitted for reasons of appearance in a particular design and are sometimes made too small in order to save money. If your house is in an area where it snows, there should be a substantial roof overhang, particularly with roofs with lower pitches. (24 inches is suggested as a nominal value.) In the South and Southwest much larger overhangs are useful because of the shade they provide against the summer sun.

Valleys

When there is a change in direction of the roof, either a ridge or a valley will be formed—ridges on outside corners, valleys on inside ones. Inept installations at valleys can result in leaking roofs, not immediately, but several years later after the builder is long gone.

With composition roofs, the easiest and least expensive way to make a valley is to simply bend the roofing material through the valley and to lay the material from the other side on top. The top layer of material is then cut in a straight line up the valley to give a finished appearance. If done properly, this is fine.

If not installed properly, rain can be blown up under the edge of the top layer of roofing material. Over time dust and particles from the roofing will also be blown under there and, sooner or later, water will accumulate and leak.

There are three ways to prevent this:

⇨ Be sure the roof is laid properly. This is hard to assess unless you're a roofer. Many builders wouldn't know the difference either.

⇨ When the roof is laid initially, the roofers should weave the two layers of material, alternating them so that there isn't a single long line of cut roofing for rain, etc., to enter.

⇨ Use a piece of specially bent metal in the valley (called a "valley W") that extends well back under the roofing material on both sides. A ridge in the metal keeps water from being blown under the roof.

It took the fifth winter before our roof developed a leak. The cost of correcting the builder's lack of supervision was considerably more than it would have been if it had been done right in the first place.

This is yet another way to tell a responsible builder from one who hire his/her subs and doesn't know whether they've done their job right or not.

This valley leaked.

This one does not.

Nooks and crannies

Where roofs from dormers meet the rest of the roof there's usually a small protected area that's attractive to birds looking for a place to set up housekeeping. If this is okay by you, fine. If you'd rather the birds took their dirty nests, noisy nestlings, and multitudinous parasitic pests to a tree or bird house, then these protected nooks and crannies in the roof should be blocked off, either with wire mesh or boards.

This can be done at any time. However, it's a good idea for the builder's crew to do this so that you don't have to shoo the birds away when they've already decided to set up nest making. (In some areas it's illegal to do anything once nesting activities have begun.) This is yet another small detail you can have the builder do or wait and take care of it after you've moved in.

And don't overlook the vent from a kitchen or bathroom exhaust system. If not properly protected, they can make inviting places for nests.

It was interesting to watch a pair of starlings set up housekeeping in the vent of the kitchen exhaust system in the house behind us. It came out the back of the house rather than going up through the roof and the birds thought it was great. By the time the owner realized what was going on, there were already nestlings. But before the next spring came around he cleaned out the duct and put in a covering that kept them out.

Concrete Work

Concerns about driveways, particularly if there is a potential snow problem, were discussed in Chapter 2. Here we look at a few more ways concrete can help—or hurt.

RV (recreational vehicle) pads

An RV pad is another item that needs to be considered. Some subdivisions do not allow them. In others, local custom may frown on the idea of storing a recreational vehicle on a residential lot. Or the lot widths may not leave room for one. If, however,

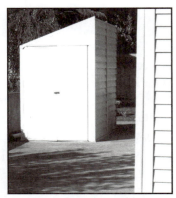

An "RV pad" is a good location for an outside tool shed.

you want and can have an RV pad, you'll have to be sure that the lot is wide enough for both it and the house. Beyond that, when the contractor is working up the cost for the house, be sure there's enough money for concrete to pour a useful driveway for the RV pad. Some driveways/RV pads are too narrow and simply cannot be used by RVs. They may, however, serve as a good location for an outside tool shed for mowers, wheel-barrows, etc.

Sidewalks

Front sidewalks can be utilitarian and ugly or smooth and flowing with lots of curb appeal. It's easier to form and finish a square-cornered walk than a gently curving one. If you don't speak up, you could get a walk that doesn't do a thing for the appearance of the house.

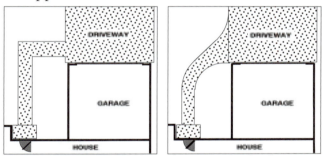

Different front walks: right angles are easier for the contractor to form and pour.

Avoid a house with a steeply pitched walk if you live where there's ever snow or ice.

Steps are better than a steep walk. But be careful with steps. If there's a possibility of someone not seeing the step, better have it well lighted and marked with white paint to avoid accidents. If you are concerned with access by people with disabilities, you'll need a gently sloping walk without steps.

Conduits under concrete

When sidewalks, driveways, and RV pads are being poured, it is nice to have enough conduits put under them. A yard irrigation system may eventually need to have a pipe go under the concrete. It's a lot simpler (and cheaper) to put an oversized pipe (conduit) under the walk or driveway when it's poured. The irrigation pipes can then be put through the conduit whenever they're needed. Alternately, the concrete subcontractor can lay a piece of 3/4-inch PVC under the concrete for the irrigation system. This is simpler but lacks flexibility.

A more common problem arises with telephone and television cables that are run from the street to your house. When these have to go under concrete, the easiest and most common thing to do is to dig them directly in the dirt. The concrete is then poured over them. If this is done, you should pray that nothing ever goes wrong with either of the cables. The methods of repair are not only expensive but unsightly, unless you don't mind the sight of wires running up the outside of your house.

If you can, have pieces of plastic conduit put under the concrete and the telephone and TV cables put in the conduit. If a cable ever needs replacing, it's then just a matter of pulling a new one through the conduit. An extra wire put in the conduit initially can be used to pull in any new cable that's ever needed.

Be sure that the ends of the conduits come up through the concrete. In one house, the builder instructed the subcontractor to put the telephone and TV cables in conduit under the RV pad. This was done but the end of the conduit wasn't brought up to the surface of the RV pad. Now that the pad is poured, the two cables come up through the concrete just as if there were no conduit underneath.

Electrical power is already run in conduits so that doing the telephone and TV cables the same way should pose no problem.

Decks and Patios

If you're planning a patio, make it as large as you want initially. It's probably not a good idea to get a small one with the intention of expanding it later because, when adding concrete to make it bigger, it is difficult to make it look as if it had been poured all at the same time. It will always look like an afterthought. (Aesthetics, again.)

Decks have similar problems. It's difficult to add on and keep anything like an aesthetically appealing appearance. So unless it's laid out for possible later expansion, it's better to be big enough initially.

In considering whether to have a deck or patio, remember that decks are much more expensive than patios by a ratio of about 6:1 and that decks will become even more expensive as the price of lumber increases. And wood deteriorates with time, concrete doesn't.

If there is gas in your home, it should be stubbed to the deck or patio area for a BBQ. Even if you don't have a gas BBQ, the guy that's looking at the house when you're ready to sell may

Gas stub and power outlets together on a deck or patio. This is how they should be.

find it a very positive feature. And make sure the deck isn't built over the gas stub as I've seen done a couple of times.

Check out the location of the gas stub as well as the electrical outlet on the back of the house. The gas stub is definitely for the BBQ and one of the electrical outlet's uses will be to power the BBQ spit motor. They should be close to each other and close to where the BBQ is likely to be used. This seems obvious, but more than one house was seen in which the two were are least 20 feet apart.

When a deck is built, it is better to have the decking put down with deck screws rather than nails. Screws allow you to remove a board and put it back down while, when nails are used, you have to buy new lumber and try to get a finish on it like the rest of the deck. And screws are also less likely to pull up when boards start to warp.

Electrical

It might be well to review Chapter 5 at this point. There you'll find several items that apply to the outside of the house as well as the inside.

Lights and lap siding

With lap siding or clapboard, each successive board overlaps the one below it. However, when decorative outside lights are mounted on it, there is a problem. The siding slopes, therefore the fixtures slope.

Better builders will fashion a small vertical surface on which to mount the lights and then install the siding around it. Insist on

A small mounting board between the light and the siding makes a smooth transition.

this, if you are getting lap siding—to do otherwise looks unfinished.

House numbers

You'll need lights on the front of your house to help guests find you and to see their way to the door. These lights should be chosen for their functional use of illumination as well as their aesthetic appearance. The lights should also light your house numbers so people can find the house at night.

They may be either decorative lights which add to the decor of the house or they may be recessed can lights mounted in boxed-in soffits.

At the urging of fire and police departments, new homes in some communities use black numbers mounted on white back-lighted plastic. These units, about 5x10 inches, are equipped with light sensors which turn them on at night.

These unattractive all-houses-alike plastic numbers are not among our suggested solutions for lighting house numbers. It's a simple matter to select fixtures that shine on the house and then to put the numbers in the light. Be sure to have

Unless you go into hibernation at night, get lights that illuminate the house numbers.

this done. In over 40 percent of houses surveyed the house numbers were not lighted.

Outside outlets

In 1993 the National Electrical Code (now incorporated into the International Residential Code) changed the number of required outside outlets from one to two. With this change, you don't have to run an extension cord to the back of the house to get power for your Christmas lights or electric lawn mower.

If you have an RV pad, you'll want at least one outlet there. If you plan to have an outside barbeque with a spit or use an electric barbeque starter, be sure the outlet in the back of the house is close to where the barbeque will most likely be located.

These outside outlets must be GFCI protected. And it's probably a good idea for them to have their own 15-ampere or 20-ampere circuit.

If you're planning for a spa in the backyard, there should be a separate circuit for it. According to one interpretation of the code, the outlet for the spa doesn't have to be GFCI protected. However, it's a good idea to do it. Anytime you're going to be near a ground or a water pipe and power at the same time, you can't be too careful.

Under the House

In houses with slab floors and in houses that have basements under them, there is no crawl space to be concerned about. Where there is a crawl space, both access and drainage are major considerations.

Crawl-space room

If the design of a house uses a crawl space, be sure there's enough room to crawl, not just slither. The floor beams may sit even with the top of the foundation wall but heating ducts and drain pipes go under the beams, thus cutting into the available space. Heating ducts are large and wrapped with insulation, making them even larger.

If the builder uses manufactured joists (Chapter 12), there is another consideration. In an effort to keep the houses from sitting too high off of the ground, builders will lower the foundations to allow room for the manufactured joists. You need to be sure that the foundation is high enough above ground level so that there is room under the house for the joists and well-insulated heating ducts and still leave room to get around under there. Building codes should protect you but inspections are too often hurried, sloppy or nonexistent. When you buy an existing house, new or previously owned, your own home inspector should check this out for you.

Crawl-space drainage

Codes don't require drain lines around a house with a crawl space. To handle a potential water problem, the builder grades the dirt under the house to a low spot and installs either a drain or a sump pump.

The dirt under the house is then covered with a heavy plastic polyethylene sheet (Visqueen). Vents around the foundation make it so that the space above the plastic is kept dry, even though the ground underneath may be wet. This keeps the wood under the house from getting dry rot, a fungus that can rot wood in a moist environment.

In most places, water doesn't collect under the house and builders and code inspectors get pretty sloppy about what they do and what they allow. When a house is built on a lot with a ground water problem, this sloppiness can become serious.

Consider this example:

Construction on a new house was started when the soil was still saturated from the winter rains. The dirt inside the foundation was sloped, more or less, toward one corner of the house. (In actuality, the dirt was really just mud that was pushed around with a bulldozer to get something resembling a slope.)

At the low corner a drain pipe was put just under the footing but was several inches above the dirt it was supposed to be draining The plastic sheet was laid down over the mud and water and the house was built.

Ground water seeped through the foundation wall, oozed up from below, and collected at the low corner of the crawl space under the house, below the level of the drain. The plastic sheet sank to the bottom of the water and the crawl space turned into a lake.

The problem should never have occurred. The drain pipe, according to the code, should have been at the lowest spot under the house. It wasn't. *Caveat Emptor.*

Where's the sump pump?

To solve a problem with water under a house, sump pumps are sometimes needed to keep the water from collecting. But they can be noisy. In a neighbor's house, the pump was installed right under the master bedroom. Now in the rainy season our neighbors have to turn the sump pump off so they can sleep at night and then turn it on the next morning—and hope that the crawl space keeps dry enough to prevent dry rot.

The builder wasn't thinking of the homeuser when the work for the drainage under the house was being done. Vigilance is necessary. If a sump pump is needed, try to have it located away from the bedroom areas of the house.

Internet Resources

These resources are all in terms of the URL's where additional information may be found. It is suggested that the easiest way to use them is to go to <www.BetterHousesBetterLiving.com> and click on "Internet Resources" where they will be listed with direct links to the websites. That will be much easier than typing in the often awkward addresses.

And there's another reason for doing this. Because of the fluid nature of such things, the URL's listed below may not be current by the time you need to use them so we will try to keep the links on <www.BetterHousesBetterLiving.com> current for a given resource. If you find one that doesn't work right, please let us know. Thanks.

Ch.

1
1A. http://www.fanniemae.com/homebuyers/homepath/index.jhtml?p=Homepath
1B. http://www.abanet.org/publiced/practical/books/family_legal_guide/chapter_4.pdf
1C. http://www.freddiemac.com/homebuyers/
1D. http://www.ashi.org
1E. http://www.nahi.org
1F. http://www.realtor.com
1H. http://www.rebac.net
1J. http://www.BetterHousesBetterLiving.com/supplements/f.htm
1K. http://www.mortgagebankers.org/about/factsheet.html
1L. http://www.namb.org/about_namb/mission.htm
1M. http://www.fanniemae.com
1N. http://www.freddiemac.com
1O. http://www.freddiemac.com/homebuyers/school/credit_report.html
1P. http://www.equifax.com
1Q. http://www.creditexpert.com
1R. http://www.transunion.com
1S. http://www.BetterHousesBetterLiving.com/supplements/e.htm
1T. http://www.nahb.org/
1U. http://www.nari.org/
1V. http://www.iccsafe.org/e/prodcat.html?catid=I-Codes&stateInfo=EfdZdhdcvVdbTldJ9349l1
1W. http://www.arello.com
1X. http://www.hud.gov
1Y. http://www.homeloans.va.gov/

2
2A. http://www.nari.org/
2B. http://www.sips.org/
2C. http://www.ownerbuilderbook.com/
2D. http://www.ownerbuildercenter.com/
2E. http://www.buildingsystems.org/
2F. http:// www.nudura.com/
2G. http://www.askthebuilder.com/449_Modular_Homes.shtml

3
3A. http://www.BetterHousesBetterLiving.com/supplements/h.htm
3B. http://www.aibd.org
3C. http://www.aia.org
3D. http://www.aia.org/consumer/overview.asp
3E http://www.aia.org/consumer/index_residential.asp

3
con't
3F. http://www.mascord.com/
3G. http://www.crds-pa.com
3H. http://www.DreamHomeSource.com
3I http://www.home-inspect.com/

4
4A. http://www.BetterHousesBetterLiving.com/supplements/d.htm
4B. http://www.homeownerassoc.com/

5
5B. http://www.leviton.com
5C. http://www.us.kohler.com/onlinecatalog/detail.jsp?item=290002&prod_num=4649 module=&frm=

6
6A. http://www.arwa-tech.com/
6B. http://www.gotankless.com/tech_1.html
6C. http://www.eemaxinc.com/index.htm
6D. http://www.rinnaiamerica.com

7
7A. http://www.BetterHousesBetterLiving.com/supplements/a.htm.

8
8A. http://www.regency-fire.com/
8B. http://www.cpsc.gov/cpscpub/prerel/prhtml02/02248.html
8C. http://www.hearth.com/what/specific.html
8D. http://www.heatnglo.com/
8E. http://www.oilstoves.com/
8F. http://www.endtimesreport.com/kerosene_stoves.html
8G.http://www.firelogs.com/FAQ.htm#Gas%20Logs%20-%20Vent%20Free
8H. http://hearth.com/what/unvented.html

9
9A. http://www.marvin.com/   )
9B. http://www.pella.com/   ) *See* the disclaimer note
9C. http://www.peach99.com   ) at the end of Chapter 9
9D. http://www.therma-tru.com/   )

10
10A. http://www.pella.com/products/windows_patiodoors/default.asp?path=/products/hurricane
10B. http://www.askthebuilder.com/240_Certified_Vinyl_Windows_-_The_Only_Way_to_Go.shtml
10C. http://www.nfrc.org/
10D. http://www.nfrc.org/label.html
10E. http://www.energystar.gov/
10F. http://www.ibhs.org/
10G. http://www.freedomseal.org

11
11A. http://www.adt.com/divisions/residential/index.cfm
11B. http://www.monitronics.com/
11C. http://www.brinkshomesecurity.com/ab_history.asp

12
12A. http://www.owenscorning.com/around/sound/products/wallframing.asp
12B. http://www.nahb.org/generic.aspx?genericContentID=293
12C. http://www.nofma.org/faq.htm#installationq4
12D. http://www.mohawkcarpet.com/
12E.http://www.carpet-rug.com/drill_down_2.cfm?page=2&sub=4&request timeout=350
12F. http://www.armstrong.com/ressheetna/article5193.asp
12G. http://www.woodfloorsonline.com/

12H. http://www.woodfloorsonline.com/woodspecies/woodspecies.html

12I. http://www.ifloor.com/group_5667/Cork-Flooring/APC-Cork-Floors/Prefinished-Planks-Glueless-Click-.html

12J. http://www.ifloor.com/brand_1353/Bamboo-Flooring/Westhollow-Bamboo-Flooring.html

12
con't

12K. http://www.ifloor.com/

12L. http://www.nofma.org/faq.htm#installationq4

12M. http://www.ifloor.com/articles/lam/basics.html

12N. http://www.ifloor.com/articles/lam.brands.html

12O. http://www.usfloorsource.com/

13A. http://www.monticellogranite.com/granite-colors.html

13B. http://www.kitchens.com/

13C.http://interiordec.about.com/cs/kitchencountertop/tp/tp_kitcounter.htm?iam=sherlock_abc

13D. http://www.cosentinousa.com/1_info/info.htm

13E. http://www.zodiaq.com/

13F. http://caesarstoneus.com/

13G. http://www.vmcind.com/

13H. http://www.formica.com/

13

13I. http://www.corian.com/

13J. http://www.avonite.com/

13K. http://www.theswancorp.com/

13L. http://www.wilsonart.com/

13M. http://www.quarrystone.net/welcome.htm

13N. http://www.diygranite.com/

13O. http://www.stonecare.com:80/

13P. **GONE** http://olytops.com/solid_surfacing_veneer.htm

13Q. http://www.isdesignet.com/Magazine/J_F'98/srssv.html

14

15A. http://www.sears.com/sr/javasr/category.do?BV_UseBVCookie=Yes&vertical=APPL&cat=Refrigeration

15B. http://www.amana.com/amana/jsp/homepage.do

15C. http://www.whirlpool.com/cgi-bin/ncommerce3/CategoryDisplay?cgmenbr=181&cgrfnbr=920&catname=Refrigerators

15

15D. http://www.subzero.com/subzero/default.asp

15E. http://www.kitchenaid.com/

15F. http://www.geappliances.com/shop/prdct/rfr_frz/

15G. http://www.lowes.com/lkn?action=productSection&catalogId=T050600

15H. http://www.energystar.gov/

16A. http://www.thehardwarehut.com/cabinet_hinges.php

16 B. http://www.diamond2.com/diamond/home.htm

16 C. http://www.kraftmaid.com

16 D. http://www.medallioncabinetry.com/

16

16 E. http://www.edgewatercab.com/

16 F. http://www.aristokraft.com/aristokraft/home.htm

16 G. http://www.canyoncreek.com/

16 H. http://www.soss.com/

16J. http://www.msue.msu.edu/msue/imp/mod02/01500096.html

17
17A. http://www.imperialhoods.com/
17B. http://www.kitchensource.com/kau/hoods.htm
17C. http://www.broan.com/product-category.asp?CategoryID=508
17E. http://hyperphysics.phy-astr.gsu.edu/hbase/sound/phon.html
17F. http://www.vikingrange.com/welcome.html

18
18A. http://store.faucet.com/cgi-bin/fcom/products?id=35L5sXJj&mv_arg=ISESTS00&mv_pc=1
18B. http://www.homecenter.com
18C. http://www.moen.com/Consumer/catalog/product_search.cfm?ptype=r
18D. http://www.insinkerator.com/
18E. http://www.nkba.org/
18F. http://www.kitchens.com

19

20
20A. http://www.icpa-hq.com/
20B. http://www.askthebuilder.com/
20C. http://www.avonite.com/consumer/consumer_prod_complist.html
20D. http://www.basins.com/
20E. http://www.us.kohler.com/pr/n_seamless.html

21
21A. http://www.littlegiantladders.com/typeIA.htm
21B. http://www.wernerladder.com/

22
22A. http://www.energystar.gov/index.cfm?c=clotheswash.pr_clothes_washers

23
23A. http://www.BetterHousesBetterLiving.com/supplements/d.htm
23B. http://www.nahb.org/generic.aspx?genericContentID=293
23C. http://www.masoniteclaims.com/woodruf/index.html
23D. http://www.growinglifestyle.com/article/s0/a92767.html

Glossary

This listing is intended to help you understand what you're reading about in this and other books dealing with houses. It is not all-encompassing. Many terms used in the industry are omitted because they don't generally involve the homeuser.

3-way switch—Uses two switches that permit a light or outlet to be turned on or off from either switch. The term "3-way" refers to the three ways which the switches can be set: 1) OFF, 2) ON from switch A, or 3) ON from switch B.

4-way switch—Similar to a 3-way switch except that there are three switches instead of two. The light can be turned on or off from any of the three.

A—Ampere. A measure of electric current, used with a number (15A, for example) to indicate the capacity of a circuit, fuse, or circuit breaker.

ac—In today's houses this usually means the air conditioning unit. It can also mean alternating current to differentiate it from direct current.

ABR—Accredited Buyer Representative. Designation of REBAC[1H]

AIA—American Institute of Architects[3C]

AIBD—American Institute of Building Designers[3B]

Air switch—A switch that uses an air tube between the acuating button and the electric switch.

ARELLO—Association of Real Estate License Law Officials[1W]

ASHI—American Society of Home Inspectors[1D].

Amp—(*See* A.)

backerboard—A special rigid board used under tile.

backfill—Dirt that's pushed back against the house foundation after the house is finished.

backsplash—Area just behind and above a countertop, usually covered to prevent water from splashing on the wallboard.

baseboard—Piece of material used to hide the joint where the floor meets the wall; may be wood, plastic, or rubber.

base molding—Molding used as a baseboard.

batten—Narrow piece of material used on the outside of a house to cover joints in walls.

bearing wall—Wall that supports a ceiling joist, floor joist, or roof. May be an outside wall or an inside partition.

bifold doors—doors that fold into two sections when opened.

board and batten—Siding made up of vertical boards the joints of which are covered with batten slats.

board foot—Amount of lumber in a piece 1" thick by 12" wide by 1-foot long. A piece of 1"× 12" that is 8 feet long has 8 board feet. A 2"× 6" that is 8 feet long also has 8 board feet.

boot—Piece of formed sheet metal used to interconnect a heating/cooling duct and a register.

BR—Bedroom. Could also mean brick.

branch circuit—Electrical circuit with its own circuit breaker in the service panel.

brick veneer—Brick facing on an exterior wall or fireplace.

building codes—Generic term relating to codes for buildings. (*see* codes.)

building designer—A person who designs buildings. May or may not be an architect. May work individually or be a part of a company that makes building plans.

building inspector—A government employee who inspects buildings to determine if they are code compliant.

building official—A government official with the responsibility for generating codes and/or enforcing them. May supervise building inspectors.

bullnose—The rounded outside edge of a tile counter.

butt—Describes how the ends of two boards or the edges of sheet materials meet so that their ends or edges touch in a continuous line. Also describes the end of a board.

CABO—Council of American Building Officials. Now amalgated into the International Code Council.

CAD—computer aided design.

can light—An incandescent light in a metal can. The can is flush with the surface in which it is mounted. The light itself may be recessed.

Casablanca fan—(*See* ceiling fan.)

casement window—Windows that hinge in or out for opening.

casing—Trim for a window, door, or opening.

caulking—Refers to the compound used to make joints weatherproof and waterproof or simply to make them smooth.

CC&Rs—Covenants, Conditions, and Restrictions. Appended to deeds. (*See* Supplement D²ᴬ.)

ceiling board—Like wallboard (which *see*) but more rigid so that it won't sag when installed horizontally in a ceiling.

ceiling fan—Large ceiling-mounted fan. Also known as a paddle fan or Casablanca fan. Although Casablanca is the name of one manufacturer of ceiling fans, the name is also used generically.

center mullion—In some cabinets, the vertical piece of wood on the front that divides the opening into two parts.

CFM—cubic feet per minute. A measure of air flow.

chase—A boxed-in shaft, usually vertical, through which pass various pipes, drains, ducts, and flues.

chipboard—A board made of wood chips that are glued together under pressure

CI—Cast iron.

clapboard—A siding, usually cedar, made of overlapping horizontal boards. Largely replaced by lap siding.

cleanout—Part of a fireplace from which ashes may be removed from the fireplace.

codes—A group of legal documents that define many building parameters. (*See* Supplement B.)

comps—Comparables; describes the process of comparing the values of different pieces of property. Used by appraisers as a major tool in determining property values.

conduction—heat transfer through a solid material.

conduit—A pipe or tube through which wires or smaller pipes can be run.

construction loan—A short-term loan made to a builder to finance the construction of a building. Money is loaned only to cover the builder's costs for materials and labor as it is spent.

convection—heat carried by a gas through a space.

cop—Copper, as in copper pipe.

CPVC—chlorinated polyvinyl chloride

crawl space—Space between the bottom floor of a house and the ground under it.

crown—Piece of molding around the top of a room.

CRS—certified residential specialist. A real-estate designation.

D—Dryer.

deck—1) the flat area around a bath tub, *see* also surround; 2) with post and beam construction, the flat wooden surface on top of the beams; 3) a wooden platform on the exterior of houses used for outdoor living.

diag—Diagonal.

dim—Dimension.

dimensional lumber—Single pieces of lumber that are sawed to standard dimensions as opposed to that which is "manufactured."

dimmer—an electrical device used to dim a light.

direct vent—A type of gas fireplace that vents the burned gas directly to the outside of the house.

dn—Down, as in stairs.

door light—The small vertical window(s) on one or both sides of an entry door.

double-hung—Two-window sash where each window slides up and down.

downdraft—a vent type where the exhaust is pulled downward off of a stovetop.

DR—Dining room.

draw—A payment made to builder against a construction loan.

drawer boxes—The boxes in cabinet drawers to which are attached the facing piece drawer slides.

dry—Dryer.

drywall—(*See* wallboard).

duct—A pipe, usually metal, used to carry heating or cooling air.

ductless—a kitchen exhaust scheme where the fumes, steam, heat, etc., are run through a charcoal filter and blown back into the room.

duplex outlet—The standard electrical outlet in a home. (Two separate plugs can be plugged in, hence the term "duplex.")

DW—Dishwasher.

easement—an area of a lot where drains, power lines, etc. owned by another party may be run.

eating bar—A counter,usually a part of an island or peninsula in a kitchen, part or all of which can be used to seat people who are eating.

eaves—The part of the roof that overhangs the outside wall of a building.

EIFS—A synthetic stucco which causes serious problems if it is not installed properly.

el—Elevation.

elevation—A drawing showing the straight-on exterior view of a building.

empty nester—Refers to an older couple whose children are gone, leaving them with an empty house.

Energy Star—An EPA designation for appliances that designed to use less energy.

enviromental hazard—A material or substance which is potentially dangerous to humans.

ent—Entrance.

entry level—(*See* starter house.)

EPA—Environmental Protection Agency. A government department.

European-style—Describes a style of cabinet without a face frame, also called "box" cabinets. Also used to describe a particular type of hinge needed for this style of cabinet. The hinge is not visible from outside the cabinet.

exfiltration—Leakage of air from the inside to the outside of a building.

ext—Exterior.

face frame—A term used to identify the ring or frame of wood that goes around the front opening of western- or face-frame style cabinets.

fascia—Board covering ends of the roof rafters.

fenestration—Refers to windows and the way they are arranged in a building.

FHA—Federal Housing Authority. A part of HUD[IX].

fl—Floor.

flip switch—Electrical switch that is operated by moving the control up/down rather than pushing or tapping on it (as differentiated from a rocker switch, which *see*.)

footing—The base on which a building's foundation sits.

FP—Fireplace.

Fanny Mae—a federally chartered lender[1M].

Freddie Mac—a federally chartered lender[1N].

FSBO—for sale by owner.

gable—Describes a triangular section of a wall that extends up from the level of the eaves to a roof peak. The roof line is straight, not curved or broken.

gar—Garage.

gel coat—a special surface added to cultured marble countertops.

GFCI—Ground-fault circuit-interrupter.

grout—A kind of mortar used to fill between tiles, marble, or stone.

gl—Glass. Used on drawings to show sliding glass doors.

glazed—From the verb glaze meaning to fit a window with glass panes. Double glazed is used to describe a window with double panes.

GRI—Graduate, Realtor Institute.

ground water—water in the ground.

gyp board—(*See* wallboard.)

gyp rock—(*See* wallboard.)

gypsum—A white mineral. (*See* wallboard.)

hardboard—A material made from wood fibers that may be made into sheets or pieces to simulate wood.

heat pump—Part of a heating and air-conditioning (HVAC) system. Pumps heat into or out of the house.

hollow-core door—A door whose interior is mostly empty.

hose bibb—An outside faucet to which a hose may be connected.

HUD—Department of housing and urban development[IX].

hugger—A type of ceiling fan that uses a minimum of vertical space. Used with low ceilings.

HVAC—Heating, ventilation, and air conditioning.

ICC—International Code Council[IV].

in—Inch or inches.

infiltration—Leakage of air from the outside to the inside of a building.

IRC—International Residential Code, one of the codes developed by the ICC.

joist—A horizontal beam supported by a bearing wall. Usually used to support floors and/or ceilings.

kiln-dried lumber—Lumber that has been dried in a kiln or oven. Differentiated from lumber that may be wet when used and then dries after the house has been erected.

kit—Kitchen. Also used to designate a home which is shipped in kit form to a site for erection.

knife hinge—A face-frame cabinet hinge that is hidden when the door is closed.

laminate—A plastic surfacing material used on countertops and, rarely, in tub and shower surrounds. Popularly known by the trademarked name Formica.

landing area—The horizontal area where items coming from or going into an appliance may be set.

lap siding—Boards of wood or composite material used horizontally on the outside of houses in which the bottom of one piece is made to overlap the top of the piece below it.

lazy Susan—a circular or semi-circular shelf that rotates. Used in cabinet corners.

light—(*See* door light.)

lin—Linen closet.

lndry—Laundry.

LR—Living room.

MBA—The Mortgage Bankers Association of America[1K].

MBR—Master bedroom.

mechanical—Dealing with heating, ventilating, and air conditioning as in "mechanical subcontractor." (In some parts of the country, mechanical is used to refer to electrical and plumbing as well as HVAC items.)

melamine—A hard plastic that is used to cover shelves.

Mello-Roos—Refers to special assessments districts in California formed to pay for streets, sewers, etc., in new subdivisions. Can add significantly to the tax bill.

miter—Used to describe how two boards meeting at right angles are cut so that cut ends do not show. Miters are usually 45-degree cuts.

MLS—(*See* multiple listing service.)

modular house—A made-to-order factory-built house that is not constrained to pre-determined designs.

mold—A fungus that grows in a damp environment on suitable materials. It can be toxic to people.

molding or moulding—Strips of wood, usually decorative, used as trim. May be painted or stained and finished.

move-up house—The next step above a starter house. A house for a growing family.

mullion—A vertical piece at the center of a cabinet against which the cabinet doors close.

multiple listing service—A service provided by the local real estate agents that lists all properties for sale in an area along with many of their more pertinent features.

NAHI—National Association of Home Inspectors[1E].

NAMB—National Association of Mortgage Brokers[1L].

NAR—National Association of Realtors[1F].

NAHB—National Association of Home Builders[1S,1T].

no duct—(*See* ductless.)

nosing—The front edge of a stair tread that extends or noses over the riser.

no vent—(*See* ductless.)

NV—No vent. (*See* ductless.)

O—Built-in oven.

OC—(*See* on center.)

on center—Used to specify distance from the center of one piece of material to another. Most frequently used to describe the distance between studs or joists.

OD—Outside dimensions.

orange peel—Refers to a wallboard finish that resembles the texture of an orange peel.

OSHA—The Occupational Safety and Health Administration. A federal agency.

owner-builder—A home where the owner is the builder or general contractor.

P—Pantry.

paddle fan—(*See* ceiling fan.)

panelized—a form of building where walls are factory made and shipped to the construction site.

party wall—A wall or fence that sits on a property line and is a common responsibility of both parties or land owners.

particle board—Similar to chipboard except that the pieces are smaller (particles rather than chips). Has a higher density than chipboard.

pass through—An opening in a wall to pass dishes through. Usually between kitchen and breakfast nook or dining room.

PB—Polybutylene. One type of plastic pipe.

PE—Polyethylene. One type of plastic pipe.

Pergo—A company which makes laminate flooring. Used colloquially for laminate flooring in general.

pitch—May refer to the sticky stuff that exudes from lumber but more likely has to do with the slope or pitch of the roof. A 4/12 pitch, for example, means that there is 4" of vertical rise for each 12" of horizontal run.

plasterboard—(*See* wallboard.)

plate—The bottom or top piece of a wall. Studs sit on the bottom plate and are capped by the top plate.

pocket door—An interior door that slides into a pocket in a wall.

polymer—A big molecule, usually organic, strung together to get specific properties. Many building materials are polymers, whether they're called poly--- or not.

pot mark—Marks made on surfaces by aluminum and other metal pots and pans.

pre-owned—a house which has been lived in.

production house—One made on site in a factory-like production-like envivonment where it is one of many essentially identical houses. Usually in tract subdivisions.

PWR—Powder room or half-bath (not power).

R—Range, when used in kitchens.

radiation—the emission from a hot object. A means of heat transfer across space.

r—Radius.

REBAC—Real Estate Buyers Agency Council. A part of the National Association of Realtors®[4R].

R-value—Resistance to heat flow. (*see* Supplement A.)

recirculating—*See* ductless. May also refer to a recirculating hot-water system that provides immediate hot water to faucets in the house.

ref—Refrigerator.

register—The part of an HVAC system where heated or cooled air enters a room.

resilient channel—A channel (ususably steel) run across wall studs under wallboard to reduce sound transmission through the studs.

riser—The vertical boards between the steps of a stairway.

riser height—The vertical distance from the top of one step of a set of stairs to the top of the next.

rm—Room.

rocker switch—An electrical switch which is operated by tapping the top or bottom of the control plate (as differentiated from a flip switch, which *see*.)

roof pitch—a measure of the slope of a roof.

RV pad—A concrete pad specifically intended for storing a recreational vehicle.

sawn lumber—(*See* dimensional lumber.)

sconce—Wall-mounted light fixture.

scr—Screen.

semi-custom—A house in a development where the buyer has a number of design and material options.

shake—A thick wood split shingle, usually cedar, used for roofs and siding.

sheet rock—(*See* wallboard.)

sidelight—(*See* door light.)

sillcock—(*See* hose bibb.) (This term is seldom used in the west.)

soffit—The underside of eaves. Also used to designate the space between cabinets and the room ceiling. May be closed (boxed-in) or open.

solid-core door—A door whose interior is filled as differentiated from a hollow-core door.

solid surface—Generic name to a family of materials used for counters, shower stalls, etc. These materials (acrylic, polyester or a mix) are the same throughout, i.e., not just on the surface.

solid-surfacing veneer—A laminate of a thin solid-surface material laid on a particle board or plywood backing.

Soss—a type of hinge used on face-frame cabinet where the hinge is completely hidden when doors are closed[16H].

soundboard—A special board used under wallboard to reduce sound transmission through the wall.

spa—(*See* whirlpool tub.)

spec—A house built on speculation with the expectation of finding a buyer for it. Differentiated from a custom or build-to-order house for a which there is a buyer before building starts.

special assessment—A assessment levied against a piece of property by a local government to pay for streets, sewers, etc.

specs—Specifications.

SSV—(*See* solid-surfacing veneer.)

starter house—A family's first house. Usually small and low-cost.

stock plans—A stock a company which specializes in designing and selling house plans.

stor—Storage.

studs—The uprights used in walls. Usually 2"×4"s or 2"×6"s. Usually wood in residential construction but may be metal.

stucco—A siding material made with Portland cement that is spread on in several layers over a metallic mesh.

subcontractor—A company or person employed by the builder to do a specialized part of the house construction.

subdivider—A company or person who divides land into lots to sell or on which to build houses. Usually includes streets and utilities in the process.

subfloor—What's under the finished floor. Refers to the rough material laid across the floor joists to support the rest of the floor. Also can refer to the sheathing, plywood, or particle board, used to give a smooth surface for the finish flooring.

sump pump—A pump installed under a house to remove any water that may accumulate there.

surround—Refers to the material that surrounds a bathtub or shower. Tub surrounds may be only the flat area around the tub (the deck) or may include a facing on the front of the tub as well as a backsplash.

swagged chandelier—a hanging light fixture where the electric cord is draped across the ceiling.

T1-11—A hardboard (Masonite) exterior siding with vertical grooves to simulate boards. Comes in 4' × 8' or 4' × 10' panels.

T111—(*See* T1-11.)

T&G—(*See* tongue and groove.)

TC—(*See* terra cotta.)

terra cotta—A red low-fired tile. Used extensively for roofing in the desert southwest but now being superseded by concrete tile because of concrete's greater strength.

tongue and groove—Lumber with a small groove down one side of each board and a protruding piece (the tongue) that fits into the groove when the boards are installed.

toxin—a material which can be unhealthy for people who breathe or ingest it.

tract—A land development area, typically with models of houses for sale.

tread—The flat part of a stair step.

tread width—The front-to-back width of a stair step exclusive of the nosing.

typ—Typical, as in a typical stud arrangement.

type-B vent—vent used on fireplace or stove where the exhaust goes directly outside.

unvented—A type of gas fireplace or stove that doesn't vent the spent gasses outside but dumps them back into the room.

U-value—Used to quantitatively describe the amount of heat a door or window conducts between inside and outside air. (*see* Supplement A.)

VA—**V**eterans **Adm**instration. A federal govenmental department[4T].

vaulted ceiling—Arched ceiling.

V-Cap—A special piece of ceramic tile used at the edge of a counter to prevent liquids from running off. Name comes from underside shape which is a V.

vent—the means of removing unwanted combustion products or other gases from a space.

visqueen—Polyethylene sheet used to cover the ground in a crawl space.

VT&G—Vertical tongue and groove.

W—Clothes washer.

walk-through—Joint action taken by the buyer and builder at completion of the house to find those items that have not been done properly and need to be fixed by the builder.

wallboard—Strictly speaking, refers to all wall materials that come in sheets including plywood and Masonite hardboard. We use "wallboard" here to mean sheets of compacted gypsum (a mineral) with a paper exterior. This is, by far, the most commonly used wallboard. Also called dry wall, sheet rock, gyp rock, gyp board, gypsum board, plasterboard and probably more.

walk-in closet—A larger closet made to be entered as differentated from one that is reached into.

WC—Water closet or toilet.

western-style—Describes a cabinet with a face frame around its front opening.

whirlpool tub—More popularly known by the trade name Jacuzzi and also called spa. A tub with jets of water flowing into it to give a whirlpool effect.

WR—Washroom.

X—Marks a location.

yd—Yard.

zero lot line—A house has a zero lot line when it is built with one wall on the edge of the lot. This wall is frequently a common wall with the adjacent house.

Index

More Help for Home Buyers

The website **www.BetterHousesBetterLiving.com** has a wealth of information which is put there to help home buyers, builders and remodelers even after they have the book. There is the list of 140+ Internet Resources, given here in the book, but as hot-links on the website that make it easier to get to them. And on the website changes in the URL's will be updated.

There is also a section of the website for "what readers say." You are encouraged to read it from time to time to see if there any additional hints others may have. And you are urged to share with others if you find something that's not covered in the book that you think could be of help to people going through the same process as you.

Because we are dealing with an environment where improvements are continually being made, we have included a page we call "Updates" where you can find the latest in changes in materials, form, and building techniques.

The process of buying a home, whether new or pre-owned, is not the primary focus of *Better Homes, Better Living.* For readers who would like an introduction to the players beyond what is in the first chapter of the book, 8 supplements can be found on the website **www.BetterHousesBetterLiving.com.** Their format is PDF which should make them easier to copy if you want.

> ⇨ Supplement A. Energy Considerations
> Energy savings are an ever-increasing part of our culture. Here we take a quick look at the meanings of some of the terms and what they may mean in your home.
>
> The pluses and minuses of "tight" house are touched upon.

> ⇨ Supplement B. Building and Energy Codes
> Building and energy codes, as they apply to home building are reviewed to give the reader more understanding of what's involved both in the actual codes themselves and in their enforcement.

> ⇨ Supplement C. Environmental Hazards
> The discussion of the four main toxins - radon, asbestos, lead and molds - found in houses today includes what they are and what we can do about them.
>
> It is emphasized that knowledge is your best protection.

> ⇨ Supplement D. Deed Restrictions
> Deed restrictions can come as a surprise the first time a homebuyer runs into them, not realizing how much they can add to the value of his property both aesthetically and financially. But there is a down side because these same restrictions can keep the homeowners from doing things they'd like to do both inside

and outside the house.

⇨ <u>Supplement E. Home Builders</u>
The problems builders face.

What consumers can expect from builders - at least most of them.

The problems consumers face because of builders' ignorance, ineptness, resistance to change, and/or stress on the bottom line.

The national builder organization (NAHB) and what it does and doesn't do - but could.

⇨ <u>Supplement F. Realtors</u>
The way the National Association of Realtors®, the local real estate agencies and the individual agents fit together is reviewed.

The question of agency, just whom an agent represents in a given transaction, is explained along with the importance of having an agent that only represents you and not the seller when you are buying a house.

One of the things you'll have to do is decide whether you should buy your home on your own, i.e., without an agent. And, if you do use an agent, should you use a full-service agency, a discount agency, or use services available on a consulting, i.e., fee-for-service, basis.

All of these are are discussed here.

⇨ <u>Supplement G. User Friendliness</u>
Here we take a look at what user-friendliness is in a home and what you can do to get it. Examples of several widely different unfriendly things are given along with where you can go for further discussions to help you make user-friendliness a part of your thinking in your decisions about your new home.

⇨ <u>Supplement H. The Players</u>
This is a brief introduction to some of the key players you'll meet when you set out to get your home. Internet references are given to sources of more information.

Are You a Building Industry Professional?

Builder
Remodeller
Architect
Designer
Realtor®
Loan Officer

Consider

Better Houses, Better Living

as a gift to customers buying, building or remodelling a home:

◊ To show them that you have their best interests in mind.

◊ To solidify your relationship.

◊ To give impetus toward those downstream referrals that are so important to your success.

Call, write or Email to find out about the quantity discounts
that are available to you.

Home User Press
1939 Woodhaven Street NW
Salem, OR 97304

1-800-530-5105

mefhup@open.org